SHADOW FORCE

SHADOW FORCE

Private Security Contractors
in Iraq

DAVID ISENBERG

PRAEGER SECURITY INTERNATIONAL

Westport, Connecticut • London

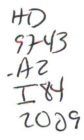

Library of Congress Cataloging-in-Publication Data

Isenberg, David.
  Shadow force : private security contractors in Iraq / David Isenberg.
    p. cm.
  Includes bibliographical references and index.
  ISBN 978–0–275–99633–8 (alk. paper)
  1. Private security services—Iraq. 2. Private military companies—Iraq. 3. Government contractors—Iraq I. Title.
  DS79.76.I82 2009
  956.7044'3—dc22   2008033208

British Library Cataloguing in Publication Data is available.

Library of Congress Catalog Card Number: 2008033208
ISBN: 978–0–275–99633–8

First published in 2009

Praeger Security International, 88 Post Road West, Westport, CT 06881
An imprint of Greenwood Publishing Group, Inc.
www.praeger.com

Printed in the United States of America

The paper used in this book complies with the
Permanent Paper Standard issued by the National
Information Standards Organization (Z39.48-1984).

10 9 8 7 6 5 4 3 2 1

This is my first book, and I regret that three important people in my life are not alive to see its publication.

First and foremost are my parents, Joseph and Carol Isenberg. My father, who died in 1983, has always been an inspiration to me. Like many men of his generation, he was a doer, not a talker. He graduated at the top of his class at City College of New York, put himself through Harvard Law School, and served in the Army during WWII. Despite many setbacks in his life—whether the loss of his business or physical illness—he never lost his determination, facing whatever life threw at him (and life threw many difficulties at him) with composure and unfailing good humor. He did exactly what he was supposed to do: love his wife, raise a family, and conduct himself with integrity, courage, and honor. Unlike many people today, when he made a promise, he kept it. He was also a man of enormous intelligence and erudition. His love of reading and pursuit of knowledge rubbed off on me at an early age, helping to explain why I read books such as the *Odyssey* and *Iliad* in elementary school. Whatever qualities of intellect, discernment, insight, reason, and judgment I have—and have hopefully brought to bear in writing this book—came from him.

My mother, who died in 2007, grew up during the Depression. She knew great poverty and tough times. When she met and married my father, it was like a real-life Cinderella meeting her Prince Charming. Their long love for each other despite the vicissitudes of life was a constant that could always be counted on. When my father became ill, she went back to work, despite the responsibility she already bore of being a full-time mother to three children. She taught me to respect other people and to see the good in them, listening sympathetically and being thankful for what I have even when it is not easy to do so. She also taught me to pick myself up and to keep going after dealing with life's difficulties. Her love for me and her pride in me have sustained me through many difficult times.

Not a day goes by that I do not think of my parents.

I also think of Martin Blum, my mother's brother, my Uncle Buddy, who died in 2008. His goodhearted ebullience, gregariousness, innate decency, enthusiasm, zest for life, and lifelong devotion to his beloved sister, my mother, have been an enormous comfort to me. The advice he gave my mother enabled her to live comfortably after my father died. The interest he showed in me, and his pride in my accomplishments over the years, made life much more bearable.

Contents

Preface

Why did I write this book? My rationale is simple. I wrote it to fill a void. It is a sad fact that much of the debate over private military and security contractors is, to borrow from *Macbeth*, a tale told by idiots, full of sound and fury; signifying nothing. The tale is made worse by the fact that much of those doing the telling have highly partisan axes to grind.

In general there has been far too much sensationalistic, sometimes misleading coverage of how and why tasks formerly done in-house by the U.S. military have been outsourced, especially in regard to Iraq. Now that PMCs are becoming embedded in popular culture via film, popular books, cartoons, and television, the time is long overdue for a factual, dispassionate accounting of both the good and bad of the subject.

A quick note on terminology is in order. In this book I am writing about private security contractors (PSCs). These are firms that employ people who carry weapons to protect their clients and use them when necessary. Such firms are often labeled "private military contractors," although that more accurately refers to firms doing unarmed logistics work, such as KBR. PSCs are generally considered a subset of PMCs. Academics have spent years arguing over the appropriate terminology. I largely consider it an academic distinction that doesn't have much relevance to real-world discussion of the subject. For the sake of convenience—because the acronym is already firmly embedded in popular culture and discourse—I generally use PMC, although I am writing specifically about PSCs, an acronym I use as well.

I wrote this book because I have been following the industry since the early 1990s, long before most contemporary writers even realized there was a PMC sector, and therefore have a substantial store of knowledge and experience on which to draw. As time passed, it became clear that an interesting, indeed, fairly important subject—the role and impact of outsourcing traditional military and other national security functions—was degenerating into a politicized debate.

This book is simply a modest attempt to bring some facts into view and let the chips fall where they may. Although I do have opinions on the pros and cons of governmental use of private military contractors, I am neither a diehard supporter nor fervent opponent of their use. I have no dog in the fight over outsourcing things that used to be considered governmental functions. As Mr. Spock used to tell Captain Kirk on the original *Star Trek* series, I consider it a fascinating phenomenon, worthy of continuing study.

Some people consider PMCs (or PSCs) simply patriotic Americans willing to do their part in supporting America, just like regular military forces. But others consider them thinly veiled mercenaries. Typical is this view by Yale English professor David Bromwich:

> A far more consequential euphemism, in the conduct of the Iraq war—and a usage adopted without demur until recently, by journalists, lawmakers, and army officers—speaks of mercenary soldiers as contractors or security (the last now a singular-plural like the basketball teams called Magic and Jazz). The Blackwater killings in Baghdad's Nissour Square on September 16, 2007, brought this euphemism, and the extraordinary innovation it hides, suddenly to public view. Yet the armed Blackwater guards who did the shooting, though now less often described as mere "contractors," are referred to as employees—a neutral designation that repels further attention. The point about mercenaries is that you employ them when your army is inadequate to the job assigned. This has been the case from the start in Iraq. But the fact that the mercenaries have been continuously augmented until they now outnumber American troops suggests a truth about the war that falls open to inspection only when we use the accurate word. It was always known to the Office of the Vice President and the Department of Defense that the conventional forces they deployed were smaller than would be required to maintain order in Iraq. That is why they hired the extracurricular forces.[1]

Putting aside the fact that, historically speaking, *mercenary* hasn't always been a dirty word, the truth is more complex. There are both good and bad aspects to private military contracting, and I've mentioned both in past writings.

Admittedly, the line between the two is often hard to discern. One British commentator noted:

> When I asked an official at the Foreign Office a question about mercenaries last week, he replied "they're not mercenaries, they're private security companies." "What's the difference?" "The difference is that a private security company is a properly registered company, not an individual getting a few friends together." In other words, you cease to be a mercenary by sending £20 to Companies House.[2]

And it is true that there are connections between the worlds of classic mercenaries and security contractors.

For example, consider Simon Mann, a former British Army officer, a South African citizen, and a mercenary.[3] In 2004 he was accused of planning to overthrow the government of oil-rich Equatorial Guinea. His coup attempt was viewed as a real-life version of the 1974 novel *The Dogs of War* by Fredrick Forsyth, which chronicled the efforts of a company of European mercenary soldiers hired by a British industrialist to depose the government of a fictional African country. Interestingly, in recent years, after the release of once-secret British government documents, Forsyth was forced to admit his own role in financing a similar, and similarly failed, coup against Equatorial Guinea in 1973.

Mann is a former associate of Lieutenant Colonel Tim Spicer, the chief executive of the British private military contractor Aegis Defence—one of the biggest security firms currently in Iraq—having worked with him in another private security firm, Sandline International. Forsyth was an investor when Spicer first set up Aegis, and he reportedly made quite a bit of money from his investment.[4]

But Mann also helped establish Executive Outcomes. That firm was the mother of all private security contractors and the missing link between the "Wild Geese"–style mercenaries of old and the new generation of PMCs. Executive Outcomes was renowned around the world in the 1990s for fighting against rebel leader Jonas Savimbi in Angola and against the murderous Revolutionary United Front rebel group in Sierra Leone.

But as a U.S. military veteran, I believe there is another side to the use of private security and military contractors that few people care to talk about publicly. The reality is that private contractors did not crawl out from under a rock somewhere. They are on America's battlefields because the government, reflecting the will of the people, wants them there.

As one editorialist noted:

It's fashionable to look down on the civilian contractors employed by firms such as Halliburton and Blackwater. When contractors make the news, it's usually in the context of stories about waste and fraud in reconstruction or service contracts, or human rights abuses committed by private security contractors. So when civilian contractors die in Iraq, most of us don't waste many tears. These are guys who went to Iraq out of sheer greed, lured by salaries far higher than those received by military personnel, right? If they get themselves killed, who cares?

But we should all care. Not because it's our patriotic duty to support the lucrative corporate empires that employ the thousands of civilian contractors in Iraq, but because most of the men and women employed by these corporate giants are in Iraq at our government's behest.[5]

The reason we have such reliance on private contractors is simple enough. Even though the Cold War is over and the Soviet Union is a historical memory, the United States still reserves the right to militarily intervene everywhere. This, however, despite the so-called Revolution in Military Affairs that Defense Secretary Donald Rumsfeld championed, is a highly people-powered endeavor. And most people have decided that their children, much like Dick Cheney during the Vietnam War, have "better things to do."

Looking at it historically, however, it wasn't supposed to be this way. As one scholar noted,

> When the U.S. military shifted to an all-volunteer professional force in the wake of the Vietnam War, military leaders set up a series of organization "trip wires" to preserve the tie between the nation's foreign policy decisions and American communities. Led by then Army Chief of Staff Gen. Creighton Abrams (1972–74), they wanted to ensure that the military would not go to war without the sufficient backing and involvement of the nation. But much like a corporate call center moved to India, this "Abrams Doctrine" has since been outsourced.[6]

But, given the downsizing the U.S. armed forces had undergone since the fall of the Berlin Wall, the military turned to the private sector for help.

My own view of the world is that the international order will continue to be roiled and disrupted for some time to come. Thus, there will be a void in international politics. And, just as in nature, which abhors a vacuum, private contractors will step in to fill it.

Personally, I think the outsourcing of military capabilities left the station decades ago. It has taken this long for public perception to catch up—and people still only see the caboose.

If people don't want to use private contractors, the choices are simple. Either scale back U.S. geopolitical commitments or enlarge the military, something that will entail more gargantuan expenditures and even, some argue, a return to the draft down the road.

Personally, I prefer the former. But most people prefer substituting contractors for draftees. As former Marine colonel Jack Holly said, "We're never going to war without the private security industry again in a non-draft environment."[7]

Still, what I would really like to see is a national debate on this. Instead, we bury our heads in the sand and bemoan the presence of private contractors. That is a waste of time. Private security contractors, after all, are just doing the job we outsourced to them. And, like them or hate them, they are going to be around for a long time.

As Paul Lombardi, CEO of DynCorp, said in 2003, "You could fight without us, but it would be difficult. Because we're so involved, it's difficult to extricate us from the process."[8] And as Professor Debra Avant noted, "A lot of the companies in the 1990s were small, service-based companies. Now they're small services-based wings of large companies. Defense contractors have been buying up these companies like mad. This is where they think the future is."[9]

Acknowledgments

Any half-decent nonfiction book builds on the writings of others. In that regard, this book is no different, even though I have been studying and writing about private security and military contractors since the early 1990s, long before it became the politically fashionable issue that it is today. Thus, I want to acknowledge some of those whose ideas and analyses have helped inform me.

First, I want to thank a former employer, the British American Security Information Council, and especially its former director, Ian Davis, who gave me permission to use a report I wrote while working there—*A Fistful of Contractors: The Case for a Pragmatic Assessment of Private Military Companies in Iraq*—as the basis for this book. If I had not had the opportunity to write that report, this book would never have been published. I have also drawn on other papers I wrote while working at BASIC: *The Good, the Bad, and the Unknown: PMCs in Iraq* and *A Government in Search of Cover: PMCs in Iraq* (which was subsequently published as a chapter in *From Mercenaries to Market: The Rise and Regulation of Private Military Companies* [Oxford University Press, 2007]). I am also drawing on a chapter I wrote for *Private Actors and Security Governance*, published in 2006.

In 2008 I began writing a column for United Press International on this subject, and I have drawn on some of those columns as well.

This book would not have been possible without the information and comments made on the e-mail lists devoted to the international trade in private military services that are run by Doug Brooks, founder of the International Peace Operations Association. He has taken a lot of grief over the years, often being unfairly characterized as a shill for the PMC industry, but he has always been willing to discuss any and all aspects of the industry without hedging. Other trade associations could learn a great deal from him.

In recent years, especially since the United States' 2003 invasion of Iraq, there have been a slew of books published on the subject. Many of them are not worth the paper they are written on, but a few have been well reasoned, insightful, and downright brilliant. These include Robert Young Pelton's *Licensed to Kill: Hired Guns in the War on Terror*; Deborah Avant's *The Market for Force: The Consequences of Privatizing Security*; and Peter W. Singer's *Corporate Warriors: The Rise of the Privatized Military Industry*. Pelton, in particular, has been a veritable one-man cyclone of irreverent but always perceptive and well-informed commentary on the subject. Those wishing to follow the subject in detail would be well advised to read his *IraqSlogger* Web site.

There has also been a torrent of periodical literature, which is a pleasant change from the days of the early 1990s, when one could scour databases for months and come up with only a fewscore references. A complete listing would merit several books alone, but I have tried to list some of the most relevant in the bibliography, including many from law journals. These make for eye-glazing reading, but considering how often the debate on private security and military contractors focuses on issues of oversight and accountability, they merit reading, even if only to understand the shades of gray that envelop the subject.

Some (although not many) good television and film documentaries have been made on this subject. And in terms of raw material, in an age when one can find video clips of contractor convoys posted on *YouTube* and discussions of the finer points of looking for work in Iraq on chat forums such as *Lightfighter*, getting information about security contractors has never been easier.

There has also been some very fine press reporting over the years. Considering the sensationalism that this subject engenders and the personal risk that some reporters have taken in covering the actions of PSCs in war zones, I would be remiss if I did not mention a few of them. These include Steve Fainaru and Renae Merle of the *Washington Post*, T. Christian Miller of the *Los Angeles Times*, Jay Price and Joseph Neff of the *News & Observer*, David Pallister and Julian Borger of the *Guardian*, Robert Fisk of the *Independent*, Thomas Catan of the *Financial Times*, David Phinney of *CorpWatch*, Sharon Behn of the *Washington Times*, Katherine McIntire Peters and Shane Harris of *Government Executive*, William Matthews of *Defense News*, and Jim Krane and Deborah Hastings of the Associated Press. There are many more who should be mentioned, but space does not permit it.

The fact that Steve Fainaru won the 2008 Pulitzer Prize in the international reporting category for his series on private security contractors in Iraq is well-deserved confirmation that much of the truly accurate information we know about the industry is made available by the dogged efforts of a very few enormously determined reporters.[1]

I also want to thank Adam Kane, my editor at Greenwood, for helping shepherd this book all the way from contract negotiation to fruition. He patiently answered all the questions of a first-time author and extended my deadline when family crises forced delays. Additional thanks go to Laura Mullen for her work in publicizing this book. Though I've read many books published by Greenwood over the years, I never dreamed that Greenwood would publish one I wrote. I am delighted that it gave me the opportunity to do so.

And my thanks go also to Publication Services, Inc., which edited this book. The jury may still be out about whether outsourcing works in the military world, but there is no question that it works in the publishing world. My thanks go to Lisa Connery, project manager, and her colleagues at Publication Services. Their work was the very embodiment of professionalism and made a difficult job vastly easier.

Finally, I have benefited enormously over the years that I have followed this subject by the conversations and correspondence I've had with numerous contractors, both those in the field and those working in the company headquarters. Some, because of the nondisclosure agreements in their contracts, could speak or write only off the record. But they all generously and patiently shared time and information with me to help me better understand the truth of what is often a murky gray reality. I thank them all.

Most private security contractors are not saints, but neither are they sinners. They are men—and yes, in the private security world, it is still all men—who try to do a difficult job in dangerous situations. They are doing the proverbial dirty jobs that no one else wants to do. The industry they work in is a rough one, and although they don't ask for special treatment, most of them do deserve a more accurate depiction of their work than they currently receive. I hope that in some small way, this book helps give them that.

Overview of the Military Issue

Cry "Havoc!" and let slip the dogs of war.[1] But whose dogs?

Traditionally, the ultimate symbol of the sovereignty of a nation is its ability to monopolize the means of violence—in other words, raising, maintaining, and using military forces. Although there have always been exceptions, such as partisans and guerrilla forces, the evolution of the international system over the centuries has been such that military conflict has been conducted using state-raised forces. Of course, even during that evolution private actors played significant roles. Some of the same criticisms made against private contractors today were made against the East India Company back in the 17th to 19th centuries. Indeed, it was the East India Company that pioneered the shareholder model of corporate ownership.[2]

In modern times these forces have been motivated by issues of nationalism and ideology, in opposition to earlier traditions of fighting for whoever could pay. The evolution of national military establishments has also been accompanied by changes in international law that, though often belatedly and imperfectly, seek to regulate the means by which military force is used, including the types of military units considered legitimate.

The standard explanation for the rise of private military contractors (PMCs) is that the end of the Cold War gave states a reason to downsize their military forces, freeing up millions of former military personnel from a wide variety of countries, many of them Western. At the same time, the end of the Cold War lifted the lid on many long-simmering conflicts held in check by the superpowers. Because markets, like nature, abhor a vacuum, PMCs emerged to fill the void when conflicts emerged or wore on with no one from the West or the United Nations riding to the rescue.

Even the UN once thought seriously about turning to a PMC:

As it happens, the UN did once consider hiring mercenaries. It was in the wake of the Rwanda genocide, when the killers were hiding among refugees in eastern Zaire. Kofi Annan, the UN secretary general who was then the man in charge of peacekeeping, wanted to disarm the fighters so the humanitarian assistance could flow to the civilians. He appealed to governments for help; they spurned him. So he considered the mercenary option, only to drop it because the UN's member states were horrified by the idea.[3]

PRIVATIZATION PROLOGUE

In an era when governmental downsizing and free market philosophy are sweeping much of the world, it is not surprising that governments have turned to the private sector in search of services traditionally provided by the public sector.

In the United States, the 1993 Commission of Roles and Missions, whose mandate was to avoid duplication among the armed services, focused on privatization. A 1995 Defense Science Board report suggested that the Pentagon could save up to $12 billion annually by 2002 if it contracted out all support functions except actual warfighting. In 2001, the Pentagon's contracted workforce exceeded civilian defense department employees for the first time.

In the mid-1970s, Vinnell became the first U.S. firm to sell a military training contract directly to a foreign government when it signed a contract to train Saudi forces to defend Saudi Arabian oil fields.

Although logistics support by private firms is not the focus of this book, it should be noted that such work long precedes the contract awarded to Halliburton.

For example, DynCorp has supported every major U.S. military campaign since Korea. It provided aviation support to the Army in Vietnam from 1964 to 1971 and aviation maintenance services and logistics support to the U.S. Army and Marines during Desert Shield/Desert Storm from August 1990 to December 1991.

In 1951, DynCorp International's predecessor, then known as Land-Air, Inc., was awarded the first Contract Field Team (CFT) contract by the U.S. Air Force. The CFT's concept was providing a mobile rapid-response workforce of highly skilled aircraft technicians to provide maintenance support to the U.S. Air Force at remote locations. Land-Air and DynCorp have held the Contract Field Teams contract continuously since then and currently maintain rotary and fixed-wing aircraft for all branches of the U.S. armed forces throughout the world.

DynCorp also has two significant worldwide contracts in support of the military under which its personnel have been periodically stationed in Iraq and Afghanistan: the Army C-12 Program and the Air Force War Reserve Material (WRM) contract.

In March 2003, DynCorp supported combat operations in Iraq under the WRM contract by establishing a reception center for war reserve material in the

Middle East to support the onward movement of military forces. Maintenance of U.S. Army aircraft was provided by the CFT and C-12 contracts as the Army conducted deployment and combat operations.[4]

The Logistics Civil Augmentation Program (LOGCAP), an Army program established in 1985, is an initiative for the use of civilian contractors in wartime and during other contingencies. It includes all preplanned logistics and engineering/construction-oriented contingency contracts and includes everything from fixing trucks to warehousing ammunition to doing laundry, running mess halls, and building whole bases abroad.

The first comprehensive multifunctional LOGCAP Umbrella Support contract was awarded in August 1992 and was used in December 1992 to support all U.S. services and United Nations (UN) forces in Somalia. Other areas where LOGCAP has been implemented include Rwanda, Haiti, Saudi Arabia, Kosovo, Ecuador, Qatar, Italy, southeastern Europe, Bosnia, Panama, Korea, and Kuwait.

According to estimates from the International Peace Operations Association, the total industry value of the global "Peace and Stability Operations Industry" is $20 billion for all companies providing services in the field.

Of that number, private security contractors (PSCs) make up only about 5 to 10 percent of the total (approximately $2 billion annually of total industry value). Although the normal peacetime number would be closer to 5 percent for PSCs, events in Iraq have driven the number up.

But the industry is seen as a growth sector. In September 2005 the Stockholm International Peace Research Institute said that the industry is likely to double in size over the next five years, confirming predictions that industry revenues will hit $200 billion in 2010.[5]

And, in truth, leaving aside normal military–industrial contracting, recent events in Iraq are far from the first time the U.S. government has turned to the private sector for help. Before the 1990s privatization push, private firms had periodically been used in lieu of U.S. forces to enforce covert military policies outside the view of Congress and the public. Examples range from Civil Air Transport and Air America, the CIA's secret paramilitary air arm from 1946 through 1976—prominently used during the Vietnam War—to the use of Southern Air Transport to run guns to Nicaragua in the Iran–Contra scandal.[6]

Historically speaking, in fact, the story goes back even farther. Privateers, or private ships licensed to carry out warfare, helped win the American Revolution and the War of 1812. In World War II, the Flying Tigers, American fighter pilots hired by the government of Chiang Kai-shek, helped defeat the Japanese.

The only point I try to make with these figures is that the use of civilians in American military operations goes back to the founding of the country. Beyond that, any comparisons are problematic because of differences caused by the changes in military control. For example, none of the eras cited used volunteer armies. Civilian workers in the Revolutionary War were sutlers. These were merchants traveling behind the columns who each night would sell the troops extra items not supplied by the military (jam for the hardtack, liquor, better shoes, and so on). They were not

Table 1.1 Civilian Participation in Conflict[7]

War/Conflict	Civilians	Military	Ratio
American Revolution	1,500 (est.)	9,000	1:6 (est.)
Mexican/American	6,000 (est.)	33,000	1:6 (est.)
Civil War	200,000 (est.)	1 Million	1:5 (est.)
World War I	85,000	2 Million	1:20
World War II	734,000	5.4 Million	1:7
Korean Conflict	156,000	393,000	1:2.5
Viet Nam Conflict	70,000	359,000	1:6

part of the war effort in the way we talk about today, and they certainly did not provide a personal security detail for General George Washington.

Thus we can say that private military industry is neither as new nor as big as is frequently claimed. Also, it is evident that civilians have always been instrumental to military operations and have often been in harm's way in support of the military.

It seems that private contractors are an inevitable part of the American military future, especially in light of today's continuing revolution in military affairs, with its emphasis on the use of high-technology systems. As an *Atlantic Magazine* correspondent noted,

> The more technological the military sphere becomes, the greater the emphasis on the quality of personnel, rather than on their number. And the private sector can offer trained personnel, whether on land or at sea. Rather than go back to a military draft, we're more likely to see the further privatization of war.

> Indeed, the private sector is so interwoven with our military that we've been indirectly outsourcing killing since the early days of the Cold War. Many corporations with classified units work intimately with uniformed personnel on weapons systems and so forth. This trend will gain momentum in a century of cyber warfare, when geeks with long hair and glasses working for computer companies will become part of the killing machine. Actually, setting guidelines for good old boys with guns could be the easy part.[8]

So what is new? Specifically, the past two to three decades have seen increased prominence given to the reemergence of an old phenomenon: the existence of organizations working solely for profit. The modern twist, however, is that rather than being ragtag bands of adventurers, paramilitary forces, or individuals recruited clandestinely by governments to work in specific covert operations, the modern firm is solidly corporate. Instead of organizing clandestinely, such firms now operate out of office suites, have public affairs staffs and Web sites, and offer marketing literature.

But although they like to call themselves private security firms, such organizations are clearly quite different from the traditional private security industry that provides watchmen and building security. Business flourishes wherever there is a need for security, both in developed and in failed states.[9]

Furthermore, the movement from bodies to technology from the 1980s onward, as well as today's movement back to emphasizing bodies—at least in the U.S. military and the U.S. Department of State's transformation diplomacy efforts—has developed a capacity gap that will take at least a decade or two to fill. The capacity "refill" is only possible if the associated government has not only the political will to increase overhead and government personnel costs and positions, but also the ability to retain employees. Because this is far from assured, the dependence on security contractors will continue.

MERCENARIES Я U.S.?[10]

The truth is, although perhaps the birds and bees don't do it, throughout human history just about every nation that has gone to war *has* done it. The Hittites did it, the Egyptians did it, and so did the Carthaginians, Persians, Romans, Syrians, Egyptians, Greeks, Romans, Germans, French, British—and yes, we Americans—to name just a few.

"It" is a nation's hiring of people other than their own countrymen to pick up weapons to fight on their behalf.

The history of warfare from the Greek and Roman times is inextricably linked with individuals providing combat services for others outside their community.[11] A few examples include the Greek and Roman recruitment of hired units, European free companies during the Hundred Years' War, Italian condottierri, the Scots in 18th-century Russia, Hessians in the American Revolution, Swiss mercenary units—including the Swiss Guard at the Vatican that continues to this day—and the Dutch and English East India Companies.

Such people have been called many things throughout human history, acting as soldiers of fortune, condottierri, free companies (the root of the modern term *freelancers*), and, thanks to William Shakespeare's *Julius Caesar*, dogs of war.

The history of mercenaries' formation and use is one too long and complex to be covered here, though it is worth noting that the formation of mercenary companies in the Middle Ages was, in some senses, the earliest antecedent of what we would now call the private sector. Let's just say that war and business are very familiar and intimate partners.

Nowadays, people tend to label anyone who carries a gun while not a member of a regular military establishment a mercenary. Such people are supposedly uncontrollable rogues who commit unspeakable atrocities and wreak havoc. As a member of an industry trade group put it, "The term 'mercenary' is commonly used to describe the private peace and stability operations industry by opponents and those who lack a fundamental understanding of exactly what it is that the industry does. Regardless, it is a popular pejorative term among those who don't particularly care for the private sector's role in peace and stability operations."[12]

Well, war is war and violence is an inextricable part of it. But even the worst of classical mercenaries from ancient times or the Middle Ages would have a hard time rivaling the record of human and physical destruction achieved by regular military forces.

Mercenaries did not invent concentration camps, firebomb cities from the air, use chemical or biological weapons, or use nuclear weapons on civilian cities. In fact, the bloodiest century in recorded human history was the twentieth, courtesy of regular military forces. Not even the most bloodthirsty mercenaries of centuries past could have imagined committing the kind of carnage that contemporary regular military forces routinely plan and train for.

Nowadays, various countries—most notably the United States, thanks to its invasion of Iraq, although it is hardly the only nation—have brought back into the spotlight the role of what in our times is euphemistically called the private security and military sector.

It is a fact that much of the debate over private military and security contractors sheds more heat than light. The tale is made worse because many of those doing the telling, both pro and con, have their own partisan agendas. Because so many people, at least in Western nations, are relatively unfamiliar with military affairs, the concept of people willing to place themselves in harm's way, primarily in pursuit of profit, means only one thing: mercenary.

Put aside for a moment the reality that as nations have frayed, private security contractors are far from the only type of group that has taken a bite out of the monopoly of violence traditionally assumed by states: think gangs in urban ghettos or factions in failed states, for example.[13] The truth is that defining a mercenary is a bit like defining pornography; it is frequently in the eye and mind of the beholder. From the viewpoints of *accountability* or *regulation*, words that have been cited innumerable times over the past few years in regard to private security contractors, the only definition that counts is the legal one.

The most widely if not universally accepted definition is that in the 1977 Protocol I to the Geneva Conventions. Article 47 puts forward six criteria, all of which must be met for a combatant to be considered a mercenary. Accordingly, a mercenary is any person who:

(a) is specially recruited locally or abroad in order to fight in an armed conflict;

(b) does, in fact, take a direct part in the hostilities;

(c) is motivated to take part in the hostilities essentially by the desire for private gain and, in fact, is promised, by or on behalf of a Party to the conflict, material compensation substantially in excess of that promised or paid to combatants of similar ranks and functions in the armed forces of that Party;

(d) is neither a national of a Party to the conflict nor a resident of territory controlled by a Party to the conflict;

(e) is not a member of the armed forces of a Party to the conflict; and

(f) has not been sent by a State that is not a Party to the conflict on official duty as a member of its armed forces.

So why wouldn't someone working for a private security contractor in Iraq—for example—meet that definition? Well, for starters, a majority of those working for private security contractors are Iraqi, and as such are nationals of a party to the conflict, so they don't qualify.

Second, not all private security workers take a direct part in the hostilities. There are at least 200 foreign and domestic private security companies in Iraq, ranging from major firms such as Aegis Defence Services, ArmorGroup, Blackwater USA Group, DynCorp, and Triple Canopy to far smaller ones. Not all their employees are out there toting guns. Some of their consultancy services are extremely white-collar, involving work such as sitting in front of computer consoles at Regional Operations Centres and monitoring convoy movements.

Plus, one might note that there are tens of thousands of people serving in the American military who aren't even American, at least not yet. The number increased from 28,000 to 39,000 from 2000 to 2005 alone.[14]

Many of them applied under a fast-track process approved by President Bush in 2003 and enacted in October 2004. Under the new rules, people in the military can become citizens without paying the customary $320 application fee or having to be in the United States for an interview with immigration officials and naturalization proceedings.

The President also made thousands of service members immediately eligible for citizenship by not requiring them to meet a minimum residency threshold, as civilians applying to be citizens must do, although they must still be legal residents of the United States.[15]

In late 2006 it was reported that the U.S. military, struggling to meet recruiting goals, was considering opening up recruiting stations overseas and putting more immigrants on a faster track to U.S. citizenship if they volunteered.[16] Such proposals have been catching on among parts of the establishment. Michael O'Hanlon, a senior fellow at the Brookings Institution in Washington, and Max Boot, a senior fellow at the Council on Foreign Relations in New York, have proposed allowing thousands of immigrants into the United States to serve for four years in the military in exchange for citizenship.[17]

In any event, such immigrants are fighting—and in some cases dying—for a country of which they are not a part, but we don't call them mercenaries. As of March 2008, more than 100 foreign-born members of the U.S. military had earned American citizenship by dying in Iraq.[18]

The United States, as it has done in every major conflict since the Civil War, is making it easier for legal resident aliens to become U.S. citizens if they choose to fight.[19] To that end, a bill was introduced in Congress called the Development, Relief and Education for Alien Minors (DREAM) Act, which targeted children of undocumented immigrants resident in the United States for more than five years but not born within its border. Such children would be granted legal status and become eligible for citizenship if they graduated from high school, stayed out of trouble, and either attended college for two years or served two years in the armed forces.[20]

But the fact that someone working for Blackwater or any similar firm isn't a mercenary—as the word is legally defined—doesn't mean we should be altogether comfortable with their use, either.

PSC operations in Iraq tread a difficult line in providing protection in a manner that meets the intricate demands of corporate, military, and government ethics and comes at significant cost, posing many questions.

Effective contracts require coordination between different departments within the U.S. government, something that has not always been forthcoming. Academic Deborah Avant, who has written extensively on the subject, noted that Triple Canopy could not appropriately execute its contract with the State Department to protect State Department employees in Iraq with the requisite armed personnel, because the Office of Defense Trade Controls (also at the State Department) did not issue a license to export the required weapons. The company was forced to choose between acquiring weapons illegally in Iraq or failing to be in compliance with the terms of its contract.[21]

UNANSWERED QUESTIONS

Some questions, despite being increasingly asked over the past few years, are still unanswered: How many private security firms work in Iraq? How many contractors do they employ? How many contractors have been wounded or killed? What cost is incurred in such operations? But such questions have worked their way up the political chain over time. For example, in February 2007, senator and presidential candidate Barack Obama (D-IL) introduced the Transparency and Accountability in Military and Security Contracting Act (S. 674) as an amendment to the 2008 Defense Authorization Act, to require federal agencies to report to Congress numbers of security contractors, types of military and security equipment used, numbers of contractors killed and wounded, and disciplinary actions taken against contractors.

For the first three years of Operation Iraqi Freedom, the U.S. government had no accurate count of its contractors. As recently as December 2006, the Iraq Study Group estimated that only 5,000 civilian contractors worked in Iraq. The same month, however, Central Command issued the results of its own internal review: about 100,000 government contractors, not counting subcontractors, were operating in Iraq. Then, in February 2007, the Associated Press reported 120,000 contractors working in Iraq.[22]

A Government Accountability Office (GAO) report released in July 2005 said that investigators identified more than $766 million in government spending on private security companies in Iraq through the end of 2004.[23] The report noted that neither the Department of State, the Department of Defense, nor the U.S. Agency for International Development has complete data available on the costs of using PSCs.

In December 2006 the *Washington Post* reported that about 100,000 government contractors were operating in Iraq, not counting subcontractors—a total approaching the size of the U.S. military force there. That finding, which includes Americans, Iraqis, and third-party nationals hired by companies operating under U.S. government contracts, was significantly higher and wider in scope than the Pentagon's only previous estimate, which claimed that 25,000 security contractors were in the country. It is also 10 times the estimated number of contractors that were deployed during the Persian Gulf War in 1991.[24]

Reporting a major milestone, the *Los Angeles Times* wrote in July 2007 that the number of U.S.-paid private contractors in Iraq exceeded that of American combat troops. More than 180,000 civilians, including Americans, foreigners, and Iraqis, were working in Iraq under U.S. contracts, according to State and Defense Department figures. The numbers include at least 21,000 Americans, 43,000 foreign contractors, and about 118,000 Iraqis. That number, by the way, is still bigger than U.S. military forces, even after the United States increased the number of forces during its 2007 "surge."[25] Furthermore, private security contractors were not fully counted in the survey—so the total contractor number was even larger.

At the end of Q1, FY 2008 (December 2007), the U.S. Central Command reported that approximately 6,467 Department of Defense (DoD)-funded armed PSCs were in Iraq. Of that number, 830 were U.S. citizens, 7,590 were third-country nationals, and 1,532 were local/host-country nationals. This number, of course, was hardly the total PSC number, leaving out as it did those working for the State Department, as well as private companies doing reconstruction. Still, it does illustrate the point that the number of American PSCs is only a small proportion of the total.[26]

The Pentagon released a report in 2005, required by the FY 2005 Defense Authorization Act,[27] that noted that there was no single-source collection point for information on incidents in which contractor employees supporting deployed forces and reconstruction efforts in Iraq have been engaged in hostile fire or other incidents of note.[28]

At that time, the only existing databases for collecting data on individual contractors were the Army Material Command Contractor Coordination Cell (CCC) and Civilian Tracking System (CIVTRACKS).[29]

The CCC is a manual system dependent on information supplied to it by contractors. The CCC identifies contractors entering and leaving the theater, companies in the area of responsibility (AOR), and local contracting officer representatives (CORs) and enables local authorities/CORs to report contractor status, providing a means of liaison among the local COR and the assigned airport point of debarkation and helping to reconcile contractors with companies.

CIVTRACKS answers the "who, when, and where" of civilian deployments. CIVTRACKS accounts for civilians (Department of the Army civilians, contractor personnel, and other civilians deployed outside the continental United States in an operational theater).[30]

It was not until May 2006 that the Army Central Command and Multi-National Force–Iraq undertook a new effort to develop a full accounting of government contractors living or working in Iraq, seeking to fill an information gap that remains despite previous efforts. A memorandum issued by the Office of Management and Budget's Office of Federal Procurement Policy asked military services and federal agencies to assist Central Command and Multi-National Force–Iraq (MNF-I) by providing information by June 1, 2006.

The request sought data for contractors, including the companies and agreements they worked under, the camps or bases at which they were located, the services—such as mail, emergency medical care, or meals—they obtained from the military, their specialty areas, whether they carried weapons, and government contracting personnel associated with them.[31]

In October 2006 it was reported that an Army effort to count the number of contractors working or living in Iraq, pursuant to a call from the Office of Management and Budget, had foundered.[32]

The truth is, for most of the time since the United States went to war in both Afghanistan and Iraq, the Pentagon simply didn't know how many contractors

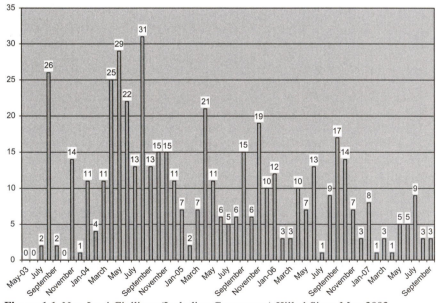

Figure 1.1 Non-Iraqi Civilians (Including Contractors) Killed Since May 2003

Table 1.2 Logistics Personnel in Iraq and Kuwait

Civilian Personnel	38,305
U.S. expatriates	11,860
Third-country nationals	900
Host-country nationals	35
Subcontractors and labor brokers	25,510
U.S. Army Combat-Service-Support Personnel	**45,800**

worked in the U.S. Central Command's area of responsibility, which includes both countries. In summer 2007, the Pentagon kept tabs on about 60,000 contractors with its Synchronized Predeployment and Operational Tracker (SPOT). By the end of the year, it planned to use SPOT to register all contractors who work in the Central Command's area of responsibility.[33]

Of course, even with all these data collection efforts, keeping track of contractors will likely be difficult, for contractors rotate in and out of theater more often than soldiers do.

There are few good, comprehensive public sources of information about contractor casualties, including fatalities. Thus, even though these graphs suffer certain limitations, they also merit examination.[34]

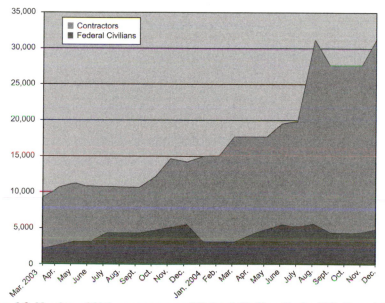

Figure 1.2 Number of U.S. contractors and Federal Civilians in the U.S. Central Command Area of Responsibility

The U.S. government, predictably, has not gone out of its way to help make information available to the public. From the viewpoint of some in the industry, the U.S. government is not eager for transparency in contracting activities. According to Doug Brooks, the President of the International Peace Operations Association, a trade group for contractors,

> Oftentimes, the clients, which is [to say] the state governments, like to control the message going out, and they will tell the company, essentially, you know, "If there is a media contact or something, it should come through us"—which would be the State Department, [the] Department of Defense.[35]

Of course, private security companies themselves, regardless of what their clients want, are not exactly known for volunteering information, either. Sometimes they are reticent for legitimate reasons, such as concerns of operational security. But the companies are also private, and—with rare exceptions, such as the British firm ArmorGroup—they're not seeking out much publicity.

In November 2005, the *Los Angeles Times* filed a lawsuit seeking U.S. government records related to the presence of private security firms in Iraq. Earlier that year, the *Times* asked for a database of reports contractors in Iraq submit after involvement in violent incidents. The newspaper asked for the records to be released under the Freedom of Information Act, a request that was partially denied, with the *Times* receiving only a heavily redacted version of the data omitting the names of security team members as well as the names of armed forces members and government employees.[36] In July 2006, a federal judge ruled that the U.S. government can keep secret the names of private security contractors involved in serious shooting incidents in Iraq.[37]

In February 2006 it was reported that 505 civilian contractors had died in Iraq since the beginning of the war. Another 4,744 contractors have been injured, according to insurance claims on file at the Department of Labor.[38]

As of December 2006, at least 770 contractors had been killed in Iraq and at least 7,700 wounded.[39]

According to U.S. Labor Department statistics, the first three months of 2007 brought the highest number of contract worker deaths for any quarter since the beginning of the Iraq war. At least 146 contract workers were killed, topping the previous quarterly record of 112 killed at the end of 2004. From August 2004 to the beginning of June 2007, 138 private security workers were killed, and 451 were wounded.[40]

In May 2007 the *New York Times* reported the total number of contractors killed in Iraq to be at least 917, along with more than 12,000 wounded in battle or injured on the job. Those statistics suggested that for every four American soldiers who die in Iraq, a contractor is killed.[41]

By the end of June 2007, the number of contractors killed in Iraq reached 1,001. But these numbers were likely understated, for the data only showed the number of cases reported to the Labor Department, not the total number of injuries or deaths that occurred. The Department broke down 776 contractor deaths by company, leaving out almost a fourth for unspecified reasons, and did not include all companies whose employees or contractors have died in the war.[42]

In November 2007 it was reported that nearly one-third of all U.S. contractor deaths in Iraq since the war began in 2003 have been employees of San Diego–based Titan and its new parent L-3 Communications, which had a multibillion-dollar contract with the Pentagon to provide thousands of translators and interpreters to soldiers in the battlefield and elsewhere in the Middle East. At that time, it had 216 employees killed in the Iraq war, more than any other entity except the U.S. military. Also at that time, 665 employees of private contractors had died in the war, according to casualty statistics released by the Labor Department.[43]

Numbers like these tend to confirm the view long held by many observers of the industry that one reason government likes to turn to contractors is that it lowers their political costs. Bluntly put: if you are not on active duty in the U.S. military—even if you were for 10 to 20 years previously—and even if you are contributing to the war effort, nobody beyond your immediately family cares if you get killed.

A study by the Project for Excellence in Journalism searched the coverage in 441 mainstream media outlets—400 newspapers, 10 national network and cable TV outlets, 24 magazines, different feeds from 2 wire services, 4 Web sites, and 1 radio outlet—from the beginning of the war on March 20, 2003, through April 1, 2007. Less than one-quarter of those outlets—only 93 of them—ever mentioned private military contractors beyond a brief account of a death or injury. Moreover, 61 of those 93 outlets ran only a single story on the subject. In other words, only 32 news outlets, or 7 percent of the outlets examined, have delved into the issue of PSC forces more than once, beyond a brief mention in a story about casualties or incidents.[44]

In total, out of well over 100,000 stories dealing with the war over that period, PEJ found only 248 stories dealing in some way with the topic of PSCs, and most of that coverage could be characterized as tangential references to private security contractors or companies inside larger stories about other Iraq-related issues or events. Even the total of 248 stories overstates the coverage, in a sense. Some of those were the same story that ran in different outlets, or a repeated airing of the same story. In June 2006, for example, CNN aired eight stories on PSCs, but five of those airings were actually the same report re-aired over three days. Of those 248 stories, 20 were also op-eds, meaning that they were submitted by outside writers or written by editorial boards and meant as commentary.[45]

From the start of the war in March 2003 through December 31, 2007, 123 civilian contractors are known to have died in Iraq, according to the U.S. Labor Department; 353 civilian contractors working for the U.S. government were killed in Iraq in 2007, a 17 percent increase over 2006. How many of these were security contractors is not known, for the Labor Department does not distinguish between logistics and security contractors.[46]

WHAT IS A PMC?

What is a private military company? It is a sign of the confusion and controversy surrounding the idea of private-sector firms carrying out military and security missions of many different kinds—from combat service support and military training to personal protection—that hardly anyone uses the term the same way. It is a definitional morass. The media invariably uses the term to include non-weapons-bearing firms such as Halliburton and its Kellogg, Brown & Root (KBR) subsidiary.

But it makes no sense to lump military logistics services firms such as KBR in with the likes of Blackwater or ArmorGroup. Anybody who has ever logged on to a relevant listserv or industry chat board knows that one of the easiest ways to start a virtual war is to call ArmorGroup or Control Risks a private military company.

Even among those firms that employ armed personnel, whose mandate includes shooting if necessary, there exist very wide gulfs. A firm such as Blackwater, whose employees have often found themselves in the midst of armed attacks, have little in common with a group such as Erinys, whose main function was providing on-site security for fixed petroleum-sector infrastructure such as pipelines, primarily by training over 14,000 Iraqis in security operations.

In Iraq, many of the private firms, unlike the now-disbanded Executive Outcomes of South Africa, which fought in Angola and Sierra Leone in the 1990s, are actually acting as bodyguards, rather than as combat military units.

Let's be honest about this. The fact that we are dealing with an industry that has really only been in the public eye for a bit over a decade, depending on who and where you count, makes drawing conclusions difficult. Quite simply it is, despite notable consolidations in recent years, an industry in flux. Ten years ago, most public commentary focused on just three companies, Executive Outcomes and Sandline of Great Britain (both of which no longer exist) and U.S.-based MPRI (now a subsidiary of L-3).

But since the initial invasion by the United States–led coalition, Iraq has become the poster child for the private military and security sector. Certainly, the role of such firms has inspired a torrent of popular and academic writing on the subject.[47] Moreover, most people nowadays will at least recognize firms such as Halliburton, Blackwater, DynCorp, ArmorGroup, Triple Canopy, and such others, something that would not have been the case just three years ago.

Now, in Iraq alone, probably hundreds of private military and security firms of all shapes and sizes (most of them *not* employing armed personnel) have operated in Iraq since the start of the 2003 U.S. invasion. And the current PMC sector, contrary to liberal claims, is not a Bush administration initiative either.

The military's growing reliance on contractors is part of a government-wide shift toward outsourcing that goes back decades. During the Clinton administration, it was promoted as "Reinventing Government" by former Vice President Al Gore, an initiative that promised that cutting government payrolls and shifting work to contractors would improve productivity while cutting costs.[48] In early 2005, the federal government was spending about $100 billion more annually for outside contracts than on employee salaries. Many federal departments and offices—NASA and the Department of Energy, to name just two—have become de facto contract management agencies, devoting upward of 80 percent of their budgets to contractors.[49]

Not to be outdone, in 2000, presidential candidate George W. Bush promised to let private companies compete with government workers for 450,000 jobs. As recently as 2003, Defense Secretary Donald Rumsfeld said that as many as 320,000 jobs filled by military personnel could be turned over to civilians.

By even the narrowest interpretation, the PMC sector dates back at least 15 years, to when the then-little-known South African firm, Executive Outcomes, started gaining world attention for its operations against Jonas Savimbi's UNITA in Angola.[50] But there has certainly been a recent expansion.

In the United States one can trace the push for outsourcing of military activities back to the 1966 release of the revised Office of Management and Budget (OMB) Circular A-76.[51] Private contractors were prominent in the "nation-building" effort in South Vietnam and grew significantly over the decades that followed.[52]

Certainly, the use of private contractors by the U.S. military has been an increasing trend.

In the United States the PMC industry was fueled by the same zeal for market-based approaches that drove the deregulation of the electricity, airline, and telephone-service industries. The military was considered to be particularly well-suited to public-private partnerships, because the need for its services fluctuates so radically and abruptly. In light of such sharp spikes in demand, it was thought, it would be more efficient for the military to call on a group of temporary, highly trained experts in times of war—even if that meant paying them a premium—rather than to rely on a permanent standing army that drained resources (with pension plans, health insurance, and so forth) in times of peace.[53]

Table 1.3 Estimated Numbers of Contractors Deployed to Theaters during Conflict[54]

Conflict	Contractors	Military	Ratio
Gulf War I	9,200	541,000	1:58
Bosnia	1,400	20,000	1:15
Iraq	21,000	140,000	1:6

Since the first civilian contractors started operating in Iraq in the aftermath of the United States–led invasion of Iraq, there has been growing public scrutiny of their activities. Although the biggest number of contractors are doing reconstruction work (Parsons, Fluor) or helping with logistics support for U.S. and other coalition forces (Halliburton and its former KBR subsidiary), the glare of media attention has focused on the shooters, the men—and they are all men—who carry and use weapons.

This is not to say that the outsourcing of military logistics functions is not an issue worthy of concern. As the old saying goes, amateurs talk about strategy, but military professionals talk about logistics.

Consider, for example, that in 2004 the overall contract held by Halliburton was worth, over its total life, as much as $13 billion. That cost is 2.5 times the total amount that the United States spent for the first Gulf War, and "the equivalent, in current dollars, to what the U.S. government paid, in total," for the Revolutionary War, War of 1812, Mexican War, and Spanish–American War, combined.[55]

Still, important as they are, logistics contractors are not the focus of this book. Growing attention and concern has been paid to the operations of those private military and security firms who provide security for reconstruction and logistics firms, as well as for the former Coalition Provisional Authority (CPA) workers and various U.S. officials and agencies in Iraq and various nongovernmental organizations and Western media. The U.S. military is now so dependent on these firms that it can't function without them. Like the American Express Card commercial, it simply can't leave home without them.

To paraphrase another old commercial—for Virginia Slims cigarettes—PMCs have come a long way. Whereas as little as a decade ago they were limited to African war zones, they have now assumed a leading role in the activities of the world's sole military superpower, as well as being a front-and-center actor in the daily life of Iraq. If there were an Oscar category for combat participants, PMCs would certainly win the nomination for best supporting actor.

The past five years have seen increased attention and publicity paid to the activities and role of private contractors in Iraq, especially those providing security and military functions.[56] Some of the coverage of these firms has been sensationalist. Journalists frequently characterize PMC employees as corporate mercenaries, though they have almost nothing in common with the image of mercenaries depicted in popular culture or the mercenaries of the last days of the colonial era, involving characters such as "Mad" Mike Hoare, Bob Denard, and Jean Jacque Schram.

In fact, in the current age, in which modern state militaries are staffed by volunteer recruits largely joining in peacetime—many for the pay and benefits—the difference between the private and public soldiers appears to revolve largely around the form of employment contract.[57]

Indeed, considering that the U.S. military is increasingly accepting immigrants, whether legal or illegal, into its regular armed forces, one could make a case that in some respects the United States has a hybrid professional/mercenary military.[58]

PMCs and their conduct are now out in the open, officially above the horizon of public awareness, although concerns about transparency, openness, and regulatory oversight remain. Their relative numbers in the two Gulf Wars illustrate the increase in the use of PMCs: during the first Gulf War in 1991, for every 1 contractor there were 50 military personnel involved. In the 2003 conflict the ratio was 1 to 10.

The U.S. military had been planning to dramatically increase its long-term reliance on the private sector in 2003, independent of Operation Iraqi Freedom. The plan, overseen by then-Army Secretary Thomas E. White, was known as the "Third Wave" within the Pentagon, because there had been two earlier competitive sourcing initiatives. During the first wave, which began in 1979, the Army reviewed 25,000 positions for competition. The second wave was undertaken as part of the Defense Reform Initiative Directive. During the second wave, as part of the late 1990s' reinvention of government initiatives, the Army competed 13,000 jobs; 375 civilians were involuntarily separated as a result of these competitions.[59]

The Third Wave had three purposes: (1) to free up military manpower and resources for the global war on terrorism, (2) to obtain noncore products and services from the private sector to enable Army leaders to focus on the Army's core competencies, and (3) to support the President's Management Agenda. The Third Wave not only asked what activities could be performed at less cost by private sources but also asked on what activities the Army should focus its energies.

In March 2002, a year before the beginning of the Iraq war, then–Secretary of the Army Thomas White told top Defense Department officials that reductions in Army civilian and military personnel, carried out over the previous 11 years, had been accompanied by an increased reliance on private contractors about whose very dimensions the Pentagon knew too little. "Currently," he wrote, "Army planners and programmers lack visibility at the Departmental level into the labor and costs associated with the contract work force and of the organizations and missions supported by them."

But the initiative came to a temporary standstill in April 2003 when Secretary White resigned after a two-year tenure marked by strains with Defense Secretary Donald H. Rumsfeld.[60] White has claimed that in a memorandum dated March 8, 2002, he warned the Department of Defense undersecretaries for army contracting, personnel, and finances that the Army lacked the basic information required to effectively manage its burgeoning force of private contractors.[61]

Though more than two years after White ordered the Army to gather information, it remained uncollected.[62] It ran afoul of the 1995 Paperwork Reduction Act, becoming bogged down in assessments of the associated burden and benefits.

In April 2004, the Army told Congress that its best guess was that the Army had between 124,000 and 605,000 service contract workers. In October, the Army announced that it would permit contractors to compete for "non-core" positions

held by 154,910 civilian workers (more than half of the Army's civilian workforce) and 58,727 military personnel. It should have been no surprise, then, when
contractors were needed to meet the surge of wartime reconstruction, that the
Pentagon itself was hard pressed to estimate the numbers of its contract employees in Iraq.[63]

In September 2004 Defense Secretary Donald Rumsfeld told the Senate
Armed Services Committee that he had identified more than 50,000 positions
now filled by uniformed personnel "doing what are essentially nonmilitary jobs."
At the same time, he said, the Army was so short-handed it had to call up tens of
thousands of reservists to fight in Iraq. Rumsfeld said he intended to assign the
troops to military jobs and hire civilian workers or contractors to take the nonmilitary jobs. "We plan to carry this conversion out at a rate of about 10,000 positions per year," Rumsfeld told the committee.[64]

Raymond DuBois, then Defense deputy undersecretary for installations and
environment, said in an October 25, 2004, memo to defense agencies that in
spring 2005 the annual inventory that marks jobs as inherently government or
commercial would be used to identify military jobs that can be converted to civilian positions in addition to filling various reporting requirements.[65]

In 2003, the Pentagon for the first time used the inventories to identify
which military jobs would be given to civilians. The inventories are required
each year of all federal agencies by the 1998 Federal Activities Inventory
Reform Act.[66]

In fact, the role of PMC operations within the U.S. military has been growing for some time. One Department of Defense (DoD) guide notes:

> The use of civilian contractors for support within the US military is not new. Up to
> World War II, support from the private sector was common. The primary role of con-
> tractors was simple logistics support, such as transportation, medical services, and
> provisioning.
>
> As the Vietnam conflict unfolded, the role of the contractor began to change. The
> increasing technical complexity of military equipment and hardware drove the Ser-
> vices to rely on contractors as technical specialists, and they worked side by side with
> deployed military personnel.

Several factors have driven this expanded role for contractors:

> Downsizing of the military following the Gulf War; [g]rowing reliance on contractors
> to support the latest weapons and provide lifetime support for the systems; DoD-
> sponsored move to outsource or privatize functions to improve efficiency and free up
> funds for sustainment and modernization programs; and increased operating tempos.
> Today contractor logistics support is routinely imbedded in most major systems main-
> tenance and support plans. Unfortunately, military operational planners have not been
> able to keep up with the growing involvement of contractors.[67]

Another paper noted:

The notion, much less the requirement, of placing contractors on the battlefield is the cumulative effect of reduced government spending, force reductions/government downsizing, privatization of duties historically performed by the military, low retention rates—particularly in high technology positions[—]reliance upon increasingly complex technology, higher mission requirements, low military salaries, and recruitment shortfalls all within a booming economy and budgetary surplus projections.[68]

The drive to shift activities from the public to the private sector for military activities is largely ideologically motivated. A *New Yorker* article noted:

The notion that government is fundamentally inefficient and unproductive has become conventional wisdom. It had always had a certain hold on the American imagination, but it gained strength with the ascendancy of conservatism in the eighties and nineties. Second, Washington fell for the era's biggest business fad: outsourcing. For most of the twentieth century, successful corporations were supposed to look like General Motors: versatile, vertically integrated, huge. But by the nineties vertical integration had given way to "core competency": do only what you do best, and pay someone else to do the rest. The Pentagon decided that it should concentrate on its core competency "warfighting."[69]

But whether ideology is supported by the facts is still an open question.

[Outsourcing support functions is] a tidy picture: the Army becomes a lean, mean killing machine, while civilians peel the potatoes and clean the latrines. But there's a reason that companies like General Motors existed in the first place. Effective as outsourcing can be, doing things in-house is often easier and quicker. You avoid the expense and hassle of haggling, and retain operational reliability and control, which is especially important to the military. No contract can guarantee that private employees will stick around in a combat zone. After the Iraq war, some contractors refused assignments to dangerous parts of the country. That left American troops sitting in the mud, and without hot food . . .

Outsourcing works well when there's genuine competition among suppliers; that's when the virtues of the private sector come into play. But in the market for big military contracts the bidders tend to be the usual few suspects, so that the game resembles the American auto or steel industries before Japan and Germany became major players: more comfortable than competitive. Sometimes the lack of competition is explicit: many of the contracts for rebuilding Iraq were handed out on a no-bid basis. And many of them are "cost-plus" contracts. This means that the contractors' profit is a percentage of their costs, which gives them an incentive to keep those costs high. That's hardly a recipe for efficiency or rigor.[70]

Indeed, in the view of some, contractors have become virtually a fourth branch of government, raising the same questions about propriety, cost and accountability that the other three branches experience. As a *New York Times* investigation noted:

- Consider that competition, intended to produce savings, appears to have sharply eroded. An analysis by The New York Times shows that fewer than half of all "contract actions"—new contracts and payments against existing contracts—are now subject to full and open competition. Just 48 percent were competitive in 2005, down from 79 percent in 2001.
- Agencies are crippled in their ability to seek low prices, supervise contractors and intervene when work goes off course because the number of government workers overseeing contracts has remained level as spending has shot up.
- The most successful contractors are not necessarily those doing the best work, but those who have mastered the special skill of selling to Uncle Sam. The top 20 service contractors have spent nearly $300 million since 2000 on lobbying and have donated $23 million to political campaigns.
- Contracting almost always leads to less public scrutiny as government programs are hidden behind closed corporate doors. Companies, unlike agencies, are not subject to the Freedom of Information Act.[71]

The numbers for at least one contractor seem to indicate that for at least one major PSC, full and open competition is more an ideal than a reality.

Total dollars: $1,059,633,363

Total number of contractors: 1

Total number of transactions: 724

Extent of Competition

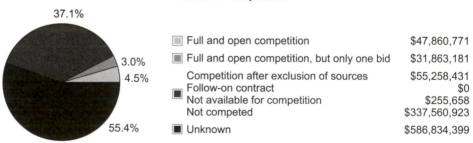

Full and open competition	$47,860,771
Full and open competition, but only one bid	$31,863,181
Competition after exclusion of sources	$55,258,431
Follow-on contract	$0
Not available for competition	$255,658
Not competed	$337,560,923
Unknown	$586,834,399

37.1%
3.0%
4.5%
55.4%

(source: FedSpending.org)

Figure 1.3 Summary for Blackwater Security's Contracts with the U.S. Government, 2000–2007[72]

Only some $47 million–plus dollars of that government contract money was won outright in competition with other firms. That leaves some $1 billion–plus dollars in contracts that Blackwater received without any competition—or without any competition that we know of—from other firms.

In the past Blackwater itself acknowledged that the cost–benefit claim is still undecided. This was seen in the October 2, 2007, hearing of the U.S. House Oversight and Government Reform Committee at which Erik Prince, the founder and head of Blackwater, testified. Mr. Prince was asked about the cost–benefit of using private contractors:

> MR. PRINCE: I don't know what those numbers are, sir, but that would be a great fully burden cost study that Congress could sponsor. They don't have to do the whole thing, just take some key nodes and really study it.[73]

What little cost–benefit analysis there has been to date has focused on narrow economic cost comparisons and has generally avoided addressing equally important political factors, such as avoiding tough political choices concerning military needs, reserve call-ups, and the human consequences of war.

A professor at the U.S. Naval Academy has written that even if there are cost savings, inevitable contractual hazards sharply limit the combat/combat support role of these companies.[74]

An economic professor wrote that "[e]xcessive use of private contractors erodes checks and balances, and it substitutes market transactions, controlled by the executive branch, for traditional political mechanisms of accountability. When it comes to Iraq, we've yet to see the evidence of a large practical gain in return; instead, use of contractors may have helped to make an ill-advised venture possible."[75]

One military officer wrote

> The increasing belief since the 1990s that private is better rests on the assumption that free-market capitalism is operating. This assumption, however, is often unfounded; there are several relevant dissimilarities. First, free market capitalism requires a competitive environment, yet over the last 5 years over 40% of DoD contracts have been sole source single bidder contracts. Second, free markets rely on numerous customers, yet the military in particular or the government in general is often the only customer. Finally[,] free market capitalism rests on the assumption that consumers cannot pass on economic inefficiencies, but the military can pass these losses to the federal government and eventually the taxpayers. In other words, there is not the same market incentive to require utmost efficiency.[76]

Scholars such as Peter Singer at the Brookings Institution have long worried that privatization is automatically considered a good thing. Writing in the journal *Foreign Affairs*, Singer noted

A third lesson is self-evident but has often been ignored: privatize something only if it will save money or raise quality. If it will not, then do not. Unfortunately, the Pentagon's current, supposedly business-minded leadership seems to have forgotten Economics 101. All too often, it outsources first and never bothers to ask questions later. That something is done privately does not necessarily make it better, quicker, or cheaper. Rather, it is through leveraging free-market mechanisms that one potentially gets better private results. Success is likely only if a contract is competed for on the open market, if the winning firm can specialize on the job and build in redundancies, if the client is able to provide oversight and management to guard its own interests, and if the contractor is properly motivated by the fear of being fired. Forget these simple rules, as the U.S. government often does, and the result is not the best of privatization but the worst of monopolization.[77]

Many academics who examine the issue of the relative cost of private versus public point to the politics behind the various ways one can measure cost. What you include or exclude in your study can be a complicated political exercise. Economists disagree on how to answer this question, at least in part because they use different variables when measuring cost. When you measure the savings of using retired special operations forces personnel, do you factor in the hundreds of thousands of tax dollars used to train these ex-soldiers? This is a valid economic variable worth including, but no study yet published seems to have done so. Even more difficult can be attaching a dollar value to in-house military 'services.' Because military establishments often have a 'monopoly' of service delivery and information regarding cost, getting accurate comparative information is not easy.

Privatization has been touted as one way to actually allow a government the ability to see cost comparisons between, say, what the army will charge and what a private provider would charge. It is not a bad idea, but problems arise when cost reductions are assumed, or when statistics measuring savings from outsourcing are based on hypothetical projections.

Furthermore, 'cost' is not the only way to measure value. Logistics officers often talk about value in terms of cost/speed of delivery/quality of service. If you need it tomorrow in a war zone, you can't expect Federal Express to get it there for you. That affects quality and price. The private and public sectors might— and do—behave differently because of inherent differences between these two sectors.

The way to ensure more nearly that the use of contractors produces real cost savings and greater efficiency, and to make it more likely that commitments to the use of contractors will not be counterproductive, is to adopt a much more public decision-making process in which Congress plays a far larger active role, coupling it with robust oversight and accounting for both expenditures and performance. This means closer regulation, mandatory audit trails, regular reporting, and greater public access to nonsensitive records, and it will require a much more nearly coherent body of laws and regulations than we now have.

The fact that outsourcing of military functions from the public to the private sector has not been proven to be more cost effective has not stopped people from claiming that it is so. Typical of this is the statement by Doug Brooks, president of the International Peace Operations Association, that "[c]ontractors are cost effective. Although the popular perception is of huge salaries for cushy jobs, the reality is that contractors live along side military personnel and generally cost the government far less in the long run."[78]

In February 2005, Erik Prince, the founder of Blackwater USA, proposed raising a "contractor brigade" to supplement regular U.S. military forces. "There's consternation in the DoD [Department of Defense] about increasing the permanent size of the army," said Mr. Prince. "We want to add 30,000 people, and they talked about costs of anywhere from $3.6bn to $4bn to do that. Well, by my math, that comes out to about $135,000 per soldier," he added. "We could do it certainly cheaper."[79]

Regardless, the PMC sector has been undergoing a significant quantitative and qualitative shift over the past decade. Professor Deborah Avant of George Washington University wrote

Private security contractors (PSCs) now provide more (and more kinds of) services, including some that have been considered core military capabilities in the modern era. This brings contractors closer to the battlefield. In Operation Iraqi Freedom, contractors provided operational support for systems such as JSTARS and Patriot, and were heavily involved in postconflict reconstruction, including in raising and training the Iraqi army and police forces. A small number of firms have provided armed personnel that operate with troops on the battlefield. Much more common, however, are PSCs that support weapons systems, provide logistics, provide advice and training, site security, and policing services to states and non-state actors. Also new is the transnational nature of the market. Private security is a global phenomenon. In the 1990s every multilateral peace operation conducted by the UN was accomplished with the presence of private military or security companies.

States that contracted for military services ranged from highly capable states like the United States to failing states like Sierra Leone. Global corporations contracted with PSCs for site security and planning and nongovernmental organizations (NGOs) working in conflict zones or unstable territories in Eastern Europe, the Middle East, Africa, Asia, and Latin America did the same.[80]

Since the September 11, 2001, attacks on the World Trade Center and the Pentagon there has been a notable increase in the formation of new PMCs. "The idea was to create a security consulting company that could work for entities such as the Department of State and the Department of Defense to deal with the situations that were going to arise in a post-9/11 world," said Jamie Smith, a former Navy SEAL who founded SCG International Risk.[81]

In 1998 Tim Spicer made headlines when his private military company Sandline International was accused of breaking UN sanctions and selling arms to Sierra Leone. In 2006 he said, "There have been a lot of changes in the way this industry works in the past ten years. What I was doing ten years ago was way ahead of its time. The catalyst has been the war on terror. The whole period since 9/11 has highlighted the need for a private security sector."[82]

Even the CIA hired contractors to bolster its paramilitary force. Johnny "Mike" Spann, the first American killed in combat in Afghanistan, on November 25, 2001, was one such CIA employee.[83] In light of the controversy over PMC involvement in the Iraqi prison scandal it is worth remembering that Spann was working as an interrogator when he was killed. Two other CIA civilian contractors, Christopher Glenn Mueller and William "Chief" Carlson, were killed in an ambush in Afghanistan on October 25, 2003, while tracking terrorists near Shkin, Afghanistan.[84] In fact, much as is the situation with PMC and regular military forces, private companies are aggressively seeking highly trained employees of intelligence agencies to fill government contracts, leading to a critical spy drain.[85]

But it was Iraq that drove the amount of world attention focused on the role of PMCs to new heights. Although noticed much less than in their post-major combat operations, PMCs were prominent during the war itself. The military relied on civilian contractors to run the computer systems that generated the tactical air picture for the Combined Air Operations Centre for the war in Iraq. Other contract technicians supported Predator unmanned aerial vehicles (UAVs) and the datalinks they used to transmit information.

The U.S. Navy relied on civilian contractors to help operate the guided missile systems on some of its ships. When the Army's technology-heavy 4th Infantry Division deployed to Iraq in 2003, about 60 contract employees accompanied it to support its digital command-and-control systems. The systems were still in development, and the Army did not have uniformed personnel trained to maintain them.[86]

The Army depends entirely on civilian contractors to maintain its Guardrail surveillance aircraft. With relatively few planes packed with specialized intelligence-gathering systems on board, the service decided it was not cost effective to develop its own maintenance capability.

As the services have increased their use of commercial off-the-shelf equipment, they have also increased their use of contractors. The Air Force and Navy used commercial communications systems throughout southwest Asia, for example—but the services don't train troops to maintain commercial systems. Instead, they hire civilian contractors.

Contractors were also used for base operations and logistics support, prepositioned equipment maintenance, generator maintenance, biological and chemical detection systems, fuel and material transport, and medical services.

All of this was predictable. In fact, *Fortune Magazine* published an article two days before the war began, auguring that if America went to war against Iraq, private military companies would play a bigger role than ever before.[87]

Even the U.S. Special Operations Command, the umbrella organization for all U.S. special operations forces, has sought the help of private contractors to make slick multilingual audio, video, print and Web packages to support its global psychological war against terrorism.[88]

What do PMCs do in Iraq? Researchers have argued endlessly for years trying to come up with a framework describing their functions. To read various academics, the search for an appropriate "typology" is a bit like the quest for the Holy Grail. But the truth is that there are no hard and fast categories. Because PMCs are businesses, their core mission is to make a profit. As such, they will bid on whatever business they think they can get—and thus their mission and function will change accordingly.

There is no consensus on what constitute a PMC, but three main categories of their activities stand out:

- *Military combatant companies*—Firms that actually provide military forces capable of combat are fairly rare and only constitute a minority of PMCs, even though such firms tend to receive the most publicity. Examples include the now disbanded PMCs Executive Outcomes of South Africa and Sandline of the United Kingdom; none are currently operating in Iraq.
- *Military consulting firms*—These traditionally provide training and advisory services, though some have expanded into personal security and bodyguard services. Examples include Blackwater, MPRI, DynCorp, and SAIC of the United States.
- *Military support firms*—These provide nonlethal aid and assistance, such as weapons maintenance, technical support, explosive ordnance disposal, and intelligence collection and analysis. Examples include Halo Group, Vinnell, and Ronco of the United States.

Regardless of category, none of the firms provide services that could be called inexpensive. For example, Charlotte, North Carolina–based Zapata Engineering was one of 10 companies working on a $1.47 billion contract for explosives demolition in Iraq. The first one-year contract the company received in September 2003 totaled $3.8 million for five management positions in Iraq. The single liaison officer cost taxpayers not just the $350,000 in salary, but $850,000 in overhead, insurance, and profit costs.[89] Four project managers were budgeted for a total of $2.7 million, which includes $275,000 in annual pay for each and a total of $1.6 million for overhead, insurance, and profit. In February 2004, the Army Corps of Engineers awarded Zapata another one-year contract worth $32.5 million to hire as many as 108 technicians and support staffers to oversee a munitions depot in Iraq. In Zapata's $32 million contract extension, security forces accounted for 50 of the 108 positions, but there's no way of telling the exact cost to taxpayers.[90]

Breaking these categories down is nearly impossible for the simple reason that a contractor can do more than one task and offer more than one capability. Military consulting firms, in particular, are capable of offering a wide variety of services—and if they don't have the capability in hand when they win a contract, they simply go out and hire it. That is what is done by most contractors in the military industrial and national security realms. Although it affords them great flexibility in competing for contracts, it also makes classifying them very difficult. That may explain why the services they advertise (risk management, protective security, security training, risk consultancy, risk management, and so on) on their Web sites are so nondescript.

Aegis Defence calls itself a "British security and risk management company." DynCorp International advertises itself as "a multifaceted, global enterprise that provides innovative solutions to the diverse technology and professional services needs of government and commercial industry worldwide." Blackwater "efficiently and effectively integrates a wide range of resources and core competencies to provide unique and timely solutions that exceed . . . customers' stated needs and expectations." ArmorGroup is "a leading provider of defensive and protective security services." Triple Canopy "mitigates risk and develops comprehensive security programs."[91]

Academics such as Chris Kinsey write, "You can only distinguish between different activities. Some companies will continue to operate within their core competency, such as ArmorGroup and CRG. Other companies may decide to move around the market depending on market opportunity."[92]

Rather than working directly for the U.S. government or the old Coalition Provisional Authority, most PMCs are subcontracted to provide protection for prime contractor employees or are hired by other entities such as Iraqi companies or private foreign companies seeking business opportunities in Iraq.

Of 60 PMCs that the CPA identified as working in Iraq, only eight had direct contracts with the CPA for obligations then totaling about $147 million.

Not only were PMCs critical, if relatively unnoticed during major combat operations in 2003, they became even more important afterward.[93] U.S. armed services relied on civilian contractors to run a number of military systems. In 2007, 34 percent of the $21 billion allocated for Iraqi reconstruction was diverted to security—an increase from a planned $4.56 billion to $6.31 billion. For private reconstruction contractors, the cost of security was running at an average of 12 percent for each contract.[94]

In August 2007, the *Washington Post* reported that the U.S. military has paid $548 million over the past three years to two British security firms, Aegis Defence Services and Erinys Iraq, that protect the U.S. Army Corps of Engineers on reconstruction projects—payment of more than $200 million over the original budget.[95]

And even if there are major U.S. troop withdrawals from Iraq, PMCs are going to be in Iraq and neighboring countries for years to come. Aside from Iraq, just about every informed observer expects that the Pentagon will still spend an increasing amount of money paying private sector firms to perform specialized tasks.[96]

To this day, nobody knows for certain how many PMCs are operating in Iraq, although we now have better estimates than we did when the United States first invaded. Uncertainty over the number springs partly from matters of definition. Not everyone agrees what a private military contractor is. Some people take the PMC category to encompass everyone—including those doing logistics work: serving food in the mess halls, driving supply trucks, doing the laundry.

As one knowledgeable reporter noted in an online interview,

> The commonly used number is 20,000, but that has been circulating for more than three years. The issues are the lack of regulation and the diffuse nature of the contracts—which are written by the military, the State Department, and various companies, and often are under many layers of subcontracting. So it's hard to count.[97]

But such people, although critical to the war effort, are not what the general public has in mind when talking about the industry. Inevitably, they are talking about the shooters; the heavily muscled men in 511 gear sporting buzz cuts and mirrored sunglasses, fingers on the trigger guards of their weapons.

Early on, in response to a request from Congress, a Coalition Provisional Authority (CPA)–compiled report listed 60 PMCs with an aggregate total of 20,000 personnel (including U.S. citizens, third-country nationals, and Iraqis), but even back then the list was incomplete. Missing, for example, were companies implicated in the Abu Ghraib prison scandal. Most of the armed personnel were the 14,000 Iraqi guards who staffed the oil field security contract for Erinys.

In March 2006, the Director of the Private Security Company Association of Iraq estimated that approximately 181 private security companies were working in Iraq, employing just over 48,000 workers.

Back then, Global Risk Strategies was said to be the largest PMC in Iraq, employing 1,000–1,200. Blackwater had about 600, SOC-SMG 300, Triple Canopy about 350, Control Risks Group 750, Olive 265, and DynCorp 175.

The total number of non-Iraqi PMC personnel is certainly less than 20,000, and despite claims to the contrary, PMCs do not constitute the second- or third-largest Army in Iraq, are not coordinated into one cohesive whole, and do not engage in offensive operations.

The lure of higher salaries is causing an exodus of U.S. and British special forces to PMCs just as these military forces are being asked to play an increasing role in combating terrorism and helping to conduct nation-building operations worldwide. Competition over elite troops from private companies is so intense that U.S. and British military commanders have created new pay, benefits, and educational incentives to try to retain them.

In early 2005, the Pentagon approved an unusual incentives package aimed at retaining Special Operations Forces personnel such as Green Berets and Navy SEALs. The Pentagon planned to budget over $100 million a year for bonuses and special pay for junior and senior Special Operations Forces (SOF) members who agree to stay in the force.[98]

PMCs in Iraq

PMCs were prominent during the war in 2003 and of course afterwards as hostilities continued.[1] U.S. armed services relied on civilian contractors to run a number of military systems. And PMCs are going to be in Iraq for some years to come. As Iraqis assume increasing responsibility for policing their own country, U.S. companies plan to play a large and profitable role in training and assisting the locals.[2]

PSCs work for many different clients: the U.S. government, the British government, the Iraqi government, and a myriad of private firms, most of them doing reconstruction work. Some PSCs work directly as subcontractors to a prime contractor; others work two, three, four, or even more levels down the contracting chain, which makes oversight that much more difficult. This problem is compounded by the fact that it is each firm's responsibility to provide security for its personnel and the projects under its domain.[3]

WPPS CONTRACTS[4]

One of the bigger contracts is for the protection of U.S. Department of State (DOS) personnel. To appreciate the State Department's use of PSCs, one has to go back 20 years. In the mid-1980s, after the bombing of the U.S. Embassy in Beirut and in conjunction with the Diplomatic Security and Antiterrorism Act of 1986, private companies were afforded the opportunity to compete for security contracts at U.S. overseas missions.

As a result, the State Department's Bureau of Diplomatic Security (DS) began using civilian contract personal security specialists (PSSs) to fulfill this priority. DS first deployed PSS contractors in September of 1994 during a prolonged period of unrest in Haiti. In the intervening period, the department has fielded PSS contractors in Bosnia, Afghanistan, Israel, Haiti, and Iraq.

In March 2000, recognizing that there was a consistent and sustained need for PSS contractors, the department developed and awarded the first iteration of the Worldwide Personal Protective Services (WPPS) contract. WPPS I was awarded to DynCorp International to provide services in the former Yugoslavia and was subsequently used for deployments in the Palestinian Territories beginning in July 2002 and in Afghanistan for the Karzai Protective Operation in November 2002.

In early 2004, additional task orders were added to the WPPS contract to provide PSS support for the U.S. Embassy in Baghdad when it opened on July 1, 2004. DynCorp was unable to meet the full requirements of the expanding mission, and a second service provider was established through a contract with Blackwater USA. Another company, Triple Canopy, was subsequently awarded a contract to protect the Regional Embassy Office in Basrah, Iraq. At the same time, the State Department drafted and released a competitive contract covering an increasing requirement for protective services throughout the world.

In June of 2005, DynCorp, Blackwater USA, and Triple Canopy were awarded contracts under what is now known as the WPPS II contract. Personnel qualifications, training, equipment, and management requirements were substantially upgraded under WPPS II because of the ever-changing program requirements in the combat environment of Iraq.

The current contract was awarded in July 2005. DS utilizes the WPPS II umbrella contract under which it issues task orders to the three qualified companies: Blackwater USA, DynCorp, and Triple Canopy. The bulk of the contractors come from Blackwater. The contract has a ceiling of $1.2 billion per contractor over five years (one base + four option years). There are currently seven active task orders under WPPS II: Jerusalem, Kabul, Bosnia, Baghdad, REO Basrah, REO Al Hillah, and REO Kirkuk (including USAID Erbil). An eighth operational task order for aviation services in Iraq was awarded to Blackwater USA on September 4, 2007, and performance was to begin in late November 2007. Task Order 1 covers the contractors' local program management offices in the Washington, D.C., area.

Security contractors working for DOS perform a narrow range of tactical duties, including protection of certain foreign heads of state, high-level U.S. officials (including members of Congress), and U.S. diplomats under Chief-of-Mission authority. As such, the department requires that security contractors working for DS meet stringent requirements for employment and sustain high performance standards once employed. Candidates undergo a screening process by their employer or contractor before submitting their applications to the State Department. After the applications are submitted, the Department of State performs a background investigation on each American-citizen contractor employee, who must qualify for a U.S. government security clearance at an appropriate level. The department requires a similar process for foreign national contractors, who, likewise, must qualify to receive a clearance appropriate to their assignments. DS special agents oversee security contractors who are trained to DS specifications by DS-vetted trainers. Before deploying, the PSS contractors receive 164 hours of DS-approved instruction and training. Only successfully trained and qualified contractors are deployed.

The Department of State requires that each person working on a private security contract meet specific experience requirements delineated by position title and description. Before each person is approved, the security firm contractor must verify that he or she possesses the experience and training required by the contract. The DS High Threat Protection (HTP) Program Office individually reviews and approves candidates for key leadership positions. The contractor certifies that all other personnel meet the requirements. The Program Office may review qualifications and remove individuals not meeting contract requirements at any time.

Qualification statements for a Personal security specialist (PSS) require a minimum of one year of experience in protective security assignments. This experience and background may have been gained in any of the following assignments:

- U.S. Department of State Diplomatic Security Service
- U.S. Secret Service
- U.S. Federal Agencies, e.g., FBI (former Special Agents with protective-security background)
- U.S. Special Forces or Special Operations
- U.S. Military Infantry (Army or USMC)
- Commercial Executive Protection Services with Military or Police Background
- Law Enforcement Experience (U.S. Military Police/Criminal Investigation Division or in an Emergency Services, Special Weapons, or Tactical Operations Type Unit of a Local or State Law Enforcement Agency)

All PSS personnel are trained in accordance with the requirements in the WPPS II base contract, which contains the qualifications and requirements for both facilities and instructors providing PSS training. PSS personnel must attend and successfully complete predeployment training that consists of 164 hours of instruction delivered by instructors previously vetted by DS. PSS training covers the following topics:

- Terrorist Operations
- Organization of a Protective Detail
- Protective Services Formations and Standard Operating Procedures
- Protective Security Advances
- Driver Training
- Vehicle Dynamics

- Evasive Maneuvers
- Armored Vehicle Dynamics
- Basic Motorcade Operations
- Radio Procedures
- Countermeasures
- Emergency Medical Training
- Firearms
- Defensive Tactics
- Land Navigation

In addition to DS-provided course materials, contractor-developed lesson plans must be approved by the DS HTP program office and the DS Training Center. DS HTP personnel visit contractor facilities and observe training to ensure compliance with contract requirements.

State Department reliance on PSCs has dramatically increased in recent years. In October 2007 the press reported that although the amount of money the State Department pays to private security and law enforcement contractors had soared from $1 billion to nearly $4 billion a year, the department had added few new officials to oversee the contracts.[5]

BRITISH CONTRACTS

It is not just the American government that uses PSCs. In September 2006 the British Foreign and Commonwealth Office (FCO), in response to a Freedom of Information Act request, revealed how much it had spent per financial year on PSCs since the start of the conflict.

May 2003–March 2004: £19,121,598

April 2004–March 2005: £45,765,639

April 2005–March 2006: £47,818,682

April 2006–June 2006: £8,766,917

This money was spent on Control Risks Group, ArmorGroup, Kroll Security Group, and Edinburgh Risk Security Management. In addition, the FCO had a contract with ArmorGroup to provide international police advisors in Iraq. This contract's costs were as follows:

April 4–March 5: £3,700,172

April 5–March 6: £8,417,242.80

April 6–August 6: £3,331,102[6]

PAY[7]

If you have it heard it once you have heard it countless times, that private security contractors make far more than regular military personnel. This is a sound bite and far from the whole story. This so-called pay gap creates low morale and jealousy in the regular armed forces and causes friction between them. It also supposedly contributes to problems with retaining people in the military, as many of them reportedly leave at the end of their enlistment to take up jobs in the PSC sector.

This would be most distressing if it were true. Soldiers, marines, airmen, and sailors make tremendous sacrifices on behalf of the country. They deserve to be well compensated, both in direct terms and relative to the civilian population.

As it turns out, they are. A study on regular military compensation (RMC) released by the Congressional Budget Office (CBO) in June 2007 looked at all the factors to which each service member is entitled, such as basic pay, housing and subsistence allowances, and associated tax advantages. The Pentagon has used RMC as a fundamental measure of military pay since at least 1962.

Another, more complete measure includes noncash and deferred cash benefits, such as healthcare for current service members and their families, the healthcare and other veterans' benefits that members can receive once they leave the military, and retirement pay and health benefits for members who serve for at least 20 years or become seriously disabled. Military personnel and their families are also eligible for subsidized child care and groceries, the use of physical fitness and recreational facilities, free legal and financial counseling, and other family-support programs.

Finally, even within the confines of purely cash compensation, service members can receive special pays, bonuses, and allowances that are not counted in RMC. Special and incentive pays are usually awarded for particular skills or for hazardous duty, including deployment and combat. Members may also earn bonus payments when they reenlist for several more years, especially if they have occupational skills that are in short supply. But because all of those types of pay are either earned by relatively few specialists or are earned irregularly, they are not generally included in the RMC measure.

Admittedly, it is hard to make exact comparisons, given the inherent differences between military and civilian life, but it appears that regular military forces do not do that badly. According to the CBO, a 20-year-old high school graduate with no dependents who had reached the pay grade of E-3 earned about $33,000 in cash compensation in 2006, as well as $28,000 in noncash and deferred benefits. A similar member in grade E-6 with 12 years of service received a total of about $96,000 in pay and benefits, and a 40-year-old E-8 earned total compensation of about $127,000.

Other studies in recent years have come out with similar numbers. In a 2004 analysis, the CBO estimated total compensation per service member at $107,600. A 2004 study by the Center for Naval Analyses estimated average compensation at $94,900 for Navy personnel. In a 2005 report, the Government Accountability Office (GAO) estimated that compensation for active-duty service members averaged

$115,500. That higher figure was partly attributable to continued increases in military compensation. An unpublished Pentagon study from 2005, which included the costs of military training and travel as well as expenditures outside the DoD budget, estimated compensation at $138,000 per service member in fiscal year 2005.

According to Cindy Williams, a former assistant director of the Congressional Budget Office, where she led the National Security Division, overall "job security is better" for regular military forces, given that their career could span 20 years, whereas a PSC has only a limited contract. She also said that "the benefits package, including healthcare and retirement, is better."

There has been more confirmation that the alleged pay gap is a myth. On March 12, 2008, the Pentagon released its Tenth Quadrennial Review of Military Compensation. The findings confirm that military member compensation is competitive. Military personnel's annual compensation meets or exceeds the 80th percentile when compared to their civilian peers of like age and education.

This confirms what some have previously said. For example, an article published in *Serviam Magazine*, an industry publication, noted:

> The active duty E-6 has an annual base pay of $33,976 plus basic allowances for housing and subsistence, for a total of $44,863. Adding special duty pay, a reenlistment bonus aggregated over four years, and other allowances, minus federal taxes, the total net cash compensation comes to $63,340.

> The independent security contractor, who in this instance earns a base pay of $165,000, receives no other benefits. Because he is rotated in and out of Iraq every 90 days, he cannot claim the income tax exemptions that he could if he was stationed abroad for a full tax year. In his high tax bracket, he must pay $69,300 in federal taxes—more than 50 times what the sergeant must pay.

> That still leaves the contractor with a net cash compensation of $95,700, or about 38 percent more than the sergeant.

> Then we factor in noncash benefits such as health care, installation-based benefits, subsistence in kind, family housing and barracks, education, and other benefits. For the sergeant, these benefits can total $22,765. The sergeant is also entitled to retirement pay accrual, Veterans Administration (VA) compensation and pension, VA health care, and related health benefits, amounting to $34,269 per year in deferred benefits. Total compensation for the staff sergeant after taxes can equal $126,734.

> The contractor in this illustration receives none of the noncash benefits or deferred benefits of the sergeant. Now the tables are turned: $126,734 in total compensation for the staff sergeant, and $95,700 for the contractor.

> But wait—there's more. If the contractor wants the noncash and deferred benefits such as health care, housing, and retirement contributions, he must pay out of his pocket. His $95,700 take-home pay, minus the equivalent $22,765 in noncash benefits and the $34,629 in deferred benefits, leaves him with a net cash compensation equivalent of a paltry $38,306.

> By contrast, the staff sergeant walks away with a net cash contribution of $69,340.

Table 2.1 Net Cash and Noncash Compensation Comparison[8]

Active Duty E-6, 10-Year Service Member	Cash Compensation	Security Independent Contractor	Cash Compensation
30 Days Paid Leave per Year		*Months per Year Actually Working = 11*	
Basic pay °	33,976	Base pay	165,000
Basic allowance for housing (BAH) *	8,507	Housing allowance	—
Basic allowance for subsistence (BAS) *	2,380	Subsistence allowance	—
Basic pay + BAH + BAS	**44,863**	**Basic pay + "BAH" + "BAS"**	**165,000**
Special duty pays **	12,060	Special duty pays	—
$45k capped reenlistment bonus °°	11,250	Reenlistment bonus	—
Other allowances *	2,441	Other allowances	—
Federal tax due °	(1,274)	Federal tax due	(69,300)
Net cash compensation	**69,340**	**Net cash compensation**	**95,700**
*Federal tax advantage *(not included)*	*4,538*	*Federal tax advantage (not included)*	*(0)*
Noncash Benefits		**Noncash Benefits**	
Healthcare *	6,829	Healthcare	—
Installation-based benefits *	3,700	Installation-based benefits	—
Subsistence in kind *	2,455	Subsistence in kind	—
Family housing and barracks *	2,221	Family housing and barracks	—
Education *	466	Education	—
Other benefits *	7,093	Other benefits	—
Total noncash benefits	**22,765**	**Total noncash benefits**	**0**

Table 2.1 (*Continued*)

Deferred Benefits	Cash Compensation	Deferred Benefits	Cash Compensation
Retired pay accrual	9,072	Retired pay accrual	—
VA compensation and pension *	7,839	VA compensation and pension	—
VA healthcare *	7,303	VA Healthcare	—
VA other *	771	VA other	—
Healthcare accrual *	9,643	Healthcare accrual	0
Total deferred benefits	**34,629**	**Total deferred benefits**	**0**
TOTAL COMPENSATION	**126,734**	**TOTAL COMPENSATION**	**95,700**
Total noncash benefits *	(22,765)	Total noncash benefits *	(22,765)
Total deferred benefits *	(34,629)	Total deferred benefits *	(34,629)
Net cash compensation	**69,340**	**Net cash compensation less USG equivalent noncash and deferred benefits**	**38,306**

* GAO-05-798 military compensation (2005)
** DOD military pay chart (2007)
° OSD military compensation Web site (2007)
°° Official Navy SEALS Web site (2007)

Now consider just a few aspects of the security contractor. Companies enforce on their employees unpaid mandatory leave out of country every few months for rest and recharge; although for some this vacation is tax-free, under U.S. law citizens are still liable to U.S. tax if they reside within the United States for more than one month in the year.

As the International Peace Operations Association noted in 2004:

> For example, a typical PSC contractor earning $500/day in Iraq might expect to work about 270 days in a year and gross $135,000 [if] they remain outside the United States for the mandated tax minimum of 330 days and thus qualify for the first $81,000 of income to be tax-free. They would still expect to pay some $16,000 in federal income taxes, and $9,000 in self employment taxes on the remainder. More typical are those who will not qualify for the tax break since in these extremely high-risk jobs it is important seeing the family as often as possible—just in case the worst happens. They can expect to pay over $62,000 in total taxes, thus a net of about $74,000 in this example.[9]

A contractor may work for a firm that actually cares about his well-being, or he may not. For example, the typical contract for an Erinys contractor ran for just under four months: three months on, then three weeks off before rotating back. The company provides a round-trip ticket for home leave. And unlike some firms, the company provides all the necessities: weapons, body armor, tactical gear, and clothing. A small canteen provides three meals a day. All new hires—regardless of experience—go through a mandatory training program and receive additional weapons qualifications.[10]

But if the experience of those who were killed in Fallujah in 2004 while working for Blackwater tells us anything, companies may be more interested in holding down expenses than in giving their employees all the resources (such as properly armored vehicles, required tail gunner) they need. And Blackwater is hardly the only firm like that.

RECRUITING PERSONNEL FROM AROUND THE WORLD

PMCs are employing personnel from numerous countries around the world, not only the United States. Contractors come from Bosnia, Britain, Nepal, Chile, Ukraine, Israel, South Africa, New Zealand, Australia, and Fiji, not to mention those who served in the French Foreign Legion, to name just some countries.[11] Though they are doing a wide variety of tasks in Iraq, the common link is helping, in one way or another, to provide security. Personnel from one country who are recruited by a company in another country to work in yet another country are called third-country nationals (TCNs). The Pentagon says that 30 percent of contract personnel in Iraq are so-called TCNs.[12]

According to David Claridge, managing director of Janusian, Iraq has boosted British military companies' revenues from £200 million ($320 million) before the war to over £1 billion, making security by far Britain's most lucrative postwar export to Iraq.[13]

Early on, more than 1,500 South Africans were believed to be in Iraq under contract to various PMCs, including members of the South African Police Services' elite task force and former members of the South African National Defence Force (SANDF). Reportedly some active members resigned from the SANDF to go to Iraq.[14]

South Africans were involved in some of the earliest private security work in Iraq. In 2005 news reports estimated that there were between 5,000 and 10,000 South Africans working for private military firms in Iraq as protectors of supply routes, bodyguards, and drivers of convoys in high-risk zones.[15]

Before Paul Bremer and the creation of the Coalition Provisional Authority, U.S. reconstruction efforts were headed by retired U.S. Army lieutenant general Jay Garner, who was director of the Office for Reconstruction and Humanitarian Assistance for Iraq. When U.S. commanders said they couldn't spare any troops to provide security for Garner, his aides had to hire a private firm. Among the men they found were two South Africans, nicknamed Lion and Lucky, who were veterans of the South African Special Air Service.[16]

Garner's work in Iraq ended when he was replaced in May 2003 by Paul Bremer and a new police trainer, Bernard Kerik, the former New York police commissioner. The South Africans suddenly found themselves out of work. But because Kerik would need bodyguards of his own and help with his police-training operation, Garner made an arrangement for the South Africans to be police trainers for the organization within the Ministry of Interior. For the purpose of doing business with the U.S. government, the South Africans organized under the name Meteoric Tactical Solutions.

In June 2003 Meteoric was awarded a $600,000 U.S. government contract. It was the first of two contracts totaling over a million dollars the South Africans received that summer from bodyguard and police-training services. Under the terms of the contract, the Meteoric employees were to be vetted by the State Department and were to qualify for secret clearances, but Meteoric's work was never completed. In their eagerness to employ bodyguards and trainers, Garner, Kerik, and their colleagues did not think to check the legality of the South Africans' work in Iraq. As it turned out, the South African government had prohibited former soldiers from hiring themselves out without prior authorization. Thus Meteoric was actually breaking South African law by signing a contract with the U.S. government.

Bernard Kerik left Iraq after only three months on the job, but the story did not end there. In March 2004, Lorenz Horn, the bodyguard Jay Garner knew as Lucky, was arrested in Zimbabwe and charged with involvement in a plot to overthrow the government of Equatorial Guinea. The coup attempt was allegedly a private venture to be carried out by former South African and British soldiers. Lorenz Horn was ultimately released by the authorities in Zimbabwe, but he was subsequently convicted in South Africa of having violated the antimercenary laws.

Because South Africa is one of the few countries in the world that has actually passed national legislation to regulate the use of PCSs, the employment of South Africans in Iraq has been controversial.[17] South Africa's legislation was criticized for its suspected unconstitutionality, its contentious exemptions, its extraterritorial jurisdiction, and its ban on even humanitarian assistance. For example, some saw a contradiction between the South African government paying for private security firms to carry firearms and protect the South African Police Service (SAPS) and the same government outlawing South Africans from doing much the same abroad.[18]

In late 2004 the South African government said that close to a hundred South Africans were being investigated for working in Iraq without permission.[19] It has also been reported that PMCs have illegally hired, in violation of a ban on Indian citizens traveling to Iraq, 1,500 ex-combat Indian troops as private guards to protect installations in Iraq.[20] In addition, the Pakistani media reported that authorities there stopped U.S. civil and military contractors from recruiting Pakistani ex-servicemen for carrying out noncombatant security operations in Iraq. Two illegal recruitment facilities being used by U.S. contractors to recruit the retired security personnel in Lahore and Rawalpindi were reportedly shut down.[21]

Security firms are also believed to be employing veterans of anti-insurgency conflicts in Colombia and Algeria and former soldiers who fought in the Russian government's war in Chechnya.[22] People recruited from Colombia are a particular concern because some analysts worry that firms may hire battle-hardened paramilitary fighters searching for jobs now that their factions were being disbanded.[23]

Throughout Latin America there have been numerous press reports of contracting and subcontracting firms recruiting in Chile, Colombia, Nicaragua, Guatemala, and El Salvador. Each of the countries has had recent—and in Colombia's case, ongoing—wars, which make for large pools of experienced military and police.[24]

In 2005 Jeffrey Shippy, who used to work for DynCorp, advertised on an Iraq jobs Web site, "For hire: more than 1,000 U.S.-trained former soldiers and police officers from Colombia. Combat-hardened, experienced in fighting insurgents and ready for duty in Iraq." Shippy said the Colombians were willing to work for $2,500 to $5,000 a month, compared with perhaps $10,000 or more for Americans.[25]

In May 2005 Honduras's Labor Ministry announced an offer it had been asked to relay from U.S. firm Triple Canopy, which was willing to pay comparatively high salaries to recruit 2,000 Hondurans to work as security guards in Iraq and Afghanistan. Assistant Labor Minister Africo Madrid said the company had contacted the government, saying it wanted Hondurans with military training and was willing to pay 10 times the going rate for similar jobs in Honduras.[26] Although Triple Canopy said that accounts of what it was willing to pay were wildly inflated, it did not deny recruiting.[27]

However, in 2006 the Honduran government fined the local subsidiary of a U.S. company, Your Solutions, $25,000 for allegedly training more than 300 Hondurans and foreigners, Chileans and Nicaraguans, in 2005 to work in Iraq.[28]

Triple Canopy recruited nearly 400 former members of the military and police from Peru to work in Iraq. A copy of the contract showed neither Triple Canopy nor the U.S. government to be responsible in the case of employees' being injured or killed in the line of duty. The contract also stated that the insurance policy covering the company's personnel would not provide coverage in case of an incident occurring when employees were off-duty or outside their place of work. If employees were attacked by insurgents at home, for instance, they would receive no compensation.[29]

The press reported that 200 of the Triple Canopy recruits had been trained in FAME, the Army's weapons and munitions factory. According to a contract between the Army and Gun Supply, the Army provided the trainers with the ammunition needed for target practice. The Army, which has suffered drastic budget cuts, accepted the arrangement with Gun Supply, which represents Triple Canopy in Lima, as a means of obtaining much-needed cash.

Triple Canopy recruited men from El Salvador to be guards, paying them a minimum of U.S. $1,700 a month.[30] The problem is that not everyone recruited had a military or even security background. One person recruited in El Salvador used to be a mason's assistant.[31]

In February 2005 it was reported that the Brazilian government was investigating efforts by an American private security firm, Inveco International Corp., to recruit Brazilian soldiers and ex-military men to work in Iraq.[32] Inveco denounced these reports as a "smear campaign," asserting that it did not have "any current contracts with the United States or Iraq Governments for providing Security Services in Iraq, NEITHER do we have any teams currently deployed in Iraq!" Of course, that is not the same as denying that it was recruiting people to work as security contractors, a point it actually acknowledged.[33]

In September 2006 it was reported that about three dozen former Colombian soldiers were engaged in a pay dispute with Blackwater USA, saying their salaries for security work in Iraq turned out to be one-quarter what they had been promised by recruiters in Bogota. The Colombians alleged that recruiters had promised them salaries of $4,000 a month. They said it was only when they were given their contracts barely hours before leaving Bogota that they learned they would be paid $34 a day, or about $1,000 a month.[34]

Although the morality of such recruiting is often debated, the economics are clear-cut, as Geoff Thale of the Washington Office on Latin America said in a radio interview in 2004:

It's sort of the overall point here is that in Latin America and elsewhere in [a] third world country, you can make four or five times working as the cook in a mess hall or the security guard for an embassy or the security for truck convoy delivering supplies, you can make four or five times there what you can make in your home country. In Salvador, as a matter of fact, people are quitting military jobs, jobs in the Salvadoran armed forces to line up for and volunteer for the jobs with private security firms, because they will make four or five times what they earn, and on the flip side, the U.S.

companies involved in recruiting are going to pay them one-quarter of what they would have to pay if they were recruiting a U.S. citizen to do this work. So there's a market logic. The Pentagon privatizes this work, and saves in the budget. The employer recruits abroad, and improves their bottom line. And people in these countries are earning more than they might earn working domestically. So, if you look on the strictly sort of economic logic, everybody is making money and the free market is at work. If you ask about the morality of this, it's a kind of a frightening thing.[35]

Africa is another region that has been a fertile recruiting ground for PSCs. According to Doug Brooks, who heads the International Peace Operations Association, a trade group for private security companies, "They tend to be much cheaper than Americans or Westerners, and maybe by a factor of five or six. You know, should the U.S. government only hire Americans to do these sorts of jobs, the cost would be just insane."[36]

Concerns about these companies peaked in Namibia in September 2007, when a Nevada-based private security firm called SOC-SMG started recruiting. Namibians need jobs, but when news spread about the risks they'd face in Iraq, there was public outcry, and in October Namibia kicked the company's officials out of the country. SOC-SMG said it had been in Namibia with the approval of the government and the U.S. embassy, and it intended to comply with local laws. U.S. companies have also looked for new hires in countries such as Angola, Uganda, and Mozambique.[37]

Asia, while more of a recruiting ground for logistics contractors, has also supplied personnel for security firms. In 2006 the author received the following e-mail from a Ram Gurung of Kailash International Manpower (P) Ltd. of Nepal:[38]

Subject: Proposal for Supplying of Nepalese Workers in Iraq and Afghanistan

Our firm, Kailash International Manpower (P) Ltd., a sister concern of Sunrise Hotel (P) Ltd. and Pashupati Carpets (P) Ltd. solely own by Gurung Family, is one of the leading overseas employment agencies in Nepal. It was established in 2003 and is been operated by a team 4 professionals of Gurung Family. The team works in the global job market by recruiting skilled, semi-skilled, and unskilled workers from the Nepal region. Our main target for staffing has been Afghanistan and Iraq. The workers we specialize in are Ex-British Army Gurkha Personnel, Ex-Indian Army Gurkhas, Ex-Royal Nepalese Army along with cooks, waiters, chefs, bakers, captains, and cleaning crew.

Board of Directors:

Bamay Gurung (Chairman)

Kalu Gurung (Managing Director)

Thakur Prasad Gurung, Ex-British Army (Recruiting Director)

Ram B. Gurung (Director, Business Development)

How We Work:

Because of the ongoing political instability in Nepal, we have opened our branch offices in New Delhi, India and Kabul, Afghanistan. We can mobilize more than 500 Army personnels [sic] and other catering workers from Delhi and the same number from Kabul as we have the candidates on standby.

Expected Salary Structure to work in Iraq for Security Guards:

Most of the guards will be either who have worked in British Army Gurkha Brigade or Indian Army Gurkha Brigade. Ex-British Army Gurkhas are good at English so supply most of them as security supervisors and Ex-Indian Army as guards to work under the command of Ex-British Army.

Expected Salary for security supervisors = 2000$

Expected salary for normal guards = 1250$ to 1500$

Expected Salary Structure to work in Iraq for Catering Workers:

1. Commis = 1000$ to 1250$

Commis Helper = 500$ to 700$

Cleaners & dishwashers = 550$

Our guarantee: If any worker sent by our company to our client is found not to be up to standard, we have the policy to send another worker on our company's expenses.

Should you require more information or wish to discuss the issue, please do not hesitate to contact us without any obligation. We shall always be looking forward to have an opportunity to serve your manpower needs.

Thank you

Ram B. Gurung

Director, Business Development

Kailash International Manpower Pvt. Ltd.

Kathmandu, Nepal

DIFFERENCES BETWEEN COMPANIES FOR DIFFERENT COUNTRIES

As the old saying goes, different strokes for different folks. PSCs are influenced by various factors; some are universal, such as international law (which they all, in theory, must comply with), and some are nation-specific, depending on the laws of the books.

Companies may also be influenced by the culture of the country in which they are headquartered. Although companies may hire workers from anywhere in the world, often the supervisory and highest management personnel are citizens of the country in which the firm is headquartered.

Yet because it is a global industry, there is a curious inversion of the old saying that a chain is only as strong as its weakest link. Since most of the truly profitable contracts are issued by Western governments and companies, any firm that wins the contract has to take great pains to live up to the strictures of that contract, and the contracts that such companies issue can be written to comply with laws that are far more stringent regarding the use of force and respect for human rights than those issued by companies or governments in developing nations. Thus, security contractors, at least in theory, can be significantly influenced and driven by their clients. For example, regardless of where it is headquartered, any PMC that operates under a U.S. government contract must adhere to U.S. law.

Hopefully, as companies interconnect and dialogue with each other in the future, a general standard will be established that all can and will adhere to. This has long been a goal of trade groups like the International Peace Operations Association.[39] In fact, numerous trade associations are currently in existence, many of which regulate and promote standards for security countries in their respective countries.[40]

A newer group is the Private Security Company Association of Iraq (PSCAI), headquartered in Baghdad. Its Web site states, "It was formed and maintained to discuss and address matters of mutual interest and concern to the industry conducting operations in Iraq. The PSCAI seeks to work closely with the Iraqi Government and foster a relationship of trust and understanding."[41] Newer yet is the British Private Security Company Association, launched in February 2006.[42]

ADVANTAGES OF USING PMC PERSONNEL

Many PMC personnel who are hired as independent contractors (ICs) are not merely ex-military but also former members of elite units, usually in the special operations forces (SOF) community.[43] In the United States that means former Rangers, Green Berets, Delta Force, and SEALs.[44] In the United Kingdom it means members of the former Special Air Service (SAS),[45] former police officers from Scotland Yard's royalty protection squad (SO14), who specialize in close protection work, and members of the Special Boat Service (SBS), the Royal Navy equivalent of the SAS.[46] Even members of the former Spetsnaz, the Soviet equivalent of U.S. special operations forces, have been included.

Why SOF? If not in special operations, the types of individuals working as security contractors who escort convoys or providing static and roving protection of individuals and installations are far more likely to have a background in the combat arms sector, or at least in policing. As security operators they are able to bring a lifetime of training and experience to a specific job.

Most of the actual security teams operating on the ground frequently are composed of former and retired senior noncommissioned officers (NCOs), men in their 30s and early 40s. This level of experience contributes to a more relaxed environment that simplifies operations. Leaders trust that their operators will automatically ensure that basic tasks have been performed and that their staff is highly professional and disciplined. In contrast, a young Army soldier or marine, recently graduated from his or her basic training and specialty school, is just that: young and inexperienced.

British operators are particularly prized because they are thought to operate with a lower profile (low pro) than those from other countries. One observer who spent a week with the British security firm Diligence, which employs ex-SAS and ex-SBS soldiers, said: "They use battered saloon cars with engines tuned up beyond belief. They wear local check shirts and keep their automatic weapons out of sight, so they're not in anybody's face. And they don't brag."[47]

Why are British companies so strong in this area? First, they entered the market early. The collapse of Britain's empire after World War II led to a flurry of enquiries from newly independent states in search of security and training from the former occupying power.

Second, British companies recruit from the British Army, whose soldiers are considered to be good at keeping the peace by showing force without using it. Kroll, an American company that has a security arm based in Britain, reckons that soldiers trained to patrol Northern Ireland's perilous streets without shooting civilians make the best troops for delicate overseas security work.[48]

The typical SOF soldier is far more accustomed to interacting with foreign nationals than the average service member. Language skills and cultural appreciation are taught in their military training and carried over into the professional approach taken as a civilian specialist. Reconnaissance and tactical analysis of intelligence are a basic part of any special operations mission; within the conventional military, analysis is the realm of a limited few.

Because they work in a local environment, less isolated than that of military personnel, security contractors can establish relationships with members of the community that are denied to the military locked up on a base. Although they lack a strategic or "big picture" view, in most instances that is unnecessary. They have more intimate knowledge of the issues that pertain to their small area of responsibility: protecting their clients and assets.

DISADVANTAGES OF RELYING ON PMCs

There are a number of legal concerns surrounding the use of PMCs, and these are discussed in more detail in other chapters. Here I focus on some of the economic disadvantages, from a U.S. governmental and corporate perspective, in employing private contract staff in Iraq. Arrangements for the provision of insurance, issues surrounding pay, and the problem of retention of personnel in the armed services are three of the more problematic issues.

Insurance

Make no mistake about it: life in Iraq is dangerous. The tens of thousands of Iraqis who have died since 2003 is testament to that reality. And life for foreign contractors, especially security contractors, is also dangerous.

If they get killed, their dependents can get insurance, but there will be no letters from a military commander or the president commending them for their service to the country. No chaplain shows up at their door to offer consolation.[49] Contractors with head wounds and fist-sized holes in their sides have had to fly back to the United States on commercial jets for medical care.[50]

Titan Corp., for example, which provides translators, had an employee beheaded by insurgents while he was posted to a U.S. Army unit in Baghdad.[51] "If the insurgents catch us, they will cut off our heads because the imams say we are spies," said Mustafa Fahmi, age 24, an Iraqi interpreter with Titan Corp. "I've been threatened like fifteen times, but I won't quit. A neighbor saw me driving and said, 'I am going to kill you.'"[52]

On April 23, 2005, 13 security contractors were killed in two days during which 6 U.S. contractors employed by Blackwater and 2 Filipino guards were among 11 killed when a Bulgarian commercial helicopter was shot down north of Baghdad.

Another American also working for Blackwater was killed near Ramadi when a roadside bomb blew up near his vehicle. And the previous day one employee from Aegis Defence Services was killed and another wounded when a bomb exploded as their car headed from the capital toward the airport. This followed another ambush along the same road the day before when an American, an Australian, and a Canadian working for British-based Edinburgh Risk security firm were killed when vehicles in their convoy came under small-arms fire.[53]

On May 18, 2005, insurgents attacked a security detail from British security company Hart Security Ltd. Of 18 Iraqi and international guards, 12 were killed in the attack, in which insurgents ambushed a convoy escorting cargo for the U.S. forces from Baghdad to a base in al-Asat, about 90 miles west of the city. Once resistance from the security team ended, the attackers moved in to finish off the wounded, then, according to sources, piled several of the bodies on top of a bomb so they could not be removed without setting off an explosion.[54]

Deborah Dawn Klecker, 51, an international police liaison officer serving in Iraq with DynCorp International under contract to the State Department, had been in the country only two months when she was killed on June 27, 2005, by a roadside bomb.[55] On January 23, 2007, Blackwater lost five contractors when a Little Bird helicopter was shot down by insurgents, killing all four aboard, and a gunner on another Little Bird was also killed.[56] Robert Jason Gore was killed in April 2005 at the age of 23 when Iraqi insurgents shot down the civilian helicopter he was aboard. Gore was a sergeant with the Iowa National Guard's 186th Military Police Company, but he was performing a six-month tour of duty as a private security contractor for Blackwater USA when he died.[57]

In November 2006 four Americans and an Austrian employed by Crescent Security Group, a small private security firm, were seized when a convoy of over 37 tractor-trailers stretching for more than a mile on southern Iraq's main highway was ambushed in broad daylight. An investigation by the *Washington Post* found that Crescent had violated U.S. military regulations while being paid millions of dollars to support the United States–led mission in Iraq. The company routinely sacrificed safety to cut costs. On the day of the kidnappings, just seven Crescent guards were protecting the immense convoy as it drove through southern Iraq, a force that security experts described as inadequate to fend off a major attack. In March 2008 the Australian and three of the Americans were confirmed dead after U.S. authorities received five severed fingers, four of which belonged to the Crescent contractors.[58] Subsequently, the fourth American was also confirmed killed.

Although Iraqis employed by U.S. contractors in their country are eligible for American workers' compensation insurance, collecting it can be daunting. Most Iraqis were not accustomed to filing claims under Saddam Hussein's regime. Those working for subcontractors do not always give their real names. Others move or lose their homes in a war zone. They might not have the proper birth and marriage documents, doctor reports, or other documentation of job-related injuries.[59]

Some companies that employ foreign nationals may neglect to report the injuries or deaths of their employees. The system, in other words, is totally based on the transparency and honesty of the contracting firm to do what the law says it must do.

It is not just Iraqis who may have problems. In May 2005 it was reported that 100 Ugandan recruits were headed for security jobs in Iraq. A Kampala lawyer named Bob Kasango of Hall Partners claimed that he had been contracted by the Nevada-based Special Operations Consulting-Security Management Group Inc. (SOC-SMG) to recruit the men for noncombat duties in Iraq. However, when contacted, Janelle Lehmann of SOC-SMG denied that the company was recruiting in Uganda. When pressed, she only said, "To my knowledge, SOC-SMG has not recruited in Africa because the company recruits mostly in the USA." That begs the question of what happens should any of the Ugandans get seriously injured or die in Iraq.[60]

The majority of claims are for work injuries, not death claims. Still, in April 2005, although Halliburton had the most overall claims, the largest number of death claims, 122, was submitted for employees of Titan Corp.

U.S. employers are required to provide limited insurance to all employees in war zones under the Defense Base Act (DBA), which was enacted in 1941 and is administered by the Department of Labor (DOL).[61] DBA insurance is a workers' compensation policy that was created by Congress as World War II loomed to insure workers at remote bases. At the time, no one envisioned a war in which the number of contractors would nearly match the number of troops and would be performing jobs once handled by the military.

The requirement to obtain DBA insurance covers all employees, including U.S. citizens, third-country personnel, and local nationals (unless DOL grants a waiver for a country, which would normally apply only to foreign nationals). The contracting company must prove that it has purchased the mandatory insurance before it can be awarded the contract. DBA insurance is required of all contractors operating abroad, even when they will be working in peaceful countries with low security risks. But the cost for DBA insurance can vary depending on the level of risk an employee will be exposed to. DBA benefits cover the cost of medical treatment as a result of injuries received while a contractor is performing the job. The insurance also reimburses wages lost because of injury and offers beneficiaries disability and death benefits.[62]

Despite that fact, contracts from the Pentagon have often excluded Defense Base Act clauses, the very clauses that provide the bare minimum of insurance protection for civilian contractors.[63]

Little noted is the fact that workers' compensation insurance is a hidden cost of the Iraq war for U.S. taxpayers. The government reimburses contractors for the insurance premiums, but nobody breaks out this cost from other expenses submitted to the government for payment. Also, DBA policies differ from conventional workers' compensation in one major way: domestic workers' compensation is heavily regulated and analyzed, but the contractors' insurance is not. The U.S. Department of Labor monitors the number of claims and resolves disputes over benefits, but it has no authority over pricing or availability.

In the first Gulf War, seven contractors were killed. As of October 2006, 646 U.S.-financed private contractors had been killed in Iraq. Because most deaths resulted from acts of war, the insurance companies were allowed to ask the U.S. Department of Labor to pay all future benefits and reimburse the insurers for all payments, plus 15 percent for processing the claims. From 2000 to 2006 insurance companies filed 186 such claims, 140 of them from Iraq. The Department of Labor made reimbursements in 81 of the cases. The average reimbursement was $48,412; this figure does not include ongoing payments the government will make.[64]

Whether DBA insurance is cost-effective seems to be a riddle. A 2005 GAO report found:

> It is difficult to aggregate reliable data on the cost of DBA insurance due in part to the large number of contractors and the multiple levels of subcontractors performing work in Iraq. Lacking reliable aggregate data, we were unable to calculate the total cost of DBA insurance to the government or the impact of DBA insurance costs on reconstruction activities in Iraq.

. . .

It is difficult to determine whether all DBA insurance is purchased in a cost-effective manner or if agencies' implementation challenges hinder their effectiveness in providing workers' compensation coverage under DBA. Lack of reliable information on numbers of contractors and cost of DBA insurance restricts the ability of agencies to make informed decisions on purchasing strategies for DBA. Additionally, confusion over when DBA applies and difficulty in enforcing DBA and processing claims remain largely unresolved problems, despite actions taken by agencies. Finally, new challenges, such as growing numbers of contractors, have arisen since 1941, when DBA was passed. These factors highlight the need for a coordinated effort among affected agencies to identify actions that can address such challenges.[65]

Such coverage is usually limited to $4,000 a month in the event of death or disability.[66] Under the DBA, lifetime payment and death benefit calculation and benefits can be $1.8 million plus permanent total disability benefits to one worker, and $2 million if the worker is killed and has a spouse and two dependents.[67]

The dependents of three out of four of the Blackwater contractors—Wesley Batalona, Scott Helvenston, and Michael Teague (Jerry Zofko left no dependents)—killed in the 2004 ambush in Fallujah have begun receiving lifetime payments of $1,100 per week tax-free.[68]

Policies for additional coverage, which have risen in price, are often needed to attract workers to Iraq, with potential payments ranging from $250,000 to more than $1 million.[69]

In June 2005 the *Los Angeles Times* reported that financial services giant American International Group Inc. (AIG) repeatedly sought to derail an effort by the Pentagon that could save millions of dollars on reconstruction work in war zones like Afghanistan and Iraq. For more than a year, AIG and industry allies fought an initiative to cut the rates for workers' compensation insurance that U.S. contractors operating overseas are required to carry. Rates had soared since the war in Iraq began, raising suspicions among government officials that the companies may be overcharging contractors and, ultimately, the taxpayers who foot the bill. Pentagon officials said their suspicions grew after the insurance companies began charging rates as much as 30 times higher in Iraq than in developing countries. As the DBA reimburses any combat-related claims, the insurance companies don't have to bear the risk. They would only be liable for claims resulting from routine workplace accidents. Thus the rates shouldn't be directly affected by the violence.[70]

Insurers claim that rates adjust lower over time as contractors and their insurers get a better handle on risk factors and risk-mitigation responses. They also say there is no economic incentive for fighting the payment of covered claims; any claim that has to be litigated automatically becomes more costly to the insurer, with or without war hazard reimbursement.

The Pentagon announced that it planned to impose tighter discipline on the program by centralizing its administration under one prime contractor. In response the insurers threatened not to compete for the business.[71]

But insurance-related problems persist. In June 2007 a Los Angeles investigation found a pattern of repeatedly blocked claims for treatment of psychological injuries sustained by civilian workers in Iraq and Afghanistan. Such action would be a clear violation of Department of Labor rules, which state, "First payment of compensation is due 14 days of the first day of disability." As the DBA benefit includes medical coverage, even if there is no lost time or lost time is less than three days (and therefore no indemnity compensation payments are due the worker), the carrier is responsible for any and all related medical treatment.[72]

Although insurance companies paid for counseling for many workers, they also fought more claims for psychological treatment than for other types of injuries, according to data compiled from Department of Labor records. Though contractors claiming psychological problems made up about 4 percent of nearly 1,400 serious reported injuries from 2003 to 2005, such workers accounted for 13 percent of the cases fought out in courtrooms.

In fighting claims, the insurance companies have relied on doctors with questionable expertise, according to court records and claimants' attorneys. In one case, an insurance company psychiatrist who specialized in pharmacological research broadly dismissed psychology as "baloney." In another, a psychologist hired by AIG for his supposed expertise in post-traumatic stress disorder (PTSD) had seen only 10 to 15 cases in a decade of practice.[73]

According to Pentagon and Veterans Affairs officials, the federal government, which has paid billions of dollars to corporations for services in Iraq since the war began, has not examined the issue of mental health problems among private workers. Contract workers who are wounded or disabled in the war zone are treated in military hospitals in Iraq and Germany, but once home, they are not eligible for care in the military or Veterans Affairs system. And unlike troops, they are not routinely evaluated for mental or stress disorders after their tours.[74]

In May 2008 a Department of Labor official testified to Congress that in 2006 the department determined that the DBA community needed to focus more on PTSD cases coming from Iraq.

> Relatively clear-cut PTSD situations were being reported by DBA contract employees—such as individuals who witnessed bombing attacks which killed several co-workers—and claim resolutions were not being obtained swiftly enough. Media reports also indicated that contract workers were not always receiving the kind of de-briefing and counseling following such traumatic events that uniformed military personnel receive, and of course it was understood that these DBA-covered employees do not have recourse to Department of Veterans Affairs psychological services upon their return to the United States.[75]

Liability and insurance concerns are one of those unglamorous but critical issues that greatly concern PSCs. As Alan Chvotkin, senior vice president and counsel of the Professional Services Council, testified to Congress:

> Even if a contractor performs in accordance with the contract, the contractor may be vulnerable to claims that services in support of a war effort are inherently risky. Poor

performance of systems support services (e.g., calibrating a weapon) could result in casualties or fatalities involving the military members using those weapons as well as unintended civilians. Air Force General Counsel Guidance Document Deploying with Contractors: Contracting Considerations, November 2003, at 9. Under current circumstances, particularly in Iraq, commercial liability insurance is still often unavailable, insufficient or unreasonably expensive. In addition, many commercial policies often exclude "war risks" or risks associated with terrorist activities. Furthermore, as we know from PSC's [sic] continuing work in this area, insurance companies are increasingly concerned about their ability to insure against the full range of risks associated with performing work in an area that is experiencing violent extremism against U.S. military forces, contractor personnel and the local citizenry. The increasing number of well publicized lawsuits filed in the U.S. by third parties against contractors alleging wrongful death support the concerns of both contractors and insurance companies.

If commercial liability insurance is insufficient, unaffordable or unavailable to contractors (and particularly to those performing fixed-price work) the number and quality of the contractors willing to accept such financial risks will decline. Boards of Directors, corporate officers, and audit committees—particularly of publicly traded companies— will decide that they cannot assume the full risk of a potential, catastrophic incident and may decline to pursue such work. As a result, the DoD will lack full access to the depth of experience and resources these contractors could otherwise provide.[76]

A review by the House Committee on Oversight and Government Reform found that, in regard to the DBA requirement to obtain insurance, three agencies— the State Department, USAID, and the Corps of Engineers—conducted a competition to select an insurance carrier to offer this insurance at low rates to their contractors. The Defense Department has taken a completely different approach. It allows contractors to negotiate their own individual insurance contracts. "This approach has produced a boondoggle for the insurance companies and the private contractors, and saddled the taxpayer with enormous costs. Typically, insurers offering workers compensation pay out as much in claims and expenses as they take in through premiums. The carriers make their real money off of investment returns they earn during the interval between when they receive premiums and pay claims and expenses."[77]

This was the experience of the State Department, USAID, and the Corps of Engineers. In fact, the company that won these contracts, CNA, actually paid out 8 percent more in claims and expenses than it had received in premiums. But these contracts represent only 10 percent of the insurance market in Iraq and Afghanistan.

Ninety percent of the DBA market is controlled by the Pentagon, and that experience has been completely different. Under the DoD approach, private contractors negotiate with private insurers but bill the taxpayers for the costs. This arrangement has been exceptionally lucrative for the private insurers and the contractors. Over the last five years, the four largest private insurers made underwriting profits of nearly 40 percent. That's almost $600 million in profits.

As noted above, the Pentagon does have a single-insurer pilot program with the Army Corps of Engineers, which has reduced DBA rates since 2005, but it has not yet implemented similar efforts throughout the department.

According to May 2008 testimony by a GAO official, the GAO previously reported that eight DoD prime contractors paid from $10 to $21 per $100 of salary cost, which was significantly higher than the rates paid by State Department and USAID contractors—$2 to $5 per $100 of salary cost—through the agencies' respective single-insurer programs.

The following example illustrates the impact of these rates on cost. In July 2005 security employees providing protection to civilians in vehicle convoys could earn from $12,000 to $13,000 per month. Assuming a DBA insurance rate of $10.30 per $100 of salary cost and assuming that security employee salaries remained the same, the contractor could bill the government $1,236 to $1,339 per security employee per month. In addition, DoD reported that it had 12,258 security contractors in Iraq as of December 31, 2007.[78]

The LOGCAP troop support contract, the largest single contract in Iraq, illustrates what's going on. Kellogg, Brown & Root (KBR) paid an insurance company, AIG, $284 million for workers' compensation coverage. Since KBR's contract is a cost-plus contract, this $284 million premium, plus a markup for KBR of up to $8 million, gets billed to the taxpayers, bringing the total cost to the taxpayers of $292 million.

Out of this amount, just $73 million actually goes to injured contractors, and AIG and KBR pocket over $100 million as profit. According to Rep. Henry Waxman (D-CA), chairman of the Oversight and Government Reform Committee, "this is really disgraceful. The taxpayer is paying nearly $300 million to deliver less than $75 million in benefits to injured contractors. Rube Goldberg could not design a more inefficient way to help employees—wounded or injured in Iraq."[79]

The Pentagon argues that Iraq's status as a war zone justifies the high costs of the insurance program. But under the Defense Base Act, the taxpayer, not the insurance company, has to pay the costs when a contractor is wounded in action. The insurance companies only pay for the types of injuries that could occur at any work site.

When Congress passed a law in 2006 requiring the Defense Department to rethink its approach, the department reported that it would be too expensive to collect the necessary data. The GAO reported in May 2008 that DoD continues to lack reliable aggregate data on the total cost of DBA insurance. Although the State Department, USAID, and Army Corps of Engineers can obtain aggregate DBA cost data for their respective single-insurer programs, DoD reported that it has not collected these data for the entire department.

A report by the U.S. Government Accounting Office in April 2005 found that monitoring of civilian contractors in Iraq was so poor that there was no way to determine how many contractors are working on U.S.-related security and reconstruction projects in Iraq or how many had been killed.[80]

At the end of January 2005, a quarterly report sent to Congress by the inspector general appointed to audit U.S.-funded work in Iraq found that at least 232 civilians had been killed while working on U.S.-funded contracts in Iraq, and the death toll was rising rapidly. It cited U.S. Labor Department statistics showing that companies had filed 232 compensation claims under the Defense Base Act for workers killed there, an increase of 93 percent in the fourth quarter of 2004.[81]

In this sense outsourcing is advantageous for the administration. For example, it allows the administration to push costs that would otherwise be incurred by Veterans Affairs not just off the books but out of government altogether, at least for now. Although those costs may be hidden in the short term and deferred in the middle term, they will have to be borne eventually. But instead of being addressed in a comprehensive, cost-effective way, the problems will be diffused and the burdens carried by individual families and communities. Think of the long-term social costs associated with the veterans returning from Vietnam, but without the government and social service available to veterans. Those services have rarely been as generous as Vietnam veterans deserve, but at least we had a framework and means for providing such services.

Some say that contractors, motivated perhaps by profit, deserve less than the troops. But had it not been for contractors, we would have needed more troops. So we would have had to pay the price one way or the other. However, part of the reason for using contract workers in Iraq was to avoid the political ramifications of calling up and paying for the number of troops that were actually needed.[82]

At most, contractors who are killed get an obituary buried in the back pages of their hometown newspaper, based on a press release by their employer, or perhaps a brief mention by a government spokesman if the contractor's client was a U.S. government agency.[83]

Most PSC operators' contracts have language like what was in the contract for the Blackwater contractors killed in Fallujah in 2004. The contract detailed that the area in which the work would be done was "volatile, hostile and extremely dangerous" and listed a number of risks, including

being shot, permanently maimed and or killed by a firearm or munitions, falling aircraft or helicopters, sniper fire, landmine, artillery fire, rocket propelled grenade, truck or car bomb, earthquake or other natural disaster, poisoning, civil uprising, terrorist activity, hand-to-hand combat, disease, poisoning, etc.[84]

And normally the workers sign a release giving up most of their rights to sue their employer if something bad happens to them. Their families and their estates can't sue, either.

It bears noting that some contractors, at least for the purpose of accounting, don't think they have much responsibility toward those that work for them. Consider, for example, the letters and memorandum released March 10, 2008, by the

House Committee on Oversight and Government Reform chaired by Rep. Henry A. Waxman (D-CA).[85]

Waxman sent letters to the Internal Revenue Service, the Small Business Administration, and the Department of Labor to request investigations into whether Blackwater has violated federal tax, small business, and labor laws. He wrote that in late 2007 his committee had obtained evidence that Blackwater may have improperly designated its security guards as "independent contractors" rather than "employees" to avoid paying and withholding federal taxes. The committee estimated that Blackwater failed to pay or withhold up to $50 million under its contract with the State Department. That in itself was old news, having been previously reported.

But Waxman alleged further violations. For example, despite the fact that Blackwater is one of the largest private security contractors, receiving nearly $1.25 billion in federal contracts since 2000, it has sought and received special preferences normally reserved for small businesses. For example, according to the government's contractor registry, Blackwater's aviation services subsidiary, Presidential Airways, is a veteran-owned small business. This makes it eligible for small-business set-aside competitions, which are designed to help small companies struggling to get government work.[86]

As it did previously, Blackwater claimed that its security guards were not "employees" for the purpose of counting the company's total number of staff. As a result, Blackwater obtained small-business contracts without competing with other qualified bidders that properly designated their guards as employees. The committee staff identified at least 100 small-business set-aside contracts worth over $144 million that have been awarded to Blackwater since 2000.

Now most people might think that even if Blackwater did this, it might not be so bad—people and businesses try to dodge taxes all the time. But that would miss the point. As Waxman's memorandum noted:

> In all three instances, Blackwater has asserted in official communications that its security guards are independent contractors because the company does not exercise sufficient control over their activities in Iraq or Afghanistan. Blackwater has claimed in official communications that its security guards are "in no way directly supervised or controlled by Blackwater"; that they "do not report to any of the Blackwater entities regarding their work in the field"; and that they "do not report to Blackwater regarding their operations in country." Blackwater has also claimed that it "plays no role in the development or planning of the contractors' security missions" and "has little if any knowledge regarding the location or activities of these independent contractors." According to Blackwater, its "only real involvement is to pay the independent contractors."[87]

Of course, Blackwater's defense is laughable, if for no other reason than that it is contradicted by the public record.[88] We know, for example, from the investigation into the killing of the four Blackwater contractors in Fallujah in 2004, that

Blackwater was intensely involved in "development or planning of the contractors' security missions" or the directions on implementing them. It was Blackwater management, not the State Department, that reduced the preparation time for the ill-fated security detail so that they were dropped in place their first day on the job. It was Blackwater management that decided to send out a four-man detail instead of the usual six. It was Blackwater that decided to send the detail in soft-skinned instead of armored vehicles. It was Blackwater that decided not to give the detail machine guns as required by contract.[89]

In fact, the day before the four contractor guards died, Tom Powell, Blackwater's Iraq operations manager at the time, wrote company officials that it was time to stop the "smoke and mirror show" and provide crucial equipment for the private army in the field. "I need Comms [communications equipment]. . . . I need ammo. . . . I need Glocks and M4s. . . . Guys are in the field with borrowed stuff and in harm's way," said the e-mail.[90]

And, more than three years later, it was revealed that Blackwater had actually sent two squads through Fallujah without maps. Both of the six-man teams, named Bravo 2 and November 1, were sent out two men short. The Bravo 2 team members had protested that they were not ready for the mission and had not had time to prepare their weapons, but they were commanded to go, according to memos written by team members. The team disregarded directions to drive through Fallujah and instead drove around it and returned safely to Baghdad that evening. The November 1 team went into Fallujah and was massacred.[91]

A congressional investigation found a company that ignored multiple warnings about the dangers of traveling through Fallujah, cut essential personnel from the mission, and failed to supply its team with armored vehicles, machine guns, sufficient threat intelligence, or even maps of the area.[92] Such actions starkly contradict the claim made by Blackwater president Gary Jackson, who in an October 2006 affidavit wrote, "After being deployed, Blackwater has little if any knowledge regarding the location or activities of these independent contractors. Blackwater's only real involvement is to pay the independent contractors."[93]

This is not just a semantic distinction. The Internal Revenue Service is quite clear that, as a general rule, for someone to be considered an independent contractor[94] the employer has the right to control or direct only the result of the work done by an independent contractor, not the means and methods of accomplishing the result.[95] This was clearly not the case with the above Blackwater contractors.

Conversely, anyone who performs services for you is your employee if you can control what will be done and how it will be done. And this was the case with the Blackwater contractors. According to IRS Publication 15A: Employer's Supplemental Tax Guide, proof of the status of the employee falls into three categories:

- Behavioral control—Does the business provide the worker with:
    Instructions? An employee generally relies on a business's instructions about when, where and how to work.

Training? An employee receives specific training, while independent contractors use their own methods.

- Financial control—What is the extent of the worker's unreimbursed business expenses? Independent contractors are more likely to have unreimbursed expenses.

    Investment? An independent contractor often has a significant investment in the facilities used in performing services for someone else.

    Availability to the relevant market? If a worker performs services for several firms at the same time, that factor generally indicates that the worker is an independent contractor.

    Pay structure? Employees receive payments at designated times. An independent contractor is usually paid by the job.

    Ability to realize a profit or loss? An independent contractor can make a profit or take a loss.

- Type of relationship—Does the business provide the worker with employee-type benefits, such as insurance, a pension plan, vacation pay, or sick pay? Is there a written contract that describes the relationship the parties intended to create? How permanent is the relationship? How crucial is the worker's activity to the regular business of the company?

What's the bottom line? Hiring an independent contractor implies you are purchasing a product, an outcome. To the extent you retain the right to control the means by which that's done, the worker looks more and more like an employee.

Robert Young Pelton, author of the book *Licensed to Kill*, points out the following:

> It is clear in ALL instances of lethal force provision that there is direct input from the client (that apply under the 12 point and 24 point contractor rule) and in the case of State there is absolute control and even joint operational presence. That however makes them employees of the State and BW can make the argument that they are in effect a middleman or a MercTemp service for Unca Sam and that their income is on the vig or markup. My guess is that won't fly based on their competition converting to quasi employee status for ICs [independent contractors]. In almost every case it is the goal of the government to prove that the individual is an employee (to get tax revenue) and to punish the employer/contractor (Fines, back taxes).[96]

Perhaps the biggest irony came more than two years later when the U.S. Army said that Blackwater was not authorized to guard convoys or carry weapons.[97] That would mean U.S. taxpayer funds paid Halliburton and Blackwater for services prohibited under Halliburton's contract. At the lowest level, Blackwater security guards were paid $600 a day. Blackwater added a 36 percent markup, plus overhead costs, and sent the bill to a Kuwaiti company that ordinarily runs hotels, according to the contract. That company, Regency Hotel, tacked on costs and profit and sent an invoice to ESS. The food company added its costs and profit and sent its bill to Kellogg, Brown & Root, formerly a division of Halliburton, which added overhead and profit and presented the final bill to the Pentagon.[98]

Of course, in a classic example of the right hand not knowing what the left hand is doing, about six months later the Army confirmed that Blackwater provided armed security guards in Iraq under a subcontract that was buried so deeply the government couldn't find it. That hidden contract not only cost taxpayers money, but also might have been illegal. Halliburton's KBR subsidiary's main contract for military support services prohibited hiring subcontractors to provide armed security. That job is left to the U.S. military, unless the theater commander decides otherwise.[99]

Back in 2005 the Pentagon amended the Defense Federal Acquisition Regulation Supplement to address issues related to contract performance outside the United States. Many observers noted that the rule appeared to shift too much risk to contractors. One respondent noted that the use of the term *inherently dangerous* in paragraph (b) of the clause could jeopardize a contractor's ability to obtain insurance coverage under the Defense Base Act and other provisions.[100]

The issue of shifting risk actually has been controversial, though it rarely breaks into public view. The defense industry and the Pentagon have tried to clarify how to split up responsibilities between deployed troops and the contractors helping them, as contractors increasingly find themselves in combat situations. For example, when the Pentagon was amending acquisition rules in 2004, it received many comments. One response raised was how much risk contractors must accept. The government's proposed rule states that carrying out a contract for deployed forces is "inherently" dangerous. "The Contractor accepts the risks associated with required contract performance in such operations," the proposed rule states. But Alan Chvotkin, the senior vice president and counsel of the Professional Services Council, a group representing 165 companies that perform communications, engineering, and scientific services, interpreted that to mean that the contractor must assume all the risk and said the government should share some responsibility.[101]

Another consideration is that most of the security contractors are not American. Even though that is not supposed to make a difference under DBA, in reality it does. Some companies that employ foreign nationals may neglect to report the injuries or deaths of employees.

Adding to the difficulty of monitoring how many contractors die in Iraq is the fact that there is no organization keeping an official tally of civilians working there. Such an accounting would be difficult because the workers come from dozens of countries.[102] If nobody reports the incident to the Department of Labor and the family does not file a claim, it has no way of knowing what has happened. In short, the system is totally based on the transparency and honesty of the contracting firm to do what the law says it must do.

Like military personnel who receive special compensation if injured or killed as a result of active military duty, contractors operating in a war zone are extended additional protections beyond DBA insurance under the War Hazards Compensa-tion Act (WHCA). If an injury or death claim is related to a "war-risk hazard," the WHCA provides for government reimbursement to insurance carriers.[103]

Whereas the DBA covers injuries sustained only during the course of an employee's performance of duties, the WHCA extends round-the-clock coverage to employees who are subject to war-risk hazards and covers injuries sustained while present in a combat zone, whether or not the employee was engaged in per-forming the contract. The WHCA broadly defines "war-risk hazards" and does not limit them to actual declarations of war. Moreover, the act can also be applied to countries where war has officially ended, as in Iraq.[104]

If a contractor is injured, killed, or captured as a result of a war-related risk, the WHCA will reimburse the insurance carrier for applicable claims made by the contractor. The Employees Compensation Fund (a federally funded entity), which also pays compensation claims for federal employees, is responsible for war hazards compensation. According to the Department of Labor, the fund is allocated about $2.3 billion annually, but there is no way of knowing if con-tractor claims from Iraq and other areas of conflict will exceed the allocated amount.[105]

Firms are reluctant to reveal how much they are spending on security and insurance. It is estimated that for every $100 in salary paid by the employer, around $20 is spent on the life insurance premium. In light of the security situa-tion in past years, the insurance companies were forced to raise rates on a weekly basis.[106]

Pay

Because such information is proprietary and has privacy implications, PMCs and their parent companies usually do not make details available concerning their contracts, salaries, or number of employees. Given the obvious danger of work-ing in a war zone where personnel are potential targets, it seems reasonable that PMC personnel, especially those with highly-sought-after skills in short supply, can command high salaries. This was especially the case when PMCs first started operating in Iraq in the spring of 2003, but since then market forces have in many cases moderated salaries.

Michael Grunberg, spokesperson of a former PMC, Sandline International, put it this way:

The market is bleeding out. Payments in Iraq exceed everything known so far. The best can get up to $1,200 per diem. Small companies, like three people somewhere in an office in Washington, in need of some 250 trained former special forces and some 4,000 local support, have no chance. It's only a small reservoir of well trained former commandos world wide. People formerly earning $400 to $500 per diem from us, tell us today: "Sorry Comrade, but in Iraq I will earn $1,000."[107]

PMC personnel, especially those with highly-sought-after skills such as former SOF personnel, can still command high salaries. In 2004 British security contractors claimed that they could earn more than £80,000 a year. Reportedly, companies were offering yearly salaries ranging from $100,000 to nearly $200,000 to entice senior SOF personnel to switch careers.[108] Members of the SAS could earn three times their pay when working for PMCs.[109]

Short-term, high-risk work can bring much higher rewards. It is claimed that security personnel working a seven-day contract in cities like Fallujah can make $1,000 a day.[110] Blackwater employees are said to have been paid up to $2,000 a day, probably for a "three-day special."[111] The Steele Foundation said it pays people willing to work in Iraq anywhere from $10,000 to $20,000 dollars a month.[112]

On the other hand, figures can be somewhat misleading. Mike Battles, cofounder of Custer Battles, downplayed the level of pay: "I hear a lot of mistakes where people say, you know, a thousand dollars a day. That's not a thousand dollars a day the person is receiving. That's what someone is paying for that person, which includes insurance, equipment, travel and all of those types of things."[113]

The fact is that well-trained former U.K. and U.S. special operations forces receive premium rates of probably at most $700 a day (less than $50 an hour); Chileans, Poles, Fijians, and South Africans are getting considerably less, but still the same proportional increase over what they would earn within their national armed forces. Fijians recruited by Control Risk, a British PMC, were being paid $3,000 a month to work in Iraq in early 2005.[114] The attraction for PMC personnel is obvious, according to Duncan Bullivant, head of the small British firm Henderson Risk, which had around 40 employees operating in Iraq:

> Doing this kind of work for a year means some people have enough to retire on. Iraq is something of a goldmine at present. The profit margin is incredibly high, way in excess of the risk factor. I wouldn't give it more than another year at this level, the bubble will burst, but there's an immense drive to cash in while it lasts.[115]

However, the financial rewards can be overplayed, especially since the downsides for PMC contractors can be considerable, including the following:

- Most companies enforce regular periods, every few months, of unpaid mandatory leave out of country for rest and recharge.
- The dangers are considerable, and the work frequently demands a high level of experience and training.
- Although the pay is tax-free for some, under U.S. law U.S. citizens are still liable to U.S. tax if they reside within the United States for more than one month in the year.
- Additional insurance and retirement contributions are the responsibility of individual contractors.

A Drain on the Regular Armed Services?

The lure of higher salaries was reportedly causing an exodus of the U.S. military's most seasoned SOF members to higher-paying civilian security jobs in places like Baghdad and Kabul, just as the special forces are being asked to play an increasingly pivotal role in combating terror and helping to conduct nation-building operations worldwide.

Of course, the same problem exists in many other areas of military specialism, such as information technology. Why work in the Army's tech operations when you can get a job at three times the remuneration in the private sector?

Reportedly, exhausted American and British special forces personnel are resigning in record numbers and taking highly paid jobs as private security guards in Iraq and Afghanistan. Competition over elite troops from private companies is so intense that the U.S. Special Operations Command has formulated new pay, benefits, and educational incentives to try to retain them. "Competition with the civilian world has never been greater," said General Bryan "Doug" Brown, commander of the U.S. Special Operations Command, in congressional testimony.[116]

In early 2005 the Pentagon announced it was offering bonuses of up to $150,000 to keep elite commandos, such as Army Green Berets and Navy SEALs, in the military and prevent them from being lured away to higher-paying jobs by private security contractors in places such as Iraq and Afghanistan. The entire price tag for the effort was expected to be about $168 million over three years. The incentives are being targeted at those within a core group of some 6,000 special operators, who include 4,200 enlisted Green Berets, 1,500 SEALs, and 325 Air Force combat air controllers and pararescue specialists.[117] The bonus program paid out nearly $40 million to about 550 soldiers, sailors, and airmen in its first eight months.[118]

The same problem was faced by British special operations forces. In early 2005 a letter from the regiment's headquarters told all the SAS's 300 frontline soldiers that "it would be in everyone's best interests" if they remained in service. At that time an estimated 120 former SAS and Special Boat Service troops had left, swapping a junior NCO's wage of about £2,000 a month for as much as £14,000 a month working as a security coordinator in Iraq or Afghanistan.[119]

Things were so bad that in 2006 the British Ministry of Defence announced that soldiers were being allowed a "gap year" to work as private contractors and then to return to their Army posts at the same rank. The move was seen as a desperate attempt to stem the tide of troops quitting the Army and to ease a huge recruitment crisis. The main targets for the so-called comeback clause were elite SAS troops, paratroopers, and specialist weapons and communications experts.[120]

Senior enlisted members of the Army Green Berets or Navy SEALs with 20 years or more experience now earn about $50,000 in base pay and can retire with a $23,000 pension. Private security companies, whose services are in growing demand in Iraq and Afghanistan, are offering salaries of $100,000 to nearly $200,000 a year to the most experienced of them.[121] But there is no guarantee beyond the contracted period, and the salary is only paid when the person is deployed, that is, for only two-thirds of the year.

One retired U.S. Army officer wrote:

> It's fundamentally wrong to let contractors go head-hunting among our troops in wartime. Those in government who've elevated outsourcing to a state religion pretend it helps our war effort—with the whopper that outsourcing military functions saves taxpayer dollars.
>
> Exactly how does that one work? You get stuck with the training and security-clearance costs; the soldier lured to the private sector gets his salary doubled or tripled—then the contractor adds in a markup for his multiple layers of overhead costs and a generous profit margin, and bills the taxpayers. How is that cheaper than having soldiers do the job?
>
> The scam-artists tell us that using contractors saves money in the long run, since their employees don't get military health care and retirement benefits. But the numbers just don't add up.
>
> Contractors are looting our military—while wrapping themselves in the flag.[122]

The fact that special operators were leaving the military to join PCS also raised another concern. In August 2005 then Army Chief of Staff Peter Schoomaker said that commanders in the field were best qualified to answer questions about contracting, but he added that the use of private security firms in places like Iraq raised key issues of command and control. "I can see where, on the battlefield, there would be issues that could be problematic in terms of the rules of engagement, what kind of controls were placed on people that are roaming the battlefield," he said.[123] General Schoomaker evidently resolved his concerns, since a bit over two years later he joined DynCorp International's board.[124]

Resignations are not just limited to special operations forces personnel. Even members of the U.S. National Guard have been lured away to work for the likes of DynCorp, Blackwater, and Kellogg, Brown & Root.[125]

In the summer of 2005 Army Lieutenant General Steven Blum, the chief of the U.S. National Guard Bureau, said the government's outsourcing of certain security tasks to private firms had "unintended consequences," making it more difficult for the Guard to recruit sought-after military personnel such as special operators and military police.[126]

Similarly, British officials said more than 300 soldiers have left the armed forces in six months to take up lucrative jobs with private companies such as Olive Security, Armour Security, Global, and USDID.[127] In particular, the demand from PMCs operating in Iraq for former Special Air Service (SAS) and Special Boat Service (SBS) soldiers was such that from May 2003 to December 2004 between 40 and 60 men were expected to have sought premature voluntary release from the Army and Royal Marines. In operational terms, this could mean that the equivalent of one entire Sabre squadron out of a total of six in the SAS and SBS is on its way to seek its fortune in the new Iraq.[128]

According to one British press report, there were more ex-SAS soldiers acting as advisors for "private military companies" than were then serving in the elite, 300-man regiment based near Hereford. More than 40 regular SAS soldiers are understood to have applied to leave the Army, many because of the lure of short-term contracts in Iraq.[129]

To counter this, the British Army offered soldiers' yearlong "sabbaticals" in an attempt to staunch the long-term damage being caused by troops leaving to take up private security work in Iraq. About 500 British soldiers a month were ending their military careers early. The Army, alarmed at the loss of some of its best men, told soldiers that their jobs would be kept open for a year in the hope that they might consider returning.

It has been said by some observers that PMCs are also exhausting the supply of qualified short-term contractors willing to work in dangerous areas. Some are hired and return home within days, alarmed at the hostile environment.

As an article in *Fortune* magazine noted, once the big PMCs started competing for contracts in Iraq, the economics of the industry changed:

> They lured many of the firms' finest with what mercenaries respond to best: money. Standard wages for PSD (personal security detail) pros were previously running about $300 a day, according to people who know this market. Once Blackwater started recruiting for its first big job, guarding Paul Bremer, the rate shot up to $600 a day. Global Risk no longer had a lock on the market for Gurkhas, whose monthly wages rose from $800 to as high as $2,000 today.
>
> The big firms didn't grab all the business by any means, but they squeezed the margins and exacerbated small firms' biggest problem: a shortage of people with management skills.[130]

Largely lost in all the usual media blather about "supporting our boys" is the fact that the migration of active-duty soldiers to the PMC sector reflects an obsolete military pay system, at least in the United States. As one former U.S. marine wrote:

> Paying civilians to play soldier makes no sense. Today the United States employs between 7,000 and 17,000 civilians in infantry roles. The pay is extraordinary, hovering between $500 per day and $1,000 per day for everything from site security (for government compounds throughout Iraq) to convoy/company security to personal security (for dignitaries). This money comes tax-free in a combat zone. There are four problems here: morale deflation, gross monetary waste, tactical confusion, and direct competition for a tiny talent pool.
>
> Soldiers look at security contractors and think: Why the hell is he making eight times my salary for performing the same job? Is the military that pock-marked with overage

and inefficiency? Using bottom-up cost-accounting, the military is essentially buying out its most experienced soldiers and luring them out of the active ranks (if Stop-Loss is ever lifted, that is) with rich contracts, even as it desperately seeks new recruits. Worse, it's paying introduction fees to private security companies like Dynacorps and Blackwater for the people it recruited in the first place. How in the world did this happen?

The answer may lie in the marginal recruit. Congress just passed legislation to increase the number of soldiers by 30,000. But the Army is just barely meeting its current recruiting goals. To attract these new hires, the Army will have to come up with a pay structure that lures the 30,000th recruit. The problem is, the military pay structure is so antiquated that if you pay one soldier more money, you pay all soldiers more money. So it's not a question of paying 30,000 recruits. It's a question of paying those 30,000, then upping the pay of the other 1.4 million active members and the other 1.1 million reservists. It's an expensive prospect, this reverse Dutch auction. Perhaps it's cheaper to shift 10,000 infantry jobs over to the privateers, jack up the pay of private contractors, and pay the brokerage fee to the company . . .

This is not to denigrate contractors themselves; they are experienced soldiers who have been there and done that. Which is precisely why we need to keep them in the Army. Less than one-tenth of 1 percent of the US population chooses to become an infantryman. It is a professional public expression of commitment rather than a job. This is a tiny talent pool. We need everyone who heeds the call to carry a rifle working toward a common goal, and the best way to do that is to keep these folks in the government.

How, then, should these elite infantrymen be compensated so that the United States' Armed Forces can attract and retain the best? By revamping the military pay structure. Today the 9-to-5 corporal disbursing pay on a base in Florida earns the same salary as the corporal working 20 hours a day in Iraq who is on his third deployment in three months. As for elite infantrymen, who are needed for special security in war zones, offer them the same pay structure we give today's contractors and then take a look at re-enlistment rates. They'll skyrocket. What's more, the military will pay no brokerage fees and will retain the flexibility to reassign these men as the battlefield shifts. The military needs an escalating, bonus-based pay system that coincides with performance and hardship, not rank and time-in-grade.[131]

THE KEY PLAYERS

Many of the civilian contractors doing logistical and reconstruction work in Iraq have hired a PMC to provide protection for their personnel. The following gives a flavor of the work of some of the PMCs operating in Iraq.

Nobody knows for certain how many PMCs (and hence the number of personnel) are operating in Iraq. In response to a request from Congress, the CPA did compile a report listing 60 PMCs with an aggregate total of 20,000 personnel.[132] That number included U.S. citizens, third-country nationals, and Iraqis. But the CPA list was obviously incomplete, missing, for example, CACI (California

Analysis Center Incorporated) and Titan personnel, both implicated in the Abu Ghraib prison scandal.[133] At that time most of the armed personnel were the 14,000 Iraqi guards working the oil field contract for Erinys.

PMCs listed in the CPA report provided three categories of services:

- Personal security details for senior civilian officials
- Nonmilitary site security (buildings and infrastructure)
- Nonmilitary convoy security

The CPA report also made it clear that most PMCs do not work directly for the U.S. government. Instead, they work under subcontract to prime contractors providing employee protection, or are hired by other entities such as Iraqi companies or private foreign companies seeking business opportunities in Iraq. Of the 60 PMCs that the CPA identified as working in Iraq, only 8 had direct contracts with the CPA, for obligations currently totaling about $147 million: $8.14 million appropriated dollars and $66.5 million in funds from the Development Fund for Iraq.

In 2007 the U.S. military planned to outsource at least $1.5 billion in security operations, including the three largest security contracts in Iraq: a "theater-wide" contract to protect U.S. bases worth up to $480 million; a contract for up to $475 million to provide intelligence for the Army and personal security for the U.S. Army Corps of Engineers; and a contract for up to $450 million to protect reconstruction convoys. The Army also tested a plan to use private security on military convoys for the first time.[134]

POLITICAL CONNECTIONS

Political connections are important to PMCs when landing contracts. Diligence LLC is not an unusual example. It first set up shop in Baghdad in July 2003 to provide security for reconstruction projects.[135] That December, it established a new subsidiary, Diligence Middle East, and expanded its services to include screening, vetting, and training of local hires and providing daily intelligence briefs for its corporate clients.[136] One of its cochairs is Joe Allbaugh, President Bush's campaign manager in 2000. In late 2003 Diligence sold a 40 percent stake in its new subsidiary to Mohammed Al-Sagar, a wealthy Kuwaiti who also runs the foreign-relations committee of Kuwait's parliament.[137] In April 2004, it quietly announced it had formed a joint venture with New Bridge Strategies,[138] a consulting company headed by Joe Allbaugh and Republican lobbyist Ed Rogers that was established in 2003 to advise companies on business deals in postwar Iraq.

William Webster, the only man to head both the CIA and the FBI, founded Diligence. Mike Baker, its CEO, spent 14 years at the CIA as a covert field operations officer specializing in counterterrorism and counterinsurgency operations. Whitley Bruner, its chief operating officer in Baghdad, was once the CIA station chief in Iraq. Shortly before the U.S. invasion, he directed a covert operation for the Bush administration to convince high-ranking generals loyal to Saddam Hussein to cooperate with U.S. forces. Although that management team sounds formidable, it is the Diligence directors and advisors who are the real power in the firm.

Richard Burt, the chairman, was a former U.S. ambassador to Germany and a key advisor to the Carlyle Group, the Washington private equity fund with a string of former senior officials and for whom the first President George Bush has worked for the past 7 years. Ed Rogers, Diligence's vice chairman, was one of Bush's top assistants when he was president. Among Diligence's senior advisors are John Major, the former British prime minister and chairman of Carlyle Europe; Ed Mathias, Carlyle's managing director; and Lord Charles Powell, a former foreign policy advisor to Margaret Thatcher.

For a brief time ArmorGroup International had Stephen Kappes, a former deputy director of the CIA's clandestine Directorate for Operations, working as its Washington-based vice president of global strategy; in November 2005 it named him chief operating officer. Kappes was named deputy director of the CIA in May 2006.[139] To run the office, ArmorGroup also hired George Connell, a former marine who was also vice president of Raytheon Technical Services Company, a services unit of the U.S. defense giant.[140]

In late 2005 it was announced that Joseph E. Schmitz, the Pentagon's inspector general, would be leaving his post to take a top job at the parent company for Blackwater USA. Schmitz's new job would be chief operating officer and general counsel for the Prince Group, a firm that's divided between Michigan-based Prince Manufacturing and North Carolina–based Blackwater.[141]

Another Blackwater official is Rob Richer, vice president for intelligence; Richer was head of the CIA's Near East division—and the agency's liaison with King Abdullah of Jordan—from 1999 to 2004. In late 2004, he became the associate deputy director in the CIA's Directorate of Operations, making him the second-ranking official for clandestine operations. He left the agency for Blackwater in the fall of 2005, effectively taking the agency's relationship with Abdullah with him. The CIA had invested millions of dollars in training Jordan's intelligence services. There was an obvious quid pro quo: in exchange for the training, Jordan would share information. Jordan has now hired Blackwater's intelligence division, headed by Richer, to do its spy training instead.[142]

In the hope of cultivating contacts with the U.S. administration, Triple Canopy hired Alan Ptak, former assistant legislative counsel at the CIA, in September 2005. Ptak worked as a staffer on the Senate Select Intelligence Committee for several years.[143]

And on December 2, 2005, Triple Canopy announced the formation of its Strategic Advisory Board. Among the heavyweights it signed up are Dan Bannister, former chairman and CEO of DynCorp; David Binney, former deputy director of the FBI and former director of security for IBM; BGEN Steve Cheney, USMC (Ret.), currently the chief operating officer for Business Executives for National Security (BENS); and Catherine Lotrionte Yoran, former assistant general counsel with the Central Intelligence Agency.[144]

Other examples are the Steele Foundation and CACI. In April 2004, the Steele Foundation announced that retired U.S. ambassador Robert Frowick had joined its Executive Advisory Board as an executive director. Prior to joining the Steele Foundation, Ambassador Frowick was a career diplomat appointed to numerous ambassadorships under four different U.S. presidents.[145]

CACI, now known for its involvement in the Iraq torture and abuse scandal, is linked to U.S. Deputy Secretary of State Richard Armitage. He was elected a CACI director in 1999, when Armitage was a member of the Pentagon's Defense Policy Board and president of Armitage Associates, a consulting firm with a long list of powerful clients that included Boeing, Unocal, Texaco, Goldman Sachs, and the Brown & Root subsidiary of Halliburton.[146] And, in an interesting example of close relations between some PMCs, CACI's board of directors includes Carl Vuono and Ronald Griffith, retired generals, who are the president and executive vice president, respectively, of MPRI, which helped to train and equip the new Iraqi Army.[147]

In 2007 retired Army general Hugh Shelton, chairman of the Joint Chiefs of Staff from 1997 to 2001, joined the board of CACI International.[148]

On February 4, 2005, Blackwater USA announced that Ambassador Cofer Black, former coordinator for counterterrorism at the U.S. State Department and former director of the CIA's Counterterrorism Center, had joined its team as vice chairman.[149] Black also joined Republican presidential candidate Mitt Romney's campaign in April 2007 as senior advisor on counterterrorism and national security.

POLITICAL DONATIONS AND LOBBYING

PMCs extensively use political campaign donations and employ lobbyists to influence government officials. In 2001, the 10 leading private military firms spent more than $32 million on lobbying, while they invested more than $12 million in political campaign donations.[150] Among the leading donors were Halliburton, which gave more than $700,000 from 1999 to 2002 (95 percent to Republicans), and DynCorp, which gave more than $500,000 (72 percent to Republicans).[151]

Blackwater hired the Alexander Strategy Group (ASG) to help shape the company's public response after four employees were murdered by a mob in Fallujah in March.[152] The Alexander Group was closely connected to former House Majority Leader Tom DeLay; its chairman was Ed Buckham, his former chief of staff, who also recruited Tony Rudy and Karl Gallant from DeLay's team.[153] ASG later announced it was shutting down because of its ties to disgraced lobbyist Jack Abramoff and DeLay, who has been indicted on money-laundering charges.[154]

Similarly, CACI turned to a high-powered group of Washington lobbyists to help it deal with an investigation by the General Services Administration into whether the company violated federal contracting rules, which could have led to it being banned from future government work. The Clark & Weinstock lobby shop includes former representatives Vin Weber (R-MN) and Vic Fazio (D-CA); David Berteau, director of national security studies at Syracuse University; Edward Kutler, an aide to then-House Speaker Newt Gingrich (R-GA); and Sandra K. Stuart, assistant secretary of defense for legislative affairs in the Clinton administration.[155]

Blackwater, Triple Canopy, DynCorp, and Erinys are represented by Crowell & Moring, a high-powered international law firm.[156]

Both CACI and Titan, also involved in the Abu Ghraib torture scandal, have made political donations that favored the Republican Party. Titan has contributed $244,350 to Republicans since January 2003, more than seven times the $32,209 it gave to Democrats. Between 1999 and 2002, the company spent more than $268,000 on Republicans, again a 7 to 1 ratio relative to contributions to Democrats.

3

The Players

Many of the civilian contractors doing logistical and reconstruction work in Iraq have hired a PMC to provide protection for their personnel.

Not all PMCs are created equal. Some are divisions of larger contractors, but others are far smaller. In the beginning stages of the Iraq War, many firms were veritable Mom and Pop concerns created virtually overnight, often by retired military personnel operating out of their homes and equipped with a Rolodex of contacts and not much else.

Over time most of those firms have either left or ceased to exist. The industry has been shaking out. The good news is that the remaining firms generally have deeper pockets with more resources to draw on. The bad news is that such firms are often more inflexible and not necessarily in touch with their operators in the field. To be blunt, they may not care very much about their operators' safety.

On the other hand, some firms, through their sheer size, role, or operating culture, have carved out distinct niches, both in Iraq and in the industry worldwide.

The following is a description of a few of the many private security players. Some, such as Aegis, ArmorGroup, Blackwater, Control Risks, Triple Canopy, and DynCorp, are veritable kings of the private security landscape. Others, such as AirScan, are tiny niche players. Firms like Custer Battles became poster children for fraudulent behavior.

AEGIS DEFENCE SERVICES (U.K.)

In March 2004, in a move to make the U.S. military presence less visible after the handover of sovereignty back to Iraq, the Coalition Provisional Authority offered a $100 million contract to protect the Green Zone, the 4-square-mile headquarters area in Baghdad.[1]

Soon after major combat operations had ceased in Iraq, companies had varying access to information, and as they were in fierce competition for contracts, they resisted sharing such information. Indeed, the contract awarded to Aegis Defence was challenged by two other competitors. That competition led to Aegis's next big contract.

In May, Aegis Defence Services won a contract, despite a protest by DynCorp, another security firm, valued at a maximum of $293 million over the next three years ($92 million for the first year) to provide antiterrorism support and analysis and to serve as a clearinghouse for information between coalition forces in Iraq and security contractors.[2] Before Aegis was awarded that contract, coordination between the U.S. military and civilian contractors was handled through the Regional Operations Centre (ROC). In June 2005 the Pentagon extended the contract for a second year and expanded it. The new deal was worth about $145 million.[3]

For its money Aegis had to pay a staff of 500 based all over the country, organize the coordination of intelligence from all the security firms and the military, and also provide a central emergency hotline, so that if someone is ambushed on the road, there is one number (or radio frequency) he or she can ring for help.[4] It operates one national and six regional command centers in cities across Iraq. Staff act as a link between coalition forces and civilian contractors on security issues, passing on information on the activity of insurgents. They provide a daily intelligence service to contractors and track the position of their vehicles.

In addition, Aegis established 75 teams of eight men to provide security on all major Iraqi government projects following the handover of sovereignty. Back then it was the fifth-largest contract ever awarded by the CPA, amounting to almost 3 percent of the CPA Program Management Office's entire Iraq reconstruction budget.[5]

At that time Aegis was, at least publicly, emphasizing its clearinghouse role. As Tim Spicer,[6] cofounder and head of Aegis, said in a BBC interview:

> We're currently employing about 500 people. We're not actually responsible for everybody's security, what we're responsible for is the coordination, in a number of civil military operation centres, the coordination of the security of the reconstruction companies and its interface with military operations—the counter-insurgency operations.[7]

The award of this contract struck many observers as odd, as Aegis had no significant experience in Iraq, or the Middle East for that matter, and its expertise was largely limited to antipiracy consulting.[8]

Some industry insiders speculated that Aegis won the contract because of growing anger in Britain that U.K.–based companies have not been awarded large contracts in the reconstruction of Iraq, despite the leading role that Tony Blair's government has played in the "coalition of the willing." The only other British bid for the contract, the Control Risks Group, Erinys, and Olive Security joint venture, was disqualified because one of the partners was under investigation for undisclosed reasons at the time the bids were evaluated.[9]

Aegis Defence CEO Tim Spicer was involved in the 1997 Papua New Guinea affair,[10] which involved Sandline, a British PMC that Spicer headed. He left Sandline under a cloud and then subsequently left the shell firm SCI (registered at a public relations office) with questions over legal registration and false claims of work done hanging over his head.[11] Spicer evidently gave only the minimum amount of information required under the contract process about his past.[12] Irish Americans campaigned against the contract because of Spicer's role as commanding officer of the Scots Guards in Belfast in 1992, when two of his soldiers shot dead 18-year-old Peter McBride.[13]

Since the awarding of the contract, Aegis has deployed satellite communications and navigation equipment that allow its officials working in the operations center to maintain a digital map showing the location of security contractors across Iraq.

Aegis's intelligence operations go far beyond merely keeping track of contractors. Known internally as Project Matrix, Aegis's U.S. Army contract has multiple aims. Part of its activity includes garnering Iraqis' trust. The company, for example, runs more than a dozen Reconstruction Liaison Teams in which contractors armed with assault rifles and traveling in armored SUVs visit reconstruction projects to assess their progress and the levels of insurgent activity. Aegis also spent about $425,000 in company money and private donations on more than 100 small charity projects such as soccer fields and vaccination programs. The projects enabled the company to build relationships in the communities in which it operates and gather information at the same time.[14]

Aegis's Regional Operations Centre (ROC) has its limitations. Blackwater and DynCorp, two of the largest security firms in Iraq and both American companies, refuse to participate in the ROC, essentially making their movements invisible to other private security firms. Blackwater said that it does not need to participate because its movements are tracked by the military under separate U.S. government contracts. DynCorp said it also is monitored separately. Also, the usefulness of the center has been limited because each time a company provides intelligence, it is classified secret by the military and not distributed. This practice has deterred the private security contractors from participating, since they don't benefit from intelligence collected by the center.[15]

With the advantage of hindsight, this was an inevitable contract. Though Aegis was not the inevitable choice, the daunting task of coordinating regular military forces, Iraqi forces, and PSCs required a dedicated firm.

In 2004 Lieutenant Colonel Len McWherter, operations officer for the Multi-National Brigade Northwest, which operates in the northern sector of Iraq, said that coordinating military operations not only with the activities of the fledgling Iraqi security forces—which include Iraqi military, police, and border protection personnel—but also with the private security forces presents the "ultimate inter-operability challenge."

It is critical that the military know where the contractors are and that they operate according to established procedures, McWherter said. "We're the only one that can respond to assist them if something goes wrong. If they run into [a roadside bomb], or run into contact with insurgents, then we have a responsi-bility to react and assist as best we can."

Equally important, McWherter said, is that contractors don't unknowingly stumble into the middle of a military operation. "The difficulty comes just shar-ing that information as efficiently as possible."[16]

The award to Aegis was challenged by DynCorp, which filed two formal protests.[17] The CPA inspector general also investigated the award.[18]

On September 13, 2007, Aegis won the Reconstruction Security Support Ser-vices contract, worth an estimated $475 million, for two more years. Under the contract, Aegis will provide a wide range of services to the U.S. Army Corps of Engineers and Joint Contracting Command Iraq, including management of six regional Regional Operations Centres (ROCs) and a headquarters operation in Baghdad. In addition, the firm will provide close protection details, static guard forces, and employee vetting services. The main client for the contract is the Corps of Engineers Gulf Regional Division (GRD).[19]

This was essentially a continuation of the services in the contract Aegis was previously awarded, despite challenges by both Blackwater and Erinys.[20] In its written challenge, Blackwater wrote that the Army's decision to exclude it was "defective" and "meaningless," in part because the military did not explain how it evaluated the contractor's offer. Erinys contended that the Army did not thor-oughly review its proposal and failed to follow procurement rules.[21]

In part, the challenges to Aegis were dismissed because a U.S. Army veteran Brian X. Scott filed a suit in April 2007 arguing that the military's use of private security contractors is "against America's core values" and violated an 1893 law prohibiting the government from hiring quasi-military forces—the Anti-Pinkerton Act, which Congress passed more than a century ago to thwart businesses that had hired mercenaries to disrupt labor groups. The Government Accountability Office dismissed the challenges because his complaint could have forced the Army to revise the contract.[22]

Aegis is hardly the only PSC to have been challenged over winning an award. Yet, by and large, challenges are rejected. A review by the Associated Press found that the GAO, a sort of court of first resort for those competing for federal work, usually rejects corporate claims of contract irregularities and improprieties. Of the 1,327 bid protests lodged with the GAO in 2006, only 249 got as far as an offi-cial decision. In 71 percent of those cases, the office sided with the government and denied the complaint.[23]

Ironically, in what is apparently a case of life imitating art, Aegis shareholder Frederick Forsyth, who wrote the classic mercenary novel *Dogs of War*, owned 414 shares, giving him 3.1 percent ownership of the company.[24]

Life for Aegis since first winning the contract has not been without controversy. In 2005 the Office of the Special Inspector General for Iraq Reconstruction criticized Aegis for its work, saying the British firm had failed to verify that employees were properly qualified for the job. Among problems cited in the audit were that Aegis could not provide the correct documents to show that its employees were qualified to use weapons and that many Iraqi employees were not properly vetted to ensure they were not a security threat.[25]

Private contractors have also provided intelligence directly to the military. In 2007 the Abraxas Corporation, founded and run by the former director of the CIA's Europe division, Richard "Hollis" Helms, landed a contract to supply analysts to the First Intelligence Battalion of the First Marine Expeditionary Force (1 MEF), which was administering Al Anbar province while training the 1st and 7th Divisions of the Iraqi Army.[26]

It is clear that there has been friction between clients and contractors on numerous occasions in this field, notably over coordination. It has been a delicate issue. Some feel that some in the regular military are jealous of the higher salaries contractors earn. There have reportedly been many cases of "blue on white" incidents in which soldiers have been in conflict with contractors.[27] In one publicized case, a 19-man security convoy, including 16 Americans, from Zapata Engineering, a company hired to destroy enemy ammunition such as shells and bombs, was taken into custody for three days on suspicion of shooting at the Marine tower. The contractors felt they were unfairly arrested and, once in the military prisons, said they were treated with physical abuse and disrespect. According to one Zapata contractor who was held:

> I know what they did was wrong. I worked Camp X-Ray in Guantanamo so I know the military procedure for these things. What I am saying is I don't feel like I was beat. Most of the harassment I received was not physical in nature. Some of the guys had it worse and some not so bad but the focus should be on the fact that while we were detained they didn't allow us to contact anyone, even our company. They would not allow us to talk to the Red Cross. They would not tell us why we were being detained. They would not let us have legal representation. Nothing. All of this and more was not allowed. Even when we spoke to a chaplain, who still falls under military control and orders, and pleaded with him to let our families know that we were not dead, nothing was permitted.
>
> It's one thing if we were insurgents. I can understand not getting to "make a phone call." These guys knew we were Marines. Hell, I think 10 out of the 16 were former Marines. While I was being cuffed, my tattoo showed and the guard pointed at it and said "how cute."[28]
>
> —Darrell Cleland, former contractor with Zapata Engineering

While the Zapata detail was in custody, one of the marines reportedly said, "How do you like your contractor money now?"[29] To this day we do not know what really happened.[30] The contractors were later cleared of all charges.[31]

A July 2005 GAO report described two incidents in which gunners in the middle of U.S. military convoys opened fire on passing private security convoys, even after the front of the military convoy had passed without incident.[32]

A GAO official testified to Congress that during the five-month period of January through May 2005, the ROC received reports of 20 friendly-fire incidents. It is likely that the number of actual incidents during that time period was higher, since some providers said they stopped reporting these types of incidents.[33]

A past GAO report found the following:

> While the U.S. military and private security providers have developed a cooperative working relationship, actions should be taken to improve its effectiveness. The relationship between the military and private security providers is one of coordination, not control. Prior to October 2004 coordination was informal, based on personal contacts, and was inconsistent. In October 2004 a Reconstruction Operations Center was opened to share intelligence and coordinate military-contractor interactions. While military and security providers agreed that coordination has improved, two problems remain. First, private security providers continue to report incidents between themselves and the military when approaching military convoys and check-points. Second, military units deploying to Iraq are not fully aware of the parties operating on the complex battle space in Iraq and what responsibility they have to those parties.[34]

Many U.S. military officials have not been happy with the presence of security contractors. Colonel Peter Mansoor commanded the First Brigade, First Armored Division in Iraq and Germany from July 2003 to June 2005, to include 13 months in combat in support of Operation Iraqi Freedom. In a 2007 interview with *Jane's Defence Weekly*, he said that the "U.S. military needs to take a real hard look at security contractors on future battlefields and figure out a way to get a handle on them so that they can be better integrated—if we're going to allow them to be used in the first place. If they push traffic off the roads or if they shoot up a car that looks suspicious, whatever it may be, they may be operating within their contract (but) to the detriment of the mission, which is to bring the people over to your side. I would much rather see basically all armed entities in a counter-insurgency operation fall under a military chain of command."[35]

Another GAO report in 2006 found that one of the main problems the U.S. military has in dealing with private security teams, which include non-Americans, is in screening them for criminal records.

The Pentagon has a policy that requires biometric screening of most non-U.S. private security providers who need to access U.S. military bases in Iraq. But, according to the GAO, "Biometric screening is not as effective as it could be because the databases used to screen contractor employees include limited international data. Based on its work to date, GAO believes that incomplete criminal background screening may contribute to an increased risk to military forces and civilians in Iraq, and the military would benefit by reviewing the base security measures to ensure that the risk private security contractors may pose has been minimized."[36]

Another major PMC in Iraq, Triple Canopy, also had several friendly-fire incidents in Iraq in which military personnel shot at them.[37]

Although there have been numerous incidents of friction between contractors and regular military in Iraq, the overall trend has been downward. Contractors clearly recognize that they are subordinate to regular military forces and when so directed must obey the orders of the commanders under whose jurisdiction they fall. To the extent there are still incidents, they are probably the result of new troops being rotated into the theater who are unfamiliar with working with contractors and who may have some resentment fueled by reports in the media of the higher salaries of contractor personnel.

Although U.S. military forces do monitor the whereabouts of all contractors and will respond, if possible, when contractors are in distress, they do so at their own discretion. It is worth noting that the U.S. military is able to monitor all security details thanks to the systems set up by Aegis Defence. Its Regional Operations Centre (ROC) and Tapestry software system allows the U.S. military to see every transponder-equipped security convoy, although not all security convoys use transponders. Ever since the Blackwater contractors were killed at Fallujah in 2004, the U.S. government requires private security vehicles to carry transponders. Drivers who are attacked hit a panic button, and Tapestry transmits an SOS to every military operations center in Iraq, the security company's operations center, and the ROC that coordinates the private–military response.[38] But it is only a one-way system. The military can see the contractors, but the contractors do not know where the military is.

There has also been friction between U.S. PSCs and military and PSCs from other countries. John Geddes, an ex-SAS soldier who wrote a book titled *Highway to Hell*, says, "I've had conversations with many [U.S. security contractors] and regular U.S. soldiers who are evangelical Christians who see themselves in a crusade against the Muslim hordes. In my view, they're not much different to the Iraqi militiamen and foreign fighters who see themselves at the heart of a jihad against the Christian crusaders."[39]

On the subject of American PSCs he also wrote

I think they're a wonderful people but they do have a couple of serious attitude problems when they're in a conflict.

Their biggest problem is communication with anyone who doesn't speak English.

Outside the U.S., a lot of Americans can be insular, arrogant and paranoid, relaxing only when accosted in a familiar language, especially if the accent is British.

They are the new empire but they don't know how to deal with it. While the Brits, with hundreds of years of colonial experience—know when to keep their heads down, the Americans are high-profile all the way.

Their PMCs move their clients across the warscape headfirst, in large convoys with as many as 20 armed guards, an armoured scout car front and back, and sometimes air cover in the form of a helicopter gunship.

They treat all Iraqis as potential insurgents and I've seen their PMC convoys strafe junctions with machinegun fire or shoot at any vehicle they feel is suspicious.

Some British companies involved with U.S. clients are contractually obliged to take the same approach, and like their American counterparts they regularly get whacked by insurgents because the tactics simply scream out: "Attack me." It's not a way I travel. I don't mind a scrap but I draw the line at mooning at the enemy and inviting him to shoot at my backside.

. . .

American PMCs feel no qualms at all about infuriating ordinary Iraqis by setting up roadblocks to give their convoys priority. They also make a habit of forcing other vehicles off the road by ramming them from behind or forcing them over from the side.

This is especially true in Baghdad, where they will actually fire at any vehicle they don't like the look of. I know it's suicide bomb central, but I believe such behaviour has alienated moderate Iraqi citizens.

In fact, I'm certain that a fair percentage of attacks on U.S. contractors in Baghdad have been made by locals fired up with what amounts to road rage.[40]

AIRSCAN INC. (U.S.)

The Coalition Provisional Authority awarded a $10 million contract to the Florida-based AirScan Inc. for aerial surveillance of the pipelines in support of Erinys. AirScan provided night air surveillance of the pipeline and oil infrastructure using low-light television cameras. Under terms of the lease, the Iraqi government had the right to buy the equipment after two years and then use Iraqi pilots.[41]

AKE (U.K.)

CNN used a company called AKE, a British security firm with its roots in the SAS. Certainly, with CNN's high-profile correspondents and camera equipment ripe for pillaging, it is not hard to understand why they would seek efficient security.

ARMORGROUP (U.K.)

The British-owned company ArmorGroup is the company now chaired by Sir Malcolm Rifkind, the former Tory foreign and defense secretary who was a fierce opponent of the Iraq War. Rifkind took on the job in 2004 and is paid £31,000 a year by the firm. In addition to his basic salary, he had the option of buying 38,685 shares in ArmorGroup every year for the next three years at 14.8p a share.[42]

Specifically, ArmorGroup, once Defence Systems Limited, was bought by U.S.-based Armor Holdings, Inc and then rebought by ArmorGroup Management, which is basically composed of the board of directors and private investors led by the Granville Baird Capital Partners with additional financial support from Barclays Bank PLC. This partnership allowed ArmorGroup to become the first independent, international security firm to be traded on a stock exchange; in 2004 it floated stocks in London.[43]

ArmorGroup originally was contracted by U.S. construction firm Bechtel to guard sites and deal with unexploded ordnance across Iraq. ArmorGroup had an £876,000 contract to supply 20 security guards for the Foreign Office. That figure rose by 50 percent in July 2004. The firm also employed hundreds of Gurkhas to guard executives with the U.S. firms Bechtel and Kellogg, Brown & Root.[44]

Armor also recruited extensively from Fiji through a company called Homeland Security. In Fiji the security industry is booming. In January 2005 the Labour minister in the previous government described the Iraq industry as "a good thing" and a Band-Aid for high unemployment. When recruiting began in Fiji in 2003, three years after Fijian soldiers returned from a United Nations peacekeeping mission in Lebanon, "there was a willing pool of recruits in the South Pacific," according to a report by Melbourne's Nautilus Institute on the privatization of Fiji's military. It concluded: "The boom in recruiting for Iraq and Kuwait has raised many issues for the Government of Fiji: the unregulated role of private recruitment contractors, the social impacts on family life, and the capacity of government to support workers with pay disputes or post-deployment health problems."[45]

Although Armor made big profits from its work in Iraq, which provided half its work, it was not enough to keep it going. In March 2008 it announced that it was being bought by the giant security firm G4S. The buyout came just six months after a scandal involving contractors for rival Blackwater, who were accused of killing Iraqi civilians, cast a pall over the sector.[46]

BLACKWATER (U.S.)

Blackwater was founded by former Navy SEAL Erik Prince. In 2002 it signed a $35.7 million contract with the Pentagon to train more than 10,000 soldiers in force protection at its 6,000-acre training range in Moyock, North Carolina.[47]

Blackwater has emerged as one of the 800-pound gorillas of the private security industry. The value of its federal contracts has risen steadily.

Value of Blackwater's federal contracts in 2001: $736,906

Value in 2002: $3.4 million

Value in 2003: $25 million

Value in 2004: $48 million

Value in 2005: $352 million

Value in 2006: $593 million

Total value of all Blackwater contracts at the end of 2006: $1 billion

Percentage growth since 2001: 80,453[48]

Its services and capabilities go beyond the work it does in Iraq. They include

A burgeoning logistics operation that can deliver 100- or 200-ton self-contained humanitarian relief response packages faster than the Red Cross.

A Florida aviation division with 26 different platforms, from helicopter gunships to a massive Boeing 767. The company even has a Zeppelin.

The country's largest tactical driving track, with multi-surface, multi-elevation positive and negative cambered turns, a skid pad, and a ram pad for drivers learning how to escape ambushes.

A 20-acre manmade lake with shipping containers that have been mocked up with ship rails and portholes, floating on pontoons, used to teach how to board a hostile ship.

A K-9 training facility that currently has 80 dog teams deployed around the world.

A 1,200-yard-long firing range for sniper training.

A sizable private armory.

An armored personnel carrier called the Grizzly.[49]

In Iraq, Blackwater personnel guarded L. Paul Bremer, the head of the CPA, among other duties. In August 2003, Blackwater was awarded a $21 million no-bid contract to supply security guards and two helicopters for Bremer.[50] It later assisted in providing security for former U.S. Ambassador to Iraq John Negroponte.

Iraq, at least in the first year of the U.S. occupation, was economically very good for Blackwater. At a ribbon-cutting ceremony in October 2004 for a new target manufacturing plant, Blackwater president Gary Jackson said he was astounded by the growth of his company. "The numbers are actually staggering. In the last 18 months we've had over 600 percent growth," he said.[51]

The killing and mutilation of four Blackwater employees in Fallujah at the end of March was an extraordinarily high-profile event, causing the U.S. marines to launch a siege of the city for about a month.[52] That incident was one of the iconic moments for the PSC industry in Iraq. It has been written about so much in subsequent years that it won't be dealt with here. But there are a few aspects worth noting.

First, the contract that the Blackwater employees were working on when they were killed, guarding convoys that carried food for U.S. troops in Iraq (although, ironically, in that particular mission there was no actual food being transported), serves as an example of how easily and quickly the costs can mount up.

According to the North Carolina newspaper *News & Observer*, which has done some of the best reporting in the world on Blackwater, here is how it worked:

> Jerry Zovko's contract with Blackwater USA looked straightforward: He would earn $600 a day guarding convoys that carried food for U.S. troops in Iraq.
>
> But that cost—$180,000 a year—was just the first installment of what taxpayers were asked to pay for Zovko's work. Blackwater, based in Moyock, N.C., and three other companies would add to the bill, and to their profits.
>
> In Zovko's case: Blackwater added a 36 percent markup, plus its overhead costs, and sent the bill to a Kuwaiti company that ordinarily runs hotels. That company, Regency Hotel, tacked on its costs for buying vehicles and weapons and a profit and sent an invoice to a German food services company called ESS that cooked meals for the troops.
>
> ESS added its costs and profit and sent its bill to Halliburton, which also added overhead and a profit and presented the final bill to the Pentagon.
>
> It's nearly impossible to say whether the cost for Zovko doubled, tripled or quadrupled. Congressional investigators and defense auditors have had to fight the primary contractor, Halliburton, for details of the spending. The companies say the subcontracts are confidential and won't discuss them.[53]

Such calculations call into question the claims regularly made by PSCs that they are more cost-effective than regular military forces.

The killings also highlighted a legal issue, which didn't get much attention then and hasn't to this day: namely, are security contractors civilians or combatants?[54] The answer is that they seem to fall in a murky area between the two. The four men who died were American citizens with some past military affiliation. As employees of a government contractor, Blackwater, they were agents of the U.S. government, although they formally worked for a private company.

They carried weapons, but unlike soldiers, they presumably had orders only to use them in self-defense within the scope of their contract and the coalition's rules of engagement. In addition, they had a quasi-military mission to defend convoys from Iraqi insurgents. As such they clearly were not civilians as defined in the Fourth Geneva Convention Relative to the Protection of Civilian Persons in Time of War, which defines noncombatants as those "[p]ersons taking no active part in the hostilities."

For these reasons, even though it's clear that the four men were not U.S. military personnel, they may have been combatants for the purposes of international law. Thus, horrifying as their deaths were to many, they could be considered acts of war, not crimes.

Another problem is that upholding the Geneva Conventions is not mandatory for private contractors as it is for soldiers. This may mean that the conventions should be amended, as has been done in the past. But that is a lengthy process that will take many years.[55]

Still, Blackwater has also, on more than one occasion, performed above and beyond the call of duty or contract. In April an attack by hundreds of Iraqi militia members on the U.S. government's headquarters in Najaf was repulsed not by the U.S. military, but by eight Blackwater commandos. Blackwater Security Consulting sent in its own helicopters amid an intense firefight to resupply its commandos with ammunition and to ferry out a wounded marine before U.S. reinforcements could arrive.[56]

Or at least that is what many people have thought. Now, we need to revise that account, according to the book *Wiser in Battle* by Lieutenant General Ricardo Sanchez, former commander of coalition forces in Iraq.[57] Sanchez writes that he began receiving radio reports from a marine major that he and his men were under attack, had been abandoned by Spanish forces, and needed help. The situation sounded so dangerous that Sanchez immediately ordered close air support. But when the fighters flew over the area, they could see no enemy activity. Sanchez radioed the major back, who said they were still under attack. "Fighting everywhere. This may be the last radio call we can make before we get overrun. Send help."

Sanchez decided, given the conflicting reports he was receiving, that he needed to go in person to find out what was happening. While en route he continued to get dire reports of the troops being under attack. But when the helicopter arrived, he found no major firefight. When he asked the major how he was getting his reports on enemy attacks, he was told, "These Blackwater and CPA guys are telling me what's happening."

When Sanchez went up to the roof of the compound to see for himself, he was informed that there was occasional fire by a sniper but nothing serious. Sanchez then went to see the Spanish brigade commander whose troops had allegedly deserted their posts and left the Americans to fend for themselves. "Not true, sir," the commander replied. "Those Blackwater and CPA guys wanted us to put all of our troops backs and surround their building. But we didn't need to do that, because there was never any threat of being overrun. Besides, it was better for us to protect the entire compound rather than just one building."

Before leaving Najaf, Sanchez told the marine major that, contrary to his information, he had not been under attack by hundreds of Iraqis, the Spanish had not deserted him, and he had been in no danger of being overrun. "Those civilians were not providing you with accurate information," Sanchez said.

After returning to Baghdad, Sanchez met with Bremer and briefed him on what happened. "Although the Ambassador didn't want to believe it, what had really happened was that the CPA personnel had panicked and the Blackwater civilians were aggravating the situation by having the young major relay bogus information."

Generally, Blackwater, because of its size and prominence, has become a target of criticism for those who just don't like the concept of private security contractors. Unease about Blackwater became a subject of international concern on September 16, 2007, when 17 Iraqis were killed and at least 18 wounded in Baghdad as Blackwater contractors were escorting a convoy in the western Baghdad district of Mansour near Nisoor Square.[58] Blackwater claimed the convoy was attacked by armed insurgents. A spokesman for the U.S. embassy said that the shooting occurred after a car bomb exploded while U.S. diplomats were nearby.

Iraqi officials disagreed. Iraq's Ministry of Interior said that Blackwater contractors fired an unprovoked barrage, and he concluded that the dozens of foreign security companies in Iraq should be replaced by Iraqi companies and that the law that has given the companies immunity for years should be scrapped.[59] In fact, in late October 2007 the Iraqi government approved draft legislation lifting immunity for foreign private security companies, although to date it has not actually been passed.[60]

U.S. military reports from the scene indicated that Blackwater guards opened fire without provocation and used excessive force against Iraqi civilians. The reports came to light as an Interior Ministry official and five eyewitnesses described a second deadly shooting minutes after the incident in Nisoor Square. The same Blackwater security guards, after driving about 150 yards away from the square, fired into a crush of cars, killing one person and injuring two, the Iraqi official said.[61]

A *New York Times* article noted that the cascade of events began when a single bullet apparently fired by a Blackwater guard killed an Iraqi man whose weight probably remained on the accelerator and propelled the car forward. The car continued to roll toward the convoy, which responded with an intense barrage of gunfire in several directions, striking Iraqis who were desperately trying to flee. Minutes after that shooting stopped, a Blackwater convoy—possibly the same one—moved north from the square and opened fire on another line of traffic a few hundred yards away, in a previously unreported separate shooting.[62]

Reportedly American investigators were told that during the shootings at least one Blackwater guard continued firing on civilians while colleagues urgently called for a cease-fire. At least one guard apparently also drew a weapon on a fellow guard who did not stop shooting.[63]

Reportedly FBI agents found that at least 14 of the shootings were unjustified and violated deadly-force rules in effect for security contractors in Iraq.[64] The case has supposedly focused on one Blackwater turret gunner.

Iraqi officials subsequently canceled Blackwater's operating license, even though the license was no longer valid. Blackwater technically did not need it to operate; the State Department position has long been that Blackwater does not need a license from the Iraqi government to protect American officials because its contract is directly with U.S. authorities to provide diplomatic security.

Specifically, Blackwater shares with DynCorp and Triple Canopy the Worldwide Personal Protective Services contract awarded by the U.S. State Department in 2004. The contractors doing this work are considered State Department employees and thus enjoy the same immunity from prosecution as any other State Department employee in a foreign country. They do not require a license.

This fact was confirmed by a September 1, 2007, report from the Iraqi Ministry of Interior that listed all the licensed foreign and Iraqi private security companies operating in the country. There was no mention of either Blackwater or DynCorp, though Triple Canopy was included.

This omission reflected a deliberate business strategy by Blackwater and DynCorp to put all their contract eggs into the single State Department basket. Triple Canopy, however, chose to be more diversified and sought out other commercial work, such as protecting logistics contractors, and thus took the time and effort to get a license.

It bears remembering that Blackwater gets far more work from the State Department than does any other U.S. government client. According to federal spending data compiled by the independent Web site FedSpending.org, the State Department's Blackwater contracts vastly exceed those of the Pentagon. From 2004 through September 2007, the State Department paid Blackwater $833,673,316, compared with Defense Department contracts of $101,219,261.[65]

In any event, any ouster of the company from Iraq likely would require the support of the State Department, which depends on Blackwater for security. Indeed, some say that the State Department was partly to blame for the Nisoor Square shootings, given that Blackwater operated under State Department authority that exempted the company from U.S. military regulations governing other security firms.[66]

A document entitled "Diplomatic Security—Use of Contractors for Protective Security," obtained by The Spy Who Billed Me blog, outlines the total annual costs of the State Department's outsourced security. According to the document, the approximate current annual costs under the Worldwide Personal Protective Services II contracts for all areas of operation worldwide are as follows:

Blackwater $339,573,391
DynCorp $47,145,172
Triple Canopy $15,550,133
[Total] $402,268,696

The approximate total costs for Iraq only, inclusive of all contractors, is $350,119,545.11.

Blackwater USA provides 7 times the services in terms of dollar amounts than DynCorp and nearly 22 times the amount of Triple Canopy. The contract amount as provided by Blackwater indicates that it is highly unlikely that one of the other two contractors could fill the void if Blackwater were expelled from Iraq. No other U.S. firms are positioned to provide specialized services on such a large scale.[67]

Some in the industry believe, for instance, that the immunity Blackwater gets from its State Department contract encourages it to emphasize its mission—the protection of its clients—to the exclusion of all other considerations: a sort of "shoot first, ask questions later" attitude.

Such an attitude has been criticized even by other parts of the government. Secretary of Defense Robert Gates said in a news conference that the mission of many contractors in Iraq—to protect their U.S. government employers regardless of other consequences—was "at cross-purposes to our larger mission in Iraq. As I see it, right now those missions are in conflict, because in the objective of completing the mission of delivering a principal safely to a destination, just based on everything I've read and what our own team has reported, there have been instances where, to put it mildly, the Iraqis have been offended and not treated properly."[68]

The State Department reportedly overlooked repeated warnings from U.S. diplomats in the field that guards were endangering Iraqi civilians and undermining U.S. efforts to win support from the population.[69]

ABC News obtained internal State Department e-mails showing that top officials were extensively briefed in 2005 about repeated incidents of Blackwater security guards killing innocent civilians, and complained about a lack of a compensation program for civilian victims.[70]

In fact, Blackwater's contract with the State Department contains a clause not to engage with the media, as noted in a congressional hearing:

MR. PRINCE: By contract, we are not allowed to engage with the press.

REP. CUMMINGS: All right. And why is that?

MR. PRINCE: That's part of the stipulations of the WPPS contract.[71]

That would help explain why Blackwater withdrew from the International Peace Operations Association (IPOA), run by Doug Brooks, on October 10, 2007, even though Blackwater was a founding member. IPOA provides legitimacy because of its commendable but unenforceable code of conduct, which emphasizes respect for human rights, ethics, transparency, and corporate accountability. However, Blackwater's withdrawal called into question IPOA's ability to police its membership.

According to Robert Young Pelton, author of *Licensed to Kill*, the company's departure from IPOA may be the result of pressure from the State Department to keep a lower profile following the September 16 shootings. "Doug Brooks is pretty vocal in the media. State is usually the one that smacks Blackwater in the back of the head to say, 'Shut the fuck up! You're not supposed to talk while there's a pending investigation.' So, my guess is that this is a State-mandated decision, which is why Doug is saying nothing about it."[72]

Such contract-mandated silence can become burdensome even for Blackwater. In an interview Erik Prince said, "For the last week and a half, we have heard nothing from the State Department. From their senior levels, their PR folks, we've heard nothing—radio silence. It is disappointing for us. We have performed to the line, letter and verse of their 1,000-page contract. Our guys take significant risk for them. They've taken a pounding these last three years."[73]

In fairness, the "shoot first" attitude is one that security contractors share with the American military, one that elevates "force protection" to something approaching an absolute. This, critics say, has the effect of valuing the saving of American lives above avoiding risk to innocent Iraqis. However, after some of the most damaging incidents in Iraq, especially the killing by U.S. marines of 24 Iraqi civilians in Haditha in November 2005, the American command ordered new restraints on force escalation that sharply cut incidents in which troops opened fire on civilians.[74]

Admittedly, the problem of overaggression is probably worse among contractors. Since they are not tasked with defeating the insurgency, they do not have to take into account the feelings of the locals, as soldiers are supposed to do. All they have to do is to get their convoys or VIPs safely to their destinations.[75]

Nor is Blackwater the only contractor that has killed innocent Iraqi civilians. On October 9, 2007, guards from Unity Resources Group, an Australian-run firm, opened fire on a white sedan in downtown Baghdad, killing two Iraqi Christian women who were driving home from work. The firm was employed by RTI International, a nonprofit organization that does governance work in Iraq on a contract for the U.S. Agency for International Development.[76] This was the same firm whose guards had shot and seriously wounded a man driving a van three and a half months earlier on the same Baghdad thoroughfare.[77]

Still, it did not help Blackwater when the press reported that the State Department interceded in a congressional investigation of Blackwater, ordering the company not to disclose information about its Iraq operations without approval from the Bush administration.[78] The State Department official, Kiazan Moneypenny, wrote Blackwater vice president Fred Roitz to "advise" him of Blackwater's obligations under the State Department's contract. Among them was this statement: "All documents and records (including photographs) generated during the performance of work under this contract shall be for the sole use of and become the exclusive property of the U.S. government." These obligations, according to the contract, exist in perpetuity, not just until the contract expires. As a result, Moneypenny told Roitz to make "no disclosure of documents or information generated under [the contract] unless such disclosure has been authorized in writing by the Contract Officer."[79]

But Rep. Henry Waxman (D-CA) pointed out that the State Department has no authority to compel Blackwater to obstruct a congressional investigation, unless President Bush is prepared to say that the terms of Blackwater's contracts or its operational doctrine is covered under executive privilege.

Blackwater is hardly the only company without a current license. Few foreign security companies hold current licenses, most simply not bothering to renew their one-year permit after 2005 elections because the new government's policy was unclear.[80] Some foreign security contractors in Iraq say they operate without licenses because the corrupt government officials who issue them demand bribes of up to $1 million.[81]

The issue of immunity in this incident is ambiguous. If the Blackwater contractors did shoot without cause, it is not true that there is no way to prosecute them. Some claim that the June 2003 Coalition Provisional Authority Order 17, which states that contractors "shall be immune from any form of arrest or detention," grants the firms blanket immunity from any and all crimes. Such thinking ignores section 5 of the order, which states that the contractors' immunity from prosecution "may be waived" by the "sending state"—in this case the U.S. government. Still, the shootings set into motion a wave of investigations and rules that continue to ripple.

Initially, until it became apparent that it was a public relations farce, the FBI team traveling to Iraq to assist in the investigation was supposed to be guarded by Blackwater. However, the State Department realized that the ensuing conflict of interest would be too egregious and said that security for the team would be handled by the department's Diplomatic Security Service.

In late September 2007 Defense Secretary Robert Gates ordered U.S. military commanders in Iraq to crack down on any abuses they uncover by private security contractors. In a three-page directive to the Pentagon's most senior officers, Gates's top deputy, Deputy Defense Secretary Gordon R. England, ordered them to review rules governing contractors' use of arms and to begin legal proceedings against any that have violated military law.[82] The memo listed seven steps, including a requirement that commanders ensure that private guards are authorized to carry their weapons and that those who are not are disciplined. It also requires commanders to stop guards who commit felonies from leaving the country. Commanders must also ensure that guards follow rules on escalating force and deadly force. They should also "review periodically the existing RUF"—Rules on the Use of Force—"and make any changes necessary to minimize the risk of innocent civilian casualties or unnecessary destruction of civilian property."[83]

Another development took place October 29, 2007, when it was revealed that potential prosecution of Blackwater guards may have been compromised because the guards received immunity for statements they made to State Department Bureau of Diplomatic Security officials investigating the incident, even though they did not have the authority to do so. Prosecutors at the Justice Department, who did have such authority, had no advance knowledge of the arrangement.[84]

On October 30 it was announced that all State Department security convoys in Iraq would fall under military control. The military would assert greater control over contractor training, rules for the use of force, employment standards, and movements around Iraq, although details had not been worked out at the time of the announcement.[85]

Ironically, the Pentagon had already coordinated its outsourced security details through its Regional Operations Centres, which track movement of security convoys to make sure they and the military don't conflict with each other. Presumably the ROCs would be expanded to monitor State Department PSCs. But the ROCs are themselves outsourced, through the contract to the British firm Aegis Defence.[86]

Whether these measures will have any real impact is open to question. Military personnel who have worked with the ROCs have said they're virtually useless in real time but are good at providing historical data of where contractors have been. Establishing minimum training standards is also unlikely to make any difference because the WPPS II contract itself already requires a rigorous training program.[87]

Gates's order contrasted with the reaction of State Department officials, who were slow to acknowledge any potential failings in their oversight of Blackwater.[88] In October 2007, however, the State Department announced that it would now send its own personnel as monitors on all Blackwater security convoys in and around Baghdad. The department would also install video cameras in Blackwater armored vehicles to produce a record of all operations that could be used in investigations of the use of force by private security contractors. In addition, the State Department would save recordings of all radio transmissions between Blackwater convoys and military and civilian agencies supervising them in Iraq. These measures were based on the initial recommendations of Patrick F. Kennedy, the department's director of management policy. Kennedy is the leader of a team that Secretary of State Rice appointed to look at the way Blackwater and other private security contractors operate in Iraq.[89]

These measures likely will work better in theory than in practice. Peter Singer of the Brookings Institution noted, in regard to the ride-alongs, that we have the odd outcome of the government "embedding" government employees inside a private operation that is carrying out a government mission. These State Department persons will be essentially like "chaperones" for the team, but not in operational command of it and not empowered to take any contractual or legal action. These observers will also reportedly only be for Blackwater, which seems to dodge the broader problem of contracting gone too far, since Blackwater is not the only security contractor in Iraq and not the only one to have had problems.

Second, with regard to video cameras mounted on the dashboard, not all incidents happen to the front. Third, many companies already had these. Most importantly, having video footage of incidents doesn't mean much if the State Department refuses to act on it. An example would be the footage from the Aegis "trophy" video.

The State Department's announcement is also highly ironic considering that the department cited legal concerns in turning down a 2005 request from Blackwater to install cameras in official U.S. motorcades protected by its employees. The company first asked the State Department's Bureau of Diplomatic Security to take that step on May 17, 2005, "in response to a false accusation against one of our teams in Baghdad."[90]

Moreover, in regard to better coordination of radio frequencies with the military, this was already supposed to be happening. It doesn't solve the actual problem of overly aggressive behavior in any way.[91]

About the same time the Pentagon released a report that found considerable frustration among U.S. military commanders, who complained that contractors working for non-Pentagon agencies, including the State Department, often behave arrogantly, traveling through areas of military operations without prior notification and setting up their own checkpoints and roadblocks.[92]

The inevitable lawsuit has already been filed. On October 11, 2007, a U.S.-based legal team filed a civil lawsuit against Blackwater. The team includes the Center for Constitutional Rights in New York and the law firms of Burke O'Neil and Akeel & Valentine. The suit was filed in federal court in Washington, D.C., on behalf of an injured survivor and the families of three men who were killed in the incident. It claims that Blackwater violated U.S. law and "created and fostered a culture of lawlessness amongst its employees, encouraging them to act in the company's financial interests at the expense of innocent human life."[93]

On November 27, 2007, an amended complaint was filed that added two families of killed Iraqis and an injured survivor to the list of plaintiffs. The amended complaint also alleges that Blackwater routinely deploys heavily armed "shooters" in the streets of Baghdad with the knowledge that up to 25 percent of them are chemically influenced by steroids or other judgment-altering substances, that it fails to take effective steps to stop and test for drug use, and that the Blackwater personnel who fired on the innocent civilians had ignored directives from the Tactical Operations Centre (TOC), which was manned by both Blackwater and Department of State personnel, to stay in another area with State Department personnel until further instructed to leave.[94]

On October 24, 2007, Richard Griffin, the assistant secretary of state for the Bureau of Diplomatic Security, resigned. Just a day earlier, Secretary Rice, accepting the results of a review, ordered a series of measures to boost government oversight of the private guards the department uses to protect its diplomats in Iraq, including more explicit rules on when and how to use deadly force.[95] That review implicitly rebuked Griffin's office for insufficient oversight. Yet shortly after Griffin's resignation, ABC News reported that two key deputies who worked closely with the security contractors, Kevin Barry and Justine Sincavage, received quiet promotions.[96]

Reportedly federal authorities convened a grand jury to investigate multiple shootings involving private security contractors in Iraq. Federal prosecutors issued grand jury subpoenas to some of the Blackwater employees present at the September 16 shooting.[97]

Despite all the controversy and criticism Blackwater has received since the September 2007 shootings, it continues planning for an expansion that would put its forces in hot spots around the world doing far more than guard duty. Erik Prince wants to take advantage of the movement to privatize all kinds of government security. The company wants to be a one-stop shop for the U.S. government on missions to which it won't commit American forces. For example, the Pentagon tapped Blackwater to compete for parts of a five-year, $15 billion budget to fight terrorists with drug trade ties.[98]

CONTROL RISKS GROUP (U.K.)

Control Risks Group (CRG) has been one of the largest British security companies operating in Iraq, with staff mainly drawn from former members of the British Army, SAS, and Royal Marines.

The U.K. government's largest contract with Control Risks Group has reportedly earned the company £23.5 million.[99] It won the contract to distribute the new Iraqi currency when it was issued, a job it also carried out in Afghanistan.[100] Its proposal to use former Fijian soldiers to do so was attacked as improper by human rights groups.[101]

Control Risks Group was also on the ground early and was used by the Office of Reconstruction and Humanitarian Assistance (ORHA), the now-disbanded body established by the United States in the war's immediate aftermath, to plan and direct U.S. entry into Iraq. The company says ORHA's successor agency, the CPA, as well as a wide range of other agencies, including the U.S. Department of Defense, USAID, and the UN, similarly employ it.

Control's CEO, Richard Fenning, wrote this statement in a letter to *The Guardian* newspaper:

> Our role is not to act as a substitute for the military or to be an adjunct to the campaign. Rather, it is to provide reconstruction agencies and those companies involved in the rebuilding process with on the ground risk assessment and security support to enable them to work as safely and effectively as possible in difficult circumstances. This is not the "privatisation of war," but an established private-sector activity in many parts of the world: Iraq is different only for the scale and complexity of the assignment.[102]

In May 2006 hundreds of British contractors considered resigning en masse the next month over a pay dispute. At that time Control Risks, whose 450 employees in Iraq provide close protection for British diplomats and aid workers, had its contract renewed by the Foreign Office, but only after it reduced charges by cutting salaries to some frontline staff by 19 to 37 percent. The move prompted a furious response by Control Risks staff, who are recruited mainly from the British military and police. An e-mail obtained by the *Times* in London said that there was overwhelming support for mass resignations starting June 24.

> We can now count on 68 per cent support from CRG [Control Risks Group] operators in Baghdad alone. This figure may well rise as the news spreads and people on

leave check their e-mails. We firmly believe that a figure in excess of 75 per cent resignations is wholly achievable. As support grows in Basra and Kirkuk we hope that similar figures can be called upon. This being the case, then we believe this is enough to make CRG's position untenable regarding the FCO contract.[103]

A spokesman for the employees said, "In Baghdad, CRG no longer stands for Control Risks Group. It now reads Cheap Rate Guys. Given the dangers we face on a daily basis, pay cuts are unacceptable."[104]

CUSTER BATTLES (U.S.)

Custer Battles was a very new company, in existence for only nine months before its work in Iraq. Its first assignment involved guarding Baghdad's airport.[105] It had no experience in the security industry when it landed that $16 million contract. In winning it, it beat more experienced companies such as DynCorp and ArmorGroup, primarily by promising to have 138 guards on the ground within two weeks, faster than the others.[106]

It also won a contract in August 2003 to provide logistical support for a massive currency exchange in which Iraqis turned in trillions of old dinars for the nation's new currency.[107] That contract committed the Coalition Provisional Authority (CPA) to paying for all the company's costs for setting up centers where the exchanges would take place, plus a 25 percent markup for overhead and profit.

Custer Battles purchased trucks, equipment, and housing units to carry out the contract. It then created a series of "sham companies" registered in the Cayman Islands and Lebanon.[108] The companies were used to create false invoices that made it appear that they were leasing the trucks and other equipment to Custer Battles. The scheme inflated the 25 percent markup allowed under the contract.

Those were hardly the only ways Custer Battles gouged the CPA. A $33,000 food order in Mosul was billed to the United States–led interim government of Iraq at $432,000. Electricity that cost $74,000 was invoiced at $400,000. Even $10 kettles got a 400 percent markup. The company billed the government nearly $10 million for dozens of items, including food, vehicles, and cooking pots. The total cost to Custer Battles was less than $4 million—a profit margin of 150 percent, far higher than the 25 percent margin allowed under its contract.[109]

In October 2003, company representatives accidentally left a spreadsheet in a meeting, and it was later discovered by CPA employees. The spreadsheet showed that the currency exchange operation had cost the company $3,738,592, but the CPA was billed $9,801,550, a markup of 162 percent.

In another case, a Custer Battles employee wrote in a report that a $2.7 million invoice was based on "forged leases, inflated invoices and duplication." In yet another case, Custer Battles billed the government $157,000 to build a helicopter pad that cost $95,000. When the case was first filed, lawyers for the two men suing Custer Battles said the firm's fraudulent charges amounted to $50 million.[110]

Attorneys for Custer offered a novel defense that the firm could not be sued under the False Claims Act, a key federal anticorruption law, because the allegedly stolen money belonged to Iraqis, not Americans. That precedent-setting claim could undercut fraud claims involving billions of dollars in reconstruction contracts that were issued by the United States–led CPA and paid for with money belonging to the Iraqi people.

They also argued that the CPA, which had ruled occupied Iraq, should not be considered a U.S. agency, and thus any fraud committed was against the CPA and not the U.S. government.[111] During the trial the lawyer for Custer Battles argued that "the funds that were used were Iraqi funds, not U.S. funds." "The fact that CPA was in temporary possession of the money and distributed it does not form a basis for a false claim."[112]

The trial made clear that government oversight of contractors was woefully deficient, something that had been apparent for years. Court filings in the case detailed how CPA officials in Baghdad were ill-equipped to write, much less oversee, the processing of millions of dollars in contracts. For example, since the agency couldn't wire money to Custer Battles and its other contractors, it sometimes advanced them millions of dollars in cash.[113]

Consider these excerpts from a segment on the *60 Minutes* television program:

> Colonel Richard Ballard, the top inspector general for the Army in Iraq, was assigned to see if the company was living up to its contract.
>
> The contract looked to me like something that you and I would write over a bottle of vodka, complete with all the spelling and syntax errors and annexes to be filled in later, presented it the next day and then got awarded about a $15 million contract.
>
> . . .
>
> KROFT: (Voiceover) As for the bomb sniffing canine teams:
>
> Col. BALLARD: I eventually saw one dog. The dog did not appear to be a certified trained dog. And the dog was incapable of operating in that environment.
>
> KROFT: What do you mean, incapable of operating in that environment?
>
> Col. BALLARD: He would be brought to the checkpoint and he would lie down and he would refuse to sniff the vehicles.
>
> KROFT: What about the handler? Did he have a handler?
>
> Col. BALLARD: The handler had no certificate, no evidence.

KROFT: So neither the dog nor the handler were qualified?

Col. BALLARD: I think it was a guy with his pet, to be honest with you.

. . .

KROFT: (Voiceover) In a memo obtained by 60 MINUTES, the airport's director of security wrote to the Coalition Authority, "Custer Battles have shown themselves to be unresponsive, uncooperative, incompetent, deceitful, manipulative and war profiteers. Other than that, they're swell fellows."

. . .

KROFT: (Voiceover) Philip Wilkinson was a colonel in the British Army assigned to the Coalition Authority's Ministry of Finance and charged with providing security to convoys that travel all over Iraq, loaded with $3 billion in cash. The trucks were supplied by Custer Battles.

Mr. WILKINSON: And you can imagine open trucks with that sort of money on the back was just a red hot target for not only terrorists but criminals. And therefore, we needed trucks that were going to work. When those trucks were delivered to us, some of them were physically dragged into our compound.

KROFT: They were towed into the camp?

Mr. WILKINSON: They were towed into the camp.

(Footage of Kroft interviewing Wilkinson)

KROFT: (Voiceover) And Custer Battles' response?

Mr. WILKINSON: When questioned as to the serviceability of the trucks, was, "We were only told we had to deliver the trucks. They didn't—the contract doesn't say they had to work." Which, I mean, when you're given that sort of answer, what can you do?[114]

Unfortunately, change comes slowly. A GAO report released in March 2008 said that the Pentagon relies too much on contractors who often work alongside their government counterparts, cost more, and sometimes take on responsibilities they are not supposed to. The report said that as the government's workforce has shrunk, its demand for services has mushroomed and procurement deals have become more complex and hard to manage. That has forced agencies to hire more contractors. In 2007 the Defense Department spent $158.3 billion on services, a 76 percent increase over the past decade and more than what it spends on supplies, equipment, and major weapons systems.

The GAO looked at the Army Contracting Agency's Contracting Center of Excellence (CCE), which does procurement for 125 divisions at the Pentagon. It found that 42 percent of the Army's CCE procurement specialists are contractors, up from 24 percent in fiscal 2005. The report said that relying so much on contractors creates "the risk of loss of government control over and accountability" for government programs.

Ironically, nearly all of the contracting specialists, who often perform some of the same functions as their government counterparts, work for CACI International.[115]

Although the jury initially found Custer guilty and ordered it to pay $10 million in fines, a federal judge threw out the verdict after concluding that the now-defunct CPA was not a U.S. government entity. Although he did not dispute that Custer submitted "false and fraudulently inflated invoices," he found that the nature of the CPA precluded a fraud claim.[116]

Even after Custer Battles had been banned from further government contracts, former executives continued doing contracting work and formed new companies to bid on such projects. According to federal regulations, individuals suspended by the military are banned from acting as principals on subsequent government contracts.[117] Subsequently it was reported, according to a sealed federal lawsuit obtained by the Associated Press, that ex-employees accused two former Pentagon officials, former acting Navy Secretary Hansford Johnson and former acting Navy Undersecretary Douglas Combs, of plotting with Custer Battles to set up shell companies that, among other things, sold arms on the Iraqi black market—weapons that could have been used against American troops.[118]

Custer reportedly hired former Polish GROM commandos. GROM personnel deployed with U.S. and British forces during the main combat operations of the war. London-based Global Risk Strategies Ltd later won the airport contract.

Custer was also one of the earliest firms whose employees were alleged to have shot innocent Iraqi civilians. *NBC News* reported in February 2005 that four former Custer Battles security contractors, retired U.S. military veterans, watched as innocent Iraqi civilians were fired upon, and one was crushed by a truck. They claimed that heavily armed security operators on Custer Battles' missions—among them poorly trained young Kurds, who have historical resentments against other Iraqis—terrorized civilians, shooting indiscriminately as they ran for cover, smashing into and shooting up cars. They were so upset by what they saw that three quit after only one or two missions.[119]

Lost in all the media coverage about the court case was the fact that, according to one former CPA official, the contract should never have been awarded in the first place. Consider the testimony of Franklin K. Willis, former deputy senior advisor for Iraq's Ministry of Transportation and Communications, before a Senate committee:

> In late June 2003, a decision was made to open Baghdad International Airport to limited scheduled civilian aircraft service beginning July 15. A USAID contract had been awarded earlier to a company named Skylink to manage the airport. It is unclear to me why Skylink, the airport manager, was not made responsible, under the AID contract, for providing, by itself or through subcontracting, security for civilians using the new service. Nonetheless, a decision was taken to issue an

immediate Request for Proposal (RFP) allowing respondents some three or four days to submit their proposal, and the RFP mandated that respondents would be required to have their security team in place by July 15. Several respondents requested more information as to scope, one established service said it could be ready within six weeks but that July 15 was an impossible deadline, and CusterBattles said it could be ready by July 15.

It is not clear to me whether CusterBattles existed prior to this RFP, or had any experience providing security services anywhere, but since they said they would be ready by July 15, they were picked. They were paid $2 million at the end of June and $2 million more at the end of July out of DFI funds from the vault in the basement under the $16 million contract (originally $13 million) they were awarded. I arrived in mid-July and by that time the decision to open Baghdad International had been rescinded for security reasons. There was a small amount of charter traffic, but Baghdad International was never opened for scheduled civilian traffic in the life of the CPA.

Thus the reason for the CusterBattles contract had disappeared, and their presence required searching for a new scope. The contract had not been definitized and consisted solely of their proposal.[120]

Put more simply, Custer Battles never should have received its first no-bid contract. It didn't have any money, didn't have a viable business, and didn't have any employees. Bremer's CPA had overlooked these shortcomings and forked over $2 million anyway, in cash, to get them started, simply ignoring long-standing requirements that the government certify that a contractor has the capacity to fulfill a contract.[121]

Custer Battles also recruited Fijians. The company was threatened with $50,000 in penalties by the Fijian government if it, through a new subsidiary Custer Battles Fiji,[122] hired 250 local former soldiers without complying with regulations in regard to overseas employment.[123] Reportedly Custer offered up to $390 a day for three-month contracts.[124]

Custer provided security for Fluor Inc., CH2M Hill Cos., Washington Group International, and the Berger Group.[125] Custer also reportedly offered to help the United Nations secure its headquarters in Baghdad after the war, more than three months before the August 2003 truck bombing of its headquarters there that destroyed the building and killed 23 people, including Sergio Viera de Mello, the top United Nations diplomat in Iraq.[126]

DYNCORP (U.S.)

DynCorp International was prominent for hiring police officers in the United States to train police recruits in Iraq.[127] In April 2003 the U.S. State Department awarded DynCorp a one-year contract in a limited competition against SAIC worth up to $50 million to support law enforcement functions in Iraq.[128] In May 2003, under the Department of State Advisory Support Mission (DASM) contract, DynCorp International deployed, supported, and equipped U.S. law enforcement personnel to provide police presence, enhance public security, and assist in reestablishing the Iraq National Police by providing necessary training to local police. SAIC was brought in by DynCorp to cooperate in the contract delivery.[129] The United States Investigative Services (USIS) also played a role.[130] Under the contract, up to 1,000 civilian technical advisors with 10 years of domestic law enforcement, corrections, and judicial experience, including at least 2 years in specialized areas, were to help the government of Iraq organize effective civilian law enforcement, judicial, and correctional agencies. Advisors would work with Iraqi criminal justice organizations at the national, provincial, and municipal levels to assess threats to public order and mentor personnel at all levels of the Iraqi legal apparatus.[131] They also were to train 32,000 Iraqi recruits at a rebuilt military base at Muwaqqar in neighboring Jordan.[132] The contract paid $75,000 to $153,600 to those it hired on yearlong contracts.[133]

In February 2004, Computer Sciences Corporation won a State Department contract for civilian police (CIVPOL) services worth about $1.7 billion over five years. On July 15, 2004, functions being performed in Iraq under the DASM contract were shifted to the CIVPOL contract, which was one of three planned contracts that were awarded under the State Department's Civilian Police Program. CSC was to recruit up to 2,000 experienced American law enforcement specialists to serve in civilian policing missions overseas.[134]

Initially the training of Iraqi police forces was a haphazard affair. The Pentagon began to rebuild the Iraqi police with a mere dozen advisors. Overmatched from the start, one was sent to train a 4,000-officer unit to guard power plants and other utilities, a second to advise 500 commanders in Baghdad, and another to organize a border patrol for the entire country.[135]

Before the war, the Bush administration dismissed as unnecessary a plan backed by the Justice Department to rebuild the police force by deploying thousands of American civilian trainers. After Baghdad fell and a majority of Iraqi police officers abandoned their posts, a second Justice Department proposal calling for 6,600 police trainers was reduced to 1,500, and then never carried out. At that time DynCorp had already located 1,150 active and retired police officers who had expressed interest in serving in Iraq.[136]

Field training of the Iraqi police, the most critical element of the effort, was left to DynCorp, which received $750 million in contracts. When it became clear in 2004 that the civilian effort by DynCorp was faltering, American military officials took over police training, relying on heavily armed commando units that had been established by the Iraqis. Within a year, members of the Sunni Muslim population said some units had been infiltrated by Shi'ite Muslim militias and were kidnapping, torturing, and executing scores of Sunni Muslims.[137]

Subsequently, in the spring of 2006, three years after administration officials rejected the large American-led field training effort, American military commanders adopted that very approach. Declaring 2006 the year of the police, the Pentagon dispatched a total of 3,000 American soldiers and DynCorp contractors to train and mentor police recruits and officers across Iraq.[138]

DynCorp says that many concerns about its performance are related to the officers recruited for the Iraqi or Afghan police forces, which is not the company's responsibility. The company hired public relations firm Qorvis Communications to help deal with the attention.[139] Qorvis also teamed with Patton Boggs to help Halliburton navigate congressional probes and handle media inquiries.[140]

DynCorp also received a contract from the State Department to recruit veteran U.S. law officers who would serve as "mentors" and train Iraqis to guard their borders.[141] Some U.S. politicians, such as Governor Janet Napolitano of Arizona and New Mexico Governor Bill Richardson, worried that the effort distracted from the mission of securing the U.S. border.[142]

DynCorp achieved a brief moment of notoriety when its personnel commandeered an Iraqi gas station and gave CNN journalist Tucker Carlson an AK-47 while escorting him.[143] In a separate incident, eight DynCorp personnel accompanied Iraqi police who raided the Baghdad home and offices of former U.S.-favored Iraqi politician Ahmed Chalabi on May 20. Their participation in a raid the U.S. government has insisted it did not order is thus far unexplained.[144]

Another DynCorp contractor, talking about his work in Iraq, was quoted this way in a news report:

[S]ome tactics can anger Iraqis. The convoys barrel through this city's chaotic traffic creating their own right of way. In a traffic jam, security contractors may hop out of the vehicles and order Iraqis out of the way or hold up all traffic at busy intersections and traffic circles to let their vehicles pass. They simply can't afford to be a sitting target for someone with an assault rifle, bomb or rocket-propelled grenade.

Most of the times I've been with the security teams on the ground, they behave very professionally and without really antagonizing the locals. However, the driving is a whole different story. We cruise through the streets fast and furious and without much regard for the locals. That would piss me off, and I imagine it does the Iraqis too.[145]

An account from the actor Sean Penn, in describing a trip he made to Baghdad, demonstrates how hyperbolic the discussion of PMCs can be:

As the rifle concussion vibrates through my head, so does the name DynCorp. I've since done a little research, and here's what I found: DynCorp is a ubiquitous presence in Baghdad. A PMC, or private military corporation, DynCorp was started in the late '40s and given a big recruiting boost by the post-Church Commission firings of thousands of CIA operatives by President Carter in the late '70s.

PMCs, and there are many of them, tend to be staffed and directed by retired generals, CIA officers, counterterrorism professionals, retired Special Air Service men, Special Forces guys and so on. DynCorp is a subsidiary of the benignly named Computer Sciences Corp. DynCorp forces are mercenaries. Their contracts have included covert actions for the CIA in Colombia, Peru, Kosovo, Albania and Afghanistan.[146]

Of course, none of DynCorp's contracts have been covert. All the activities that Penn cites were widely covered in the media.

However, a 2005 State Department audit claimed that DynCorp International employees overcharged the U.S. government $685,000 to provide fuel for a police academy in Jordan used to train Iraqi security forces. The audit found that a DynCorp driver, in collusion with two other employees, inflated the amount of fuel. DynCorp said the three workers were fired. The company reimbursed the State Department and filed suit to recover the money in a Jordanian court.[147]

One DynCorp contractor, Thomas Nelson Barnes III, made news in September 2005 when he was charged with distributing identity badges that control access to Baghdad's heavily fortified Green Zone to people not allowed to receive them, including an Iraqi woman he was dating.[148] Ironically, on September 2 DynCorp was awarded a $9,872,005 firm-fixed-price contract for Access Control Badge System Services. This was a sole source contract initiated on August 6, 2005.[149]

In May 2006, Barnes pled guilty to one misdemeanor count of theft/embezzlement of U.S. property and was sentenced to 30 days in jail at the direction of probation followed by 1 year of supervised release and 30 days of home confinement. He also had to pay a $25 special assessment and was debarred for four years, ending on December 4, 2010.[150]

In another case involving DynCorp, the special inspector general for Iraq reconstruction reported to Congress that an audit requested by the Bureau of International Narcotics and Law Enforcement Affairs (INL) estimated that DynCorp may have overcharged the government as much as $600,000 in providing fuel to the INL-administered police academy in Amman, Jordan. The State Department inspector general's audit of the contract confirmed INL's estimate of overcharges and found a basis for an additional claim of $85,000.[151]

In October 2006 a U.S. government review of Iraqi police training concluded that there were no accurate means to verify the operational capabilities of more than 120,000 officers reported to have passed through DynCorp and U.S. Army classes.[152]

Questions were also raised about the competence of some of DynCorp's managers in Iraq. Some employees contended that flawed decisions by DynCorp managers repeatedly put employees at lethal risk. Among their concerns was the fact that Dyncorp sent employees into war zones without adequate weapons and protective equipment. In another case, a manager took his unit's only armored vehicle for personal errands, leaving his employees to drive in hostile areas with "soft-sided" passenger cars. Another ordered his staffers to drive along one of Iraq's most attack-prone routes to purchase liquor for his personal consumption. At one point in 2006, a U.S. Army general ordered the company to temporarily halt operations because too many people were being killed.[153]

In December 2006 a consortium of DynCorp International and McNeil Technologies was awarded a five-year Army contract worth up to $4.6 billion to provide linguists to the U.S. military in Iraq.[154]

In 2007 an audit by the special inspector general for Iraq (SIGIR) noted that DynCorp's contract called for it to build a camp to house its trainers. Auditors found that the company performed $4.2 million worth of work that had not been authorized by the contract, including building a pool and 20 VIP trailers at the behest of Iraqi officials. Because of security concerns, the camp was never used. The State Department ordered work on the project stopped in September 2004, shortly after issuing the contract, because of concerns that the location was too dangerous for DynCorp's trainers. DynCorp initially told the department that the camp had already been completed, but more than a year later said it wasn't.[155]

The report also said that the department cannot account for $36.4 million of weapons and equipment, including armored vehicles and body armor, because DynCorp's invoices were vague. "DynCorp invoices were frequently ambiguous and lacked the level of detail necessary to identify what was procured."[156]

In 2007 DynCorp was one of the companies awarded the Army's LOGCAP IV contract, worth up to $150 billion. The other two were Fluor Intercontinental and KBR, Halliburton's former contracting arm, which had previously held the contract. DynCorp won it in 1997 to do work in East Timor and the Philippines.

The contract is considered one of the biggest deals in the contracting services industry. It has ballooned in value from $2 billion when it was first awarded in 1992 to $23 billion under the previous LOGCAP III contract.[157]

Another report released by SIGIR in October 2007 found that the State Department so terribly managed a $1.2 billion contract for Iraqi police training that it can't figure out what it got for the money spent.[158] Because invoices and records on the project were in total disarray and the government was trying to recoup money paid inappropriately to DynCorp, auditors temporarily suspended their effort to review the contract's implementation. In April 2007 SIGIR released a follow-up report that found improvement in the overall administration of the contract.[159]

ERINYS (S.A.)[160]

At the best of times running an oil-exporting complex isn't easy. With thousands of kilometers of pipelines, refineries, and pumping stations, many things can go wrong. Add in the fact that people are literally blowing up portions of pipelines on a regular basis, and you have a real problem.

When it was awarded the original contract, Erinys was a little-known, small Johannesburg-based company headed by a South African, Sean Cleary, a former senior official in pre-independence Namibia and a senior political advisor to the Angolan rebel leader Jonas Savimbi. He was one of the most vocal opponents of Executive Outcomes, the former South African–based PMC that had fought against Savimbi on behalf of the Angolan government.[161]

At the time Erinys was barely a year old, and although its Web site named five managers and directors, most of whom were affiliated with Armor Holdings,[162] a Florida-based security company, its ownership structure was opaque.[163] Erinys Iraq, an affiliate of South African Erinys International, formed in 2001, had the responsibility of protecting Iraq's oil infrastructure.

The company originally obtained a nearly U.S. $40 million contract in August 2003 to supply and train 6,500 armed guards charged with protecting 140 Iraqi oil wells, 7,000 kilometers of pipelines and refineries, and power plants and the water supply for the Iraqi Ministry of Oil. But that contract proved to be inadequate. Subsequently, the CPA modified the contract, increasing its value to $100 million, to provide for the air surveillance and to increase the force.

The contract calls for an audit of the security requirements of each oil region and the vetting, training, and hiring of the estimated 14,000 Iraqi guards needed to do the job.[164] Erinys's Iraqi partners and many of its recruits were close to associates of Ahmed Chalabi and Faisal Daghistani, leaders within the Iraqi National Congress (INC), which before the war was the main umbrella resistance group for Iraqis opposed to Saddam Hussein's rule.[165]

Larger competitors questioned whether Erinys had the infrastructural size and financial reserves to handle the contract, though given that the CPA had extended the scope of its contract, it seems to have handled it well enough.

The July 25, 2003, CPA solicitation for bids provided no details of what would be required to provide security for Iraq's "multibillion-dollar oil infrastructure." It did, however, ask that the bidder submit "a list of five contracts of the same or similar type to demonstrate previous experience." Yet Erinys had never handled a job as large and complicated as this one, and its partner firm, Nour, had never worked in the security area.

At that time Erinys was deploying 12,165 guards, the vast majority of them Iraqi nationals, under the command of just over 100 Western soldiers, to serve as a lightly armed guard force whose job was to secure static sites, pipelines, and personnel working on those sites. The force grew to a peak of 14,500 before dropping slightly to 14,000 men. Most of the guards came from the former Iraqi Army.

Around 2,000 guards were deployed north of Baghdad, where they protected power plants, oil fields, refineries, and the northern pipeline to Turkey. The rest were stationed in the south, home to the Basrah oil terminal, through which passes more than 80 percent of Iraqi oil exports. U.S. soldiers also helped guard the terminal.[166]

Erinys operated throughout the country under a north-center-south regional structure, each with its own independent headquarters, and a further 14 subsidiary sectors each with its own headquarters. Its regional headquarters were in Mosul, Kirkuk, Baghdad, and Basra. Overlying this was a management and communications infrastructure that enabled nationwide VHF (very high frequency), HF, and satellite voice/data communications. Each sector and regional headquarters, along with national headquarters, operated a 24-hour operations center.[167]

The oil security forces were working under Task Force Shield, a project overseen by the U.S. Army Corps of Engineers and executed by Erinys on behalf of the Oil Ministry. Erinys trained recruits for Task Force Shield, building on the old system whereby tribal leaders were responsible for protecting the oil pipelines for now-deposed dictator Saddam Hussein. Now the Iraqi interim government pays leaders to watch over the remote pipelines.

The Iraqi National Guard took over responsibility for protecting the key northern oil fields around Kirkuk in November 2004.[168]

In 2006 the special inspector general for the reconstruction of Iraq issued an audit report that said Task Force Shield's use of private security companies to protect Iraq's oil and power infrastructure had collapsed amid reports of possible fraud, missing weapons, and destroyed documents. The companies were ARS (a Greenbelt, Maryland, company hired to protect Iraq's electrical grid) and Erinys.

According to the audit, Erinys was paid $104 million to train at least 14,400 guards. Government auditors could find evidence of only 11,400 guards who had been trained. They also could not determine the location of more than 6,000 AK-47s purchased for the guards.

Erinys said it had trained 16,000 guards and turned over boxes of documentation to the Iraqi Oil Ministry detailing weapons, training, and inventory purchased under the contract. But it did provide a report acknowledging that Erinys management had continual problems with the ownership, contractual oversight, and tasking of the oil security force.[169]

Working for Erinys was not without risks. Among the Erinys expatriates, the name for all non-Iraqis working in Iraq, the fatalities included:

November 11, 2003—An Erinys team was attacked while traveling from Latafiya to Baghdad. James Wilshire and Majid Hussain Jasim were killed. Another bodyguard was injured.

January 28, 2004—Francois Strydom was killed when an ambulance vehicle-borne improvised explosive device was detonated in the vicinity of the Shaheen Hotel in Baghdad. He worked for SASI, an Erinys subcontractor.

April 12, 2004—Hendrik "Vis" Visagie, 29, a former member of the South African Pretoria Task Force, died after being critically injured during an ambush.

ERINYS EMPLOYMENT CONTRACT

All employees of Erinys Iraq Ltd are required to sign the following declaration as a condition of their employment with Erinys Iraq Limited.

Erinys Iraq Limited reserves the right to submit the names of employees, or prospective employees, to the appropriate government agencies of the employee's country of residence or citizenship, for the purpose of vetting to determine the suitability of that person for employment or prospective employment with Erinys Iraq Limited.

DECLARATION

I _____ HEREBY DECLARE:

1. That I am not a serving member of the armed forces, police service or any other government agency or office of my country of residence and/or citizenship and that I am free to take up employment with Erinys Iraq Ltd.
2. That I have not been convicted of a criminal offence, in person or absentia, in the country of my residence or citizenship or any other country recognised as having an independent judiciary by the International Court of Human Rights in the Hague, Netherlands.

For citizens or residents of the Republic of South Africa:

1. That I have not been convicted of any offence, in person or absentia, under the Regulation of Foreign Military Assistance Act, 1988.
2. That I am not subject to any restrictions to my employment by a private company as a security manager, consultant or officer, or any related security appointment or title by virtue of my having been granted immunity from prosecution by the Truth and Reconciliation Commission in person or absentia.

For citizens or residents of the United States of America:

1. That I have not been convicted of any offence, in person or absentia, under the Lautenberg Amendment 5 USC Section 922 (g) (9) which pertains to the charge of a Misdemeanour Crime of Domestic Violence.

• Certified by the declaring person as a true and accurate statement

Signed . . . .

Date . . . .

Witness . . . .

Date . . . .

Erinys was also sued for allegedly causing the death of an American soldier. The suit alleges that specialist Christopher Monroe was on guard duty in southern Iraq on October 25, 2005, when he was struck and killed by a speeding Erinys vehicle.[170]

GLOBAL RISK STRATEGIES (U.K.)

The United Kingdom's largest private security firm in Iraq, Global Risk Strategies, helped the Coalition Provisional Authority and the Iraqi administration to draft new regulations. It has had between 1,000 and 2,000 personnel, including 500 Gurkhas, operating in Iraq.[171] It was also known for recruiting people from Fiji to do security work in Iraq.[172] In 2003 it established a branch in Fiji to recruit over 500 former and serving Fiji soldiers to travel to Iraq and provide security for oil fields, installations, and government buildings.[173]

In fact, so many Fijians have gone to work in Iraq that Global Risk, along with providing troops for UN peacekeeping missions, was earning nearly as much money as Fiji earned from tourism, its top foreign exchange earner.[174] In fact, in 2006 Fiji Reserve Bank governor Savenaca Narube confirmed that the figure now stands at around $500 million a year—well surpassing Fiji's $400 million a year from tourism.[175]

So many Fijians are available to work for PSCs because the Fiji Army has a proud international reputation with a long tradition of supporting UN peacekeeping operations around the world. Republic of Fiji Military Forces (FMF) soldiers and Fiji police have served in global hot spots like Sinai, Cyprus, Namibia, Kosovo, Zimbabwe, Bougainville, Timor, and Lebanon. For many years, FMF soldiers in Lebanon played a central role in the United Nations Interim Force in Lebanon (UNIFIL), which operated from 1978 until Israel's withdrawal in May 2000. During that period, hundreds of FMF soldiers provided much-needed jobs and remittances.

Since many serving and reserve Fijian soldiers had Middle East experience, there was a willing pool of recruits in the South Pacific. The United Nations and the Fijian military could not compete with the salaries offered by security corporations, which were desperately seeking experienced personnel to protect infrastructure from Iraqi insurgent attacks and guard the supply trucks that carry goods to U.S. forces from Kuwait. As one recruiter explained:

The Government knew that the UNIFIL commitment was coming to end way before the 2002 deadline and many soldiers leaving Lebanon were wondering "What next?" On arrival in Fiji they were demobilised and what eventually happened was that overnight we had a glut of highly-skilled, highly-trained soldiers doing nothing, despite being skilled in military duties. Members of one reserve battalion were given security duties with Morris Hedstrom supermarkets, but at the end of the day the soldiers realised that what they were being paid was not enough compared to what payment they could demand using their skills. Many of them opted to join security companies, securing work contracts in Iraq and Kuwait.[176]

Around 300 former Fijian soldiers planned to sue Global Risk in a class-action lawsuit for failing to pay them the lucrative salaries they were promised.[177] A total of 408 Fijians were also recruited to protect UN offices, VIPs, and oil fields.[178] It was reported that "Global need only pay around £35 a day to its 1,300 force of otherwise unemployed Fijians and Gurkhas."[179] Fijians may still have earned enough to send $7 million back home to their families in the first year of operations.

In 2004 Global Risk won from Custer Battles the protection contract for the Ministry of Transport.[180] It is recruiting Fijians through its subsidiary Global Risk Strategies Fiji.

Global Risk also had the distinction of being the firm whose contractors went on strike for two days in June 2005 as part of a contract dispute between their employer and the Iraqi government, shutting down most of the country's civil aviation. Global employed some 500 people just at the airport.[181] Its employees also went on strike for a day in September 2005 in another attempt to force the Iraqi government to pay what it said were months of unpaid bills.[182] That shutdown nearly led to a standoff between American military forces and Iraqi soldiers when U.S. forces rushed to the airport to prevent Iraqi troops from taking it over.[183]

KROLL (U.S.)

Kroll Inc., the U.S. corporate security firm, secured a contract with USAID and hired Aldwin Wight, a former head of Britain's elite Special Air Service regiment, to take charge of its operations in Iraq.[184] Alastair Morrison, the founder (in 1981) of one of the earliest PMCs, Defence Systems Ltd., and previously associated with Armor Holdings, is now head of Kroll's security division. Marsh & McLennan, a huge insurance broker, bought Kroll for $1.9 billion.[185]

METEORIC TACTICAL SOLUTIONS (S.A.)

The South African firm Meteoric Tactical Solutions (MTS) had a £270,000 contract with the British Department for International Development's (DfID) to provide bodyguards and drivers for DfID's most senior official in Iraq and his small personal staff.[186] MTS is based in Pretoria and run by former members of South African Special Forces. Meteoric also landed a big contract to train a private Iraqi security force to guard government buildings and other important sites formerly protected by U.S. soldiers.[187]

To prevent future legal proceedings in South Africa under its antimercenary law, Meteoric and other South African security companies submitted an authorization request at the ad hoc ministerial committee. But they never received a response.[188]

It was reported that some of those accused of planning an alleged coup in March 2004 in Equatorial Guinea also worked for Meteoric. Two of the firm's owners were arrested in Zimbabwe in March, accused of attempting to buy weapons for a coup plot.[189]

MPRI (U.S.)

MPRI, a unit of L-3 Communications, has been training U.S. active-duty military soldiers on a course in Kuwait on how to run convoys on supply routes, where U.S. troops are most vulnerable to ambushes, roadside bombs, land mines, and accidents.[190] MPRI also supported the CPA with staff and technical support and provided training support to the New Iraqi Army Training Program.[191]

MPRI also has the distinction of being the firm that literally wrote the book on rules for contractors on the battlefield. Under contract to the U.S. Army's Training and Doctrine Command (TRADOC), it produced the latest version of Field Manual 100-21, titled *Contractors on the Battlefield*.[192] This was officially published January 3, 2003, shortly before the United States invaded Iraq.[193] According to the company's Web site, the manual "established a doctrinal basis directed toward acquiring and managing contractors as an additional resource in support of the full range of military operations."

SCIENCE APPLICATIONS INTERNATIONAL CORP (SAIC) (U.S.)

Since the war began, SAIC has been awarded contracts to reshape the oil industry, rebuild the prison system, advise on democracy, act as liaison with the United Nations, and analyze intelligence. SAIC even launched and ran Iraq's first post-Saddam television network, although that task—under an $82 million contract headed by the Pentagon's psychological warfare division—ended December 2003 amid complaints that the network was mainly a propaganda tool for the occupying forces.[194]

STEELE FOUNDATION (U.S.)

Steele is unusual in that you almost never hear it mentioned in the media. The Steele Foundation has provided protection for construction firms. Two of its agents died in January 2004 while fighting during an attack by guerillas against a convoy. In another incident, three of its agents were wounded in an attempted ambush of one of their clients, a construction consultant.[195] Steele employs around 500 agents in Iraq, about one-third Westerners and the rest Iraqis.[196]

TITAN (U.S.)

Titan had a contract with U.S. Army Intelligence and Security Command since 1990 to provide translators.[197] In its 2003 annual report, Titan listed its translator services as its single biggest source of income, accounting for 10.3 percent of its $1.8 billion revenue.[198] The company is supplying 4,200 linguists to the Army under that current contract.

Titan provided translators in a contract worth $402 million to support both reconstruction efforts and military interrogation in Iraq (as revealed in the scandal over torture and inhumane treatment of Iraqi prisoners at Abu Ghraib prison).[199]

Titan was challenged by Northrop Grumman Corp. and L-3 Communications Holdings. In June 2004, the U.S. Army Intelligence and Security Command was deciding its next five-year worldwide translation contract, worth up to $2.5 billion.[200] But that process was canceled in July after a small business protested that the Army's procurement criteria unfairly excluded small businesses.

Titan was involved in the DoD's scandal over inadequate systems for documenting its billing of the Pentagon for labor costs and for tracking the work of non-American consultants. The Defense Contract Audit Agency threatened to withhold $4.9 million in fees until it fixed accounting deficiencies.[201]

In June 2004 Titan announced a reduction in its charges of $937,000 for overbilling and withdrew its demand for $178,000 toward costs submitted for the Titan employee and the subcontractor employee named in connection with potential "abuses" at Iraq's Abu Ghraib prison.[202]

One Titan translator, an Arabic interpreter who handled classified material while working for the last two years with U.S. military units in Iraq, was arrested after FBI agents discovered that he had so completely fabricated his identity and background that they were unsure of his true name. The interpreter, who claimed to be a Lebanese citizen who fled to the United States from Beirut in the late 1970s after his home was bombed, was deployed to Iraq in late 2003 after being hired by Titan. The interpreter fraudulently accessed "classified information of the United State Military" while assigned to various units, including "an intelligence group in the 82nd Airborne Division."[203]

Titan's involvement in Abu Ghraib did not seem to hurt its business. In October 2004 the North American Aerospace Defense Command (NORAD) awarded it an information technology contract (one base year, plus four option years) with a potential value of $169.9 million through August 2009, if all options are exercised.[204]

In June 2005 the U.S. Army said it planned to extend by eight months beyond its September 30, 2005, expiration date, at a cost of $380 million, the $600 million worldwide translation contract held by Titan to allow for an "orderly transfer" after completing a competition for the next contract.[205]

In 2005 Titan was acquired by major defense contractor L-3 Corporation. L-3 also owns MPRI, a private military training firm.[206]

A December 2006 U.S. Army award handed the five-year, $4.65 billion contract for Iraq-related translation and interpretation services to Global Linguistic Solutions LLC (GLS), a joint venture formed by security contractor DynCorp International (51 percent) and McNeil Technologies. But a GAO protest put the process on hold. The process was resolved after almost a full year, with L-3 providing all translation services in the interim, when the contract was again awarded to GLS in December 2007. And for the second time L-3 filed a protest challenging the award.[207]

Even though Titan is not a security contractor, many of its employees have paid the ultimate price. As of July 2005, Titan and its subcontractors have lost 169 employees, more than any other contractor in Iraq, according to the U.S. Department of Labor. The company's fatalities then outnumbered the casualties of any coalition force other than those of the United States and Iraq.[208]

TRIPLE CANOPY (U.S.)

Triple Canopy Inc. was founded in September 2003 by veterans of the U.S. special force's Delta unit.

Early in 2004, Triple Canopy won government contracts to guard 13 Coalition Provisional Authority headquarters throughout Iraq. The renewable six-month deals were worth, in all, about $90 million.

On November 4, 2005, it was reported that "British-based Global Strategies Group lost the contract" to defend Baghdad's Green Zone "in an open bidding process and handed over responsibility" to Triple Canopy Inc.[209]

Triple Canopy was the defendant in a lawsuit filed by three former employees who worked for Triple Canopy under a contract for KBR.[210] Former Army ranger Shane Schmidt and former marine Charles L. Sheppard III claimed in the lawsuit that on July 8, 2004, while en route to the Baghdad airport, their shift leader, 29-year-old ex-marine Jacob C. Washbourne, declared he was "going to kill someone today" and shortly afterwards stepped out of the vehicle and fired rounds of his M4 rifle through the windshield of a stopped truck. The suit goes on to claim that the shift leader said, "This didn't happen, understand?" Soon after, the shift leader stated he had "never shot anyone with my handgun before" and then fired his handgun through the windshield of a parked taxi, killing the driver.

When Schmidt and Sheppard reported the incident, they were fired by Triple Canopy. The shift leader was sent back to the United States. Triple Canopy has not denied that the incident occurred, but it argues that no violation of Virginia law occurred and that Schmidt and Sheppard were "at-will" employees and could be fired for any reason.

But the case became even more labyrinthine when another member of the PSC detail, Fijian army veteran Isireli Naucukidi, said that Sheppard, who was driving, cut off the taxi on Washbourne's orders, giving him a better shot.

Naucukidi said the three American guards laughed as they sped away, disregarding the fate of the unknown Iraqi taxi driver. According to Naucukidi, Schmidt told Washbourne, "Nice shot."

Naucukidi also said that Schmidt was responsible for an earlier shooting incident that afternoon involving a white civilian truck, and that he believed Schmidt and Sheppard had blamed Washbourne to cover up their own potential culpability. Schmidt denied responsibility for that shooting but acknowledged in an interview that he had fired a warning shot.[211]

Triple Canopy also has been noted for recruiting heavily in both the Philippines and Latin America, mostly from Peru,[212] Chile, Colombia, and El Salvador.

On June 15, 2007, Triple Canopy announced its acquisition of Clayton Consultants, Inc., a crisis management security consultancy offering incident response services and security consulting for threats like kidnappings, ransoms, and extortion against their clients.[213]

VINNELL (U.S.)

Vinnell, owned by Northrop Grumman, is technically in charge of training the new Iraqi Army, having long done the same in Saudi Arabia. Vinnell won a one-year contract to train nine battalions of 1,000 men each, with an option to train all 27 battalions if it performed well. Its contract was worth $48 million. But by the end of 2003 Vinnell was viewed as having performed badly, even though it had been paid $24 million and had subcontracted some of that work to other American PMCs. The CPA decided to use the Jordanian military to train Iraqi officers and to use other PMCs to train Iraqi noncommissioned officers (NCOs).[214]

For several reasons the number of police officers and soldiers trained was far below expectations. One year after the first training contracts were issued, the Iraqi Army had only 6,700 troops, and fewer than half of them had received training. The first real sign of trouble came in December 2003, when more than half of Vinnell's first battalion deserted. Some of the remaining soldiers had not mastered such basic skills as marching in formation or responding correctly to radio calls.[215]

Vinnell's subcontractors are MPRI, SAIC, Eagle Group International, Omega Training Group, and Worldwide Language Resources.[216]

4

Control and Accountability

Some companies early on argued that greater care should be taken in vetting the qualifications of their employees. Back in September 2004, ArmorGroup, the London-based company, published a white paper arguing that companies offering armed guards abroad should be vetted under the 2001 Private Security Industry Act. At that time only companies offering services within the United Kingdom were covered by the law.[1]

Specifically, ArmorGroup recommended that the United Kingdom's Security Industry Authority (SIA) be empowered to establish

- categorization of companies according to services offered
- fully transparent structures, including the vetting of company directors and proof of insurance, both corporate and for employees
- fully transparent operating practices, including comprehensive ethics policies and codes of conduct, include rules of engagement if weapons are to be carried
- clearly defined government department and agency responsibilities

Christopher Beese, director of ArmorGroup International, said, "It seems extraordinary that the doorman for a nightclub, catering for a particular clientele in a particular part of town may have to be vetted and licensed, when the same man can be equipped with a rifle and an armoured vehicle and be engaged to protect diamond concessions for a foreign regime in clear breach of public interest and perhaps even in contravention of human rights, but needs no such regulation."[2]

About six months later a spokesman for ArmorGroup said: "We are demanding regulation. It is extraordinary that door supervisors have to be licensed but any Joe Public can get a Kalashnikov and work with a security company abroad. This is an issue of accountability, as these companies can be set up so quickly."[3]

Of course, what constitutes proper vetting is debatable. In March 2006, five years after Mr. Beese's statement, British Foreign Secretary Jack Straw said that armed U.K. security guards working in Iraq could be checked by the Security Industry Authority, the same body that vets British pub bouncers.[4]

Because there is no uniform government requirement for vetting of contractors, it is easy to understand that the quality of the process varies. Some companies are very thorough. DynCorp, for example, carefully scrutinizes prospective hires for its civilian police program in Iraq:

> We review each application for completeness, job history, technical training and skills, certifications and licenses, past experience, and medical history. During this initial review, we inform each candidate of the screening and vetting processes, which vary according to contract requirements and may include a pre-employment drug test, medical and dental exams, psychological assessment, criminal records and credit check, and background investigation.
>
> DynCorp International (DI) utilizes experienced screeners to review all incoming resumes and determine if the applicant's work experience meets the minimum qualifications for the position. Each applicant whose resume passes this initial screen receives an Abbreviated Hiring Packet (AHP). Once the applicant receives the AHP, the applicant must sign and return the consent forms for the credit/criminal history check and employer interviews.
>
> Depending on the position, the candidate may be required to take an online psyche test which is normally required for personnel that will be required to be armed while performing their duties. No background investigation will begin until the preliminary consent forms are returned to the recruiting unit.
>
> **Background Investigation**
>
> The background investigation process begins with the submission of the criminal records and credit check request. This review of criminal and financial records using nationwide databases ascertains the candidate's financial stability and criminal history. This check reflects the current status or disposition of any misdemeanor or felony case associated with the individual in question within the last seven years. A social security number search produces a report of aliases and documented jurisdictions associated with the applicant. A credit history report includes an electronic verification of the applicant's current credit file information. The report indicates the number of trade account ratings and public record information, including civil court judgments or liens and collection information. When the report is returned to DynCorp International, a trained recruiter reviews the information and determines if the applicant's criminal and credit history is acceptable based on established minimum

criteria, if there are any pending issues that can be resolved, or if the report precludes further consideration.

If there are pending issues that can be resolved, the candidate is notified and advised of the procedures to seek resolution. The following criteria will cause a candidate to be disqualified:

— Criminal convictions for any felony by jury or a judge. It also includes a plea of guilty or no contest.
— Misdemeanor convictions which demonstrate a pattern of alcohol or drug abuse, crimes of moral turpitude, or sexual harassment. Other misdemeanors will be judged on a case-by-case basis.
— A bankruptcy that has not been discharged by a court within five years of its filing.
— Indebtedness that is not being paid off (classified on their report as bad debts).
— Tax liens and court judgments that have not been paid or satisfied.

Negative indicators, such as excessive debt, open litigation in civil or criminal court, or other reports of past criminal history are all indicators that may contribute to a decision to disqualify the candidate. Information about the candidate's integrity, honesty, resourcefulness, attitude, willingness to accept added responsibilities, and general demeanor provide DynCorp International with an in-depth view of the candidate's suitability for the demanding and unique environment of international policing missions.

For those programs requiring a detailed background check, DynCorp International actively recruits candidates that would best meet the solicitation criteria. After the initial screening, applicants are divided into three general categories: new applicants, rehires, and foreign nationals. A corresponding investigation is then conducted. DynCorp International investigators perform telephone interviews with the references indicated in the applicant's new hire documentation and collect information from current and former employers. The particular investigation requirements for each category are described below:

New Applicants—Interviews are conducted and documentation is provided for each new applicant as follows:

— Initial applicant interview.
— Interviews with family and/or close relatives (such as spouse, significant other, parents, siblings).
— Interviews with personal references.
— Supervisor interviews.
— Co-worker interviews.
— For law enforcement candidates, Internal Affairs Reports from each law enforcement agency worked within the past ten years, weapons qualification records (most recent or within one year prior to the application date), performance evaluations, and documentation from the Police Officer Standards and Training (POST) office, or the agency that certifies the applicant's training records, are also included.

Rehires—Investigators will conduct the following checks for the time period from the end of the previous contract to the present.

— Re-hire interview.
— References from family, friends and close relatives.
— If law enforcement, obtain Internal Affairs Reports and supervisor interview.
— Exit interview eligibility recommendation from the DynCorp International Site Manager.

Foreign Nationals—The DynCorp International Recruiting Manager solicits resumes from third party recruiting agencies worldwide.

— Third party recruiting agencies provide resumes of interested candidates which are screened for minimum requirements.
— Potential candidates undergo an MK Data Denial check to identify any persons that may have participated in human rights or international law violations, or engaged in acts of terrorism.
— A pass/fail online Mission Compatibility Assessment is given to each applicant.
— All remaining candidates are given a New Hire Packet and must have a medical exam.
— Each candidate must provide a criminal history report from their local law enforcement agency.

Security Clearances

For those positions requiring a security clearance, DynCorp International will assist potential candidates with obtaining the required clearance. The candidate must provide fingerprinting cards, a current passport, a copy of DD-214 if prior military, and an IRR letter if current reservist. Once the passport is verified as valid and a Security Clearance Request Form is filled out and signed by the Recruiting Manager, the DynCorp International Security Department begins clearance processing.

Civilian Police (CIVPOL) Candidates

Upon completion of the initial screening and background investigation process, all CIVPOL candidates undergo a 10-day Police Assessment, Selection and Training (PAST) which includes orientation, evaluation, and rigorous fitness and agility testing at the Crucible Learning Center in Fredericksburg, Virginia.

The 10-day PAST class completes the CIVPOL candidate's application process and certifies the candidate as capable of deploying and performing on an International Police Mission.

PAST Orientation/Evaluation consists of processing personnel for deployment and includes in-country briefings, medical evaluations, oral psychological assessments, management interviews, physical fitness and agility testing, firearms qualification, and other required training on the following topics:

— Professional and Ethical Standards of Conduct.
— Human Resource Policies.
— CIVPOL Program organization, leadership authority and relationships.

— Policies and procedures relative to the CIVPOL Program; Foreign National Police, Justice, and Prisons Programs; and Coalition Forces.
— Disciplinary Procedures.

PAST Testing is validated by a thorough job task analysis that is appropriate to mission requirements and all applicable Department of State standards. Testing includes the specific evaluation of a candidate's:

— Endurance or aerobic capacity
— Strength and power
— Flexibility
— Agility and reaction time
— Overall health (blood pressure and lung function)
— Psychological stability
— Firearms proficiency
— Capacity to work in a team environment

All personnel are qualified, tested, and trained on the various weapons applicable to a CIVPOL mission. This includes qualification on the Berretta 9-mm pistol, M-4, and a familiarization course involving the AK-47.

Section Summary

All employment contracts are contingent on the employee's proven ability to meet the established physical and mental health requirements to perform his or her obligations in an overseas mission. Candidates recruited by DynCorp International for service in Iraq must proceed to the CONUS Replacement Center (CRC) at Fort Bliss, Texas, and meet Department of Defense requirements in order to be deployable. DynCorp International's experience has resulted in a 99 percent pass rate for all candidates trained at the CRC.[5]

Triple Canopy notes that its screening process requires a minimum of four years of experience in military special operations assignments or four years of advanced police experience, current shooting skills, and excellent health and physical fitness. Its recruiting team conducts phone interviews and checks multiple references, not from friends or peers but from the former supervisors of each candidate. It also conducts criminal and credit checks. And once candidates arrive at its training site, the screening process continues with drug tests and a physical fitness test. The team also conducts a comprehensive battery of psychometric evaluations, including the Profile XT, Wonderlic Personality Test, Short Employment Test Battery, and Inwald Personality Inventory.[6]

On the negative side, the Government Accountability Office noted that its observations on the background screening of contractor employees suggests

that private security providers and DOD have difficulty conducting comprehensive background screening when data are missing or inaccessible. When doing background screenings of those living in the United States, private security providers use public information available at the county, state, or federal level and search state criminal information repositories and commercial databases such as those that collect information on incarcerations. None of these types of searches, however, guarantees a comprehensive background screening. Screening host nation and third country national employees can be difficult because of inaccurate or unavailable records in some countries. In addition, officials from some background screening firms told us that some foreign laws restrict access to criminal records. Finally, DOD's biometric screening of most non-U.S. contractors (including employees of private security providers) accessing U.S. installations in Iraq is not as effective as it could be because the databases used to screen contractor employees included only limited international data.

No U.S. or international standards exist for establishing private security provider and employee qualifications. During our review for our 2005 report, we found that reconstruction contractors had difficulty hiring suitable security providers. Contractors replaced their security providers on five of the eight reconstruction contracts awarded in 2003 that we reviewed. Contractor officials attributed this turnover to various factors, including their lack of knowledge of the security market and of the potential security providers and the absence of useful agency guidance in this area.[7]   .

Such testimony understates the difficulties of vetting third-country nationals. According to officials from international background screening firms, one problem is that they are relying on the applicant to provide all prior addresses. Since some countries, such as India, maintain criminal data at the local level, persons doing the background screenings may miss crimes that were committed in other locations within the country if the applicant did not reveal all previous addresses. Those doing screenings face other challenges as well. For example, some countries lack criminal records or the records are unreliable because of high levels of corruption. Additionally, some countries maintain records for only three to five years, which some in the background screening industry consider to be insufficient. Also, many countries lack national identification numbers, which makes it difficult to know if the person being screened was the person who committed the crimes cited in the court or police records.

In the first few years of the occupation of Iraq, there was undeniably a certain gold rush mentality, as PSCs were feverishly rushing to hire anyone they could get. Then, after the supply of well-trained and experienced professionals was exhausted, they took whoever they could get. Dale McIntosh, an American security contractor, said that when he first trained for security work in Iraq, the selection progress was "rigorous." The firm that hired him considered only highly skilled and experienced soldiers who were former special operators. It was like a tryout for a professional football team.

But those standards disappeared.

"By the time I left Iraq, we would've begged for the guys who were cut from that first group," says McIntosh. "We were one of the first companies to go in there, and within a couple of months we saw the quality drop off. Now it seems like the only require- ment to get into the contracting business is you have to get past Level Six on the Delta Force video game."

He realized how far the standards had fallen one day when he walked into a U.S. military base PX and saw one of the new private contractors. He was wearing a full- length black leather coat in the middle of the Iraqi summer, with a pony tail, screw- you sunglasses and two revolvers placed backward in holsters on his hips.

"First of all, no professional would dress like that," says McIntosh. "He just wanted to look cool. There are efficient ways to draw a weapon. He'd have to throw open his jacket, cross draw two revolvers that may have had only six to eight rounds. Those are the people who get into trouble and make a bad name for everyone."[8]

ArmorGroup was hardly the only company concerned about weeding out gunslingers. At a conference at Oxford University in December 2004, Colonel Tim Spicer, chairman of Aegis Defence, and Harry Legge-Bourke, who runs Olive Security, argued that the security industry should be tightly regulated and new restrictions placed on their operations.[9]

Of course, the big companies also had a self-interested motive in doing this, namely, eliminating the competition. The smaller security companies took away huge chunks of the pie. When an industry becomes highly regulated, it drives the smaller firms out because of administrative and compliance costs.

Motivation aside, not all companies share ArmorGroup's diligence. In the past the Pentagon said it is not in the business of policing contractors' hiring prac- tices. According to *Mother Jones* magazine:

Richard Goldstone, a retired justice of the Constitutional Court of South Africa, said he was revolted when he learned that some apartheid-era veterans are now employed in Iraq under U.S. government contracts. "The mercenaries we're talking about worked for security forces that were synonymous with murder and torture," says Goldstone, who also served as chief prosecutor of the United Nations war crimes tri- bunals for the former Yugoslavia and Rwanda. "My reaction was one of horror that that sort of person is employed in a situation where what should be encouraged is the introduction of democracy. These are not the people who should be employed in this sort of endeavor."[10]

The need for better supervision of contractors has been apparent for years. It is not just a matter of law. There are, actually, quite a few laws and regulations governing the use of contractors. The problem is that there are not enough audi- tors to monitor contracts.

For example, back in late 2004 the Defense Contract Management Agency went on a hiring spree. It needed 200 civilian employees experienced in oversee- ing contracts and producing items needed by the military services. The agency wanted people experienced in contract management so they could be deployed to various hot spots, including Iraq, 90 days after they were hired.[11]

Control and Accountability at Abu Ghraib

Arguably one of the most controversial aspects of PMC activity in Iraq, with the exception of the shooting of Iraqi civilians by Blackwater contractors in September 2007, surrounded events at the notorious Abu Ghraib prison. Even though these were translators and interrogators, not private security contractors, and relatively few of them compared with the far greater number of regular military personnel, the involvement and actions merit inclusion here if only because of the issues they raised regarding accountability and oversight.

The torture and abuse scandal at Abu Ghraib horrified people around the world and raised controversy over the role and activities of PMC personnel in the intelligence and interrogation process.[1] Ironically, long before Abu Ghraib, Defense Secretary Rumsfeld was preaching the virtues of using contractors in prisons. The secretary said at a town hall meeting in August 2003 that the Army pays $20,000 to $40,000 to hold a prisoner each year, whereas it costs Kansas only $14,000 per year. "I don't think of running a prison as a core competency of the United States military," he said.[2]

How many PMC personnel were at Abu Ghraib? One British news report said there was a team of about 30 people from CACI,[3] and during congressional testimony Defense Secretary Rumsfeld said there were 37 interrogators from private contractors in the prison.[4]

In the eyes of some critics, the events at Abu Ghraib are proof that PMCs in Iraq cannot be held accountable. For example, Rep. Jan Schakowsky (D-IL), in a letter to President Bush demanding the suspension of all contracts involving the security, supervision, and interrogation of prisoners pending an investigation into Abu Ghraib, wrote in May 2004:

It has been reported that, more than two months after a classified Army report found that contract workers were implicated in the illegal abuse of Iraqis, the companies that employ them (CACI International Inc. and Titan Corp.) say that they have heard nothing from the Pentagon and that they have not removed any employees from Iraq . . .

It has been reported that the Military Extraterritorial Jurisdiction Act (the Act), passed in 2000, may provide "some basis" for the Justice Department to investigate and prosecute private military contractors who engage in illegal activity. Please tell me if your Administration directed the Justice Department to take such action under the Act. Finally, if you believe the United States currently lacks statutory authority to prosecute illegal actions of contractors under US hire in Iraq, I urge you to ask the Congress for that authority.

I maintain that the use of private military contractors by the United States is a misguided policy that costs the American people untold amounts, in terms of dollars, U.S. lives and is damaging our reputation with the international community. It also impedes the ability of the Congress to conduct appropriate oversight and keeps the American public in the dark.[5]

Human Rights Watch foresaw the possibility of these events in a letter sent in April 2003 to Paul Bremer's predecessor, Lieutenant General Jay Garner:

The United States must also ensure that all U.S. and other foreign personnel hired to work in civilian law enforcement, civilian security, corrections and prisons, and reform of the justice system meet high professional and personal standards. This includes personnel hired through sub-contractors, for whom the United States remains responsible. The criteria and screening process used should be made publicly available. Foreign personnel must not be immune from disciplinary measures or prosecution for committing violations of human rights and applicable criminal law. Contracted personnel should at all times uphold relevant international standards such as the UN Basic Principles on the Use of Force and Firearms by Law Enforcement Officials.

The United States should ensure that the Military Extraterritorial Jurisdiction Act of 2000 (MEJA) applies to persons employed by the United States in Iraq.[6]

The two PMCs implicated in the scandal were Titan and CACI.

TITAN

Though Titan strongly denied that its employees managed or oversaw Iraqi prisoners, let alone tortured them, it withheld $178,000 in billings to the Pentagon for translators working at Abu Ghraib.[7] Subsequently, Titan's long-anticipated sale to Lockheed Martin imploded, due at least partly to its alleged involvement in the Iraqi prison scandal.[8] Still, Titan does not seem to have been cut out of the DoD procurement loop. On July 23, 2004, it announced that it had been awarded a contract by the Department of Defense having a potential value, with options if exercised, of over $255 million through August 2011 to provide comprehensive intelligence and information technology support worldwide.[9] And on September 17, 2004, the U.S. military extended Titan's contract to provide 4,500 translators and assistants for Army operations worldwide "for six months with an option for another six months, for a potential value of up to $400 million. At that time it was the contractor's largest single source of revenue."[10]

CACI[11]

CACI, originally called California Analysis Center Incorporated, always depended heavily on government contracts during the Cold War. After the Iron Curtain came down, CACI knew it had to diversify beyond weapons contracts to survive. Under the leadership of J. Phillip "Jack" London, it began offering tech support services that the Pentagon, as well as federal civilian agencies, needed. London worked to acquire smaller firms that had partnered on contracts with CACI. Acquisitions built up CACI's expertise in the critical areas of network security as well as information systems needed by intelligence agencies.[12]

In 2001 the private intelligence business exploded: CACI's revenue more than doubled and its stock price tripled. It had contracts worth $2.5 billion.[13] In the six months up to May 2004, CACI signed more than $300 million in open intelligence contracts and an additional $188 million in classified intelligence contracts. It inherited its interrogation work from the acquisition of Premier Technology Group in 2003.[14]

CACI's opaque chain of command ended at an obscure contracting office in the Department of the Interior at Fort Huachuca, 70 miles southeast of Tucson, Arizona.[15] This arrangement was the result of federal efforts in the 1990s to "streamline and reduce duplication" by having agencies with particular skill at administrative functions such as payroll or contracting handle those jobs for other agencies.

In this instance, the Interior Department had taken on Army contracting. In 2001, the Interior Department contracting office awarded a "blanket purchase agreement" to Premier Technology Group (inherited by CACI) for services to be provided to the Army. This agreement allowed the purchase of services from CACI International without competitive bidding—perhaps ironically, given the original intention to save contract costs. Since 2001, the department has approved 81 delivery orders, including 11 for services in Iraq.

Many of these contracts have related to information technology, but at least two involved the provision of interrogators, one for $19.9 million covering "interrogation support" and another for $21.8 million labeled "human intelligence support." Under those contracts, CACI provided 27 interrogators to work in detention centers in Iraq. Several worked at Abu Ghraib, including Steven Stephanowicz, who was named in General Antonio M. Taguba's report on events in Abu Ghraib.

Extract from CACI's Code of Ethics and Business Conduct Standards:

It is the responsibility of an employee or consultant having knowledge of any activity that is or may be in violation of this Code, any law, rule or regulation applicable to CACI's work, or any Affirmative Action Policy to promptly disclose such activity.

a. For this purpose, CACI has established Bill Clancy, Executive Vice President, as the Company Ombudsman. Bill is the Director of Business Operations, and can be reached at (703) 841-7811 or by email at **wclancy@caci.com**. Employees and consultants may report directly to him **in confidence** any impropriety of which they have knowledge whether committed by an employee of CACI, the Government, or a CACI client.

b. CACI also has available a "hotline," at (800) 928-3505, or email **gmadison@ caci.com**, where reports of potentially illegal, unauthorized or inappropriate conduct can be made confidentially at any time.

c. CACI's **Executive Vice President and General Counsel, Jeff Elefante**, is available for consultation on any question employees may have concerning their responsibilities within the Code. Jeff may be reached through (703) 841-7800.

d. Any supervisor or manager receiving a report of any impropriety will promptly report the matter to higher management, the Ombudsman, General Counsel, or Corporate Internal Audit.

e. Every employee and consultant is expected to cooperate fully with any investigation of any alleged violation of this Code of Ethics.[16]

On May 25, 2004, the Interior Department announced it had blocked the Army from hiring any new civilian interrogators in Iraq while it investigated the propriety of the CACI contract (which was for the provision of information technology but was used to hire interrogators). CACI workers already in Iraq were to continue serving at least until the contract ran out in August.[17] In a report released July 16, the inspector general recommended that, "given the improper contracting method used, these 11 [CACI] procurements should be terminated."[18]

However, on August 4 the U.S. Army announced it had awarded a new contract to CACI for interrogation services. The contract was worth up to $23 million over a four-month period. It was awarded without competitive bidding because CACI's interrogators were already on duty in Iraq and could not be replaced by the time the existing contract was due to expire in mid-August.[19]

After the news of Abu Ghraib broke, the Pentagon announced that it was preparing a new rule to increase its oversight of contracts issued by sister agencies, with requirements for more stringent guidelines and approval.[20]

In addition, in April 2003 the Pentagon hired Military Professional Resources Inc. (MPRI) to supply Arabic translators in Iraq for $1.9 million under a federal contract category designed for the employment of education and training analysts. According to company and government officials, the General Services Administration (GSA) never disciplined MPRI.[21]

The U.S. Army also violated contracting rules in late 2002 by hiring dozens of private interrogators working for a subsidiary of Lockheed Martin[22] to operate at Guantanamo Bay, again on a contract designed for information technology services. GSA officials terminated the contract in February, but the Southern Command, which administers the Guantanamo base, revived the work almost immediately by turning it over to Lockheed's existing engineering services contract with the U.S. Interior Department.[23] In June the GSA demanded that Lockheed show why the company "should remain eligible for future government contracts."[24]

In October 2003, Charles Abell, principal deputy undersecretary of defense for personnel and readiness, testified to Congress that staffing shortages had forced the Department of Defense to hire contractors not only as interpreters but also for interrogation work:

> We do use contractors as a means to hire linguists and interrogators . . . The Titan Corporation is among those. They run a background check and then, of course, the military does a more detailed check . . . In our rush to meet the requirements, the mere numerical requirements, I think folks were brought on based on those initial checks and then the more detailed checks followed as time permitted.[25]

It is, however, far from certain that the military had so few interrogators within its own ranks that it needed to turn to the private sector. Brookings Institution's Peter Singer noted:

> Interrogation is something that we haven't contracted out to private companies in any previous war. It really starts in late 2001, and just as you note, it's a response to certain needs. There are a good number of skilled interrogators within the U.S. military system who weren't sent to Iraq. So it wasn't the case that our bench was empty, we actually have a lot of these personnel that weren't sent. And interesting enough, when you talk to them, they say that they were quite surprised that we contracted out. That's worrisome here.[26]

As if all of this wasn't strange enough, it was reported that the use of private contractors as interrogators at Abu Ghraib and other prisons in Iraq violated an Army policy that requires such jobs to be filled by government employees because of the "risk to national security." An Army policy directive published in 2000, and still in effect today, classifies any job that involves "the gathering and analysis" of tactical intelligence as "an inherently governmental function barred from private sector performance."[27]

The Office of Management and Budget lists the following functions as inherently governmental: interpreting and executing laws; ordering military or diplomatic action on behalf of the United States; conducting civil or criminal judicial proceedings; performing actions that significantly affect the life, liberty, or property of private persons; and collecting, controlling, or disbursing appropriated and other federal funds.[28]

A memo signed by Undersecretary of the Army Patrick Henry at the beginning of the Bush administration cautioned against shifting responsibility for intelligence work to private military organizations. The concern was not only about a lack of adequate control, but also that PMCs may eventually work for other countries while retaining access to U.S. military secrets and tradecraft.

The December 26, 2000, memo noted:

> At the operational and strategic level, the intelligence function (less support) performed by military personnel and Federal civilian employees is a non-inherently Governmental function that should be exempted from private sector performance on the basis of risk to national security from relying on contractors to perform this function. The acquisition of intelligence-related technologies and systems, and the instruction and training of soldiers and Army civilian employees on intelligence doctrine and methods are non-inherently Governmental functions. The capabilities provided by military performing these functions also are exempted from conversion to private sector performance on the basis of risk to national security in order to retain a core capability.[29]

In July 2004 the Senate Armed Services Committee witnessed Catch-22 linguistic acrobatics by Les Brownlee, acting secretary of the Army, when he was asked how the hiring of PMC personnel for interrogation could be justified under such a memorandum:

> If these functions are performed by contract interrogators under an entity, which in this case was Central Command, or CGATF-7 specifically, then they would not be considered inherently governmental.[30]

A series of mostly internal military investigations have been conducted in the United States as a result of the revelations at Abu Ghraib. These include

- the final report of the Independent Panel to Review DoD Operations
- Army provost marshal general assessment of detention and corrections operations in Iraq, November 6, 2003 (Ryder Report)
- Joint Task Force Guantanamo assistance visit to Iraq to assess intelligence operations, September 5, 2003 (Miller Report)
- Army inspector general assessment of doctrine and training for detention operations, July 23, 2004 (Mikolashek Report)
- Fay investigation of activities of military personnel at Abu Ghraib and related LTG Jones investigation under the direction of General Kern, August 16, 2004 (see Appendix 3)
- Naval inspector general's review of DoD worldwide interrogation operations[31]
- Commander, Joint Task Force-7, review of activities of military intelligence personnel at Abu Ghraib (Taguba Report)
- Army Reserve Command inspector general assessment of military intelligence and military police training[32]

Although the Fay report dealt primarily with the actions of military police and intelligence officers, it did provide some detail on contractor activities. For example, it cited two cases in which "Civilian 21" allegedly directed soldiers to use military dogs to threaten prisoners.[33]

It also alleged that a second CACI interrogator, identified only as "Civilian 5," "grabbed a detainee (who was handcuffed) off a vehicle and dropped him to the ground. He then dragged him into an interrogation booth and as the detainee tried to get up . . . would yank the detainee very hard and make him fall again." The report says that the CACI employee refused to take instructions from team leaders and military trainers. At one point the civilian allegedly said, "I have been doing this for 20 years and I do not need a 20-year-old telling me how to do my job."[34]

While much of the most relevant material was classified, at least one report (the Taguba Report) implicates contractor personnel in the scandal.[35] General Antonio M. Taguba was tasked by General Ricardo Sanchez, commander of the Combined Joint Task Force Seven (CJTF-7), to investigate the conduct within the 800th Military Policy (MP) Brigade, whose responsibilities included running Abu Ghraib prison. Among General Taguba's findings, which were first publicly revealed in an article by Seymour Hersh in the *New Yorker* magazine, were the following charges:[36]

11. (U) That Mr. Steven Stephanowicz,[37] Contract US Civilian Interrogator, CACI, 205th Military Intelligence Brigade, be given an Official Reprimand to be placed in his employment file, termination of employment, and generation of a derogatory report to revoke his security clearance for the following acts which have been previously referred to in the aforementioned findings:

- Made a false statement to the investigation team regarding the locations of his interrogations, the activities during his interrogations, and his knowledge of abuses.
- Allowed and/or instructed MPs, who were not trained in interrogation techniques, to facilitate interrogations by "setting conditions" which were neither authorized and in accordance with applicable regulations/policy. He clearly knew his instructions equated to physical abuse.

12. (U) That Mr. John Israel, Contract US Civilian Interpreter, CACI, 205th Military Intelligence Brigade, be given an Official Reprimand to be placed in his employment file and have his security clearance reviewed by competent authority for the following acts or concerns which have been previously referred to in the aforementioned findings:

- Denied ever having seen interrogation processes in violation of the IROE, which is contrary to several witness statements.
- Did not have a security clearance.

13. I suspect that COL Thomas M. Pappas, LTC Steve L. Jordan, Mr. Steven Stephanowicz, and Mr. John Israel were either directly or indirectly responsible for the abuses at Abu Ghraib (BCCF) and strongly recommend immediate disciplinary action as described in the preceding paragraphs as well as the initiation of a Procedure 15 Inquiry to determine the full extent of their culpability.

30. In general, US civilian contract personnel (Titan Corporation, CACI, etc . . .), third country nationals, and local contractors do not appear to be properly supervised within the detention facility at Abu Ghraib. During our on-site inspection, they wandered about with too much unsupervised free access in the detainee area. Having civilians in various outfits (civilian and DCUs) in and about the detainee area causes confusion and may have contributed to the difficulties in the accountability process and with detecting escapes. (ANNEX 51, Multiple Witness Statements, and the Personal Observations of the Investigation Team)[38]

Stephanowicz himself said that Army guards at the Abu Ghraib prison kept some prisoners awake for as much as 20 hours a day at the direction of private contractors and military intelligence soldiers. Prison guards were given copies of written interrogation plans for each inmate, which were prepared by three-person teams composed of contractors or military intelligence soldiers.[39]

Stephanowicz is an example of the wrong man for the job. He was trained at the U.S. Army Intelligence Center and School at Fort Huachuca, Arizona, to inspect satellite pictures, not to be an interrogator.[40] Yet he reportedly directed the abuse in one of the most infamous incidents captured on camera at Abu Ghraib: a prisoner in an orange jumpsuit being menaced with an unmuzzled dog. He was never charged with a crime.[41]

Daniel Johnson, another CACI interrogator, interrogated an Iraqi prisoner using what an Army investigation calls "an unauthorized stress position." Two soldiers—who served as military policemen at Abu Ghraib and had already been sentenced and imprisoned for their mistreatment of detainees—told Army investigators that Johnson had directed and participated in prisoner abuse. The Army found "probable cause" that a crime had been committed and referred the case to the Justice Department for prosecution. But in early 2005, a Department of Justice attorney told the Army that the evidence in the case did not justify prosecution.[42]

News reports identified John Israel as an Iraqi-American Christian and an employee of Titan. Israel told Taguba he had no prior experience as a military translator before going to work at Abu Graib. He worked as a senior field technician for Ikon Office Solutions, a document management service with several Los Angeles offices, for 12 years before going to work for Titan.[43] Titan has said that Israel works for one of its subcontractors, SOS Interpreting Ltd.[44] As Professor Deborah Avant of George Washington University noted:

We are not even sure for whom these contractors work or worked. Other Pentagon officials cited different figures in their testimony. Nor do we know precisely what roles these contract employees had at the prison or to which group or agency they were accountable. To trace that, we would need to know the contracting agent— someone representing a group within the Army, probably, but which one? Military Intelligence? The Iraqi Survey Group (a Defense Intelligence Agency unit responsible for investigating weapons of mass destruction and reportedly in charge of the most important Iraqi prisoners)?[45]

Although the lack of a security clearance may seem to be among the lesser offenses, some feel that it indicates a lack of proper vetting of PMC personnel. Because of a lack of trained people, there was a strong suspicion that untrained, inexperienced, and unvetted individuals were being used.[46]

Although it may be much ado over nothing, Army records show that, of 15 Titan or SOS translators working at Abu Ghraib prison in fall 2003, only 1 held a security clearance. Nearly all of them were foreign-born American citizens, and most came from backgrounds that had nothing to do with the sort of government work that would require a security clearance.[47]

A report by the U.S. Government Accounting Office found that the Pentagon has a backlog of nearly 200,000 people working for contractors who are still awaiting security clearances. The report says that the average time required to grant a security clearance for a contract employee exceeds a year.[48]

Contractors don't see this as their responsibility. A *New York Times* article reported that

> every company official interviewed said he did not consider it his company's responsibility to research the backgrounds of the people it hires for government contracts.
>
> "No, we are not in the background investigation business," J. P. London, chief executive of CACI Inc., said in an interview. A CACI employee, Steven Stefanowicz, was implicated in the abuse case. Ralph Williams, spokesman for Titan, said, "It's up the government to execute" background checks.[49]

Since that time the U.S. government has managed to substantially reduce the time needed to process security clearances. A report by the Office of Management and Budget in early 2008 found that many agencies had exceeded goals for completing clearances, reducing the time it takes to process them to 118 days by the first quarter of fiscal 2008.[50]

In fact, Stephanowicz may not have been well qualified. He had no military experience in interrogation. As a junior Navy intelligence specialist, a petty officer third class, he did all of his work in an office, reading and analyzing intelligence reports.[51]

Stephanowicz would not have been the only one lacking proper qualifications. As part of CACI's contract in Iraq, it employed nearly half of the interrogators and analysts at Abu Ghraib. Roughly a third never received formal military interrogation training, and at least one civilian interrogator was hired without a resume, follow-up interview, fingerprints, or a criminal records check.[52]

In the time after the scandal broke but before Abu Ghraib was handed back to the Iraqi government, new procedures were instituted so that, when a new contract interrogator arrived at the prison, officers conducted a preliminary interview to make sure the civilian had the proper credentials and experience. The newcomer also watched an interrogation being conducted by an experienced soldier. And when the civilian started conducting interrogations, the first few sessions were closely observed.[53]

Regardless of vetting, it is hard to defend what can be only viewed as an extremely dilatory way of investigating contractor involvement in the scandal. One commentator noted:

> It's important to follow the time line here. The crimes happened in the fall. The investigation takes place in January. The news doesn't break until May. So we had in a sense four months to get this straight, and at least at the point of when the news broke, the individuals had not been criminally charged, nor had been fired yet. The companies, in fact, defended themselves saying—at the start of this, leaders of the companies said, "Well, we didn't have any people there. We don't know what you're talking about." And then when Major General Taguba's report went public and specifically identified their employees as being there, they changed their story and said, "Well, actually we've not been notified by the military of this report, so why should we have fired these guys if the military never told us to?"[54]

Titan Corp confirmed in May 2004 that it had terminated the contract of Adel L. Nakhla, who was cited in the Taguba report, on the same day the Justice Department said that it had opened a criminal investigation into "a civilian contractor" in Iraq related to the abuse of prisoners at Abu Ghraib. The inquiry marked the first move toward prosecuting civilian employees of contractors who worked as translators and interrogators at Abu Ghraib.[55]

> It also needs to be remembered that there were real crimes committed at Abu Ghraib. The published versions of all the official reports into Abu Ghraib have only been released in redacted, unclassified form. In short, this means that most of the appendices listing the really vile crimes have not been made public. A July report in Salon.com, for example, noted that an Army CID [Criminal Investigative Division] report does have an allegation, made by a detainee, of a male rape.[56]

That alleged rapist was identified as Nakhla.[57]

Torin Nelson, a key witness in Major General Antonio Taguba's report, served as a military intelligence officer at Guantanamo Bay before being sent to Iraq by CACI as a civilian contractor assigned to interrogations.[58] Nelson decided to leave at the end of January 2004 because other CACI staff became hostile to him when it became obvious he had told the truth to Taguba. One coworker told him that he was effectively dead to him and that he "better watch his back."[59]

Nelson said it was the overreliance on private firms providing inadequately trained personnel that led to the scandal at Abu Ghraib. He told *The Guardian* newspaper that the quality of the contractors sent to the prison was "hit or miss" because companies like CACI International were "under so much pressure to fill slots quickly."[60] He also said that the Pentagon "penalize[s] contracting companies if they can't fill slots on time and it looks bad on companies' records." "If you're in such a hurry to get bodies, you end up with cooks and truck drivers doing intelligence work."[61]

However, *The Guardian* subsequently published a clarification:

In the interview below, we quoted a remark Torin Nelson made about "cooks and truck drivers." Mr. Nelson has asked us to make it clear that he intended the remark to be rhetorical. He did not mean that people from those jobs were actually working at the prison as interrogators. He intended the remark to reflect what he felt was the declining quality of private interrogators at the prison.[62]

In a press release in response to this, CACI made the following claims:

The US Military specified in its contract Statement of Work how CACI must operate in Iraq and included the required qualifications for interrogators and other allied specialties. The company has followed these instructions.

The US Military required individuals with proven information-gathering and analysis experience at the tactical and operational levels and that such persons needed to possess at a minimum a Department of Defense SECRET level security clearance, which requires US government background checks on the individuals. The Statement of Work further specified that the US Military was to provide readiness training and briefings on rules of engagement and general orders applicable to US Armed Forces, DoD civilians, and US contractors.

CACI carefully screened and qualified all potential interrogators presented to the US Military in accordance with the Statement of Work. CACI reviewed nearly 1,600 job applications but approved less than 3% for submission to the US Military for final review and approval and/or rejection prior to presentation of employment offers.[63]

But a report by the U.S. Government Accountability Office found that government officials assigned to oversee the CACI's contract all but abdicated their responsibility, leaving it to the private contractor to set terms for its work. The result was multiple "breakdowns," with contractors performing jobs that went far beyond the initial contract terms and the government having no effective way of monitoring performance or controlling costs.[64]

That would seem to indicate that it was a government lapse. But according to a copy of CACI's contract released by the Pentagon, the contract called for the civilian workers to "provide oversight and other directed intelligence support to [military] screening and interrogation operations, with special emphasis on High-Value detainees."[65] However, the contract also said that CACI employees are to be "directed by military authority" and that "the contractor is responsible for providing supervision of all contractor personnel."

Nelson, incidentally, suffered for having helped investigators. Although he was one of the first to provide evidence to Major General Antonio Taguba's investigators and was not involved in any wrongdoing at Abu Ghraib, he has been unable to get work as an interrogator. His career since then has been an example of the saying that no good deed goes unpunished.[66]

Regardless of what actually happened, CACI decided it needed additional help in dealing with the public relations crisis. After initially turning to its external public relations firm for help, it realized it needed crisis management specialists to advise the company and build a custom-tailored response. The media team reviewed all news reports on the company relating to the Abu Ghraib prison scandal and sent letters to publications that it believed had incomplete or erroneous information. It also hired Washington consulting firm Clark & Weinstock to set up meetings with lawmakers and their staffs on Capitol Hill.[67]

In September 2005 CACI announced it was getting out of the interrogation business. The company said that once its existing interrogation contract with the Army expired on September 30, 2005, it would no longer provide such services.[68]

Nor is Abu Ghraib the only place where contractors may have acted illegally. The Justice Department examined the involvement of CIA officers and contract employees in three suspicious deaths of detainees, two in Iraq (one in Abu Ghraib and one at an interrogation center in western Iraq) and one in Afghanistan.[69]

However, the report of the Army inspector general's "Detainee Operations Inspection" into the Abu Ghraib scandal, dated July 21, 2004, barely mentioned contractors.[70] It determined that all CACI contract interrogators satisfied the Army's requirement for relevant experience as set forth in its statement of work criteria (work order).

It also found that the Army statement of work (work order) did not mandate "military training" as a prerequisite for assignment; other appropriate and relevant experience was also authorized.[71] But that was splitting hairs. Work statements issued under the CACI contract required all contractors to have between 5 and 10 years of interrogation and intelligence experience.[72] Given such a level of familiarity with proprietary military systems and procedures, military commanders would have expected potential contractors to be former military intelligence officers qualified in interrogation. After all, how likely is it that one is going to have military interrogation skills unless one was trained to do so while in the military?

The bar may have been set too low. The inspector general's report itself stated:

> Of the contract interrogators in OPERATION IRAQI FREEDOM (OIF), 35% (11 of 31) had not received formal training in military interrogation techniques, policy, and doctrine. These personnel conducted interrogations using skill sets obtained in previous occupational specialties such as civilian police interrogator or Military Intelligence (MI) officer. The lack of specific training in military policies and techniques has the potential of placing these interrogators at a higher risk of violating Army policies and doctrine, and decreasing intelligence yield.
>
> . . .
>
> Prior to May 2004, there was no CACI or CJTF-7 requirement for all contract interrogators to receive formal, comprehensive, military-specific interrogator training prior to performing interrogations in OIF. While in Iraq the DAI Team did not find evidence of a formal training program for contract interrogators.

In summary, contract interrogators in OIF met the requirements of the CJTF-7 C2 Interrogation Cell SOW. The SOW did not mandate military interrogation training as a prerequisite for employment. While some training may have occurred at Abu Ghraib, there is no evidence of a formalized POI for contract interrogators. All contract interrogators should receive training on specific theater and Army techniques, policies, and doctrine for conducting military interrogations. This requirement should be reflected in the CJTF-7 C2 Interrogation Cell SOW.[73]

. . .

(4) Root Cause: The CJTF-7 C2 Interrogation Cell SOW did not require contract interrogators to be trained in military interrogation procedures, policy, and doctrine. Pre-deployment and in-theater training for contract interrogators on military interrogation techniques, policy, and doctrine did not occur or was inconsistent.

(5) Recommendation: The CFLCC contracting officer representative modify the CJTF-7 C2 Interrogation Cell Statement of Work to require civilian interrogators to be former military interrogators trained in current interrogation policy and doctrine or receive formal training in current military interrogation policy and doctrine.[74]

This issue is far from being resolved. On August 12, 2004, CACI said that the U.S. Army had asked some of its 36 interrogators that worked in Iraq to leave their positions and confirmed that those personnel were no longer working for the company.[75] Yet in a press release CACI said that "the internal investigation it is conducting concerning its interrogator personnel in Iraq to date has not produced any credible or tangible evidence that substantiates the involvement of CACI personnel in the abuse of detainees at Abu Ghraib prison or elsewhere in Iraq."[76]

One irony resulting from Abu Ghraib is that the greatest one-year expansion of the Army's interrogation program, from 500 to 1,000 trainees, took place in 2005, the year after public disclosure of the scandals there. But the Army geared up for the effort by hiring private companies to handle the training. In August 2006, the service awarded contracts that could grow to more than $50 million over the following five years to three private firms to provide additional instructors to the 18-week basic course in human intelligence interrogation at Fort Huachuca.[77]

On August 25, 2004, the Pentagon released the results of its investigation of intelligence activities at Abu Ghraib. It detailed numerous examples of contractor misconduct, including abuse, which have been referred to the Department of Justice. It is clear from this report that both Titan and CACI employees were complicit in unlawful activity.

While the inspector general appeared reluctant to directly criticize contract interrogators, others felt free to do so. Brigadier General Janis Karpinski was in charge of the 800th Military Police Brigade that ran Abu Ghraib and other prisons. The Taguba report recommended that she be relieved from command and given a General Officer Memorandum of Reprimand. In an extended phone interview with a California cable television program, she had this to say regarding the control that the military had over Titan translators:

> Signal: John Israel was provided to the Army by Titan Corp, which has an estimated 4,400 translators in Iraq. Did you have Titan translators working for your MP brigade?
>
> Karpinski: Yes, I did.
>
> Signal: How does the chain of command work?
>
> Karpinski: We have no control over them at all.
>
> Signal: How does it work?
>
> Karpinski: Titan Corp. would—my guy who was the point of contact for the brigade would call them and tell them, "We need six more interpreters." And then he would say, "But here's the limitations: They're going to be working out at, for example, at Abu Ghraib; they won't be able to leave; we'll take care of feeding them, housing them, blah blah blah blah blah," and they'll find interpreters that will agree to those conditions.
>
> And they will remain at the facility because the interpreters are not vetted successfully. If you get one in there that can speak English and speak the language and he hasn't been vetted successfully or completely or at all, in most cases if they leave, they could be giving information to the insurgency or the opposition or whatever.
>
> So that was the only control. But their work schedules or their uniforms or what they did or—we had no control over them at all.
>
> Signal: There has been discussion recently that some of these contracting firms are basically acting as employment agencies for the military.
>
> Karpinski: That's exactly what they're doing.
>
> Signal: And that may not conform strictly to federal guidelines.
>
> Karpinski: No, I'm sure it doesn't. I was extremely frustrated with it because, you know, we'd look for the interpreter and we didn't have nearly enough interpreters but I'd look for one and they'd say, "Oh, he's sleeping." Or, "He doesn't usually come in on time" And we couldn't fire them, we couldn't and they were so the military in Iraq was so desperate to get more translators that they were the divisions were asking for more and more and more translators, and they were the priority, and they didn't have nearly what they needed. So these people, these contracting Titan Corp. and I guess there were similar corporations they had practically a blank check.
>
> Signal: There are chain of command issues, too.
>
> Karpinski: There was none for them.
>
> Signal: Reading through the Army regulation, "Contractors Accompanying the Force," evidently the contracting company is supposed to provide a job site manager to supervise the civilian employees, and the Army would designate a liaison to confer with the manager.

Karpinski: Right. Or Col. Jordan would.

Signal: So in the field, when contractors were assigned to the MP brigade, would the MP person in charge ever give direct orders to civilians?

Karpinski: No.

Signal: How did it work?

Karpinski: Well, if there was a problem with the interpreter or, like, for us, because we didn't have interrogators but for interpreters, they would call my point of contact in the brigade and he would try to get it resolved. And the job manager, or the site manager, was down in the CPA building. They were never out at the site. Never.

But the battalion commander or the company commander would voice those concerns to my lieutenant commander, who would work on getting it resolved. But even documentation to poor performance or poor English language skills or whatever, it was just a document. Nobody was ever fired.

Signal: And as you've mentioned, not all the translators were Americans who were shipped over there. A lot of native Iraqis were among the civilians.

Karpinski: Right. And then initially, the first ones that were brought over were from the United States, from throughout the United States. They were paid very, very well. Which is why they were like a lot of contractors over there, they agreed to work under those hostile fire conditions because they were paid extremely well.

Signal: How well is extremely well? What did they earn a month?

Karpinski: A month? At least $12,000 (to) $20,000. Sometimes they were paid $100 an hour, depending on what location they were in.

Signal: Translators?

Karpinski: Yes. Now, I don't know what the interrogators were paid. I can't

even begin to imagine.[78]

Lost in much of the debate over Abu Ghraib and contractors is the simple fact that torture and abuse are not particularly effective ways for obtaining information. But when proper techniques are used, civilian contractors are just as good as active-duty forces. For example, L-3 interrogators were part of Task Force 145, which cracked Abu Musab al-Zarqawi's inner circle, who led al-Qaeda in Iraq.[79]

The only thing that is really clear at this point, over four years later, is that the full details of exactly what PMC personnel did are still unknown. Six members of Congress wrote to President Bush in June 2004 asking for his assistance in obtaining key documents relevant to investigating abuses at Abu Ghraib and elsewhere. These included

- all contracts, subcontracts, and task orders for interrogation or translation work in Iraq, Afghanistan, and Guantanamo Bay

- all reports or assessments of contractor performance for these contracts
- all written statements of detainees, military personnel, or civilian contractors regarding the abuse of prisoners in Iraq, Afghanistan, and Guantanamo Bay[80]

Given the reluctance of the executive branch to answer such requests, it is not clear when, if at all, the congressmen can expect a reply.

Although it never got any publicity, another contractor, American Service Center (ASC) based in Qatar, was responsible for providing food for the prison and routinely fell short by hundreds of meals for Abu Ghraib's surging prison population. When the food did arrive, it was often late and frequently contaminated. Examples included rotten food crawling with bugs, traces of rats and dirt, and rancid meats and spoilt food, which caused diarrhea and food poisoning.[81]

Conventional wisdom says that private contractors are not accountable to a chain of command. What can be done to punish them if they break the law? According to one former Army officer:

A more serious way to discipline bad contractors is through "suspension" or "debarment" proceedings. Military procurement officials can decide not to consider a private contractor for future federal contracts for a certain period of time. For example, in July 2003, the Air Force suspended three divisions of Boeing from eligibility for new contracts in response to misconduct relating to the Evolved Expendable Launch Vehicle program. "Serious improper misconduct" by an employee during the performance of a contract can serve as grounds for suspension or debarment. A criminal indictment (of either an individual or a company) may be enough to support a debarment, as can an internal investigation like the one conducted by the Army at Abu Ghraib. However, if the grounds for debarment depend on an individual employee's conduct, that conduct must be attributed to the corporation, which may, say, have shown negligence in failing to investigate, train, or supervise its employees. The decision to suspend or debar a company rests with the executive agency—in the case of Abu Ghraib, the Army.[82]

In short, there are five legal options for seeking prosecution of the activities uncovered at Abu Ghraib:

- Iraqi justice
- Civil suits
- The Alien Tort Claims Act
- The War Crimes Act
- The Military Extraterritorial Jurisdiction Act (MEJA)

IRAQI JUSTICE

Contractor personnel are not totally beyond the reach of the law. The U.S. government could consent to local trials. Section 5 of the June 2003 order notes that the contractors' immunity from prosecution "may be waived by the Parent State." There are still no plans, however, to prosecute any contractors involved with the abuses at Abu Ghraib.

Contractors consistently say that the Iraqi legal system is not sufficiently impartial or robust enough to be trusted. Of course, the U.S. government had enough confidence in the Iraqi courts to try the late former president of Iraq, Saddam Hussein, so what they really mean is that they don't trust the Iraqi legal system to give foreigners a fair trial.

CIVIL SUITS

Civil suits may also be brought against the contractors and the U.S. government, as was done following the U.S. Navy's downing of an Iranian passenger jet in 1988. Using the Federal Tort Claims Act, families of the dead passengers attempted to sue the government contractors who built the USS *Vincennes* and its weapons systems. However, this lawsuit failed, in part because of a legal doctrine known as the "government contractor" defense, which shields government contractors from liability when they build something or provide services in accordance with government specifications. If their treatment is deemed part of the U.S. government's operations, this defense, and other procedural obstacles, may prevent the Iraqi detainees from suing contractors in American courts for damages resulting from their treatment at Abu Ghraib.[83]

ALIEN TORT CLAIMS ACT (ATCA)

The victims would have to show not only that they were subject to torture by the contractors but also that the contractors acted under "color of state law." Since the contractors were acting in close coordination with military personnel at the prison, this latter fact would seem clear.[84]

Under ATCA, a class-action lawsuit was filed on June 9, 2004, in federal court in San Diego, California, by the New York–based Centre for Constitutional Rights (CCR) and a Philadelphia law firm. Lawyers for Iraqis tortured while in U.S. custody have sued the two private security companies operating in the prison, as well as the three individuals who worked for the firms (Stephen Stephanowicz and John Israel of CACI and Adel Nakhla of Titan), for allegedly abusing prisoners to extract information from them with the goal of winning more contracts from the U.S. government.[85]

Another CACI interrogator mentioned in that lawsuit, although not a defendant, subsequently wrote:[86]

> American authorities continue to insist that the abuse of Iraqi prisoners at Abu Ghraib was an isolated incident in an otherwise well-run detention system. That insistence, however, stands in sharp contrast to my own experiences as an interrogator in Iraq. I watched as detainees were forced to stand naked all night, shivering in their cold cells and pleading with their captors for help. Others were subjected to long periods of isolation in pitch-black rooms. Food and sleep deprivation were common, along with a variety of physical abuse, including punching and kicking. Aggressive, and in many ways abusive, techniques were used daily in Iraq, all in the name of acquiring the intelligence necessary to bring an end to the insurgency.[87]

On June 29, 2004, however, the U.S. Supreme Court, in ruling on a previous case, said that foreigners have only a limited right to use the ATCA to sue in America over alleged human rights abuses.[88]

Another ATCA suit, *Ilham Nassir Ibrahim* v. *Titan Corp.*, was filed on July 27, 2004.[89] A consortium of trial lawyers from a number of states, collectively referred to as the Iraqi Torture Victim Group (ITVG), filed a lawsuit in federal court in Washington, D.C., on behalf of five Iraqis who claimed they were subjected to acts of murder, torture, and other abuses while they or their family members were held in Abu Ghraib.[90]

That suit was dismissed in November 2007 by U.S. District Judge James Robertson of the District of Columbia, who found that Titan's interpreters generally were supervised and under control of military officials, thereby freeing the company of blame.[91] But Robertson did let the suit against CACI proceed, rejecting the company's claim that it should be immune from such a lawsuit because it worked at the behest of the U.S. military. Robertson said he believed a jury should hear the case, in part because CACI had its own chain of command.[92]

WAR CRIMES ACT

Attorney General Ashcroft said in May 2004 that killings or abuse of military detainees in Iraq that involved civilian contractors could be prosecuted by the Justice Department under several statutes, including civil rights violations and antitorture laws. Federal criminal prosecutors can pursue cases against nonmilitary personnel and against those who have left the military.[93] If the evidence suggests war crimes, they might be charged under the U.S. War Crimes Act of 1996, which defines such crimes as any grave breach of the 1949 Geneva Conventions, such as torture or inhuman treatment and violations of the conventions' common article 3 (such as "outrages upon personal dignity" and "humiliating and degrading treatment").[94] The act gives U.S. courts jurisdiction in cases in which an American is either the victim or perpetrator of a war crime.

An analysis by the Institute for International Law of Peace and Humanitarian Law of the Ruhr-University Bochum in Germany found that perpetrators at Abu Ghraib were clearly liable to prosecution under U.S. federal law. It noted that, according to the 1996 War Crimes Act as amended in 1997,

> CIA agents and private contractors are criminally liable under US federal law . . . over offences committed whether in the United States or overseas. The US court would then need to examine whether the acts perpetrated by these CIA agents and private contractors fall within the scope of section 2441(c)(1) that provides that any act listed as a grave breach in the Geneva Conventions is to be considered as a "war crime" . . . According to articles 130 GCIII and 147 GCIV, grave breaches are violations of international humanitarian law that are committed against protected persons, i.e., prisoners of war (article 4 GC III) and persons "who are in the hands of a party to the conflict or occupying power of which they are not nationals" (article 4 GCIV) . . . one needs to point that even unconventional combatants shall be treated with humanity and be granted the full rights and privileges of a protected person (Article 5 GCIV).

> By virtue of articles 130 GCIII and 147 GCIV, torture or inhuman treatment, willfully causing great suffering or serious injury to body or health are to be considered grave breaches of the conventions. There is hardly any doubt that the rape of a detainee is regarded as a grave breach (see ICTY, Furundzija case). As for ordering guards to treat detainees in an inhumane manner, this can also be considered as falling under the grave breaches provision. Consequently, CIA agents and private contractors may be prosecuted under section 2441(c)(1) of US federal law.

> In addition, it is possible to prosecute these persons under section 2441(c)(3) of US federal law since Common Article 3 is also applicable to international armed conflict (see ICTY, Tadic Jurisdiction Appeal case). It is however unlikely that a US court would follow international jurisprudence on the subject. Nevertheless, if it would, it could prosecute private contractors for "outrages upon personal dignity, in particular humiliating and degrading treatment" that would without a doubt apply to the treatment suffered by the detainees in Abu Ghraib since the threshold of applicability is lower than the one enshrined in articles 130 GCIII and 147 GCIV.[95]

Once a federal court's jurisdiction is established, contractors can then face charges under a 1994 provision of the criminal code (PL 103-236) that prohibits U.S. nationals from engaging in acts "intended to inflict severe physical or mental pain or suffering."[96] That provision was passed to implement the 1984 Convention against Torture and Other Cruel, Inhuman, or Degrading Treatment or Punishment, which imposes on governments a duty to prosecute all instances of torture in their jurisdiction. The law holds that anyone who commits torture outside the United States shall be fined or imprisoned for up to 20 years, or if the victim died, could receive a life sentence or the death penalty.[97]

MILITARY EXTRATERRITORIAL JURISDICTION ACT (MEJA)

Another option is the Military Extraterritorial Jurisdiction Act (MEJA) of 2000 (Public Law 106-523, Amended Title 18, US Code). It was passed to establish federal jurisdiction over certain criminal offenses committed outside the United States by persons employed by or accompanying the armed forces, or by members of the armed forces who are released or separated from active duty prior to being identified and prosecuted for the commission of such offenses, and for other purposes.[98]

The fact that MEJA was created in the first place is proof that concerns over contractor accountability are not new and long predate the war in Iraq. In fact, in 1997 Congress established an Overseas Jurisdiction Advisory Committee, which spent a year analyzing the state of the law, found "significant jurisdictional gaps" in the government's ability to prosecute crimes committed abroad by contractors, and recommended legislative remedies. The committee's extensive report laid the foundation for the MEJA.[99]

Essentially, the act applies to anyone who engages in conduct outside the United States that would constitute an offense punishable by imprisonment for more than one year, the same as if the offense had been committed within U.S. jurisdiction.[100] The person must be employed by or accompanying the armed forces outside the United States.[101]

However, the Pentagon has not yet formalized or signed the implementing regulations for the 2000 law. On February 10, 2004, the Department of Defense issued its first proposed rules for MEJA implementation. The rules, however, were limited by the statutory constraints of MEJA, preventing DoD from clarifying the outstanding questions about civilians contracted by agencies outside DoD.

In May 2004 military officials said that the directives were still in the final stages of review by the Justice and State Departments.[102]

The first case under the MEJA was brought in 2003 in California against the wife of a murdered Air Force staff sergeant at Incirlik Air Base, Turkey.[103] Thus far the situation in Iraq is not encouraging. U.S. Army lawyers washed their hands of the situation in Abu Ghraib, deciding that they had no jurisdiction and leaving it up to the firms to decide how to discipline their staff.

According to Peter Singer of the Brookings Institution, the challenge on MEJA is not actually the lack of precedent, but rather the loopholes in it and the lack of doctrine around it.

The problem is essentially twofold: there are questions as to whether MEJA applies to contractors working for those agencies other than DoD and for foreign subcontractors, and more importantly, the doctrine of how, when, where, and who would apply MEJA was never established (DoD was supposed to, but never did). This is partly how you get this punting of the problem right now between DoD and DoJ, where DoD says it has no jurisdiction, while DoJ says its not going to do anything until DoD tells it. There is no specificity there and so military jurists look at it and feel that MEJA is close to useless for going after US citizen contractors, let alone what you do to a 3rd party national. The way the laws are written, or rather not written, make it somewhere between highly problematic and useless.[104]

What happened at Abu Ghraib was a good example of the limitations of MEJA as it was originally written. The definition section required that the civilians included within the scope of the act be employed by the Department of Defense or a contractor with the Department of Defense. As noted above, Steven Stephanowicz, who was a contract interrogator with CACI, was accused of giving military police instructions that he knew equated to physical abuse. Unfortunately, he worked for CACI, which had no contract with the Department of Defense. CACI's contract was with the Interior Department's National Business Center, which ran the contracting office at Fort Huachuca, Arizona, for the four years prior to the Abu Ghraib revelations. Since CACI's contract was not with the Department of Defense, the jurisdictional arm of MEJA would not reach Stephanowicz.[105] Federal prosecutors using the MEJA would have to argue that he was a *de facto* employee or contractor of the Defense Department.

A bill introduced in May 2004 by Rep. David E. Price and Rep. Christopher Shays extended the law to contractors with any federal agency, so long as they are "supporting the mission of the Department of Defense."[106] But even after that, MEJA failed to shut the barn door in at least five areas: employees and family members of other government agencies living and working abroad; misdemeanor offenses; the lack of implementing regulations that will at least provide grounds for challenge if not outright dismissal of some cases; individual citizens of, or ordinarily resident in, the host nation; and U.S. citizens working for the United States overseas but ultimately paid by other countries.

Furthermore, MEJA gives no authority to prosecute foreign nationals employed by contractors and subcontractors or U.S. citizens employed as contractors by the United Nations or foreign governments. While this may be irrelevant to Abu Ghraib, it is clearly worthy of clarification. What happens, for example, if illegal activities are carried out by in-country employees of a PMC? Given that Erinys employed over 14,000 Iraqis to protect Iraqi petroleum infrastructure, it is at least a possibility.

NEW LAWS IN RESPONSE TO THE SCANDAL

On May 18, 2004, Reps. David Price and Martin Meehan (D-MA) sponsored the Contractor Accountability Bill, which would extend the MEJA to include non-U.S. citizens working as contractors to the U.S. government.[107]

A significant development took place with presidential approval of the FY 2005 National Defense Authorization Act on October 28, 2004. Section 1088 of the act amended MEJA to substantially broaden its scope, allowing federal prosecutors to charge anyone within the law's scope with any violation of federal criminal law for which the statutory penalty meets or exceeds one year of prison. The original MEJA statute applied only to Defense Department civilian employees, their dependents, and DoD contractors (and subcontractors at any tier) and their dependents. Under the language passed by Congress, the MEJA now applied to all U.S. government contractors "to the extent [their] employment relates to supporting the mission of the Department of Defense overseas."

More than three years later, on October 4, 2007, the U.S. House of Representatives overwhelmingly passed the MEJA Expansion and Enforcement Act of 2007 (H.R. 2740), despite the Bush administration's opposition, with a vote of 389-30. The bill makes private contractors working in combat zones like Iraq and Afghanistan subject to prosecution for wrongdoing in U.S. courts.

It amended MEJA in three critical respects. First, it closed the legal gap in current law by making all contractors accountable for their actions. Previously MEJA extended U.S. federal criminal jurisdiction to felony crimes committed overseas by contractors working on behalf of the Defense Department. The bill now specified that the act would apply to all contractors regardless of the agency for which they provide services.

Second, it required the inspector general of the Justice Department to examine and report on the department's efforts to investigate and prosecute allegations of misconduct committed by contractors overseas.

Third, H.R. 2740 established ground units of the FBI to investigate allegations of criminal misconduct by contractors. At the time of the bill's passage, there was not a single investigating unit located in that country, even though more than 180,000 contractors were operating in Iraq.

However, before the bill was passed, Democrats agreed to add language specifying that it was not intended to hamper intelligence efforts. This is probably as close as we'll ever get to an admission that CIA contractors are involved in activities in Iraq that would be in violation of U.S. criminal law.[108]

The day the bill was passed in the House, the Bush administration said it had "grave concerns" about it but supported accountability and would be willing to work with Congress to change the legislation. Among its concerns, the White House called the bill "vague" about who would be subject to U.S. law, stating that this vagueness would result in "extreme litigation." It said the bill's outcome could threaten ongoing national security activities abroad. It also said that forcing the FBI to operate overseas infringes on the powers of the executive branch. And it said that the bill would burden the Department of Defense, forcing that agency to help the FBI even as it conducts a war. One might think that if the industry itself did not object to the bill that would be good enough, but apparently not for the White House.[109]

The International Committee of the Red Cross (ICRC) began preparing to implement a "triangular strategy" aimed at PMCs in areas of conflict. When they have concerns over activities or lack of training and expertise, the ICRC will approach the company, the hiring military organization, and the company's government to bring to bear the need for compliance.[110]

Subsequently, the Swiss Federal Department of Foreign Affairs and the ICRC launched an initiative to confirm the existing legal obligations of the actors and to develop nonbinding good practices. The initiative has the following specific objectives:

a. to contribute to the intergovernmental discussion on the issues raised by the use of private military and security companies;
b. to reaffirm and clarify the existing obligations of states and other actors under international law, in particular under international humanitarian law and human rights law;
c. to study and develop good practices, regulatory models and other appropriate measures at the national, possibly regional or international level, to assist states in respecting and ensuring respect for international humanitarian law and human rights law.

In addition, the Pentagon prepared new rules regulating contractors that went far beyond their role in the prison system. These new rules will affect all private contractors, including those providing translation services, foreign army training, security for government officials, service on reconstruction projects, weapons maintenance, base security, and information technology and communications services.

To prevent repeats of the situation in which Titan supplied interrogators through a task order off of a General Services Administration federal supply schedule contract managed by the Interior Department, the Pentagon also issued new rules so that government-wide contracts stay within regulatory guidelines.[111]

A Pentagon memo issued October 29, 2004, required Defense agencies to set specific procedures for reviewing and approving the use of contracts managed by other agencies. The procedures had to be outlined by January 1, 2005, and had to include

Evaluating whether the non-DOD contract is better at satisfying customer requirements, is more cost-effective and has better administration

Determining that the tasks or products needed are within the scope of the contract being considered

Reviewing funding to ensure that it is used in accordance with appropriations limitations

Providing unique terms, conditions, and requirements to the contracting agency so officials can incorporate them into the contract

Collecting data on assisted acquisitions for later analysis[112]

Ironically, because the Defense Department is by far the largest federal purchaser, these moves appeared likely to considerably slow federal business on government-wide acquisition contracts (GWACs) and General Services Administration federal supply schedules, which were created to streamline federal purchasing. And many Defense procurements, whether through DoD or non-DoD contracts, are likely to take longer.[113]

One likely requirement is that companies will be suspended or banned from Pentagon contract work if employees violate standards of military conduct or international conventions. Another proposed change will put the U.S. military back in charge of providing personal security for U.S. officials.

Companies that provide combat assistance in the field will also have to more fully disclose their ownership, finances, and legal histories and be subject to more thorough performance reviews and employee background checks.[114]

CONCLUSION

What does Abu Ghraib tell us about control over and accountability of PMCs? Though not all investigations have been completed and much of the most relevant material is still classified, the bulk of the evidence to date suggests that most of the abuses were carried out by regular military forces. Though several PMC contractors seem guilty of criminal behavior and merit prosecution, it does not appear that the use of translators and interrogators from private firms like Titan and CACI were part of any effort to deliberately avoid oversight. If anything, such efforts came from government agencies like the CIA, which requested the Army to keep certain prisoners off the books, that is, the so-called ghost detainees.

Abu Ghraib, like the overall slipshod, ill-planned way the United States prepared for post–major combat operations, is a reflection of broader policy failings. This has been obvious for years. Back in 2004 Stan Soloway, president of the Professional Services Council, a trade association representing some of the contractors doing reconstruction work, noted that despite the size and scope of the Iraq effort, contract specialists weren't deployed to Iraq in large numbers, creating a distance between planners in the United States and contractors in the field.[115]

In short, the Bush administration has tried to fight a war and build a nation on the cheap. It failed to commit the necessary number of trained and qualified personnel and failed to supply the necessary resources required for an occupation force under international law. In such a scenario, failure and criminal behavior by both private and public actors were virtually inevitable.

The CIA and civilian leadership higher up the chain of command in the U.S. Department of Defense (DoD) created and encouraged the culture in which such offenses occurred. In short, Iraq has shown that higher standards of accountability are required in both the public and private sector.

In addition, while Abu Ghraib has shown that certain tasks, such as prisoner interrogation, are too sensitive to be outsourced to the private sector without proper government oversight (because of the potential for human rights violations), it is a sad, current reality that the U.S. military plans to continue using PMC personnel for that task because it lacks sufficient qualified personnel of its own.

6

Control and Accountability Issues

Concerns over accountability and regulation of PMCs have long been a staple in academic discussion about the industry.[1] However, the widespread use of PMCs in Iraq brought increased publicity to and discussion of the issue.[2] One real problem in regulating PMCs is their somewhat ambiguous legal status in regard to existing international treaties relevant to conflict and war. This is partly because the whole structure of international law and relations rests on the state. The ambiguous relationship between governments and PMCs leaves companies open to arbitrary treatment by combatants or other countries if they stray over borders.[3] They are combatants under the Geneva Convention if they bear arms and are clearly working on behalf of one side in a conflict, yet they could also be treated as noncombatants if they do not wear recognizable uniforms or are not under military command.

From the day the first PMC started operating in Iraq, concerns, whether legitimate or exaggerated, have been omnipresent. Many in the PSC industry say that press coverage is biased toward the sensationalistic, what they like to call the "spicy merc" story. But with the advantage of hindsight one can say that there is reason for concern. War zones have a nasty habit of producing situations that are not normally covered in standard operating procedures. When you add in something of such recent vintage as the private security industry, you can count on problems, even if you have people with the best of intentions.

The problem for contractors is that since 2003 there have been many reported incidents of contractors wounding or killing Iraqi civilians. Sometimes the incidents were relatively straightforward; for example, a car came too close, it did not respond to warnings to keep away, and finally, a contractor opened fire. Even if it went exactly that way, the end result was an innocent civilian: someone's husband, wife, son, daughter, father, or mother ended up dead.

Although most news stories focus on foreign security contractors, it bears noting that Iraqi private security details for government officials have also been a big problem.[4] But it is undeniable that foreign contractors have shot innumerable times and that innocent Iraqis have died as a result.

In January 2005 Abd al-Naser Abbas al-Dulaimi, age 29, who supported his mother, two sisters, and the two children of an older brother, was shot in western Baghdad while he was out looking for gas, which most Iraqis are forced to buy on the black market.[5] He was apparently shot by a three-vehicle convoy belonging to a private security company.

In March 2005 Blackwater created outrage after a memo to staff was made public stating that "actually it is 'fun' to shoot some people." Bearing the name of Blackwater's president, Gary Jackson, the electronic newsletter adds that terrorists "need to get creamed, and it's fun, meaning satisfying, to do the shooting of such folk."[6]

Long before September 2007, when Blackwater contractors shot dead 17 Iraqis in an incident in Baghdad, there had been numerous incidents, not nearly as well publicized, in which contractor personnel had killed Iraqi civilians. Consider this "warden" (warning) message the State Department sent out July 20, 2005:

On July 14, 2005 a passenger was shot while riding in a vehicle within the city of Erbil. A Personal Security Detail (PSD) team has been accused by the police of having fired the shot that struck the passenger and the vehicle. A joint US-Iraqi Police preliminary investigation has been conducted to determine the facts of the case.

The results of that investigation are in dispute.

As a result of this disagreement on the facts of the case, armed uniformed local troops have begun to stop PSD details in Erbil in an effort to identify the persons whom they believe may have been the shooters of the civilian vehicle. We are in discussions concerning this matter with senior Kurdish Regional Government representatives and continue to work with the KRG to resolve the situation.[7]

A subsequent U.S. investigation of the incident concluded that no American contractors were responsible, a finding disputed by the passenger's family, other witnesses, local politicians, and the city's top security official, who termed it a cover-up.[8] This took place in the Kurdish area of Iraq, which is relatively calm and stable by Iraqi standards. There, incidents like this are rare. In central Iraq they are far more frequent and far less investigated. There a PSD detail would never have allowed itself to be stopped by the local police.

Although there is no publicly available data, anecdotes and common sense suggest that the accidental and erroneous use of lethal force by regular military personnel is far greater than that by PSC employees. U.S. military rules of engagement favor "force protection" over any obligation to protect innocent life.[9]

There are far more shootings of innocent civilians by soldiers manning checkpoints than all the known killings of civilians by PSC personnel.

There are other examples of controversial incidents involving private security staff. In February 2006 private security workers under contract with the U.S. State Department shot and killed two Iraqi civilians city of Kirkuk.[10] Another controversy occurred when an alleged "trophy" video was posted online in fall 2005 that appeared to show security guards in Baghdad randomly shooting Iraqi civilians. The video, which first appeared on a Web site that has been linked unofficially to Aegis Defence Services, contained four separate clips in which security guards open fire with automatic rifles at civilian cars.[11] While there was much hue and cry over the shootings, it is far from clear that the guards did anything wrong. Much of the commentary by other contractors appearing on e-mail chat boards found that at least two of the shootings were justified. But that left two shootings whose validity was at least questionable.

Bloggers claim that the man with the gun in the video was Danny Heydenreycher, a South African employee of Aegis at Camp Victory.[12] The results of an investigation by the U.S. military, released June 10, 2006, although not to the public, determined that no one involved would be charged with a crime.[13]

Many viewed this incident as a case of the fox guarding the henhouse. Essentially, the contractor investigated itself. The report that Aegis shared with DoD was evidently around 200 pages, half of which was appendices. However, requests to see the report were denied. Why? The Pentagon said it wasn't their report to share. Aegis said it was corporate data and therefore not public. The Pentagon agreed with Aegis's public statement that they could not identify the shooters, which is odd considering the Blue Force trackers each of their contractors wears. Interestingly, whereas the United States didn't act, South Africa knows who sat where and moved to prosecute one of their own who was shooting in violation of that country's stringent Foreign Military Registration Act.[14]

The real significance of this incident, however, was not that it happened but how often such incidents happened. Robert Pelton, author of *Licensed to Kill*, notes:

> The entire concept that we must hire Americans and foreigners to "do our dirty work" by replacing the military with "neo-mercenaries" has engendered negative feelings among Iraqis and Afghans. It has not helped that the hard-rolling, guns-up, aggressive style of security convoys in Iraq has instilled a real sense of fear and resentment. The military operations usually are concentrated in expected areas, but an Iraqi might just be going to work and have the misfortune of driving too close to a security convoy. I don't think it's unreasonable to estimate that accidental shootings happen on a daily basis. I have personally witnessed numerous questionable incidents similar to those in the infamous AEGIS PSD trophy video in my ride-alongs with various companies.[15]

The *Los Angeles Times* reported in December 2005 that private security contractors have been involved in scores of shootings in Iraq, but none have been prosecuted, despite findings in at least one fatal case that the men had not followed proper procedures. Instead, security contractors suspected of reckless behavior are sent home, sometimes with the knowledge of U.S. officials, raising questions about accountability and stirring fierce resentment among Iraqis.

In 2005 David A. Boone brought a wrongful termination suit against Virginia-based MVM Inc. for pulling his employment contract after he reported unprofessional conduct among fellow workers and the use of illegal weapons during top-secret assignments. The lawsuit included allegations of a bungled November 2004 cover-up. Boone said that MVM guards fabricated a horrific shootout with roadside snipers and later bragged about killing three enemy soldiers. The made-up firefight with 20 to 30 enemy shooters near Baghdad's airport was a "fraudulent and false report" and a violation of MVM's government contract, the complaint said.[16]

In March 2006 a 71-year-old Australian who taught at the University of Baghdad, Professor Kays Juma, was killed by a contractor working for Unity Resources Group when Juma got too close to a convoy of four-wheel drives ferrying private contractors. He was returning from the shops and was near an entry point to the city's Green Zone.[17]

In 2006 Jay Price of the *News & Observer* reported, after analyzing more than 400 reports that contractors filed with the government, that in a nine-month period (August 2004 to April 2005) of the Iraq War, security and construction contractors reported shooting into 61 vehicles. Here's the narrative from a typical shooting report:

"1 warning shot fired in a safe direction at a black OPEL that refused to adhere to the [private security detail] signals [big torch and hand signals] to stay back. After 1st warning shot car accelerate. When he accelerate we made another 2 warning shots, no reaction from driver we had to open fire directly in to that car using AK[-47 assault rifle] and PKM [machine gun]. The car was stop after we made 23 shots from PKM and 9 shots from AK. Driver . . . survived."[18]

In their reports contractors often said that they opened fire because they believed the vehicles posed a threat to their lives. Still, in only seven of the cases were Iraqis obviously attacking—carrying guns, shooting at contractors, or setting off explosives.[19]

Security analysts say that such incidents are probably vastly underreported. There is no way to tell how many civilians have been hurt or how many have been innocent.

In December 2006 an off-duty Blackwater employee, Andrew J. Moonen, who had been drinking heavily, tried to make his way into the "Little Venice" section of the Green Zone, which houses many senior members of the Iraqi government. He was stopped by Iraqi bodyguards for Adil Abdul-Mahdi, the country's Shi'ite vice president, and shot one of the Iraqis. Officials say the bodyguard died at the scene. Although Mahdi wanted the man turned over to the Iraqi government, that did not happen.[20] Blackwater fired the contractor and fined him $14,697— the total of his back pay, a scheduled bonus, and the cost of his plane ticket home.[21] However, less than two months later he was hired by another private contractor, Combat Support Associates (CSA), to work in Kuwait, where he worked from February to August of 2007. Because the State Department and Blackwater kept the incident quiet and out of Moonen's personnel records, CSA was unaware of the December incident when it hired Moonen.[22]

Blackwater subsequently acknowledged that the guard had done wrong but said there was little Blackwater could do about it. As Erik Prince of Blackwater said in a congressional hearing:

> PRINCE: (From tape) Look, I'm not going to make any apologies for what he did. He clearly violated our policies . . . we fired him, we fined him, but we as a private organization can't do any more. We can't flog him, we can't incarcerate him. That's up to the Justice Department. We are not empowered to enforce U.S. law.[23]

Nine months later a congressional report revealed that the guard was so drunk after fleeing the shooting that another group of guards took away the loaded pistol he was fumbling with. Furthermore, the acting ambassador at the United States Embassy in Baghdad suggested that Blackwater apologize for the shooting and pay the dead Iraqi man's family $250,000, lest the Iraqi government bar Blackwater from working there. According to the report, Blackwater eventually paid the family $15,000 after an embassy diplomatic security official complained that the "crazy sums" proposed by the ambassador could encourage Iraqis to try to "get killed by our guys to financially guarantee their family's future."[24]

In February 2007 three security guards at the government-run Iraqi Media Network in Baghdad were reportedly shot to death by Blackwater contractors. Although an internal investigation by the Iraqi Media Network found Blackwater responsible, nobody was charged. According to a U.S. diplomat speaking off the record, "Because they are security, everything was a big secret. They draw the wagon circle. They protect each other. They look out for each other. I don't know if that's a good thing, that wall of silence. When it protects the guilty, that is definitely not a good thing."[25] Subsequently the State Department conducted a cursory investigation and determined that the security team's actions "fell within approved rules governing the use of force."[26]

In May 2007 Blackwater guards opened fire on the streets of Baghdad twice in a single week. In once incident a guard shot and killed an Iraqi driver near the Interior Ministry. In the other a Blackwater-protected convoy was ambushed in downtown Baghdad, triggering a furious battle in which the contractors, U.S. and Iraqi troops, and AH-64 Apache attack helicopters were firing in a congested area.[27]

On October 16, 2007, two men and a woman were wounded in a Kurdish village in northern Iraq when guards from Erinys raked a crowded taxi with automatic weapons fire. At that point it was the third shooting of Iraqi civilians by a private security firm in the past month.[28]

In past years the normal standard operating procedure when a contractor was thought to have done something wrong was to ship him or her home, sometimes with the knowledge of U.S. officials. Blackwater, for example, terminated staff for personnel problems under the WPPS II contract:

Termination of Blackwater Personnel

Weapons Related Incidents 28

Drugs and Alcohol Violations 25

Inappropriate/Lewd Conduct 16

Insubordination 11

Poor Performance 10

Aggressive/Violent Behavior 10

Rules Violations 8

Failure to Report an Incident/Lying 6

Publicly Embarrassing Blackwater 4

Security Clearance/Classification Issues 3

PTSD 1

Total 122[29]

This stands in sharp contrast to the procedure followed by regular military forces. For example, the U.S. military has a commission that reviews damages claims and makes payments when troops are determined to have erred in opening fire on property or people. American troops suspected of shooting at Iraqis face trial in military tribunals. They have actually been convicted for killing Iraqis, something that has never happened with a security contractor.

Although PMC personnel have shot their weapons in hundreds of acknowledged incidents, to date not a single contractor has been prosecuted. And most of the private security companies in Iraq open fire far more frequently than has been publicly acknowledged and rarely report such incidents to U.S. or Iraqi authorities.[30]

Either every single use of force has been beyond reproach or someone is looking the other way. Given that we do not live in a perfect world, the latter seems more likely. Thus, effective public accountability, despite the increase in the number of new laws and regulations on the books that at least theoretically apply to PMCs, is still lacking. Given that PMCs are here for the foreseeable future, that situation cannot be allowed to continue.

Yet it is not clear that the U.S. government, which is, either directly or indirectly, the major client of most PSCs in Iraq, has the best of intentions. Admittedly that sounds strange. Nowadays "oversight and accountability," as well as prosecuting the guilty, are virtually sacred cows, right up there with patriotism, motherhood, and apple pie. Who could possibly be against them?[31]

In a private briefing in mid-December 2007, Justice Department officials told Congress they faced serious legal obstacles that might prevent any prosecution of the Blackwater security guards involved in the September shooting in Baghdad that left at least 17 Iraqis dead.

On January 24, 2008, U.S. government officials told Congress that the Bush administration is not prepared to manage the contractors' critical involvement in the American war effort in Afghanistan and Iraq. At this point contractors had been in both countries nearly five years. As of September 2007, there were more than 196,000 contractor personnel working for the Pentagon in those countries. But Jack Bell, deputy undersecretary of defense for logistics and materiel readiness, testified before Congress on January 24 that they "were not adequately prepared to address" what he termed "this unprecedented scale of our dependence on contractors."

Then, the *New York Times* reported on January 25 that the Bush administration will insist that the government in Baghdad guarantee civilian contractors specific legal protections from Iraqi law. This would be in lieu of a traditional status-of-forces agreement, an accord that has historically been negotiated by the executive branch and signed by the executive branch without a Senate vote. That helped explain why on February 5 the Iraqi Cabinet approved a draft bill that would subject foreign security contractors to Iraqi law, a position affirmed by Samir Sumaidaie, Iraqi ambassador to the United States. He said the future of PSCs "is one of the prime concerns that the Iraqis will put on the table."

To really understand why concerns over control now loom so high, one needs to go back to the weeks after the United States ceased major combat operations in 2003. On June 27, 2004, the Coalition Provisional Authority issued Order 17, "Status of the Coalition Provisional Authority, MNF–Iraq, Certain Missions and Personnel in Iraq."[32] The order contained this language:

> Contractors shall not be subject to Iraqi laws or regulations in matters relating to the terms and conditions of their Contracts, . . .

> Contractors shall be immune from Iraqi legal process with respect to acts performed by them pursuant to the terms and conditions of a Contract or any sub-contract thereto.

However, the order was never the blanket grant of immunity that its critics claimed, since it also stated:

> Notwithstanding any provisions in this Order, Private Security Companies and their employees operating in Iraq must comply with all CPA Orders, Regulations, Memoranda, and any implementing instructions or regulations governing the existence and

activities of Private Security Companies in Iraq, including registration and licensing of weapons and firearms.

Nothing in this provision shall prohibit MNF Personnel from preventing acts of serious misconduct by Contractors, or otherwise temporarily detaining any Contractors who pose a risk of injury to themselves or others, pending expeditious turnover to the appropriate authorities of the Sending State. In all such circumstances, the appropriate senior representative of the Contractor's Sending State in Iraq shall be notified.[33]

In fact, the legal immunity given to contractors is actually far more limited than that given to others. Section 2, subsection 1, states that "the MNF [multinational forces], the CPA, Foreign Liaison Missions, their Personnel, property, funds and assets, and all International Consultants shall be immune from Iraqi legal process." Though interpretations vary, this seems to be a blanket immunity, whereas that applied to contractors is contingent on their acting to fulfill a contract.[34]

Nevertheless, Order 17 was perceived as reducing the power of the Iraqi government to pursue legal action against foreigners working with the CPA. Depending on the interpretation, it either took power away from the Iraqi government, giving it to the CPA, or took power from the Iraqi government and gave it to individuals claiming to work in the interest of the CPA.

In addition, four days before turning governing authority back to the Iraqi interim government on June 28, 2004, CPA administrator L. Paul Bremer signed an order aimed at regulating private security companies operating in Iraq. The order, known among security contractors as Memorandum 17, states that contractors must be vetted, licensed, and registered with the Ministries of Trade and Interior.

They are subject to periodic audits by the Ministry of Interior, their weapons must be registered and licensed, and they are prohibited from performing any law enforcement functions. Also, contractors are bound by a set of rules governing the use of force. Specifically, they are allowed to use "necessary force" only in self-defense, to defend individuals they are contractually obligated to defend, and "to prevent life-threatening offenses against civilians."

Before they begin any operations, all security firms must submit a minimum refundable bond of $25,000 to the Interior Ministry (the ministry reserves the right to charge more). Any firms that violate the terms of Memorandum 17 might forfeit their bonds. In addition, firms "must submit evidence that they have sufficient public liability insurance to cover possible claims against them for a reasonable amount." If insurance is not "practicable," firms may seek an exemption from the requirement.

However, both contractors and U.S. government officials say that Memorandum 17 is impossible to implement. The Iraqi government does not yet have the personnel or the capacity to enforce the order. In addition, the scope of the memo's provisions is confusing, since the order applies to security contractors supporting reconstruction.

Even if the Iraqi government could implement Memorandum 17, it's not clear how firms would be held accountable. Many of the security firms operating in Iraq are multinational conglomerates employing foreign nationals under contract with the U.S. government or other governments, as well as private companies and nonprofit organizations. Under Memorandum 17, contractors are subject to the laws of their parent countries, but those laws might not apply to the activities of their citizens abroad, says Deborah Avant, an expert on the role of private contractors in U.S. interventions abroad.

Avant writes that although the Coalition Provisional Authority tried to specify in some of its orders, including Memorandum 17, the appropriate legal venues for holding contractors accountable, different parts of U.S. law apply to different situations. "For instance, the [2001 USA] Patriot Act applies to any crime committed by a U.S. citizen, or against a U.S. citizen anywhere U.S. forces are operating. So some of the foreign nationals working for private security firms in Iraq would be subject to the Patriot Act if they commit a crime against a U.S. citizen," but not if a foreign national commits a crime against an Iraqi.[35]

In the past some of the primary U.S. laws used to regulate contractors were inadequate. For example, the Arms Export Control Act (AECA) is a key statute in this area, although it is better known for regulating arms sales. The act gives the president full authority to promulgate regulations for this purpose and to designate items as defense articles and defense services by placing them on the United States Munitions List. Any person or organization that manufactures, exports, or imports the goods or services on the list must register with the U.S. government and receive a license for each contract. Criminal penalties can result from a failure to register properly.

But the AECA fails to effectively regulate PMC activities for three basic reasons.[36] First, it does not provide a mechanism to force presidential compliance. Second, the AECA's reporting requirements provide inadequate information for Congress to assess private military service contracts. However, if legislation passed in 2007 makes it into law, that may begin to change. Finally, the AECA provides only limited public information regarding unclassified contracts that may commit the nation to acts of war.

Because the AECA was drafted primarily to regulate one-time arms sales contracts, it does not provide adequate mechanisms for ongoing review of a service contract that may last for months or years.

Often, the activities of a PSC are closely integrated with direct American military involvement in the same region, and informal contacts between company employees and their active-duty counterparts abound. Close informal contacts between executive branch officials and private contractors, however, cannot substitute for strict accountability to Congress. Critics charge that congressional oversight is cursory at best. If the Department of Defense is directly involved, there is a whole network of congressional offices providing oversight. When these tasks are turned over to a contractor, the only oversight comes from a group of civil servants in the federal bureaucracy.

Moreover, the regulations under the AECA provide no ongoing oversight after an export license has been granted. This lack of public information makes it virtually impossible for the public to assess the practice of private military contracting. Such lack of public accountability would be less bothersome if the regulatory framework guaranteed adequate executive supervision and congressional oversight. But the level of review and inquiry that either branch gives to licensing decisions under the AECA is unclear.

The scarce public information that is available suggests that the current regulatory scheme, while constitutional, does not provide the same safeguards of ongoing executive review, in-depth congressional oversight, and public accountability that are applied to ventures undertaken by the U.S. military. Yet many of the same dangers to American interests are involved when private contractors do the work. The lack of public accountability is perhaps the most important issue because without it there is no way for voters to evaluate the adequacy of congressional enforcement provisions or oversight.

The task of getting information on the activities of private military contractors is made even more difficult by the existence of a presidential directive signed by Ronald Reagan on June 23, 1987, known as Executive Order 12600, Predisclosure Notification Procedures for Confidential Commercial Information. It stipulates that companies have potential veto power over Freedom of Information Act requests for copies of their contracts with the U.S. government.

Under this directive, private military contractors, as submitters of confidential commercial information, at the time the information is submitted to the federal government or a reasonable time thereafter, are permitted to designate any information whose disclosure they claim could reasonably be expected to cause substantial competitive harm.[37] This means that, before releasing any contract, a FOIA (Freedom of Information Act) officer must contact a PMC to ask whether there is any information that should be withheld because it constitutes confidential commercial information that could cause competitive harm if released. Withholding this information is allowed under Exemption 4 of the Freedom of Information Act, which states that records cannot be obtained if they contain "trade secrets and commercial or financial information obtained from a person and (are) privileged or confidential."

Over time, new rules, regulations, and laws have been passed in the United States to try to ensure accountability and oversight over private military contractors. In May 2005 the Pentagon issued new regulations for the conduct of civilian contractors who accompany soldiers overseas. In explaining changes in the rules, which were proposed in March 2004, Pentagon and industry officials said that the rules codified existing policies and informal practices but disagreed about whether they would be enough to address all the difficult issues that have arisen with the increased number of civilians, many of them armed, working in a war zone.[38]

This new regulation hardly settled the issue. In fact, it raised new questions over the legal status of contractor personnel. For example, the rules reaffirm that it is permissible for contractors—at the discretion of the combatant commander— to carry weapons in war zones such as Iraq. Yet the Pentagon also issued a notice saying, "The clause has been amended to caution that contractor personnel are not combatants and shall not undertake any role that would jeopardize that status. The clause already requires the contractor to ensure that its personnel who are authorized to carry weapons are adequately trained. That should include training not only on how to use a weapon, but when to use a weapon." The end result is that some contractors think they are combatants, whereas the Pentagon thinks they are not. So much for clarity.[39]

Of course, the companies themselves have hardly been passive actors. In 2005 Iraqi PSCs were pressing for the right to arm themselves with heavy military-style weapons. The Baghdad-based security manager of one company said he would like to see the companies equipped with 40-mm grenade launchers, shoulder-fired antitank rockets, and M72 anti-armor Vietnam holdovers or AT4 bunker busters.[40]

On May 5, 2005, the Defense Department finalized its "contractor accompanying the force" contract regulations. In addition, on October 3, 2005, it issued an internal instruction (DoD Instruction 3020.41) that established and implemented policy and guidance concerning DoD contractor personnel authorized to accompany the U.S. armed forces (referred to as "contingency contracting personnel").

On October 17, 2006, the Uniform Code of Military Justice (UCMJ) was amended, due to a measure introduced by Republican senator Lindsey Graham of South Carolina, to extend UCMJ jurisdiction over persons serving with or accompanying U.S. armed forces in the field in times of declared war or a contingency. The one-sentence section (number 552 of a total of 3,510 sections) in the FY 2007 budget legislation states that "Paragraph (10) of section 802(a) of title 10, United States Code (article 2[a] of the Uniform Code of Military Justice), is amended by striking 'war' and inserting 'declared war or a contingency operation.'"[41] Previously, contractors would fall under the Uniform Code of Military Justice only if Congress declared war.

This is significant because Congress is reluctant to issue a declaration of war anymore. In the case of *United States* v. *Averette*, the Court of Military Appeals set aside the conviction of a contractor in Saigon because the conflict in Vietnam was not technically a "time of declared war."[42] Technically, this means that contractors, like soldiers, can be disciplined, not just for felony crimes like murder that exist in the general justice system, but also for offenses such as talking back to an officer, viewing pornography in a country where it is forbidden, or even wearing a uniform incorrectly.[43]

Although this amendment has been hailed by many advocates of greater regulation over the industry, it is unclear how effective it can be. Since it has not yet been tested in court, whether it will hold up is anyone's guess. Even before the amendment passed, one military law journal noted that "attempts to use the military justice system to try civilian contractors are incompatible with the tradition of status-based military jurisdiction as well as the current Supreme Court's interpretation of the 6th Amendment."[44]

It wasn't always that way. Civilians accompanying military forces have been tried in military courts since at least the time of the American Revolution. Before the 1950 enactment of the Uniform Code of Military Justice (UCMJ), military prosecution of civilians was well established under the Articles of War, which codified military law in the early days of the American republic. Civilians were tried under this system during both world wars.[45]

The International Peace Operations Association, one of the industry's trade groups, put out a press release at the time, noting the following:

> Many American contractors providing logistics and support in Iraq once proudly served in uniform and operated under the UCMJ. But the overwhelming majority of private sector employees supporting Department of Defense programs are not even American; they come from countries such as Afghanistan, India, Iraq, the United Kingdom and scores of others. Requiring all nationalities to be under U.S. military law could be internationally contentious, and even more difficult to apply. Application of the UCMJ or any other disciplinary structure requires closer examination of the relationship to other applicable United States, Host Nation, and International Laws.[46]

Foreign PSCs questioned the amendment's effectiveness. A few months after it was passed, Mark Lonsdale, vice president and director of U.S. operations for Hart Security, a UK-based firm, said the UCMJ provision was a "knee jerk reaction" by legislators in response to pressure over contracting issues. "They don't take into account the complexity and practicality of the application," he said. "How are you going to make it work? How does it apply to expats working for US companies? How does it apply to non-US companies on DoD contracts?"[47]

On March 10, 2008, the Department of Defense released a memorandum regarding "UCMJ Jurisdiction Over DoD Civilian Employees, DoD Contractor Personnel, and Other Persons Serving With or Accompanying the Armed Forces Overseas During Declared War and in Contingency Operations." Issued nearly a year and a half after the extension of UCMJ jurisdiction in 2006, it states:

> When offenses alleged to have been committed by civilians violate U.S. federal criminal laws, the Department shall notify responsible Department of Justice (DoJ) authorities, and afford DoJ the opportunity to pursue its prosecution of the case in federal district court . . .

> While the DoJ notification and decision process is pending, commanders and military criminal investigators should continue to address the alleged crime. Commanders should ensure that any preliminary military justice procedures that would be required in support of the exercise of UCMJ jurisdiction over civilians continue to be accomplished during the concurrent DoJ notification process. Commanders should be

prepared to act, as appropriate, should possible U.S. federal criminal jurisdiction prove to be unavailable to address the alleged criminal behavior.[48]

In the early stages of the Iraqi reconstruction efforts, the Pentagon lacked standardized rules for most issues involving private contractors accompanying U.S. forces in Iraq, including whether they may carry arms.[49] Although the U.S. military, especially the Army because its troops are increasingly reliant on private companies for logistical and technical support, had compiled an extensive list of service and departmental regulations, doctrine, and field manuals to govern contractors' behavior on the battlefield, the regulations were more oriented to those providing logistical services and did not cover the newer private security firms.[50]

In more recent years the Joint Staff Operational Plans and Interoperability Office approved the development of a joint contracting and contractor publication known as JT4-10. The publication will give commanders guidance on the workings of a contracting organization and how to incorporate contractors deployed with a force into military operations. Another publication, field manual interim 4-93.41, which came out February 22, 2007, discusses a deployable Army Materiel Command unit approved in fall 2006 that assists with contractor management issues for deploying army contractors. Field manual 100-10-2, a discussion of contracting support on the battlefield, is also being rewritten. Originally published in 1999, FM 100-10-2 looks at how contractors on the battlefield are controlled and managed; the main participants in planning, managing, and providing these services in theater; and the relationship that influences contracting in a joint and multinational environment.[51]

Rules of engagement (ROE) apply to security contractors and coalition military personnel alike. Newly recruited PMC personnel are commonly handed a complete copy of the ROE set forth by the theater commander and prepared by the regional judge advocate general (JAG) office, which employees have to study and sign. They are often briefed on any changes or updates to the ROE, and the convoy leader or team leader reviews the ROE during each operations order and convoy brief.

One proposed provision to a Defense Department regulation required deployed contractors to follow combatant commanders' orders as long as those actions did not require the contractor employee to engage in armed conflict with an enemy force.[52] Those orders would supersede any existing contract terms or directions from a contracting officer.[53] That draft regulation also banned contract personnel from carrying privately owned weapons unless authorized by a military commander, as well as from wearing military uniforms. The policy allowed the combatant commander to issue weapons and ammunition to contractor employees.[54]

These changes were subsequently accepted in the DoD Regulation issued by the Pentagon on October 3, 2005, which was a significant development but not well covered in the press. This DoD Instruction 3020.41, "Contractor Personnel Authorized to Accompany the U.S. Armed Forces," was issued pursuant to a provision in the FY 2005 Defense Authorization Act. The 33-page document clarifies the legal status of civilians hired to support those forces in a contingency.[55] The new instruction also explains when contractors can carry weapons in areas where U.S. troops operate—for example, in Iraq, where armed contractors have been operating for years without clear regulatory guidance. The regulation ties together nearly 60 Pentagon directives and Joint Staff doctrinal statements that relate to the role of contractors on the battlefield.

From the viewpoint of the PMC industry and firms such as Blackwater and Triple Canopy, the new regulation is important because it establishes detailed criteria for civilian contractors to carry weapons, which are to be used only in self-defense. It also sets forth detailed procedures for arming contingency contractor personnel for security services.

However, the key question now is how it will be implemented. Companies that contract with the Pentagon are required to follow a set of rules known as the Defense Federal Acquisition Regulation Supplement (DFARS).[56] DFARS governs all aspects of contract enforcement, from accounting procedures to use of government property, and contains a section on "Contractor Standards of Conduct" covering proper behavior and a hotline for reporting improper conduct. Reportedly a number of DFARS rules were being modified to reflect the guidance in the new instruction. But it may be too difficult to retroactively implement all the rules and regulations spelled out in the policy to cover the contracts in effect in Iraq.

For regulation on the British front, the British Association of Private Security Companies (BAPSC) was formed by leading members of the private security industry to promote, enhance, and regulate the interests and activities of UK-based firms and companies that provide armed security services in countries outside the United Kingdom. The BAPSC is not as well known as its American equivalent, the International Peace Operations Association (IPOA), because it was launched only in February 2006, but given that British PSCs are second only to those headquartered in the United States in terms of overall numbers and worldwide presence, it will likely have significant influence. Furthermore, as the British government is more enthusiastic about transparency than the U.S. government, BAPSC, by virtue of its stated goal of working toward the "promotion of transparent relations with UK government departments and international organisations," may therefore be able to influence contractor–client relations to a greater degree.

Aside from the already mentioned CPA Order 17 and Memo 17, various rules and orders have been regulating PMCs in Iraq:

- A CPA Public Notice issued June 26, 2003, laid out the status of contractor personnel.
- CPA Order No. 3 on Weapons Control stated, "Private security firms may be licensed by the Ministry of Interior to possess and use licensed

Firearms and Military Weapons, excluding Special Category Weapons, in the course of their duties, including in public places."[57]
- CPA Memorandum 5, which implemented CPA Weapons Control Order No. 3, established a Weapons Authorization Program whereby individuals who can demonstrate a necessity to carry weapons may apply for temporary weapons authorization cards (TWC).[58]

SMALL ARMS: USE, TRANSPORT, AND PURCHASE OF ARMS

The arming of PMCs also raises a number of accountability, small-arms non-proliferation, and safety concerns. In Iraq, CPA rules restricted the weapons PMCs may use to small arms with ammunition as large as 7.62mm and to some other defensive weapons. However, some PMCs guarding foreign contractors and sensitive installations demanded the right to carry more powerful weapons. U.S. Army regulations allow contractors performing combat support services to carry weapons when required by their combatant commander.

It is not well appreciated that PMCs, at least in Iraq, are not the source of a significant amount of small arms and light weapons. They don't import many weapons into Iraq. Of course, companies do obtain fully automatic weapons, but they buy them in country, often, if not usually, on the street. Whatever they have they are required to register.

The previously mentioned DoD Directive 3020.41, "Contractor Personnel Authorized to Accompany the U.S. Armed Forces," has various provisions concerning small arms:

4.4.1. Subject to the approval of the geographic Combatant Commander, contingency contractor personnel may be armed for individual self-defense.

4.4.2. Contracts for security services shall be used cautiously in contingency operations where major combat operations are ongoing or imminent. Authority and armament of contractors providing private security services will be set forth in their contracts.

6.2.7.8. Weapons. Contingency contractor personnel will not be authorized to possess or carry personally owned firearms or ammunition or be armed during contingency operations except as provided under subparagraphs 6.3.4. or 6.3.5.

6.3.4. Force Protection and Weapons Issuance

. . . .

However, it may be necessary for contingency contractor personnel to be armed for individual self-defense. Procedures for arming for individual self-defense are addressed below:

6.3.4.1. According to applicable U.S., HN, and international law, relevant SOFAs or international agreements, or other arrangements with local HN authorities, on a case-by-case basis when military force protection and legitimate civil authority are deemed unavailable or insufficient, the geographic Combatant Commander (or a designee no lower than the general or flag officer level) may authorize contingency contractor personnel to be armed for individual self-defense. In such a case the Government shall provide or ensure weapons familiarization, qualifications, and briefings on the rules regarding the use of force to the contingency contractor personnel. Acceptance of weapons by contractor personnel shall be voluntary and permitted by the defense contractor and the contract. These personnel must not be otherwise prohibited from possessing weapons under U.S. law. The defense contractor shall ensure such personnel are not prohibited under U.S. law to possess firearms. When armed for personal protection, contingency contractor personnel are only authorized to use force for individual self-defense. Unless immune from HN jurisdiction by virtue of an international agreement or international law, contingency contractor personnel shall be advised of the inappropriate use of force could subject them to U.S. or HN prosecution and civil liability.

6.3.5.1. Requests for permission to arm contingency contractor personnel to provide security services shall be reviewed on a case-by-case basis by the appropriate Staff Judge Advocate to the geographic Combatant Commander to ensure there is a legal basis for approval. The request will then be approved or denied by the geographic Combatant Commander or a specifically identified designee, no lower than the general or flag officer level.

6.3.5.3.4. Documentation of individual training covering weapons familiarization, rules for the use of deadly force, limits on the use of force including whether defense of others is consistent with HN law, the distinction between the rules of engagement applicable to military forces and the prescribed rules for the use of deadly force that control the use of weapons by civilians, and the Law of Armed Conflict, including the provisions of reference (j).

6.3.5.3.5. DD Form 2760, "Qualification to Possess Firearms and Ammunitions," certifying the individual is not prohibited under U.S. law from possessing a weapon or ammunition due to conviction in any court of a crime of domestic violence whether a felony or misdemeanor.

6.3.5.3.6. Written acknowledgement by the defense contractor and individual contractor security personnel, after investigation of background and qualifications of contractor security personnel and organizations, certifying such personnel are not prohibited under U.S. law to possess firearms.

6.3.5.3.7. Written acknowledgement by the defense contractor and individual contractor security personnel that: potential civil and criminal liability exists under U.S. and HN law for the use of weapons; proof of authorization to be armed must be carried; contingency contractor personnel may possess only U.S. Government-issued and/or approved weapons and ammunition for which they have been qualified according to subparagraph 6.3.5.3.4; contract security personnel were briefed and understand limitations on the use of force; and authorization to possess weapons and ammunition may be revoked for non-compliance with established rules for the use of force.

In addition, a great many federal statutes, directives, and regulations dealing with contractors have been issued in the past few years. The Army prepared a

CONUS (Continental United States) Guide for Supporting Emergencies within the United States and Supporting Overseas Contingencies from CONUS Locations, as well as a guidebook for OCONUS (Outside CONUS).

Generally, the industry says it abides by all relevant national and international human rights laws.

Aside from international legal controls, private security firms are also accountable to the War Crimes Act of 1996, Victims of Trafficking and Violence Protection Act of 2000, Anti-Torture Statute, Defense Trade Controls Act, Arms Export Control Act, Gun Control Act, Export Administration Regulations, International Traffic in Arms Regulations, Defense Base Act, Foreign Corrupt Practices Act, Federal Aviation Regulations, Defense Federal Acquisition Regulations (DFAR), and General Orders of the Central Command, Multi-National Corps—Iraq and Combined Joint Task Force (CJTF) 76.[59]

But in 2006 Laura Dickinson, a University of Connecticut law school expert on military contractors who has worked with Amnesty International on the issue of PSC compliance on human rights, said she had studied 60 publicly available contracts of private companies working for the U.S. government in Iraq and found that none of them required employees to obey international human rights and humanitarian laws, provisions that could easily be added to government contracts.[60]

In Iraq the problem for PMCs has not been a lack of relevant laws, but of means. Regulations existed but were not implemented because the relevant administration existed mainly on paper. The legal infrastructure was shattered. The Ministry of Interior, for example, simply did not have the means to handle the paperwork and could not enforce the laws.

The real impact of this problem has largely been lost in public discussion. People have overlooked the fact that, without immunity, security contractors simply were not going to work in Iraq because of the likelihood that their employees would be subjected to arbitrary legal treatment. In addition, without immunity their insurers were threatening to jack up their premiums to a level they could not afford. Furthermore, because there is no status of forces agreement in place, it has never been clear in what venue legal proceedings against a contractor might take place. Such uncertainty was another reason for giving contractors immunity.

However, from a historical perspective, such concern may be unwarranted. A status of forces agreement (SOFA) generally provides immunity to contractor personnel. Some of the SOFAs drawn up for U.S. forces include protection for contractors working on behalf of the U.S. Defense Department. For example, the U.S. government linked its aid package to Colombia, a signatory of the International Criminal Court (ICC), to an agreement to exempt American military personnel and contractors from the ICC's jurisdiction.[61]

Still, the impact of all the above is ambiguous. Theoretically, even with the immunity granted by CPA Memorandum 17, contractors could still be prosecuted under various legal authorities, especially the Military Extraterritorial Jurisdiction Act. But, until recently, federal prosecutors were not that interested in using it, and local prosecutors in the states where PMCs are headquartered, and for whom MEJA holds greater relevance, normally do not have sufficient resources to use it.

Despite these rules and regulations, it is unlikely that the activities of PMCs in Iraq, numerous as they are, offer many permanent lessons for the industry as a whole. From an industry perspective, nobody believes that there is going to be another Iraq. The United States could not intervene in another country on the same scale as Operation Iraqi Freedom, even if it wanted to. The industry recognizes that whatever contracts they get in the future are going to be in countries and situations that will be quite different from those in Iraq.

There have been numerous problems with accountability of private contractors of all kinds. Consider these excerpts from a study released in February 2006 by the special inspector general for Iraq reconstruction:

> The U.S. government also experienced shortcomings in accounting for personnel deployed to Iraq—especially civilians and contractors. There was, and still is, a lack of effective control procedures at many entry and exit points for Iraq, and there is no interagency personnel tracking system. Official and contract personnel often arrived and departed with no systematic tracking of their whereabouts or activities, or in some cases, with no knowledge of their presence in country. Shortly before its dissolution in June 2004, CPA was still unable to account for 10% of its staff in Iraq.
>
> Mechanisms to track contractors supporting CPA have been left largely to the contractors' individual firms and have not been enforced.[62]

The most important factor in the risk-management trade is choosing and training the right people. PMCs generally subject potential employees to rigorous vetting.[63] But although PMCs usually have codes of conduct for their staff, government agencies do not uniformly check these codes. Thus although contractors to the U.S. government are theoretically liable to prosecution, as yet this has never happened. Disciplining contractor personnel is seen as the contractor's responsibility.

The CPA set some initial minimum standards for regulating PMCs, and subsequently the Iraqi Ministries of Interior and Trade adopted new mandatory guidelines to vet and register PMCs.

While the Iraqi government is, in a *de jure* sense, in charge, especially since the end of the Coalition Provisional Authority and handover of sovereignty back to the Iraqi government, it is a sovereignty that is still largely theoretical, given the challenges posed by the insurgency and the Iraqi government's lack of resources. Thus, from the viewpoint of the PMC sector, doing business with the relevant Iraqi ministries is extremely difficult.[64] Currently, there is nobody in the Iraqi Interior Ministry who can issue a Weapons Authorization Card. This means that security contractors are using a variety of IDs, making their own, or using none at all. When you have a variety of identification documents, there is no credibility, which undermines the point of trying to regulate.

Things become more complex when international law is considered. If nothing else, the rise of the private military sector has been good for future lawyers. In recent years articles in law journals about the relevance, or nonrelevance, of Geneva Conventions and other international laws to the PSC sector have become a veritable cottage industry.

As I am not a lawyer, a comprehensive treatment of the legal issues is beyond the scope of this book, but a few thoughts are in order.

Under the authority of international law, contractors working with the military are civilian noncombatants whose conduct may be attributable to the United States, but they may be held accountable under laws that apply extraterritorially or within the special maritime and territorial jurisdiction of the United States.

It may seem rhetorical, but it is still an unsettled question whether the duties of contractors amount to "taking an active part in hostilities." Under international law only members of regular armed forces and paramilitary groups that come under military command and meet certain criteria (carry their weapons openly, distinguish themselves from civilians, and generally obey the laws of war) qualify as combatants.

Thus, because contract employees fall outside the military chain of command, even those who appear to meet the criteria as combatants could be at risk of losing their right to be treated as POWs if captured by the enemy.

The Geneva Conventions and other laws of war do not appear to forbid the use of civilian contractors in a civil police role in occupied territory, in which case they might be authorized to use force when absolutely necessary to defend persons or property. But given the fluid nature of the current security situation in Iraq, it is sometimes difficult to discern whether civilian security guards are performing law enforcement duties or are engaged in combat.

If their activity amounts to combat, they become lawful targets for lawful enemy forces during the fighting, and, if captured by such forces or an enemy government (if one should emerge), they could potentially be prosecuted as criminals for their hostile acts.

Some have suggested that the International Criminal Court (ICC) is an appropriate venue given the instances of questionable actions and outright support or involvement in human rights abuses worldwide. Further, international courts are the most appropriate bodies to pronounce on serious breaches of international law because "they are in a better position to understand and apply international law."[65]

The upside to using the ICC is that it is an already established, though still new, international court that is prepared to investigate and try international crimes of great magnitude. The court can investigate crimes of such character, which may involve gathering evidence and witnesses from various nations. Additionally, international judges may be relatively impartial because they are not engaged by the state for which the illegal actions were committed.

Second, prosecution by the ICC would lead to the development of precedential and uniform case law regarding PSC employees. In contrast, proceedings in various national courts might lead to disparity both in the interpretation and application of that law and the penalties given to those found guilty. An international criminal trial might bring the problems of PSCs to light more so than a national trial.

Initiating prosecutions for the first time against some individual employees of PSCs (non-U.S. nationals), however, could prompt the United States to prosecute abuses by the PSC itself. The ICC is based on complementarity; that is, it only acts when a nation is unwilling or unable to prosecute individuals. In this instance, the United States seems unwilling to prosecute, perhaps out of fear of disturbing its contractual obligations with PSCs. Perhaps its desire to prevent the ICC from prosecuting individuals could prompt it into action.

The downside is that although the ICC could provide justice by prosecuting individual employees of the PSCs, it most likely will only be able to assert jurisdiction over non-U.S. nationals. The United States has signed bilateral treaties with over 80 nations (37 of which are ICC parties) to prevent them from delivering U.S. nationals or U.S. employees to the ICC. Another problem is that there is notable political opposition to the ICC, not only by the United States, but also by China, Russia, Israel, and India. These countries cite fears of politically motivated prosecutions and encroachment on sovereignty. Given this lack of support, not only will the ICC face hurdles in establishing jurisdiction, as discussed, but also enforcement may be a problem, since it depends on the cooperation of nations.

7

Conclusions

It is extremely difficult to generalize about private military and security firms. As an industry, or at least, business sector, PMCs have been around for less than 20 years. And although they have attracted growing attention from analysts, scholars, governments, and the general public in the past decade, there are still no agreements on how to define them, let alone categorize them.

Iraq elevated world attention on the role of PMCs to new heights. Reliance on PMCs increased greatly after the initial major combat operations phase, mainly because of two factors. First, the U.S. political leadership grossly underestimated the number of troops that would be required for stability and security operations. Ignoring the advice of its own military professionals, the Bush administration chose to invade with far fewer forces than were needed. As a result, companies such as Halliburton were needed just to meet the military logistics requirements of sustaining U.S. and other coalition forces.

Second, as part of the U.S. plan to bring democracy to the Middle East, Iraq was to be remade into a new country. This required a massive reconstruction project to overcome the effects of over two decades of war, against Iran and then the United States, as well as the consequences of the sanctions regime. But once again the U.S. administration miscalculated and did not anticipate the emergence and growth of the insurgency. Since U.S. forces were not available to protect those doing reconstruction work, such firms had no choice but to turn to private security contractors to protect their employees. Put another way, while PMCs provide valuable services in Iraq, monumentally poor planning created the need for them; these are not exactly the market conditions the industry can or should count on in the future.

Much of the public image of PMCs is based on perceptions that are woefully out of date, such as the activities of now-defunct groups like Executive Outcomes and Sandline.[1] Specifically, many people still think that companies undertake direct offensive combat operations such as Executive Outcomes did in Angola and Sierra Leone, which is simply not the case. They also think that the various PMCs operating in Iraq constitute a cohesive army, second only in size to the American forces there.

What is worth remembering about PMCs in Iraq is that most of what you think you know is wrong. The private security sector there is very diverse. Yes, there are thousands of Westerners carrying arms, but there are also more host nationals, such as Iraqis and third-country nationals, doing the same. Some PMCs are more low key than others in using force, but, in general, they are more disciplined and experienced than their active-duty counterparts. And their function varies depending on what the contract calls for. While the common theme for a security contractor is providing security and protection, it can take many different forms, ranging from static security for buildings and infrastructure to security details for officials and reconstruction workers.

The role and impact of private actors in providing security vary significantly according to context. Obviously, in the case of Iraq, the provision of personal security, primarily for people doing reconstruction work but also for protecting infrastructure, has been the top priority, especially given the dangers caused by the insurgency. This has put groups like DynCorp, Triple Canopy, Erinys, Hart Group, Control Risks, ArmorGroup, and Aegis Defence squarely in the public eye.

But as time goes by and the new Iraqi government seeks to establish, consolidate, and expand its powers, personal protection will assume less of a role. As Iraqi military and paramilitary forces assume security functions and as the reconstruction effort draws to a close, the emphasis will be on the training and professionalization of those forces, something the United States did not get serious about until 2005. While the U.S. military has taken back some of the responsibility for training Iraqi military forces that it originally outsourced out of dissatisfaction with the way it was being done, other PMCs—notably DynCorp, which has the contract for training Iraqi police—will continue to play a prominent role in reforming that aspect of the Iraqi security sector.

PMCs have provided three main categories of services in Iraq:

- Personal security details for senior civilian officials
- Nonmilitary site security (buildings and infrastructure)
- Nonmilitary convoy security

Breaking these categories down, say, in terms of tasks done by contractor, is no easy task. In fact, it would take an organization, for the simple reason that a contractor can do more than one task and offer more than one capability.

Military consulting firms, in particular, are capable of offering a wide variety of service.

Moreover, if they don't have the capability in hand when they win a contract, they simply go out and hire it. That is the same approach used by most conventional contractors in the military industrial and national security realms. While it affords them great flexibility in competing for contracts, it makes classifying them very difficult.

Earlier, PMCs also were involved in the retraining of Iraqi security forces, but because of problems and the increasing challenges posed by the insurgency, this task was been taken back by American military forces. However, contractors are still involved in training the Iraqi police.

Rather than working directly for the U.S. government or even the Coalition Provisional Authority (CPA) when it existed, most PMCs were and are subcontracted to provide protection for prime contractor employees or are hired by other entities such as Iraqi companies or private foreign companies seeking business opportunities in Iraq. This obviously makes PMC accountability difficult. One past Congressional Research Service report noted:

> Details of the CPA contracts and related subcontracts are not public information. This has led to questions concerning the cost-effectiveness of the contracts as well as of any obligations of the contractors under the contracts regarding the use of force. According to the CPA, "subcontracted PSCs and their parent companies generally do not make available details concerning the prices of their contracts, salaries, or numbers of employees," because "such information is proprietary and may have privacy implications. . . ." Some analysts suspect that at least a few of the contracts may detail "rules of engagement" under which contracted personnel are permitted to use their weapons as a means of protecting the personnel and other assets of the companies performing reconstruction work, as there currently is no legal framework governing the use of private weapons in Iraq.[2]

That somewhat overstates the issue of PMC accountability in Iraq. In fact, companies did and do provide enormous levels of detail on their contracts to government contracting officers. The problem is that the Bush administration has been particularly reluctant, for whatever reason, to share that information with Congress. In fact, at the time of the turnover of sovereignty to the Iraq government, the CPA gave an enormous amount of personal data on PMC employees, such as names, addresses, and contact information, to the Iraqi government, which, arguably, was a violation of the 1974 Privacy Act.[3] Furthermore, Coalition Provisional Authority Memorandum 17 required companies to provide detailed information as a condition of receiving a license to operate.

The lack of security in postwar Iraq created an enormous demand for PMC services. At least 10 to 15 cents of every dollar spent on reconstruction is for security, according to the inspector general for the CPA.[4] Other reports indicate that the cost of security was at times much higher, approaching 50 percent.[5]

Certainly, PMCs have not lacked for business. In February 2006 the British government disclosed that it had spent more than GBP £100 million on private security companies in Iraq since the 2003 invasion. U.K. Foreign Office minister Kim Howells said, "The total contractual costs of private security companies contracted to the Foreign and Commonwealth Office and operating in Iraq, between April 2003 and December 2005, was £110,342,718."[6]

Certainly, some PMCs have done very well financially.[7] A joint investigation by Corporate Watch, an independent watchdog, and *The Independent* newspaper found that British businesses have profited by at least £1.1 billion since coalition forces toppled Saddam Hussein. Among the top earners were Aegis Defence Services, which has earned more than £246 million from a three-year contract with the Pentagon to coordinate military and security companies in Iraq, and Erinys, which has won contracts for more than £86 million.[8]

In early February 2006 the British press reported that Aegis Defence had seen turnover rise more than 100-fold in three years thanks to its security contracts in Iraq. According to its CEO, Tim Spicer, turnover in 2005 was £62 million, of which three-quarters came from work in Iraq. In 2003, the firm's first full year of operation, turnover was £554,000.

Given that the U.S. military is reluctant to take on any new missions while trying both to turn responsibilities over to Iraqi military and security forces and to reduce its own presence, it is likely that any reconstruction efforts—and the Bush administration has decided to establish more reconstruction teams in Iraq's provinces to coordinate U.S. aid and fortify local governments—will provide PMCs with additional business opportunities.[9]

Some believe that Iraqis prefer foreigners for critical security tasks because international staff are harder to bribe or threaten (via vulnerable family members).[10] However, using foreigners risks strengthening distrust of Iraqi government institutions, such as the police and security services. And ultimately, only a capable, autonomous government can provide the day-to-day security that is so desperately needed in Iraq.

From a PMC perspective, most activities have been of a tactical, not a strategic, nature. That is, their day-to-day actions are not serving to transform the overall political, military, and social environments in which they operate. Their actions are mostly straightforward. The one possible way in which PMCs could help effect a strategic change would be in the training program of Iraqi military and security forces. The creation of competent, professional, and trusted forces will be essential for the formation of a central government, which is necessary if there is to be a future state of Iraq.

In that regard DynCorp International was prominent for its hiring of police officers in the United States to train police recruits in Iraq. Training was also conducted by Vinnell Corp. or one of its subcontractors.[11] Unfortunately, there is at least some reason to doubt how effective PMCs have been in this regard.[12] For example, Vinnell, helped train the new Iraqi Army. But Vinnell was viewed as having performed badly.

Some problems, however, were beyond the contractors' control. For one thing, the U.S. administration in Baghdad balked at paying the recruits more than about $70 a month, minimum wage even in Iraqi, where at least $200 is needed for a comfortable middle-class lifestyle.

But some said that Vinnell erred in that it based its techniques on its 25-year experience in training the Saudi Arabian National Guard, a relatively well-paid, well-educated fighting force that bore little resemblance to the unskilled recruits fresh off the streets of Baghdad.

Some U.S. military officials complained that the contractors had put too much emphasis on classroom studies of strategy and tactics and not enough on basic combat skills. Another problem was objections from Iraqi officials, who asked why Iraq should pay U.S. contractors to train police when France and Germany were reportedly offering such services for free. They also said it was a waste of money to hire contractors to build a training facility in Jordan when there were plenty of facilities in Iraq.

A more important problem was that Iraq's security situation became so precarious that police officers in outlying areas were afraid to travel to Baghdad or Jordan for training. From the perspective of providing security, for Iraqi society PMCs play only a small part. The true center of gravity would be the reconstruction effort itself. Unfortunately, there is reason to believe that that effort has been as badly bungled as the planning for postinvasion military operations was.[13]

Simply put, in Iraq PMCs can be divided into two types: those with guns and those without. The difference is between a security contractor and a logistic contractor. Inevitably, a security contractor is someone who has used weapons for a living, sometimes someone who has worked in law enforcement but usually someone with prior military experience. Of course, the two are not mutually exclusive; many former military personnel go into law enforcement after discharge. They are familiar with being in combat, taking and receiving fire, and living in harsh conditions.

The logistics category includes employees of the big companies such as Halliburton and its Kellogg, Brown & Root subsidiary. These are the people driving supply trucks, setting up and staffing U.S. military bases, running the mess halls and laundry services, and doing all the usual logistics that a regular military force requires. While this is an immense operation and costs many billions of dollars, it has virtually nothing to do with security or security sector reform in Iraq. It is simply the most recent iteration of the military subcontracting phenomenon.

It is often said that such firms are more cost-effective and efficient than the public sector, but the simple truth is that nobody knows for sure.[14] There are no empirical data to confirm such assertions, and there has been enough evidence of cost overruns, inflated invoices, fraud, and abuse to be somewhat skeptical.

What this implies is that whether or not a PMC is cost-effective will depend heavily on how the contract between the client and PMC is structured and what incentives it contains.[15]

Scholar Deborah Avant put it well:

> The nature of the task determines whether private contractors or civil servants will be most cost effective. Contracting makes sense if a government knows exactly what it wants and cares more about the ends than the means. Sometimes contracting can even force discipline on the government, leading to a better specification of its goals. On the other hand, if the government cares about means and wants its agents to follow a set of guidelines for how to go about providing a service, civil servants—geared to follow instructions—are superior. Furthermore, the effect of privatization is "highly dependent upon the wider market, regulatory, and institutional environment in which it is implemented."[16]

PSCs have not been immune from the corruption more commonly linked with their PMC brethren.[17] An auditing board sponsored by the United Nations recommended that the United States repay as much as $208 million to the Iraqi government for contracting work in 2003 and 2004 assigned to Kellogg, Brown & Root, the Halliburton subsidiary. The work was paid for with Iraqi oil proceeds, but the board said it was either carried out at inflated prices or done poorly.[18] As of the December 28, 2005 meeting of the International Advisory and Monitoring Board (IAMB) for Iraq, there had been no recommendation to repay the money.[19] However, the overall cost of the KBR work was subsequently reduced by $9 million.[20]

The prosecution of Custer Battles was a case in point. The trial in February 2006 was notable for being the first civil fraud case against a U.S. contractor accused of war profiteering in Iraq: specifically, bilking the U.S. government out of $50 million. It pitted two whistleblowers against two former Army officers whose company, Custer Battles LLC, won multimillion-dollar contracts in the aftermath of the fall of Saddam Hussein in 2003. The case generated extensive media coverage, including a segment on *60 Minutes,* because of the seriousness of the fraud charges and because it became the first test of whether the federal False Claims Act applies to the conduct of contractors working in Iraq. Court filings in the Custer Battles case detailed how CPA officials in Baghdad were ill-equipped to write, much less oversee, the processing of millions of dollars in contracts. On March 9, 2006, the federal jury found Custer Battles guilty and ordered it to pay more than $10 million in damages and fines. It found that Custer Battles committed fraud in 37 instances in connection with a $9 million contract to help distribute new currency in Iraq. It was found guilty of defrauding the Coalition Provisional Authority of millions of dollars.[21]

The impact of private military and security contractors in Iraq has been mixed.[22] Their impact varies according to who is viewing their activities—the

U.S. military, civilians doing reconstruction work, other U.S. government agencies, the Iraqi government, or Iraqi civilians.

If you are a logistics contractor whose life was saved by a security contractor during an attack by insurgents, you naturally think they are worth their weight in gold. If you were a prisoner at Abu Ghraib who suffered physical and emotional abuse, or perhaps outright torture, by a contract interrogator, you think they are scum. Since we do not have a full accounting of the actions of all contractors operating in Iraq, it is impossible to determine where the balance lies between positive and negative assessments.

Yet even granting that much of the criticism of PSC is sensationalistic and ill–informed, their actions in Iraq to date raise serious strategic questions about the impact of their use. A Brookings Institution study noted that their use

Allows policymakers to dodge key decisions that carry political costs, thus leading to operational choices that might not reflect public interest.

Enables a "bigger is better" approach to operations that runs contrary to the best lessons of U.S. military strategy. Turning logistics and operations into a for-profit endeavor helped feed the "Green Zone" mentality problem of sprawling bases, which runs counter everything General Petraeus pointed to as necessary to winning a counterinsurgency in the new Army/USMC manual he helped write.

Inflames popular opinion against, rather than for, the American mission through operational practices that ignore the fundamental lessons of counterinsurgency. As one set of contractors described. "Our mission is to protect the principal at all costs. If that means pissing off the Iraqis, too bad."

Participated in a series of abuses that have undermined efforts at winning "hearts and minds" of the Iraqi people. The pattern of contractor misconduct extends back to 2003 and has involved everything from prisoner abuse and "joyride" shootings of civilians to a reported incident in which a drunken Blackwater contractor shot dead the security guard of the Iraqi Vice President, after the two got into an argument on Christmas Eve, 2006.

Weakened American efforts in the "war of ideas" both inside Iraq and beyond. As one Iraqi government official explained even before the recent shootings, "They are part of the reason for all the hatred that is directed at Americans, because people don't know them as Blackwater, they know them only as Americans. They are planting hatred, because of these irresponsible acts."

Reveals a double standard towards Iraqi civilian institutions that undermines efforts to build up these very same institutions, another key lesson of counterinsurgency. As one Iraqi soldier said of Blackwater. "They are more powerful than the government. No one can try them. Where is the government in this?"

Forced policymakers to jettison strategies designed to win the counterinsurgency on multiple occasions, before they even had a chance to succeed. The U.S. Marine plan for counterinsurgency in the Sunni Triangle was never implemented, because of uncoordinated contractor decisions in 2004 that helped turn Fallujah into a rallying point of the insurgency.[23]

Though it is not popular to acknowledge it, accountability of and control over private military and security companies have, at least in a few countries, actually been a pressing concern for several years. In South Africa attempts to regulate have been largely legislative. The problem with South African legislation is that the government views PMC activity with suspicion. Since many South Africans working in this sector had their formative military experience in the apartheid era, the government often views them as potential troublemakers, both in other countries and at home.

The United States, in sharp contrast, increasingly views PMCs as part of the total force. Just like the old American Express credit card ad, nowadays the U.S. military can't leave home without them. Its concerns, bolstered by its experience in Iraq to date, tend to be administrative: how to ensure coordination between theater commanders and PMCs, how to prosecute PMC personnel if they commit a crime, how to ensure common standards for issuing and implementing contracts.

If one believes that U.S. forces may remain in Iraq for many years to come, as some politicians such as Senator John McCain have suggested, it seems that PSCs will become even more important to coalition forces than at present. If that is the case, the following suggestions merit consideration.[24]

1. Establish an Army-controlled Force Protection Command (FPC) for PSCs. The U.S. Multi-National Force–Iraq (MNF-I) should consolidate PSCs into a unified DoD-backed organization: security companies could be placed directly under the command of a field-grade officer assigned to MNF-I, with appropriate liaison staff big enough to support the needs and operations of all PSCs. This provisional FPC would be assigned the job of organizing, supporting, and regulating all PSC personnel in Iraq and making them accountable under a commissioned military commander.

2. Standardize the entire FPC force. The FPC could transform the PSC world in Iraq into a unified entity instead of dozens of individual companies guarding their own interests and those of their clients. In fact, in Iraq, the principal client is the U.S. government. All security contracts would be managed and contracted by MNF-I, including those of the State Department. Having these contract forces, MNF-I would oversee and be responsible for the protection of all U.S. activities in Iraq. Only companies willing to put their men under the FPC chain of command and meet the Army's standards would be awarded contracts.

3. Dispel the mercenary myth. As long as PSCs operate as commercial entities for commercial reasons of the owners, they will be viewed as mercenaries—mistrusted by U.S. forces and vilified in the press. A strict military command watching over, directing, and integrated with them will help dispel that myth.

4. End the mass contracting of third-country nationals (TCNs). Over time most detractors came to regard PSCs as mercenaries, especially those

bringing in large numbers of third-country nationals. TCNs were brought in largely because they would work for low wages and were ethnically distinct from the Iraqis. With the exception of a few companies that have used ex-British army Gurkhas and United Nations–trained Fijians for years, the recent trend is to strip third world armies of full battalions in order to be the lowest bidder. It lends a bit of truth to accusations that MNF-I is paying foreign mercenaries.

5. Implement strict accountability. The immunity granted to PSCs by Ambassador Bremer's CPA Order 17 should be revoked completely. It should not be expected or welcomed by the private security community. To be able to act with complete impunity encourages rogue individuals and unscrupulous entities to enter Iraq with the intent to "get some and get paid" rather than perform the mission professionally. There have been no prosecutions to date of PSCs involved in questionable shootings or even outright murder. A "What happens in Baghdad, stays in Baghdad" mentality blurs the line between the rogues and the professionals.

6. Make PSCs an integral part of the strategy, legally. Congress needs to introduce legislation that would essentially force professionalism and transparency on PSCs. This legislation would also place them in a legally binding framework and protect them under the Geneva Conventions. It should also serve as a reminder that they are being paid to represent the interests of the ultimate paying client, the American people. Of course, amending international law is not done easily, so the sooner this is started the better.

CONGRESS

During the first couple of years of PMC activity in Iraq, aside from a few members who mostly grandstanded on the issue, focusing on the misdeeds by Halliburton and KBR, there was not a lot of sustained attention paid to the issue of control and accountability of PMCs. This is bad because most firms in the industry welcome reasonable proposals in that area.

However, benign neglect is no longer a problem. In the past couple of years it seems you couldn't throw a stone in Congress without hitting a member speaking about or proposing legislation on the private military and security sector.

In April 2005 Rep. David Price (D-N.C.) reintroduced a proposed Transparency and Accountability in Security Contracting Act that would set disclosure guidelines and standards for private security firms. The first version of the bill failed the previous year during the presidential campaign, at a time when the Republicans were especially sensitive to questions about U.S. operations in Iraq.[25]

In 2005 the "Contractors on the Battlefield Regulatory Act," was part of the House-passed fiscal year 2006 National Defense Authorization Act. That title required the geographic combatant commander to plan and communicate with those contractors who are "accompanying the force" and to also reach out to those contractors "not accompanying the force" to share information about the threat environment and to communicate with both groups as much as possible. Although this title was not enacted as part of the final conference agreement, the statement of managers accompanying the conference report directed the Defense Department to review all relevant policy, guidance, and instructions to address security issues raised by contractors not accompanying the force, as well as to specifically address five enumerated issues, including integrated planning and communication of relevant threat information.

In May 2006 the Pentagon issued a revision of its policies designed to ensure that U.S. forces and the private contractors that accompany them adhere to the laws and treaties that govern their actions in overseas missions. The new policy was the first update since the United States launched major counterterrorist missions in 2001.

The "DOD Law of War Program" directive was signed May 9, 2006, by Deputy Defense Secretary Gordon England. It updates the policies and responsibilities set forth in a 1998 policy designed to ensure that the Defense Department complies with the Geneva Conventions; it also provides guidance for reporting violations committed by or against U.S. personnel.

The document states that work statements for civilians employed by private firms hired by the military must stipulate that "contractors comply with the policies contained in this directive." These firms also are "required to institute and implement effective programs to prevent violations of the law of war by their employees and subcontractors, including law of war training and dissemination."[26]

LESSONS LEARNED

Like the Chinese ideogram for crisis, the use of PMCs in Iraq represents not only crisis but also opportunity. Their activities in Iraq have made public a number of issues that heretofore concerned only academics, some journalists, and people inside the industry. These include working both for and with regular military forces, recruiting qualified personnel, maintaining high standards of training, not undercutting civil–military relations, ensuring proper competition in awarding contracts, auditing contracts, and ensuring public control and accountability over them, especially regarding the use of force.

With the advantage of hindsight, it seems clear that a lack of strategic planning affected private sector operations in Iraq in the same way it affected the regular U.S. military.

Normally, the responsibility for protecting embassy personnel and nongovernmental contractors falls to the State Department's Bureau of Diplomatic Security, which had regional security officers embedded in every government agency. In postconflict situations, these security officers normally work with U.S. Embassy Marine guards and local police. But back in 2003 and 2004, the police barely existed and U.S. military units were stretched to the breaking point. Indeed, around the time of President Bush's "mission accomplished" speech on the deck of the aircraft carrier *Abraham Lincoln*, a Rand Corp. study concluded that, based on the postwar history of Germany and Japan, Washington would need a minimum of 500,000 troops to rebuild Iraq. But coalition forces numbered only 211,000. Because the Pentagon refused to increase troop levels, the State Department was forced to sign contracts with dozens of private security firms.[27]

PMCs were badly coordinated and were not given sufficient early warning before the war about how much their service would be needed. Both the U.S. and U.K. military failed to realize the extent to which they would become reliant on PMCs after the invasion. Rear area security, perimeter security, and highway escort of supplies were once the domain of the military police and light infantry units. They now largely belong to PMCs.

It was not until the military hired a company to protect a U.S. general did it realize how useful PMCs could be. This is understandable: no one really understood what PMCs were about, and no one foresaw what was coming in terms of the insurgency. The U.K. military also failed to engage with U.K. civilian police, who later played a very important role in training local police in forensic duties.[28]

Even without hindsight, it is clear that some things should have been done that weren't. The U.S. Project and Contracting Office,[29] formerly called the Program Management Office, which manages the $18.4 billion from the United States to Iraq to support the reconstruction of Iraq's infrastructure, should have been established before the war. Similarly, the contract awarded to Aegis Defence to provide security on all major Iraqi government projects should have been foreseen before the war.

Although it is true that the private sector can scale up and adapt faster than the regular military, it is also true that the Pentagon's oversight mechanisms could not be scaled up as quickly. The shortened timeframe meant hasty tendering of contracts, which denied both the contracting PMC and the awarding organization the necessary time to make careful decisions. In addition, with the explosion of companies within the industry in Iraq and the reduced timeframes for tenders, those awarding contracts had insufficient information about the companies tendering for contracts. This was exacerbated by that fact that those awarding the contracts often had little experience of the industry or of their own organizations' security needs.[30]

Iraq also shows that some flexibility in contract pricing and delivery is required. Some fixed-price contracts, for example, have led to underbidding by less reputable companies (whereas their more reputable counterparts have given more realistic bids to include costs to cover deterioration in the security situation).[31]

PMCs also need a better understanding of the basic laws and regulations of the country they operate in. When, as in the case of Iraq, they are under contract to the U.S. government, this becomes a governmental responsibility. Some of the big companies do have a clear understanding of their legal responsibilities when operating in foreign countries. They operate around the world and understand that they are accountable to national regulation. Indeed, on one occasion ArmorGroup

took the unprecedented step of removing the scene of an accident back to the
United Kingdom so that forensic experts could determine the cause of death of
one of their employees. The scene was a hut that they had dismantled and shipped
back to the United Kingdom because the local police were unable or unwilling to
do anything about the death.[32]

There are, however, things that can be done to improve the situation. For
example, regulation can be strengthened through contract law. And outside the
marketplace there are additional legal changes that can be contemplated.

Several cases have come to light in which security contractor personnel in
Iraq turned out to be unqualified, both professionally and ethically. Though there
were far fewer of these cases than is often casually asserted in media reports,
there were enough to warrant concern.

A number of measures could be introduced to prevent this from happening,
such as increasing the number of regulators and screening PMC personnel earlier
and better. If PMCs were required to keep a register of their staff, some form of
periodical review by government inspectors would be possible, with less intrusive
oversight for those companies with a good record (as is currently the case with
export licensing). Alternatively, a purely voluntary regulatory approach might be
considered, with companies solely responsible for carrying out their own background checks, but with a system of financial and criminal penalties in place as a
"backstop" for when transgressions come to light.

Finally, lawmakers could try to tackle areas where they consider that outsourcing has gone too far, such as the use of contractors for interrogations.
Although the key consideration should be whether someone is qualified and operating legally, the reality is that some positions, such as interrogators, are simply
too sensitive to be outsourced.

AUDITING[33]

On the U.S. side, Congress should bring in auditors from other governmental agencies, such as the inspector general offices of the various military services.
If past GAO reports tell us anything, it is that too few contract officers are trying
to manage vast numbers of contracts worth billions of dollars, with predictable
results.

If private military and security contractors are motivated by patriotism, as
well as by the mighty dollar, they should welcome oversight of the way the government spends taxpayers' money. Besides, if you take the king's shilling, you
must take the king's auditor, too.

We need to be honest here. Contractors do this work for the same reason
Willie Sutton robbed banks, because that is where the money is. Anyone who tells
you otherwise is a liar. And anyone who believes it is a fool.

In the end it is all about showing the money. There is nothing wrong with
that. In a capitalist society it is foolish to expect people to voluntarily risk serious

wounds or death, when they are not in the regular military, on the basis of love of country.

The problem is that it is a government doling out the money—specifically, the U.S. government. And when the spigots to the U.S. treasury can be turned on by various contractors, then you better be sure to move quickly out of the way lest you be trampled by the resulting stampede.

Anytime a government starts awarding hundreds of billions of dollars in contracts, you must have one thing in place before you start signing contracts, and that is financial oversight. In a word, you need auditors—lots of them; you also need experienced ones.

It has long been a dirty little secret that the private military industry has far too few contracting officers, and of those it does have, there are not enough with significant experience. Moreover, those who do have experience are about to retire. This in itself is scandalous, given that military contract management has long been known to be a high-risk area. As John P. Hutton, director, Acquisition and Sourcing Management of the Government Accountability Office, testified to Congress in May 2007, "It was 15 years ago that GAO identified DOD contract management to be high-risk because of its vulnerability to fraud, waste, abuse, and mismanagement. Now, while DOD has acknowledged its vulnerabilities and taken some actions to address them, many of the initiatives are still in the early stages."[34]

According to Pentagon statistics and GAO reports, the Defense Department's civilian acquisition workforce has shrunk by about 40 percent since the early 1990s and now has about 270,000 employees, even while defense spending on service contracts increased 78 percent, to $151 billion, from 1996 to 2006. In 2007 there were 7.5 million federal contractors, 1.5 million more than in 2002, without a corresponding increase in government officials to oversee them.[35]

In case anyone had any doubts about the state of contractor management, they were answered by an Army commission report released in November 2007. The independent Commission on Army Acquisition and Program Management in Expeditionary Operations found significant failures in the Army's contracting and contract management.[36] Among other things, it found that contracting personnel received no on-the-job training until after they had been shipped out to war zones like Iraq and Afghanistan.[37]

The commission suggested improvements to the Army's contracting personnel, the reorganization of contracting in expeditionary operations and at home, training for contracting activities, and getting external assistance to ensure contracting efficiency. It also recommended that the Pentagon add up to 2,000 military and civilian contract officers, strengthen the Defense Contract Management Agency, overhaul its personnel system, and reform its procurement procedures.

Although the military gets it, the White House still seems clueless. Among the 2887 sections of the 2008 National Defense Authorization Act that President Bush signed into law in early 2008 were four provisions that, according to president, "purport to impose requirements that could inhibit the president's ability to

carry out his constitutional obligations to take care that the laws be faithfully executed, to protect national security." So his approval came with a catch: a signing
statement in which he reserved the right to ignore them. Perhaps only in the Bush
administration can protecting the American taxpayer against graft and fraud be
seen as endangering national security.

Two of these provisions were aimed at private security firms accused of
wartime abuses. One would establish an independent, bipartisan Commission on
Wartime Contracting. This was actually endorsed by no less an official than the
Pentagon's inspector general, who told Congress in a November meeting, "We're
leaning forward in the saddle, we're committed to this."

The other provision Bush waived would extend whistleblower protections to
employees of defense contractors. A whistleblower, by the way, was how the
Custer Battles fraud was revealed.

To do so would be a mistake. Experience has shown that without sufficient
auditors, private military and security contracting will, like every other industry,
continue to attract fraudsters and con men from every corner.

RECRUITMENT

PMCs should take steps to ensure that the personnel recruited from third
countries receive the same notification and training as those recruited from the
PMC home country. And PMCs should prescreen far more people than they currently do, even if it means added expense. The role of government in screening
also needs to be reviewed and strengthened.

Another strong tool for regulating PMC behavior is economic. The
lifeblood of PMCs is profit. If they can't make money, they don't exist. Thus,
creating financial disincentives should be a priority. For example, firms that
have overcharged the government in the past or have committed crimes in the
contracting process should not be hired. In that regard the guilty verdict against
Custer Battles for fraud, even though the verdict was overturned, was an
encouraging precedent.[38]

Most international law relevant to the subject was developed with mercenaries in mind. Contemporary private military and security firms assert, and right-
fully so, that what they do is not at all the same and that it is wrong to label them
mercenaries.

Contrary to popular wisdom, it is possible to think of extending court-martial
jurisdiction to civilian contractors; currently this is not the case, as one West Point
law professor has written.[39] But thinking may be as far as we can go in the near
future; the use of court-martials over civilians was found unconstitutional in *Reid
v. Covert* because it did not meet the guarantees of Article III, Section 2, or the
Fifth or Sixth Amendments.[40]

The Uniform Code of Military Justice (UCMJ) details procedures for prosecuting members of the military should they commit a crime abroad. Article 2 of

the code provides jurisdiction over "persons serving with or accompanying an armed force in the field," but only "in time of war," which the courts have held to mean a war formally declared by Congress. Somewhat ironically, it now seems that one of the results of the U.S. debate over interrogation procedures for detainees in the "global war on terrorism" is that in the future Congress will formally declare that the United States is at war. This will make it easier for the U.S. military to exert control over contractors.

Although states and PMCs disagree over the specifics of various regulatory proposals, ultimately they understand that the current state of affairs benefits no one. Companies understand that increased oversight and regulation protect them from the relatively few unsavory types who periodically crop up in the PMC world while giving them credibility with the rest of the world, which increases their future business prospects. To further ensure proper accountability, future legislation should provide a punishment system for contractors who show blatant disregard for human rights.

Notes

PREFACE

1. David Bromwich, "Euphemism and American Violence," *New York Review of Books* (April 3, 2008): 29.

2. George Monbiot, "Pedigree dogs of war," *The Guardian*, January 25, 2005.

3. This section on Simon Mann is derived from David Isenberg, "Dogs of war: Life imitating art," *UPI*, March 21, 2008,

4. Richard Kay, "Forsyth is now a fat cat of war," *Daily Mail* [London], October 25, 2005.

5. Rosa Brooks, "Deniable, disposable casualties," *Los Angeles Times*, A23, June 1, 2007.

6. Peter W. Singer, "The Dark Truth about Blackwater," *Salon*, October 2, 2007.

7. Nir Rosen, "Security Contractors: Riding Shotgun with Our Shadow Army in Iraq," *Mother Jones*, April 24, 2007.

8. Nelson D. Schwartz, "The Pentagon's Private Army," *Fortune*, March 17, 2003, http://money.cnn.com/magazines/fortune/fortune_archive/2003/03/17/339252/index.htm.

9. "The Outsourced War 'Is Here to Stay,'" Daily Briefing, NEWSMAKER Q&A, *Business Week Online*, May 24, 2004.

ACKNOWLEDGMENTS

1. http://www.pulitzer.org/citation/2008,International+Reporting/bio/. See the archive of his past coverage at http://www.washingtonpost.com/wp-dyn/content/linkset/2007/06/15/LI2007061501702.html.

CHAPTER 1

1. William Shakespeare, Julius Caesar, Act III, I, 273, in *Bartlett's Familiar Quotations*, 16th ed. (Boston, MA: Little, Brown, 1992), 188.

2. Sreeram Chaulia, "A law unto itself," *Asia Times*, January 27, 2007; and Nick Robbins, *The Corporation That Changed the World: How the East India Company Shaped the Modern Multinational* (London: Pluto Press, 2006).

3. S. Mallaby, "Mercenaries are no altruists, but they can do good," *Washington Post*, June 4, 2001.

4. Statement of Robert Rosenkranz, president, International Technical Service, DynCorp International, before the Committee on House Government Reform, Subcommittee on National Security, Emerging Threats, and International Relations, June 13, 2006.

5. "Private security industry set to double by 2010: Expert," *Brussels (ANTARA News)*, September 16, 2005.

6. William Hartung, "Outsourcing Blame," May 21, 2004, *TomPaine.com*, http://www.tompaine.com/articles/outsourcing_blame.php.

7. Colonel Stephen J. Zamparelli, "Contractors on the Battlefield: What Have We Signed Up For?" *Air Force Journal of Logistics* 23, no. 3 (Fall 1999): 12.

8. Robert D. Kaplan, "Outsourcing Conflict," *Dispatch Unbound, Atlantic Monthly*, September 2007, http://www.theatlantic.com/doc/200709u/kaplan-blackwater.

9. The preceding six paragraphs are taken from my monograph *Soldiers of Fortune Ltd.: A Profile of Today's Private Sector Corporate Mercenary Firms* (Washington, DC: Center for Defense Information, November 1997).

10. This section borrows from David Isenberg, "Dogs of war: Here to stay," *UPI*, January 25, 2008.

11. See Peter Singer, "Privatized Military History," chap. 2 in *Corporate Warriors: The Rise of the Privatized Military Industry* (Ithaca, NY: Cornell University Press, 2003).

12. J. J. Messner, "What's in a Name? The Importance of Language for the Peace and Stability Operations Industry," *Journal of International Peace Operations* 2, no. 6 (May 1, 2007): 24.

13. John Rapley, "The New Middle Ages," *Foreign Affairs*, May–June 2006.

14. Patrik Jonsson, "Noncitizen soldiers: The quandaries of foreign-born troops," *Christian Science Monitor*, July 5, 2005. See also Moni Basu, "Under a new flag: Foreign-born GIs join fight in Iraq," *Atlanta Journal-Constitution*, September 21, 2005, p. 1F.

15. Edward Wong, "Swift road for U.S. citizen soldiers already fighting in Iraq," *New York Times*, August 9, 2005.

16. Bryan Bender, "Expedited citizenship would be an incentive," *Boston Globe*, December 26, 2006.

17. Eunice Moscoso (Cox News Service), "Experts push the use of migrants to bolster the U.S. military," *Miami Herald*, November 20, 2006.

18. "Families torn by citizenship for fallen," Associated Press, March 23, 2008; and Clyde Haberman, "Becoming an American citizen, the hardest way," *New York Times*, September 18, 2007.

19. Gregg Zoroya, "Troops put lives on line to be called Americans," *USA Today*, June 30, 2005, p. 1.

20. Max Boot, "Defend America, become American," *Los Angeles Times*, June 16, 2005.

21. Deborah D. Avant, "The Privatization of Security: Lessons from Iraq," *ORBIS* (Spring 2006): 337.

22. Marc Lindemann, "Civilian Contractors under Military Law," *Parameters* (Autumn 2007): 84.

23. *Rebuilding Iraq: Actions Needed to Improve Use of Private Security Providers.* GAO-05-737, July 28, 2005, http://www.gao.gov/cgi-bin/getrpt?GAO-05-737; and Matt Kelley, "U.S. contractors spent $766M on security in Iraq, GAO says," *USA Today,* July 29, 2005, p. 7A.

24. Renae Merle, "Census counts 100,000 contractors in Iraq," *Washington Post,* December 5, 2006, p. D1.

25. T. Christian Miller, "Contractors outnumber troops in Iraq," *Los Angeles Times,* July 4, 2007.

26. Statement of P. Jackson Bell, Deputy Under Secretary Logistics and Materiel Readiness, Department of Defense, Committee on Senate Armed Services, Subcommittee on Readiness and Management Support, April 2, 2008.

27. "Public Law 108-375, Section 1206 Report," http://www.fas.org/irp/agency/dod/1206report.pdf.

28. Ibid., p. 17.

29. Ibid, p. 20.

30. Ibid, p. 20.

31. Jenny Mandel, *Government Executive,* May 19, 2006, http://www.govexec.com/story_page.cfm?articleid=34125.

32. Jenny Mandel, "Army punts on Iraq contractor census," *Government Executive,* October 20, 2006.

33. Sebastian Sprenger, "Where are the contractors now?" *Federal Computer Week,* July 9, 2007.

34. Source: *Iraq Index: Tracking Variables of Reconstruction and Security in Post-Saddam Iraq,* Brookings Institution, January 17, 2006, http://www.brookings.edu/fp/saban/iraq/index.pdf.

35. "Contract Businesses Thrive in War Times," *Morning Edition,* National Public Radio, June 25, 2007.

36. "Iraq FOIA," *City News Service,* November 23, 2005.

37. David G. Savage, "U.S. can withhold security firm data," *Los Angeles Times,* July 27, 2006.

38. Alejandra Fernandez-Morera, "Civilian contractors: Invisible casualties of Iraq," *Scripps Howard News Service,* February 23, 2006.

39. Jeremy Scahill, "Outsourcing the war," *The Nation,* May 11, 2007.

40. Anthony H. Cordesman, "Iraq's Insurgency and Civil Violence: Developments through Late August 2007," August 22, 2007, p. 56, http://www.csis.org/media/csis/pubs/070822_cordesman_iraq_report.pdf.

41. John M. Broder and James Risen, "Contractor deaths in Iraq soar to record," *New York Times,* May 19, 2007. See also Bernd Debusmann, "In outsourced U.S. wars, contractor deaths top 1,000," Reuters, July 3, 2007.

42. David Ivanovich, "Labor Dept: 1,001 contractors have died in Iraq," *Houston Chronicle,* August 8, 2007.

43. David Washburn, "L-3/Titan jobs: Deadly duty: 216 have been killed while working in Iraq," *Union-Tribune,* November 26, 2006.

44. "A Media Mystery: Private Security Companies in Iraq—A PEJ Study," June 21, 2007, http://journalism.org/node/6153.

45. Ibid.

46. David Ivanovich, "Contractor deaths up 17 percent across Iraq in 2007," *Houston Chronicle*, February 9, 2008.

47. See, for just a few examples, John Geddes, *Highway to Hell* (London: Century, 2006); Martha Minow, "Outsourcing Power: How Privatizing Military Efforts Challenges Accountability, Professionalism, and Democracy," *Boston Law College Review* (September 2005); Mark W. Bina, "Private Military Contractor Liability and Accountability after Abu Ghraib," *John Marshall Law Review* (Summer 2005); Michael N. Schmitt, "War, International Law, and Sovereignty: Reevaluating the Rules of the Game in a New Century: Humanitarian Law and Direct Participation in Hostilities by Private Contractors or Civilian Employees," *Chicago Journal of International Law* (Winter 2005).

48. William Matthews, "The Deal on Contractors: How Much Is Too Much in Providing DoD Services?" *Armed Forces Journal* (November 2004): 10.

49. Stephen Goldsmith and William D. Eggers, "Government for hire," *New York Times*, February 21, 2005.

50. Jim Hooper, *Bloodsong: First Hand Accounts of a Modern Private Army in Action, Angola 1993–1995* (London, UK: HarperCollins Publishers, 2002).

51. Valerie Bailey Grasso, *Defense Outsourcing: The OMB Circular A-76 Policy*, Congressional Research Service, RL 30392, April 21, 2005.

52. See James M. Carter, "The Vietnam Builders: Private Contractors, Military Construction and the 'Americanization' of United States Involvement in Vietnam," *Graduate Journal of Asia-Pacific Studies* 2 (2004): 44–63.

53. Rebecca Ulam Weiner, "Sheep in Wolves' Clothing," *LegalAffairs*, January–February 2006, http://www.legalaffairs.org/issues/January-February-2006/argument_weiner_janfeb06.msp.

54. Avant, "Privatization," 330.

55. Richard Mullen, "Pentagon needs better contract oversight: Thinktanker," *Defense Today*, November 9, 2004.

56. Numerous articles have been written about PMCs, especially since the invasion of Iraq. A small sample include: Barry Yeoman, "Soldiers of Good Fortune," *Mother Jones*, May–June 2003, http://www.motherjones.com/news/feature/2003/05/ma_365_01.html; Barry Yeoman, "Need an army? Just pick up the phone," *New York Times*, April 2, 2004; P. W. Singer, "Warriors for Hire in Iraq," http://www.salon.com/news/feature/2004/04/15/warriors; Thomas K. Adams, "The New Mercenaries and the Privatization of Conflict," *Parameters* (Summer 1999): 103–116; James Dao, "'Outsourced' or 'mercenary,' he's no soldier," *New York Times*, April 25, 2004; Eugene B. Smith, "The New Condotierri and U.S. Policy: The Privatization of Conflict and Its Implications," *Parameters* (Winter 2002–2003); Kim Richard Nossal, "Global Governance and National Interests: Regulating Transnational Security Corporations in the Post-Cold War Era," *Melbourne Journal of International Law* (December 2001); Ian D. Jeffries, *Private Military Companies—A Positive Role to Play in Today's International System*, http://coursenligne.sciences-po.fr/2003_2004/securite_defense/setting_scence.pdf; Deborah Avant, "Think Again: Mercenaries," *Foreign Policy* (July–August 2004); and Mariyam Hasham, "Public Wars, Private Profit," *The World Today* 60, no. 4 (June 2004).

57. Brendan O'Neill, "Is it mercenary to join military for perks, not war?" *Christian Science Monitor*, June 1, 2004, http://www.csmonitor.com/2004/0601/p09s02-coop.html.

58. Susan Carroll, "Father of fallen soldier now battling deportation," *Houston Chronicle*, August 6, 2007, p. 1.

59. Grasso, op. cit., *Defense Outsourcing: The OMB Circular A-76 Policy*, Congressional Research Service, April 21, 2005.

60. Christopher Lee, "Army outsourcing put on hold: Plan for jobs came to halt after White's resignation," *Washington Post*, January 5, 2004, p. A15.

61. Alan Green, "Early Warning: The U.S. Army Can Hardly Be Surprised by Its Problems with Contractors in Iraq," May 5, 2004, http://www.publicintegrity.org/report.aspx?aid=274&sid=200.

62. Jason Peckenpaugh, "Army Contractor Count Stymied by Red Tape," *GovExec.com*, June 3, 2004.

63. Dan Guttman, "The Shadow Pentagon: Private Contractors Play a Huge Role in Basic Government Work—Mostly Out of Public View," Center for Public Integrity, September 29, 2004.

64. William Matthews, "The Deal on Contractors: How Much Is Too Much in Providing DoD Services?" *Armed Forces Journal* (November 2004).

65. Tichakorn Hill, "DoD to tally military jobs that can be given to civilians," *Federal Times*, November 15, 2004, p. 3.

66. Ibid.

67. *Contractor Support in the Theater of Operations*, Deskbook Supplement, March 28, 2001, http://www.dscp.dla.mil/contract/doc/contractor.doc.

68. Gordon L. Campbell, United States Army Combined Arms Support Command, *Contractors on the Battlefield: The Ethics of Paying Civilians to Enter Harm's Way and Requiring Soldiers to Depend upon Them*, paper prepared for presentation to the Joint Services Conference on Professional Ethics, Springfield, VA, January 27–28, 2000, http://www.usafa.af.mil/jscope/JSCOPE00/Campbell00.html.

69. James Surowiecki, "Army, Inc.," *New Yorker*, January 12, 2004. See also Cullen Murphy, "Feudal Gestures: Why the Middle Ages Are Something We Can Still Look Forward To," *Atlantic Monthly*, October 2003, http://www.theatlantic.com/issues/2003/10/murphy.htm.

70. Ibid.

71. Scott Shane and Ron Nixon, "In Washington, contractors take on biggest role ever," *New York Times*, February 4, 2007.

72. Jim Booth, "Blackwater: Getting' Rich While the Troops Try Dyin'," September 28, 2007, http://scholarsandrogues.wordpress.com/2007/09/28/blackwater-gettin-rich-while-the-troops-try-dyin/.

73. David Isenberg, "Changes Ahead for Private Security Companies," *Oxford Analytica Brief*, October 16, 2007.

74. Eric J. Fredland, "Outsourcing Military Force: A Transactions Cost Perspective on the Role of Military Companies," *Defence and Peace Economics* 15, no. 3 (June 2004): 205–219.

75. Tyler Cowen, "To know contractors, know government," *New York Times*, October 28, 2007.

76. Marc O. Hedahl, Captain, USAF, *Outsourcing the Profession: A look at Military Contractors and Their Impact on the Profession of Arms*, http://www.usafa.edu/isme/JSCOPE05/Hedahl05.html.

77. Peter W. Singer, "Outsourcing War," *Foreign Affairs*, March–April 2005.

78. Testimony of Doug Brooks, president, International Peace Operations Association, Subcommittee on Oversight and Investigations, House Armed Services Committee, April 25, 2007.

79. Nathan Hodge, "Washington urged to save money by raising private military 'contractor brigade,'" *Financial Times* (FT.com), February 10, 2005.

80. Avant, "Privatization."

81. Kirsten Scharnberg and Mike Dorning, "Iraq violence drives thriving business," *Chicago Tribune*, April 2, 2004.

82. Matthew Lynn, "Men with guns are the new dotcoms," *The Spectator*, November 4, 2006, p. 36.

83. John J. Lumpkin, "CIA seeks guns-for-hire in terror fight," Associated Press, November 27, 2003.

84. "CIA Remembers Employees Killed in the Line of Duty," May 21, 2004, http://www.cia.gov/cia/public_affairs/press_release/2004/pr05212004.html.

85. James Bamford, "This spy for rent," *New York Times*, June 13, 2004. Outsourcing in the intelligence realm is a related but distinct subset of PMC operations. A new book on this subject worth reading is Tim Shorrock, *Spies for Hire: The Secret World of Intelligence Outsourcing* (New York: Simon and Schuster, 2008).

86. William Matthews, "Counting on contractors: Industry employees are a growing power in the U.S. arsenal," *Defense News*, April 12, 2004.

87. Nelson D. Schwartz and Noshua Watson, "The Pentagon's Private Army," *Fortune*, March 17, 2003.

88. Kris Hundley, "Wanted: Ad agency to aid global battle on terrorism: Special Operations Command seeks a private firm to put a more persuasive face on U.S. efforts overseas," *St. Petersburg Times*, December 8, 2004, http://www.sptimes.com/2004/12/08/news_pf/Business/Wanted__Ad_agency_to_.shtml.

89. Kevin Begos and Phoebe Zerwick, "Civilians working for U.S. in Iraq making a bundle: Army Corps is paying Charlotte contractor millions to dispose of munitions," *Winston-Salem Journal*, February 13, 2005.

90. See also "Iraq bomb disposal contract pays well for Charlotte engineers," Associated Press, February 14, 2005.

91. Language taken from company Web sites, accessed April 27, 2008.

92. January 13, 2006, e-mail from Dr. Chris Kinsey, lecturer, Joint Services Command and Staff College, Shrivenham, United Kingdom.

93. J. R. Wilson, "Sharing the Risk: Contractors Work Side-by-Side with War Fighters," *Armed Forces Journal* (July 2004): 26.

94. James Cameron, "Privates on Parade," *The World Today*, May 2007.

95. Steve Fainaru, "U.S. pays millions in cost overruns for security in Iraq," *Washington Post*, August 12, 2007, p. 1.

96. John T. Bennett and Jen Iosue, "Growth expected in U.S. services sector even after Iraq War," *Defense News*, July 23, 2007.

97. Steve Fainaru, "Private armies: Security contractors in Iraq," *Washington Post*, July 30, 2007. Fainaru was online to discuss his coverage of private security companies in Iraq, http://www.washingtonpost.com/wp-dyn/content/discussion/2007/07/27/DI2007072701634.html.

98. Ann Scott Tyson, "Military offers special perks in bid to retain special forces," *Christian Science Monitor*, January 21, 2005.

CHAPTER 2

1. Wilson, "Sharing the Risk."

2. James Flanigan, "In Iraq, army of private contractors is set to stay entrenched," *Los Angeles Times*, May 23, 2004.

3. Sherie Winston, Debra K. Rubin, and Andrew G. Wright, "Contractors Tailoring Protection to Projects," *ENR: Engineering News-Record* 252, no. 6 (February 9, 2004).

4. This section taken from "Private Security Contracting in Iraq and Afghanistan," Statement of Ambassador Richard J. Griffin, Assistant Secretary of State for Diplomatic Security, Testimony before the House Committee on Oversight and Government Reform (as prepared for delivery), October 2, 2007, http://www.state.gov/m/ds/rls/rm/93191.htm.

5. John M. Broder and David Rhode, "State Dept. use of contractors leaps in 4 years," *New York Times*, October 24, 2007.

6. http://www.channel4.com/news/media/2006/09/week_3/22_foi.jpg.doc.

7. Information in this section is drawn from David Isenberg, "Dogs of war: The pay gap myth," *UPI*, February 15, 2008.

8. Ann Jocelyn, "Just How Overpaid Are Private Security Contractors?" *Serviam Magazine*, November–December 2007, http://www.serviammagazine.com/mag/NovDec2007/1207_contractor_pay.htm.

9. "Making a Killing in Iraq," International Peace Operations Association op-ed, August 11, 2004.

10. Nathan Hodge, "Kalashnikovs for hire in Iraq," *Slate*, February 9, 2006.

11. "Kiwis face danger in Iraq for dollars," *New Zealand Herald*, August 11, 2006; Nick McKenzie, "Armed and ready: Private soldiers in Iraq," *The Age* [Australia], July 1, 2006; Cameron Stewart and Michael McKenna, "Eyes wide open," *The Australian*, July 17, 2007; Neil Cotter, "I was shot in the face but I was still standing and I told myself there's no way I was going to be taken alive," *The Mirror*, July 2, 2005, p. 8. Another Legionnaire, Akihiko Saito, with a distinguished combat career, was a Japanese security guard who worked for the British PSC Hart Group. He was taken hostage by the Jaish Ansar al-Sunna in Iraq in May 2005 and later died in captivity of wounds he had received in the earlier gun battle. S. Skuletic, "Hardship Induces Young Bosnians to Work in Iraq, Afghanistan for Low Pay," *Dnevni avaz* [Bosnia], Report in the Sedmica supplement: "Bosnian Invasion of Iraq and Afghanistan," May 12, 2007.

12. Gretchen Wilson, "Third World export: Security guards," *Marketplace*, March 26, 2008, http://marketplace.publicradio.org/display/web/2008/03/26/namibia#.

13. "Mercenaries: The Baghdad Boom," *Economist*, March 25, 2004.

14. "Lucrative pay lures cream of SA cops to Iraq," *Sunday Independent*, February 8, 2004.

15. Hennie Strydom, "Private Military Companies: Some Legal Issues," *Strategic Review for Southern Africa* (November 2005).

16. "U.S. Hired Mercenaries as Bodyguards in Iraq," *Morning Edition*, National Public Radio, February 15, 2005.

17. *Regulation of Foreign Military Assistance Act* (Act No. 15 of 1998), http://www.info.gov.za/gazette/acts/1998/a15-98.pdf.

Subsequently, that act was replaced by *The Prohibition of Mercenary Activities and Regulation of Certain Activities in Country of Armed Conflict Act, 2006* (Act No. 27, 2006), which was, after a considerable delay, assented to and signed by President Thabo

Mbeki on November 12, 2007. The new act also provides for two amendments to the Criminal Law Amendment Act, 1997 (Act No. 105 of 1997). The regulations to this act are still to be promulgated. Source: "South African Mercenary Legislation Enacted," January 21, 2008, http://www.iss.co.za/static/templates/tmpl_html.php?node_id=2923&link_id=5.

18. Raenette Taljaard, "New market for force," *Daily News* [South Africa], November 22, 2005, Edition 1, http://www.dailynews.co.za/index.php?fSectionId=541&fArticleId=3004793.

19. Karen Pretorius, "S Africans working in Iraq contravenes the law," *BuaNews* [Pretoria], October 27, 2004.

20. "India probes reports of ex-soldiers working illegally in Iraq," *Agence France Presse*, May 3, 2004.

21. "Pak Busts US Secret Drive to Recruit Ex-servicemen for Iraq," May 25, 2004, http://www.webindia123.com/news/showdetails.asp?id=38944&cat=Asia.

22. Harvey Thompson, "Washington Fields Mercenary Army in Iraq," May 6, 2004, http://www.axisoflogic.com/artman/publish/article_7322.shtml.

23. "US firm's pursuit of Colombians for Iraq jobs causes concern" (Associated Press), *Taipei Times*, December 16, 2004, p. 7.

24. Danna Harman, "Firms tap Latin Americans for Iraq," *Christian Science Monitor*, March 3, 2005.

25. Sonni Efron, "Worry grows as foreigners flock to Iraq's risky jobs," *Los Angeles Times*, July 30, 2005; and Edison Lopez, "Ecuador scrutinizes American entrepreneur offering mercenaries for duty in Iraq," *Associated Press Worldstream*, August 15, 2005.

26. "Honduras gets offer from US firm for Iraq security work" (Associated Press), *Dow Jones International News*, May 18, 2005.

27. "Statement by Triple Canopy, Inc. regarding employment," *PRNewswire*, May 20, 2005.

28. Freddy Cuevas, "Honduras fines U.S. subsidiary over alleged mercenary training," Associated Press (State & Local Wire), November 25, 2006. See also Matthew D. LaPlante, "Third world warriors fight U.S. wars—for dollars a day," *Salt Lake Tribune*, December 2, 2007.

29. Ángel Páez, "Veteran soldiers, police recruited for Iraq by U.S. contractors," *Inter Press Service*, October 31, 2005, http://www.ipsnews.net/news.asp?idnews=30834.

30. Eloy O. Aguilar, "U.S. company recruits Salvadorans for security jobs in Iraq," *AP Worldstream*, October 8, 2004.

31. Kevin Sullivan, "Poor Salvadorans chase the 'Iraqi Dream': U.S. security firms find eager recruits among former soldiers, police officers," *Washington Post*, December 9, 2004, p. A24.

32. Carmen J. Gentile, "Brazil Investigating Iraq Recruiters," February 7, 2005, http://www.estadao.com.br.

33. Inveco International Corporate Release, February 19, 2005, http://www.webwire.com/ViewPressRel.asp?aId=1495.

34. Bill Sizemore, "Blackwater and Colombian workers clash over pay scale," *Virginian-Pilot*, September 2, 2006.

35. "A new poverty draft: Military contractors target Latin America for new recruits," *Democracy Now*, December 23, 2004, http://www.democracynow.org/article.pl?sid=04/12/23/1541224.

36. Gretchen Wilson, "Third World export."

37. Ibid.

38. E-mail from Ram Gurang of Kailash International Manpower (P) Ltd., April 16, 2006. Gurang had mistakenly assumed that my then-employer was a private military contractor. The firm's Web page is at http://www.kailashinternational.com.

39. http://www.ipoaonline.org/home/. IPOA's Mission Statement says, "IPOA is committed to maintaining industry-wide standards to ensure sound and ethical professional and military practices in the conduct of peacekeeping and post-conflict reconstruction activities. All member companies subscribe to our Code of Conduct, based on the belief that high standards will both benefit the industry and serve the greater causes of human security and development." Source: http://www.ipoaonline.org/about/mission/.

40. http://www.privatemilitary.org/securityindustry.html.

41. http://www.pscai.org/index.html#.

42. http://www.bapsc.org.uk.

43. This section is based on e-mail comments by a PMC member in Iraq that appeared on the PMC listserv run by Doug Brooks, founder of the International Peace Operations Association.

44. Michael Stetz, "'It's who we are': War against terror gives former SEALs the chance to resurrect their skills," *San Diego Union-Tribune*, June 3, 2004.

45. For details see Pratap Chatterjee, "Ex-SAS Men Cash in on Iraq Bonanza," June 9, 2004, http://www.corpwatch.org/article.php?id=11355.

46. For a detailed examination of British PMCs and their personnel in Iraq, see the transcript of *File on 4* program "Iraq Security Firms," May 25, 2004, http://www.bbc.co.uk/radio4/news/fileon4/transcripts/fileon4_iraq.pdf.

47. "This SAS gun for hire," *Times Online*, February 20, 2005.

48. "Who Dares Profits; Private Military Companies (Britain's Private Military Companies Are Flourishing)," *Economist*, May 20, 2006.

49. David Zucchino, "Death without honors," *Los Angeles Times*, January 15, 2005, p. 1.

50. T. Christian Miller, "The battle scars of a private war," *Los Angeles Times*, February 12, 2007.

51. Dean Calbreath, "Translator hired by Titan beheaded by insurgents," *Union-Tribune*, October 12, 2004.

52. Jim Krane, (AP), "Translators working with U.S. troops in Iraq are top targets," *Arizona Daily Star* [Tucson], May 22, 2005.

53. "Paying the blood price," *Fiji Times*, April 23, 2005.

54. Sharon Behn, "Attacks hit vital security in Iraq: Contractors see rising brutality," *Washington Times*, May 23, 2005, p. 1.

55. "Government should be wary of hired guns: Expert," *Canberra Times* [Australia], June 27, 2005, p. A11; Capi Lynn, "Woman killed in Iraq recalled as mentor, friend," *Statesman Journal*, June 30, 2005; and Mike Francis, "Oregon suffers its first female casualty in Iraq War," *The Oregonian*, June 29, 2005.

56. Kim Gamel, "Helicopter shot down in Iraq; 5 killed," *Associated Press Online*, January 23, 2007; Robert Y. Pelton, "Another black day for Blackwater," *IraqSlogger*, January 23, 2007; and Joanne Kimberlin, "Blackwater contractors linked by common threads," *Virginian-Pilot*, February 1, 2007.

57. Erin Magnani, "Iowa State U. student killed in Iraq might not be named in memorial," *Iowa State Daily via University Wire*, June 23, 2005.

58. Steve Fainaru, "Private war: Convoy to darkness," *Washington Post*, July 29, 2007, p. 1; Steve Fainaru, "Five severed fingers identified as belonging to guards held in

Iraq," *Washington Post*, March 13, 2008, p. A12; and Steve Fainaru, "For missing guards' kin, an agonizing conclusion," *Washington Post*, March 30, 2008, p. A1.

59. Larry Margasak, "War's hidden cost: Workers' comp: Hundreds of American contractors and their Iraqi employees are receiving insurance benefits" (Associated Press), *Philadelphia Inquirer*, April 6, 2005.

60. Opiyo Oloya, "Death could come very swiftly in Iraq!" *New Vision* [Kampala], May 25, 2005.

61. For a good explanation of DBA, including coverage and insurance requirements, see http://www.dol.gov/esa/owcp/dlhwc/ExplainingDBA.htm. A good outline of the history, purpose, and coverage of the DBA is at http://www.dol.gov/esa/owcp/dlhwc/DBAWorkshopJAC2-22-06.pdf. A link to the key DBA and U.S. Longshore and Harbor Workers Compensation Act (which DBA is part off) claim forms is http://www.dol.gov/esa/owcp/dlhwc/lsforms.htm, the most significant of which is the LS-202, or the Employer's First Report of Injury or Occupational Disease, and http://www.dol.gov/esa/owcp/dlhwc/ls-202.pdf, which gives the carrier and DOL notice of the worker's death or injury.

62. Marta Roberts, "Working in a War Zone," *Security Management*, November 2004, http://www.securitymanagement.com/article/working-war-zone.

63. For details see Susie Dow, "Iraq, Contingency Contracting and the Defense Base Act," *EPluribus Media*, http://www.epluribusmedia.org/features/2007/20070304_contingency_contracting.html.

64. Joseph Neff, "Iraq contracts burden taxpayers," *Raleigh News&Observer*, December 24 2006, p. A1.

65. *Defense Base Act Insurance: Review Needed of Cost and Implementation Issues*, GAO-05-280R, April 29, 2005, http://www.gao.gov/htext/d05280r.html.

66. Established in 1941, the primary goal of the Defense Base Act was to cover workers on military bases outside the United States. The act was amended to include public works contracts with the government for the building of nonmilitary projects such as dams, schools, harbors, and roads abroad. A further amendment added a vast array of enterprises revolving around the national security of the United States and its allies. Today, almost any contract with an agency of the U.S. government for work outside the United States, whether military in nature or not, will likely require Defense Base Act coverage. There are five provisions in the current version of the Defense Base Act that prompt coverage: any employee working on a military base or reservation outside the United States; any employee engaged in U.S. government-funded public works business outside the United States; any employee engaged in public works or military contract with a foreign government that has been deemed necessary to U.S. national security; those employees that provide services funded by the U.S. government outside the realm of regular military issue or channels; any employees of any subcontractors of the prime or letting contractor involved in a contract like numbers 1–4 above.

Waivers: One should note that DBA coverage makes no reference to the nationality of the covered employees; thus, local nationals or third-country nationals are automatically covered under the DBA. Waivers can be granted, but they need to follow certain criteria, and only the secretary of labor is able to authorize any such waiver. Key points for gaining waivers include the following:

- The class of employee must have available alternate means of compensation such as Employers Liability, Workers' Compensation, or Social Security.

- Waivers cannot be requested for any class of employee, including U.S. citizens or those employees hired inside the United States.
- The agency letting the contract must recommend that such a waiver be granted.
- The contractor must file an application with the U.S. Department of Labor.

Coverage Issues: The courts rely on precedent when determining liability issues. Two doctrines, known as the Zone of Special Danger and Reasonable Recreation, are central to finding coverage under the act. The Zone of Special Danger doctrine requires that an employee's injury or death arises out of or in the course of employment. In addition, the Zone of Special Danger states that when unique conditions or circumstances of employment place an employee in a zone of danger, then an accident resulting in injury or death need not be strictly related to job duties. The Reasonable Recreation doctrine requires that an employee's injury or death arises out of or in the course of the employer's furnished, funded, or promoted recreational activities. Some nonsponsored activities may also be included. Please note that these two doctrines taken together do not lead to "24-hour coverage" for an employee.

Failure to obtain DBA insurance carries stiff penalties. All government contracts contain a provision requiring that bidding contractors obtain necessary insurance. Failure to do so will result in fines and possible loss of contract. The additional and most severe penalty is that employers without DBA coverage are subject to suits under common law wherein common law defenses are waived. In other words, the claimants or their heirs need only file suit and do not have to prove negligence. Lastly, all claims may be brought in federal court and are against the insured directly.

The DBA requires full disability compensation for two-thirds of a worker's average weekly earnings, up to a maximum $1,030.78 per week. Death benefits are 50 percent of an employee's average weekly earnings, payable to the surviving spouse or to one child, and two-thirds of earnings for two or more survivors, up to the weekly maximum. Benefits may be payable for life and are subject to annual cost-of-living adjustments. For further information see *Defense Base Act Workers' Compensation Insurance Coverage: Guide for US Contractors in Iraq*, http://www.export.gov/iraq/bus_climate/dba.html; and http://www.dol.gov/esa/owcp/dlhwc/ExplainingDBA.htm.

67. http://www.dol.gov/esa/owcp/dlhwc/BenefitsundertheDBA(slide).pdf. See pp. 12 and 13.

68. Joseph Neff and Jay Price, "Courts to resolve contractors' deaths," *News& Observer*, January 9, 2005.

69. Andrew Jacobs and Simon Romero, "US workers, lured by money and idealism, face Iraqi reality," *New York Times*, April 14, 2004, p. 1.

70. T. Christian Miller, "Army, insurer in Iraq at odds: The Pentagon suspects vast overcharging for workers' compensation in war zones," *Los Angeles Times*, June 13, 2005. According to the article, four companies issue the vast majority of Defense Base Act policies: New York–based AIG, Bermuda-based ACE Ltd., Chicago-based CNA, and New Jersey–based Chubb Corp.

71. Elliot Blair Smith, "Defense seeks insurance plan changes: Workers' compensation scrutinized," *USA Today*, June 14, 2005, p. 4B.

72. "Defense Base Act Insurance and Claims Administration," Department of Labor OWCP Defense Base Act Workshop, February 22, 2006, p. 7, http://www.dol.gov/esa/owcp/dlhwc/DBAAdministration.pdf.

73. T. Christian Miller, "War, red tape haunt civilian workers," *Los Angeles Times*, June 17, 2007, p. 1.

74. James Risen, "After Iraq, contractors face mental health issues," *New York Times*, July 4, 2007.

75. Statement of Shelby Hallmark, director, Office of Workers' Compensation Programs, U.S. Department of Labor, Committee on House Oversight and Government Reform, May 15, 2008.

76. Statement of Alan Chvotkin, senior vice president and counsel, Professional Services Council, before the Committee on House Government Reform, Subcommittee on National Security, Emerging Threats, and International Relations, June 13, 2006.

77. "Defense Base Act Insurance: Are Taxpayers Paying Too Much?" House Oversight and Government Reform Committee, May 15, 2008.

78. Statement of John K. Needham, director, Acquisition and Sourcing Management Issues, Government Accountability Office, Committee on House Oversight and Government Reform, May 15, 2008.

79. "Defense Base Act Insurance: Are Taxpayers Paying Too Much?"

80. Jim Krane, "Keeping track of the number of contractors dying in Iraq is proving difficult," Associated Press, May 21, 2005.

81. Sue Pleming, "232 contractors die in Iraq," Reuters, January 31, 2005.

82. Taken from http://talkingpointsmemo.com, September 17, 2006.

83. For example, after two Blackwater contractors were killed and another injured in a roadside attack in Baghdad in March 2005, State Department spokesmen Richard Boucher said, "These men were assigned to the U.S. Embassy in Iraq to protect American diplomats. They played a vital role in our mission to bring democracy and opportunity to the people of Iraq. We will always remember their courage, dedication, and ultimate sacrifice for their country in the name of freedom. We mourn the loss of these brave men and extend our deepest sympathies to their families." Press statement, Richard Boucher, spokesman, Washington, DC, March 13, 2005, http://www.state.gov/r/pa/prs/ps/2005/43343.htm.

84. Henry Weinstein, "Families of slain private security contractors sue for negligence," *Los Angeles Times*, January 6, 2005.

85. "Chairman Waxman Calls for Blackwater Investigations," Committee on Oversight and Government Reform, House of Representatives, March 10, 2008, http://oversight.house.gov/story.asp?ID=1791. See also "Evidence of Tax Evasion by Blackwater," October 22, 2007, http://oversight.house.gov/story.asp?ID=1562.

86. Elise Castelli, "Blackwater: A 'small' firm by government rules," *Federal Times*, November 12, 2007.

87. *Employment Practices of Blackwater Worldwide*, Committee on Oversight and Government Reform, House of Representatives, March 10, 2008, p. 2, http://oversight.house.gov/documents/20080310101306.pdf. On October 23, 2007, Blackwater issued its own report, available on its Web site, on the events in Fallujah on March 31, 2004. See also Glenn Kessler and Karen DeYoung, "Blackwater focused on cost, not safety, report says," *Washington Post*, September 28, 2007, p. A14.

88. See the agreement for security services between Regency Hotel and Hospital Company and Blackwater Security Consulting, Inc., dated March 12, 2004, http://www.newsobserver.com/content/news/nation_world/blackwater/20041023_blackwater1.pdf.

89. David Isenberg, "Dogs of war: Employees, what employees?" *UPI*, March 14, 2008.

90. Larry Margasak, "Blackwater e-mail outlines gear shortage," Associated Press, February 7, 2007. Note: Some, such as Charles Murray of ESS Services, one of the subcontractors in the chain between Blackwater and KBR, dispute that the Blackwater

contractors were not properly equipped. See the transcript of the hearing, *Iraq Private Contractor Oversight*, of the House Oversight and Government Reform Committee, February 7, 2007. Nevertheless, the preponderance of accounts and evidence indicates that there were serious problems for the Blackwater security contractors in getting the equipment they felt they needed in a timely manner.

91. "Blackwater deaths detailed," *Richmond Times Dispatch*, July 8, 2007, p. A7.

92. "Private Military Contractors in Iraq—An Examination of Blackwater's Actions in Fallujah, House Committee on Government Oversight and Government Reform, September 2007, http://oversight.house.gov/documents/20070927104643.pdf. See also February 7, 2007, Hearing Examining Reliance on Private Military Contractors, http://oversight.house.gov/story.asp?ID=1165.

93. Isenberg, op. cit.

94. Independent contractors should have a business license, even if they are sole proprietors, from the state in which they conduct their business. If they do not possess a business license, the IRS will most likely treat them as employees. That is, they must file a Schedule C, Form 1040, along with their personal taxes.

95. See IRS Form SS-8, Determination of Worker Status for Purposes of Federal Employment Taxes and Income Tax Withholding, http://www.irs.gov/pub/irs-pdf/fss8.pdf.

96. March 14, 2008, e-mail to author from Robert Young Pelton.

97. Joseph Neff, "Army disavows Blackwater work," *News&Observer*, September 29, 2006, p. A1.

98. Joseph Neff and Jay Price, "Waxman on warpath over Blackwater payments," *News&Observer*, December 8, 2006.

99. Larry Margasak, "After many denials, Army confirms Blackwater contract in Iraq," Associated Press, February 7, 2007.

100. David Isenberg, "Dogs of war: The pay gap myth, *UPI*, February 15, 2008.

101. "Restrictions on privately owned guns: DOD, industry debate new rules for contractors in combat zones," *Inside the Navy*, August 16, 2004, p. 1.

102. Kirsten Scharnberg, "Contractors pay unsung toll in Iraq: Over 230 killed in jobs vital to military," *Chicago Tribune*, February 22, 2005.

103. http://www.dol.gov/dol/allcfr/ESA/Title_20/Part_61/toc.htm.

104. Ibid.

105. Ibid.

106. Zvi Bar'el, "Taking Iraq to Account," *Haaretz*, April 22, 2004, http://www.haaretz.com/hasen/spages/415039.html. See also Russell Gold and Sara Schaefer Muñoz, "Security costs rise for Iraq contractors," *Wall Street Journal*, May 17, 2004, p. 3.

107. "With one foot in the grave," *Der Spiegel*, Nr. 19, May 3, 2004, pp. 142–143.

108. James Dao, "Private US guards take big risks for right price," *New York Times*, April 2, 2004.

109. Thomas Catan and Stephen Fidler, "The military can't provide security: It had to be outsourced to the private sector and that was our opportunity," *Financial Times* September 29, 2003.

110. Robert Fisk and Severin Carrell, "Occupiers spend millions on private army of security men," *Independent on Sunday* [London], March 28, 2004, p. 21.

111. Scharnberg and Dorning, "Iraq violence."

112. "Private Company Provides Soldiers' Duties in Iraq: Steele Foundation Pays Employees Up to $20,000 Monthly," April 22, 2004, http://www.nbc11.com/news/3033866/detail.html.

113. "Custer Battles—Co-Founder Interview," *Your World with Neil Cavuto*, Fox News Network, Inc., April 16, 2004.

114. "Exodus cannot be stopped," *Fiji Times*, January 19, 2005.

115. Clare Murphy, "Iraq's Mercenaries: Riches for Risks," *BBC News Online*, April 4, 2004, http://news.bbc.co.uk/go/pr/fr/-/2/hi/middle_east/3590887.stm.

116. Ann Scott Tyson, "Private firms take on more military tasks: The deaths of security workers in Falluja show risks of 'outsourcing' war-zone jobs," *Christian Science Monitor*, April 2, 2004. See also Lisa Burgess, "DOD trying to retain its special operators," *European Stars and Stripes*, March 16, 2004.

117. Tom Bowman, "Bonuses offered to elite troops: Pentagon competing with security companies for skilled commandos," *Baltimore Sun*, January 23, 2005; Thom Shanker, "Pentagon sets bonuses to retain members of special operations," *New York Times*, February 6, 2005; and Miguel Navrot, "Pararescuemen in high demand: Airmen offered $150,000 bonuses," *Albuquerque Journal*, April 5, 2005, p. 1.

118. James W. Crawley, "Stopping a special-operations exodus: Nearly $40 million has been spent to re-enlist commandos," *Richmond Times-Dispatch*, August 31, 2005.

119. Thomas Harding, "Crisis as SAS men quit for lucrative Iraq jobs," *Daily Telegraph*, February 14, 2005.

120. Christopher Leake, "A Gapyear for the soldiers of fortune," *Mail on Sunday* [London], April 2, 2006, p. 49.

121. Eric Schmitt and Thom Shanker, "Big pay luring military's elite to private jobs," *New York Times*, March 30, 2004.

122. Ralph Peters, "Blackwater vs. nat'l defense," *New York Post*, October 6, 2007.

123. Nathan Hodge, "Army chief notes 'problematic' potential of armed contractors on the battlefield," *Defense Daily*, August 26, 2005.

124. "Former Army Chief of Staff General Peter Schoomaker joins board of DynCorp International," *Business Wire*, November 9, 2007.

125. Mike Francis, "Re-enlistment a tougher sell to soldiers in Iraq," *The Oregonian*, February 7, 2005.

126. Nathan Hodge, "National guard chief: Private military contractors stymie recruitment," *Defense Daily*, July 13, 2005.

127. David Rennie and Michael Smith, "Weary special forces quit for security jobs," *Daily Telegraph*, March 31, 2004.

128. Christian Jennings, "Special forces quitting to cash in on Iraq," *The Scotsman*, February 21, 2004, http://news.scotsman.com/index.cfm?id=205892004.

129. Ian Bruce, "SAS veterans among the bulldogs of war cashing in on boom," *The Herald*, March 29, 2004.

130. John Helyar, "Fortunes of War," *Fortune*, July 26, 2004.

131. Owen West, "Private Contractors Aren't the Answer to the Army's Problems," *Slate.com*, July 29, 2004, http://slate.msn.com/id/2104305/entry/2104507.

132. Press release from Rep. Skelton's office, "DOD Responds to Skelton Inquiry on Contractors in Iraq," May 4, 2004. See http://www.house.gov/skelton/pr040504a.htm for the actual CPA discussion paper on PMCs in Iraq.

133. Robert Schlesinger, "The Imperial Pentagon," *Salon*, May 20, 2004, http://www.salon.com/news/feature/2004/05/20/secrets/print.html.

134. Steve Fainaru, "Shadow war in Iraq escalates in intensity," *Washington Post*, June 16, 2007, p. 1.

135. http://www.diligencemiddleeast.com/dme_iraq.html.

136. "Diligence, LLC expands into the Middle East: New subsidiary focuses on security in Iraq and launches comprehensive information services in region," *PR Newswire*, December 8, 2003.

137. "Allbaugh getting Diligence its due," *National Journal*, December 6, 2003.

138. http://www.newbridgestrategies.com/index.asp.

139. Mark Huband, "Ex-CIA man to lead US sales drive," *Financial Times*, April 11 2005; and "Stephen Kappes," *Wikipedia*, http://en.wikipedia.org/wiki/Stephen_Kappes.

140. "ArmorGroup Extends its Reach," *Intelligence Online*, No. 497, April 1, 2005.

141. Griff Witte, "Pentagon's IG takes job at contractor," *Washington Post*, September 1, 2005, p. D3.

142. Ben Van Heuvelen, "The Bush Administration's Ties to Blackwater," *Salon.com*, October 2, 2007.

143. "Lee Van Arsdale," *Intelligence Online*, No. 512, November 25, 2005.

144. "The People Who Oversee Triple Canopy," *Intelligence Online*, December 9, 2005.

145. "Ambassador Robert Frowick Joins the Steele Foundation as Executive Director," April 14, 2004, http://www.prnewswire.com/cgi-bin/stories.pl?ACCT=SVBIZINK3.story&STORY=/www/story/04-14-2004/0002151497&EDATE=WED+Apr+14+2004,+11:34+AM.

146. Tim Shorrock, "CACI and Its Friends," *The Nation*, June 21, 2004, http://www.thenation.com/doc.mhtml?i=20040621&s=shorrock.

147. Robert Schlesinger, "The Private Contractor-GOP Gravy Train," *Salon.com*, May 11, 2004, http://www.salon.com/news/feature/2004/05/11/private/print.html.

148. Jeff Clabaugh, "CACI Names Former Joint Chiefs' Shelton to Board," *Washington Business Journal*, April 24, 2007.

149. Blackwater press release, February 4, 2005, http://www.blackwaterusa.com/btw2005/articles/pr1.html.

150. Singer, "Warriors for hire in Iraq."

151. Ibid.

152. Jonathan E. Kaplan, "Private army seeking political advice in D.C.," *The Hill*, April 14, 2004. See also http://www.disinfopedia.org/wiki.phtml?title=Alexander_Strategy_Group; and "ASG provides PR for Blackwater," *Jack O'Dwyer's Newsletter*, September 28, 2005, p. 2.

153. Schlesinger, "Private Contractor-GOP."

154. Jeffrey H. Birnbaum and James V. Grimaldi, "Lobby firm is scandal casualty: Abramoff, DeLay publicity blamed for shutdown," *Washington Post*, January 10, 2006, p. A01.

155. Judy Sarasohn, "A contractor calls in the big guns," *Washington Post*, June 17, 2004, p. 27.

156. Daphne Eviatar, "Private military contractors count on Crowell partner," *The American Lawyer*, June 20, 2007.

CHAPTER 3

1. Robert Collier, "Global security firms fill in as private armies: 15,000 agents patrol violent streets of Iraq," *The San Francisco Chronicle*, March 28, 2004, Pg. A1. See also Walter Pincus, "More private forces eyed for Iraq: Green Zone contractor would free US troops for other duties," *Washington Post*, March 18, 2004, p. 25.

2. T. Christian Miller, "To rebuild amid danger: An alliance," *Los Angeles Times*, February 21, 2005, p. A4. The DynCorp complaint referred to the Sandline affair, in which a company where Spicer was a director sold arms to Sierra Leone in an apparent breach of a UN embargo. Spicer later caused a furor by saying he had done so with the approval of the British government. A British government investigation confirmed Spicer's account.

3. Dominic O'Connell, "Brits clinch Pentagon security deal in Iraq," *Sunday Times*, June 26, 2005.

4. Charlotte Eagar, "The spoils of war," *The Evening Standard* [London], October 15, 2004.

5. Press reports said the contract falls within the "Security and Justice" component of the CPA Program Management Office's budget. The main S&J contract, amounting to $900 million (around 5 percent of the PMO's overall budget), was given to Parsons Inc on March 26, 2004. Parsons announced the award in a press release on March 29, and some further details have since emerged on a Web page of its subsidiary, Parsons Iraq, in which three UK-based CPA partners are listed, including Control Risks Group. The PMO Web site shows that Control Risks is listed as a registered supplier in the S&J category, but there is no entry for Aegis Defence.

Curiously, there was no reference to this new major S&J contract for close protection services on either CPA or PMO Web sites. A project status report by the PMO's director on May 24 gives no indication of contract awards after the last published list on the site of March 26.

6. For Spicer's history, see Lieutenant Colonel Tim Spicer, *An Unorthodox Soldier: Peace and War and the Sandline Affair* (Edinburgh: Mainstream Publishing, 2000); and http://www.sourcewatch.org/index.php?title=Tim_Spicer#Other_points. For background on Aegis, see http://www.sourcewatch.org/index.php?title=Aegis_Defense_Services.

7. Sir David Frost interviewed Colonel Tim Spicer, private security in Iraq, "BBC Breakfast with Frost," October 3, 2004, *BBC News*, http://news.bbc.co.uk/1/hi/programmes/breakfast_with_frost/3711312.stm.

8. See Andrew Ackerman, "Tim Spicer's World," *The Nation*, January 10, 2005.

9. Pratap Chatterjee, "Controversial commando wins Iraq contract," *CorpWatch*, June 9, 2004, http://www.corpwatch.org/article.php?id=11350.

10. Sandline's best-known operation was to try to quell a nine-year armed independence movement in Bougainville, PNG (Papua New Guinea). A British firm, Defense Security Systems, informed Spicer that the government of PNG was interested in hiring a PMC to defeat the rebels. Sandline International approached Prime Minister Sir Julius Chan to train and provide logistical support to the PNGDF (Papua New Guinea Defense Force) in exchange for a stake in the Bougainville mine. The PNG National Security Council authorized a $36 million dollar contract.

In February 1997, former British soldiers led approximately 70 Executive Outcomes (a South African PMC no longer in operation) soldiers into PNG. Although the PNG government denied that Sandline personnel would participate in direct combat, Sandline confirmed frontline participation. Political disputes between PM Sir Julius Chan and PNGDF Brigadier-General Jerry Singirok, who opposed the hiring of Sandline, led to harsh criticisms against the deal. When the terms of the contract were leaked to the public, riots erupted to protest alleged corrupt dealings between Sir Julius and Sandline. By March 21, all hired Sandline workers were airlifted from PNG. Only Spicer remained to face a judicial inquiry concerning the Sandline contract. The Andrew Commission of Inquiry ruled that the contract between Sandline and the PNG government was legitimate.

Further, the commission found that Sandline's actions had appropriately complied with the terms of the contract.

Four months after the PNG affair, Singirok confessed to having accepted $70,000 in secret payments from J&S Franklin (JSF), a British arms dealer, before leading the revolt against Sandline. The payments, which Singirok admitted using for personal expenses, were reportedly to create opposition to the Sandline contract.

Prime Minister Chan was forced to step down, as was Brigadier General Singirok.

11. Peter W. Singer, National Security Fellow, Brookings Institution, made these points in a June 10, 2004, e-mail on the PMC e-mail list (http://groups.yahoo.com/group/pmcs) run by Doug Brooks. See also Peter W. Singer, "Nation builders and low bidders in Iraq," *New York Times*, June 15, 2004; and Pratap Chatterjee, "Controversial Commando Wins Iraq Contract," June 9, 2004, http://www.corpwatch.org/article.php?id=11350.

12. Mary Pat Flaherty, "Iraq work awarded to veteran of civil wars: Briton who provided units in Asia and Africa will oversee security," *Washington Post*, June 16, 2004, p. E1. See also Sinclaire Solomon, "Spicer in Iraq: Sandline mercenary fame of B'ville crisis to head private army in Baghdad," *National* [PNG], June 16, 2004, http://www.the national.com.pg/0616/nation1.htm; and Charles M. Sennott, "London firm with Iraq pact involved in past scandals," *Boston Globe*, June 21, 2004. Two British members of the Advisory Council for Aegis Defense Systems are General Wheeler and Sir John Birch, who were outspoken critics of the war in Iraq. But evidently their opposition didn't prevent them from being part of a firm making money off of it.

13. Tom Griffin, "Irish-Americans target Iraq contract," *Asia Times*, July 30, 2004, http://www.atimes.com/atimes/Middle_East/FG30Ak03.html.

14. Steve Fainaru and Alec Klein, "Iraq's private intelligence firms: Firms extend U.S. government's reach," *Washington Post*, July 1, 2007.

15. Ibid.

16. Katherine McIntire Peters, "Buck private: Meet the new face of the armed forces in Iraq: A security contractor," *Government Executive*, October 1, 2004.

17. Paul Lashmar, "Spicer's security firm in battle with DynCorp over $290m deal," *Independent on Sunday*, July 4, 2004; and Jimmy Burns and Thomas Catan, "Dyncorp seeks to overturn Iraq contract," *Financial Times*, July 21, 2004. The first protest was filed June 22, 2004, File number B-294232.001, Solicitation No. W911S0-04-R-0005, with a due date of September 30, 2004. The second protest was filed August 2, 2004, File number B-294232.002, Solicitation No. W911S0-04-R-0005, with a due date of November 10, 2004. DynCorp's challenges were denied by the GAO on September 13, 2004. See GAO report *DynCorp International LLC*, B-294232; B-294232.2, September 13, 2004, http://www.gao.gov/decisions/bidpro/294232.htm.

18. Tony Capaccio, "U.S. Inspector Probing $293 Mln Aegis Award For Iraq Security," *Bloomberg.com*, July 30, 2004.

19. Nathan Hodge, "Aegis Wins Major US Security Contract in Iraq," *Jane's Defence Weekly*, September 26, 2007.

20. Alec Klein, "U.S. Army awards Iraq security work to British firm," *Washington Post*, September 14, 2007, p. D1.

21. Alec Klein and Steve Fainaru, "Firms protest exclusion from Iraq security bid," *Washington Post*, May 5, 2007, p. D1.

22. Alec Klein and Steve Fainaru, "Judge halts award of Iraq contract," *Washington Post*, June 2, 2007, p. D1.

23. Richard Lardner, "U.S. company's effort to reverse Iraq contract award highlights difficult protest process," Associated Press, August 13, 2007.

24. July 23, 2004, *Private Eye*. Forsyth owns 414 shares in the company. The total that were issued was 13,374. Therefore, he owns 3.1 percent of the company. The shareholdings in Aegis, as filed by the company in its statutory declaration (available online at http://www.companieshouse.gov.uk), gave the following holdings:

Tim Spicer	5,000
Mark Bullough	2,500
J Day Group Ltd	2,500
Dominic Armstrong	1,250
F Forsyth	414
Saad Investments Ltd	414
Lombard Atlantic Bank NV	414
MJ & AM Donovan	138
D&T Pemberton	138
R Sale	138
AM Sladen	138
C Wood & M Lemsey	138
BAO Ltd	138
Paragon Returns SDN BHD	138
Pershing Keen Nominees	138
Royal Bank of Canada Trustees	138
Total shares issued	13,734

According to one industry analyst, the story on Aegis's incorporation and shareholders is as follows:

The executives in the company are the first four, totaling 11,250 shares, that is, 81.9 percent of the equity. Some of these, such as J Day Group (Jeffrey Day), would have received their shares in exchange for making an investment in the business. Day may have invested £500,000 for his 2,500 shares, which have a face value of £25 but which give him 18.2 percent of the ownership.

Aegis now owns Trident (Spicer's old firm) outright, that is, 100 percent of the shares in that company, making it a "wholly owned subsidiary." However, before Aegis even existed, about three years ago Spicer secured an investment in Trident from a Lloyds underwriting syndicate with which he was developing a maritime security business. They underwrite maritime risk and presumably were interested in referring their clients to Trident, which would carry out risk assessments to help them improve their security. Since this has the upside of reducing the underwriter's exposure, everyone benefits: the insured client improves security; the underwriters reduce risk; and Trident makes money. The underwriters were probably attracted by the business side of Trident's activities and decided to invest in the company to participate in the profits from this security business that they were in fact referring to Spicer.

Now, when a company makes an investment, shares are issued in the name of the company. However, Lloyds syndicates are not companies; they are partnerships. So the partners presumably chose to receive the shares in Trident in their own names (or in the names of nominees). Assuming that the partners invested between them £270,000 and Forsyth put in £45,000 of this, then he would get one-sixth of the shares issued.

Subsequently, Spicer established Aegis Defence Services Ltd and presumably set about restructuring the business, proposing to subsume Trident into Aegis. A benefit to the shareholders in Aegis, which include himself and the 12 syndicate members, is that the latter group would now participate in the wider profits that the business would generate, not just maritime contracts, and Spicer would get to tidy up his share structure. The alternative would have been to leave the 12 syndicate members with the, say, 50 percent interest they shared in Trident (he would own the balance), but the plan may have been to write all future business in Aegis so that the restructuring would become a necessity.

So, the syndicate members surrender their shares in Trident and receive shares in Aegis Defence in their stead. In this case it is agreed that they will receive between them a number divisible by 18 and closest to but less than 2,500, which equates to the investment holding of Jeffrey Day and his more recent £0.5 million and/or the 50 percent that Spicer owns in Trident, which gives him half of his 5,000 shares in Aegis. Thus, we get 2,484 shares. Forsyth receives one-sixth of this figure, equating to the proportion of his holding in the original syndicate investment in Trident, that is, 414 shares. Thus Forsyth owns 3 percent of Aegis as a result of his membership in a Lloyds insurance syndicate and that syndicate's earlier investment in Trident.

25. Sue Pleming (Reuters), "U.S. audit criticizes Aegis security work in Iraq," *Union-Tribune*, April 22, 2005.

26. "First Iraq Venture for Abraxas," *Intelligence Online*, June 8, 2007.

27. Liza Porteus, "Iraq's new war zone: American vs. American," *FoxNews.com*, July 1, 2005.

28. "FOXNews.com Readers Respond to Contractor Series," July 13, 2005, http://www.foxnews.com/story/0,2933,162162,00.html.

29. Liza Porteus, "'How do you like your contractor money?'" *FoxNews.com*, July 1, 2005.

30. David Phinney, "Marines jail contractors in Iraq: Tension and confusion grow amid the 'fog of war,'" *CorpWatch*, June 7, 2005; T. Christian Miller, "U.S. Marines detained 19 contractors In Iraq," *Los Angeles Times*, June 8, 2005; Tom Regan. "US troops, security contractors increasingly at odds in Iraq," *Los Angeles Times*, June 11, 2005, p. 1; and T. Christian Miller, "Contractors say Marines behaved abusively," *Christian Science Monitor*, June 13, 2005. The statement of Manuel Zapata, president, ZapataEngineering, on the incident can be accessed at http://www.corpwatch.org/article.php?id=12376.

31. Clint Confehr, "Blanchard cleared of wrongdoing," *Shelbyville Times-Gazette*, March 28, 2006, http://www.t-g.com/story/1145493.html; and Griff Witte and Josh White, "Navy won't file charges in Iraq contractor fracas," *Washington Post*, March 25, 2006, p. 15.

32. *Rebuilding Iraq: Actions Needed to Improve Use of Private Security Providers*. GAO-05-737, July 28, 2005, http://www.gao.gov/cgi-bin/getrpt?GAO-05-737.

33. Statement of William M. Solis, director, Defense Capabilities and Management, United States Government Accountability Office, to the Committee on House Government Reform, Subcommittee on National Security, Emerging Threats, and International Relations, June 13, 2006.

34. *Rebuilding Iraq: Actions Needed to Improve Use of Private Security Providers*, U.S. Government Accountability Office, GAO—05-737, July 2005, http://www.gao.gov/new.items/d05737.pdf.

35. Peter W. Singer, "Banned in Baghdad: Reactions to the Blackwater License Being Pulled," Wired Blog Network, September 17, 2007, http://www.brookings.edu/views/op-ed/psinger/20070917.htm.

36. "Private guards in Iraq pose challenges," *UPI*, June 19, 2006.

37. David Phinney, "Marines jail contractors in Iraq: Tension and confusion grow amid the 'fog of war,'" *CorpWatch*, June 7, 2005; T. Christian Miller, "U.S. Marines detained 19 contractors in Iraq," *Los Angeles Times*, June 8, 2005; "Marines 'beat US workers' in Iraq: Contractors say they were treated like insurgents," *The Guardian* [London], June 9, 2005, p. 15; Griff Witte, "Contractors deny they shot at Marines, allege mistreatment," *Washington Post*, June 10, 2005, p. 18; Scott Sonner, "Nevadan says Marines abused him while jailed in Iraq 3 days," Associated Press, June 10, 2005; Sharon Behn, "Security guards sent back to U.S.," *Washington Times*, June 10, 2005; T. Christian Miller, "Contractors say Marines behaved abusively," *Los Angeles Times*, June 11, 2005, p. 1; Adrian Blomfield, "Shootings may lead to security guard curb," *London Daily Telegraph*, June 11, 2005, p. 1; Tom Regan, "US troops, security contractors increasingly at odds in Iraq," *Christian Science Monitor*, June 13, 2005; and "Troops and Contractors Come into Conflict in Iraq," *Morning Edition*, National Public Radio, 7:10 AM, June 13, 2005.

38. Nir Rosen, "Security Contractors: Riding Shotgun with Our Shadow Army in Iraq, " *Mother Jones*, April 24, 2007.

39. Max Hastings, "The fatal divide at the heart of the coalition," *London Sunday Telegraph*, March 12, 2006.

40. John Geddes, "Never mind the rebels—the most dangerous gunmen in Iraq are American mercenaries: From an SAS soldier of fortune in Baghdad, a chilling warning . . . 2. Highway to hell," *Daily Mail* [London], March 27, 2006, p. 34.

41. Jackie Spinner, "Iraqi oil gets its own police force," *Washington Post*, January 17, 2004.

42. Isabel Oakshoote, "War opponent Rifkind holds stake in Iraq security firm," *Evening Standard* [London], September 9, 2005, p. A16.

43. Tirge Caps, "Private financing of private military companies," *Dailykos.com*, February 27, 2005.

44. Ibid.

45. Joel Gibson, "Security work in Iraq is a booming industry, but it's costing Fiji its young men," *Sydney Morning Herald*, June 17, 2006; and Nic Maclellan, *Fiji, the War in Iraq, and the Privatisation of Pacific Island Security*, Austral Policy Forum 06-11A, April 6, 2006, http://www.nautilus.org/~rmit/forum-reports/0611a-maclellan.html.

46. Danny Fortson, "ArmorGroup sold to G4S after sharp fall in profits," *The Independent* [London], March 21, 2008.

47. Alissa J. Rubin, "Security businesses operate in shadows," *Los Angeles Times*, April 2, 2004. An industry source says the original contract was for $6.5 million but was extended.

48. "Blackwater by Numbers: A Statistical Index," Mother Jones Blog, October 3, 2007, http://www.motherjones.com/mojoblog/archives/2007/10/5663_blackwater_by_numbers_a_statistical_index.html.

49. Mark Hemingway, "Warriors for hire: Blackwater USA and the rise of private military contractors," *Weekly Standard*, December 18, 2006.

50. "Blackwater USA," April 1, 2004, http://www.democracynow.org/article.pl?sid=04/04/01/1621244.

51. "Security contractor cites 'staggering' growth amid Iraq war," Associated Press, October 13, 2004.

52. The precise nature of the mission of the Blackwater personnel is still being debated. An article in *Time* magazine noted, "It's still unclear whether the four Blackwater

employees found themselves in Falluja inadvertently or were on a mission gone awry. Even by Pentagon standards, military officials were fuzzy about the exact nature of the Blackwater mission; several officers privately disputed the idea that the team was escorting a food convoy. Another officer would say only the detail was escorting a shipment of 'goods.'" Source: Michael Duffy, "When private armies take to the front lines," *Time*, April 12, 2004. According to one news report, Blackwater violated its own standards by sending the four men on an undermanned mission. Jay Price and Joseph Neff, "Security company broke own rules," *News&Observer*, August 22, 2004, http://www.newsobserver.com/news/v-printer/story/1552996p-7741192c.html.

53. Joseph Neff and Jay Price, "Contractors in Iraq make costs balloon: Extensive paramilitary work earns profit on several levels," *News&Observer*, October 23, 2005.

54. This section on civilian and combatant differences draws on Phillip Carter (FindLaw columnist), special to CNN.com, "What the law says about the recent killings in Iraq," *CNN.com*, April 5, 2004.

55. For detail see Renee de Nevers, "Modernizing the Geneva Conventions," *Washington Quarterly* (Spring 2006).

56. Dana Priest, "Private guards repel attack on US headquarters," *Washington Post*, April 6, 2004, p. 1.

57. The following nine paragraphs are derived from Lieutenant General Ricardo S. Sanchez (USA–Ret.), *Wiser in Battle: A Soldier's Story* (New York: HarperCollins, 2008), 336–340.

58. Adam Zagorin and Brian Bennett, "Will Iraq Kick Out Blackwater?" *Time*, September 17, 2007; Joshua Partlow and Walter Pincus, "Iraq bans security contractor," *Washington Post*, September 18, 2007, p. A1; Ned Parker, "Iraq bans U.S. security firm after deadly incident," *Los Angeles Times*, September 18, 2007; Alex Koppelman and Mark Benjamin, "What Happens to Private Contractors Who Kill Iraqis? Maybe Nothing," *Salon.com*, September 18, 2007.

59. Sabrina Tavernise and James Glanz, "Guards' shots not provoked, Iraq concludes," *New York Times*, September 21, 2007, p. 1.

60. Sinan Salaheddin, "Iraq bill would lift contractor immunity," Associated Press, October 30, 2007.

61. Sudarsan Raghavan, Joshua Partlow, and Karen DeYoung, "Blackwater faulted in military reports from shooting scene," *Washington Post*, October 5, 2007, p. A1.

62. James Glanz and Alissa J. Rubin, "From errand to fatal shot to hail of fire to 17 deaths," *New York Times*, October 3, 2007, p. 1. See also Sudarsan Raghavan, "Tracing the paths of 5 who died in a storm of gunfire," *Washington Post*, October 4, 2007, p. A1.

63. James Glanz and Sabrina Tavernise, "Blackwater shooting scene was chaotic," *New York Times*, September 28, 2007.

64. David Johnston and John M. Broder, "F.B.I. says guards killed 14 Iraqis without cause," *New York Times*, November 14, 2007; and Brian Ross, "Blackwater turret gunner 'Paul': Why I opened fire in Baghdad," *ABC News*, November 14, 2007. The turret gunner's statement given to State Department investigators is at http://abcnews.go.com/images/Blotter/Gunner_blackwater_abcnews_071114.pdf.

65. Sudarsan Raghavan and Thomas E. Ricks, "Private security puts diplomats, military at odds," *Washington Post*, September 26, 2007, p. A1.

66. Steve Fainaru, "Where military rules don't apply," *Washington Post*, September 20, 2007, p. A1.

67. R. J. Hillhouse, "Updated exclusive: The cost of private security in Iraq," *The Spy Who Billed Me*, October 8, 2007, http://www.thespywhobilledme.com/the_spy_who_billed_me/2007/10/exclusive-the-c.html.

68. Peter Spiegel, "Gates: Security contractors conflict with U.S. mission in Iraq," *Los Angeles Times*, October 19, 2007.

69. Paul Richter, "State Dept. ignored Blackwater warnings," *Los Angeles Times*, October 7, 2007.

70. "State Dept. E-Mails Say Blackwater Hurting U.S. in Iraq," *ABC News: The Blotter*, October 25, 2007, http://blogs.abcnews.com/theblotter/2007/10/exclusive-state.html.

71. "Blackwater USA; Private Security Contracting in Iraq & Afghanistan," hearing of the House Committee on Oversight and Government Reform, October 2, 2007.

72. Bruce Falconer, "Peace Out: Blackwater Splits with Trade Group That Promotes the 'Peace and Stability' Industry," *Mother Jones*, October 11, 2007.

73. Sharon Behn, "Blackwater nixes Iraq arrests," *Washington Times*, October 17, 2007, p. 1.

74. John F. Burns, "The deadly game of private security," *New York Times*, September 23, 2007.

75. Max Boot, "Accept the Blackwater mercenaries," *Los Angeles Times*, October 3, 2007.

76. Joshua Partlow and Sudarsan Raghavan, "Guards kill two women in Iraq," *Washington Post*, October 10, 2007, p. 1.

77. Steve Fainaru, "Iraqis detail shooting by guard firm," *Washington Post*, November 26, 2007, p. A1.

78. Peter Spiegel, "State Dept. intercedes in Blackwater probe," *Los Angeles Times*, September 26, 2007.

79. Spencer Ackerman, "State to Blackwater: You don't say nothin' to no one, see?" *TPM Muckraker*, September 25, 2007.

80. Paul Tait, "Shooting shines light on murky world of Iraq security," Reuters, September 18, 2007.

81. Sharon Behn, "Unlicensed security," *Washington Times*, September 19, 2007, p. 1.

82. *Management of DoD Contractors and Contractor Personnel Accompanying U.S. Armed Forces in Contingency Operations outside the United States*, Memorandum from the Secretary of Defense, September 25, 2007.

83. Ann Scott Tyson, "Pentagon team to study oversight of security firms," *Washington Post*, September 27, 2007, p. 16.

84. Karen DeYoung, "Immunity jeopardizes Iraq probe," *Washington Post*, October 30, 2007, p. A1; and David Johnston, "Immunity deals offered to Blackwater guards," *New York Times*, October 30, 2007, p. 1. For a view on why the grant of immunity would not prevent prosecution of Blackwater contractors, see Byron L. Warnken, "Blackwater, Garrity, and Immunity: What Does It All Mean?" *Jurist*, November 12, 2007, http://jurist.law.pitt.edu/forumy/2007/11/blackwater-garrity-and-immunity-what.php.

85. John M. Broder and David Johnston, "U.S. military will supervise security firms in Iraq," *New York Times*, October 31, 2007.

86. Noah Shactman, "World's Most Notorious Merc to Oversee Blackwater?" Danger Room, October 31, 2007, http://blog.wired.com/defense/2007/10/worlds-most-not.html.

87. R. J. Hillhouse, "New rules for Blackwater," *The Spy Who Billed Me*, December 5, 2007.

88. Peter Spiegel and Julian E. Barnes, "Gates moves to rein in contractors in Iraq," *Los Angeles Times*, September 27, 2007.

89. John M. Broder, "State Dept. plans tighter control of security firm," *New York Times*, October 6, 2007, p. 1.

90. Nicholas Kralev, "Blackwater call for cameras denied," *Washington Times*, October 24, 2007, p. 1.

91. Peter W. Singer, "Outlook: Break the Blackwater habit," *Washington Post Online*, October 8, 2007, http://www.washingtonpost.com/wp-dyn/content/discussion/2007/10/05/DI2007100501642.html.

92. Karen DeYoung and Ann Scott Tyson, "Blackwater faces new monitoring from State Dept.," *Washington Post*, October 6, 2007, p. 1.

93. "Abtan, et al. v. Blackwater USA, et al.," October 11, 2007, http://ccrjustice.org/ourcases/current-cases/atban%2C-et-al.-v.-blackwater-usa%2C-et-al.

94. Ibid.

95. Report of the Secretary of State's Panel on Personal Protective Services in Iraq, http://www.state.gov/documents/organization/94122.pdf. See also Ambassador Patrick F. Kennedy on the Report of the Secretary of State's Panel on Personal Protective Services in Iraq, Special Briefing, Office of the Spokesman, via teleconference call, October 23, 2007, http://www.state.gov/r/pa/prs/ps/2007/oct/94019.htm.

96. Spencer Ackerman, "After Blackwater controversy, State Dep't gave bonuses to contracting officials," *Talking Points Memo Muckraker*, December 4, 2007.

97. Steve Fainaru and Carol D. Leonnig, "Grand jury to probe shootings by guards," *Washington Post*, November 20, 2007, p. A10; and David Johnston and John M. Broder, "U.S. prosecutors subpoena Blackwater employees," *New York Times*, November 20, 2007.

98. August Cole, "Blackwater vies for jobs beyond guard duty," *Wall Street Journal*, October 15, 2007, p. 3.

99. "Britain banks on private security firms in Iraq as civilian gunned down," *Agence France Presse*, March 28, 2004. The £23.5 million fee is disputed by Control Risks Group. An e-mail from their London office stated, "As a company we do have a policy of confidentiality re: our clients which means we will never disclose who we work with. However, the Department for International Development do state on their website that we provide services for emergency aid sector. We do not disclose fees that we are paid—however, the fee you quote is incorrect and exaggerated."

100. Ibid.

101. David Pallister, "British firms on the frontline," *The Guardian* (Final Edition), December 10, 2003, p. 1.

102. *The Guardian*, December 11, 2003, http://politics.guardian.co.uk/foreignaffairs/story/0,11538,1104379,00.html.

103. Liz Chong and Richard Beeston, "Diplomatic guards may quit in Baghdad pay row," *The Times* [London], May 27, 2006.

104. Ian Bruce, "Private security staff plan strike over pay cuts," *The Herald*, May 29, 2006, p. 12.

105. David R. Baker, "In Peril: Private security guards face constant danger in Iraq," *San Francisco Chronicle*, April 2, 2004. For background on Mike Battles, one of the firm's founders, see Michael Corkery, "Newport man out to strike it rich in Iraq," *Providence Journal*, January 25, 2004, p. A-01. See also press release "Custer Battles marks successful year securing Baghdad International Airport," June 30, 2004, http://www.custerbattles.com/press/pr063004.html.

106. Neil King Jr. and Yochi J. Dreazen, "Amid chaos in Iraq, tiny security firm found opportunity: Once funded by credit cards, Custer Battles garnered millions in U.S. contracts using Gurkhas at the airport," *Wall Street Journal*, August 13, 2004, p. 1.

107. T. Christian Miller, "Military suspends firm accused of overbilling in Iraq," *Los Angeles Times*, October 9, 2004. See also Matt Kelley, "Lawsuit says Iraq security contractor defrauded U.S.," Associated Press, October 8, 2004. See also transcript of "File on 4"–Iraq," *Radio 4*, British Broadcasting Corporation, February 1, 2005, http://news.bbc.co.uk/nol/shared/bsp/hi/pdfs/08_02_05_fileonfouriraq.pdf.

108. David Phinney, "Iraq contractor accused of offshore shell game," *CorpWatch*, October 14, 2004, http://www.corpwatch.org/article.php?id=11575.

109. Jason McLure, "How a contractor cashed in on Iraq," *Legal Times*, February 28, 2005, p. 1.

110. Kelley, op. cit. Also, Erik Eckholm, "Memos warned of billing fraud by firm in Iraq," *New York Times*, October 23, 2004; and Eddie Curran, "Accusations by mobile firm spark probe of Iraq contracts," *Mobile Register*, November 8, 2004. See an early Custer Battles response to allegations in "Setting the Record Straight: Custer Battles Dismisses Baseless Allegations," http://www.custerbattles.com/press/pr101504.html.

111. T. Christian Miller, "Contractor argues U.S. fraud law does not cover Iraqi funds: Outcome of suit against a security firm may set a precedent for cases that involve other legislation," *Los Angeles Times*, December 19, 2004.

112. David Phinney, "Iraq contractor claims immunity from fraud laws: Seized oil assets paid for offshore overbilling," *CorpWatch*, December 23, 2004, http://www.corpwatch.org/article.php?id=11763.

113. Charles R. Babcock, "Contractor fraud trial to begin tomorrow," *Washington Post*, February 13, 2006.

114. "War Profiteers? Custer Battles and Other Government Contractors under Investigation for Overbilling US Government by Billions in Iraqi War," *60 Minutes*, CBS News Transcripts, February 12, 2006. See also Charles R. Babcock, "Contractor accused of profiteering: Witness says Custer Battles sent trucks that didn't work to Iraq," *Washington Post*, February 16, 2006, p. D2.

115. *Defense Contracting: Army Case Study Delineates Concerns with Use of Contractors as Contract Specialists*, U.S. Government Accountability Office, GAO-08-360, March 26, 2008; and Dana Hedgpeth, "Report faults Pentagon's reliance on contractors," *Washington Post*, March 27, 2008, p. D1.

116. Renae Merle, "Verdict against Iraq contractor overturned: Occupation authority's murky status cited," *Washington Post*, August 19, 2006, p. D1. It should be remembered that Custer Battles and its executives were suspended and debarred by the U.S. government because of "adequate evidence" of fraud. Although the jury found Custer Battles and its executives guilty of fraud against the United States, the judge set it aside because they were guilty of fraud but not necessarily against "the United States" (i.e., the Coalition Provisional Authority might not be part of "the United States").

117. Deborah Hastings, "Banned contractor soliciting Iraq deals," *Associated Press Online*, June 12, 2005; and Yochi J. Dreazen, "Employees of contractor barred from Iraq resurrect its business," *Wall Street Journal*, June 20, 2006, p. 1.

118. Froma Harrop, "In this version of Custer Battles in Iraq, we're all losers," *Houston Chronicle*, July 29, 2006.

119. Lisa Myers and the NBC investigative unit, "U.S. contractors in Iraq allege abuses: Four men say they witnessed shooting of unarmed civilians," *NBC News*, February 15, 2005, http://msnbc.msn.com/id/6947745/.

120. Statement of Franklin K. Willis before the Senate Democratic Policy Committee, February 14, 2005, http://www.socnetcentral.com/vb/showthread.php?t=42727&page=4.

121. Donald L. Barlett and James B. Steele, "The Spoils of War: Billions over Baghdad," *Vanity Fair*, October 2007.

122. "Recruits told to be cautious," *Fiji Times*, May 17, 2004, p. 3.

123. "Firm faces $50,000 fine," *Fiji Times*, May 24, 2004, p. 4.

124. Atunaisa Sokomuri, "US firm stresses groundwork done on Fiji recruitment," *Fiji Sun* Web site, Suva, in English, May 13, 2004.

125. Andrew G. Wright, "Despite a String of Setbacks, CPA Vows to Stay the Course," *Engineering News-Record* 252, no. 17 (April 26, 2004): 14.

126. Vivienne Walt, "Firm says UN office in Iraq refused security," *Boston Globe*, August 23, 2003.

127. Larry Hendricks, "The high price of security in Iraq: Former sheriff lieutenant off to train Iraqi officers," *Arizona Daily Sun*, April 2, 2004; Ben Schmitt, "Detroit cop gets a new beat: Iraq," *Detroit Free Press*, December 22, 2003; Andrew Higgins, "As it wields power abroad, U.S. outsources law and order work: DynCorp is asked to restore policing in Iraq vital to an American exit," *Wall Street Journal*, February 2, 2004, p. 1. The Web site of DynCorp International FZ-LLC (DIFZ) is http://policemission.dyncorp.com/iraq.asp.

128. "Justification for Other than Full and Open Competition," http://iraqcoalition.org/economy/PMO/State_Justification.htm.

129. Ariana Eunjung Cha, "Crash course in law enforcement lifts hopes for stability in Iraq," *Washington Post*, December 9, 2003, p. A22.

130. Spencer E. Ante, "Contractors Find Security in Iraq," *Business Week*, February 10, 2005.

131. "CSC'S DynCorp International Awarded $50 Million Contract to Support Law Enforcement Functions in Iraq," April 18, 2004, http://www.csc.com/newsandevents/news/2072.shtml.

132. Andrea Mitchell, "The Cost of Training Iraqi Police," November 4, 2003, http://msnbc.com/news/989323.asp; and Nicolas Pelham, "Jordan offers safe training haven to new Iraqi cadets," *Financial Times*, January 30, 2004.

133. "Connecticut civilians offer view from Baghdad," *Newsday*, April 18, 2004.

134. Gail Repsher Emery, "CSC wins contract for civilian police services," *Washington Technology*, February 24, 2004, http://www.wtonline.com/news/1_1/daily_news/22854-1.html. For details see "Contracting for the Iraqi Security Forces," Hearing of the Oversight and Investigations Subcommittee of the House Armed Services Committee, April 25, 2007.

135. Michael Moss and David Rhode, "Misjudgments marred U.S. plans for Iraqi police," *New York Times*, May 21, 2006.

136. Ibid.

137. Ibid.

138. Ibid.

139. Renae Merle, "Coming under fire: DynCorp defends its work in training foreign police forces," *Washington Post*, March 19, 2007, p. D1.

140. Peter H. Stone, "Iraq contractors on defense," *National Journal*, March 3, 2007.

141. Steve McVicker, "U.S. wants border patrol agents for Iraq," *Houston Chronicle*, April 30, 2007, p. 1.

142. Matthew Benson, "Border agents recruited for Iraq," *Arizona Republic*, May 19, 2007.

143. Tucker Carlson, "Hired Guns," *Esquire*, March 2004.

144. Scott Shane, "Chalabi raid adds scrutiny to use of U.S. contractors," *Baltimore Sun*, May 30, 2004; and Renae Merle, "DynCorp took part in Chalabi raid," *Washington Post*, June 4, 2004, p. A17.

145. Phillip O'Connor, "Hired guns are vital to forces in Iraq," *St. Louis Post-Dispatch*, March 11, 2004.

146. Sean Penn, "At war Sean Penn finds getting out of Iraq even tougher than getting in," *San Francisco Chronicle*, January 15, 2004.

147. Andrew Stephen, "Overcharging Uncle Sam?" *Business Week*, May 2, 2005.

148. Jerry Markon and Josh White, "Contractor charged in Baghdad badge scam," *Washington Post*, September 21, 2005, p. 19.

149. "USA: DynCorp International Awarded Contract for Badge System," Global News Wire—Asia Africa Intelligence Wire, InfoProd, September 7, 2005.

150. POGO Federal Contractor Misconduct Database, http://www.contractormisconduct.org/index.cfm/1,73,222,html?CaseID=488.

151. "Overcharges in Providing Fuel to a Police Academy in Amman, Jordan," POGO Federal Contractor Misconduct Database, http://www.contractormisconduct.org/index.cfm/1,73,222,html?CaseID=694.

152. Tod Robberson, "DynCorp has big role, little oversight in war efforts," *Dallas Morning News*, December 24, 2006.

153. Tod Robberson, "DynCorp criticized for employee deaths," *Dallas Morning News*, December 24, 2006.

154. Renae Merle, "Va. consortium wins bid to send linguists to Iraq," *Washington Post*, December 16, 2006, p. 14.

155. Griff Witte and Renae Merle, "Reports fault oversight of Iraq police program," *Washington Post*, January 31, 2007, p. D1.

156. Ibid.

157. Dana Hedgpeth, "Army splits award among 3 firms," *Washington Post*, June 28, 2007.

158. Interim Review of DynCorp International, LLC, "Spending Under Its Contract for the Iraqi Police Training Program," SIGIR-07-016, October 23, 2007, http://www.sigir.mil/reports/pdf/audits/07-016.pdf.

159. *Progress on Recommended Improvements to Contract Administration for the Iraqi Police Training Program*, SIGIR-08-014, Office of the Special Inspector General for Iraq Reconstruction, April 22, 2008, http://www.sigir.mil/reports/pdf/audits/08-014.pdf; and Dana Hedgpeth, "Inspectors progress on DynCorp audit," *Washington Post*, April 28, 2008, p. D3.

160. This section draws on David Isenberg, "Protecting Iraq's precarious pipelines," *Asia Times*, September 24, 2008.

161. David Pallister, op. cit. A useful article on how Erinys works with a dedicated Iraqi protection force, U.S. military personnel, and local tribes is Richard Giragosian, "Targeting weak points: Iraq's oil pipelines," *Asia Times*, January 27, 2004. See also Paul Sampson, "US deploys patrols, tribes for Iraq security," *International Oil Daily*, March 3, 2004; and Isenberg, "Protecting Iraq's precarious pipelines."

162. Armor Holdings Inc. used to be part of ArmorGroup, but as of November 26, 2003, ArmorGroup no longer has any connection.

163. Jim Vallette and Pratap Chatterjee, "Guarding the oil underworld in Iraq," *CorpWatch*, September 5, 2003, http://www.corpwatch.org/issues/PID.jsp?articleid=8328.

164. Thomas Catan and Stephen Fidler, "The military can't provide security," *Financial Times*, September 29, 2003; Robert Fisk and Severin Carrell, "Mercenaries are coining it in Iraq," *The Star*, March 30, 2004.

165. Nicolas Pelham, "Rival former exile groups clash over security in Iraq," *Financial Times*, December 11, 2003; and "En Route to Baghdad," *Indian Ocean Newsletter*, January 24, 2004, N. 1073. See also Knut Royce, "Start-up company with connections: U.S. gives $400M in work to contractor with ties to Pentagon favorite on Iraqi Governing Council," *Newsday*, February 15, 2004; and Joe Cochrane, "Guarding a Vital Asset: Are Iraqis Ready to Protect Their Valuable, Vulnerable Oil?" *Newsweek*, February 16, 2004, p. 30.

166. George Orwel, "Iraq: Guarding the oil," *Energy Compass*, December 17, 2004.

167. Isenberg, "Protecting Iraq's precarious pipelines."

168. "Iraq national guard takes over protection of northern oilfields," *AFP*, November 23, 2004. For a chronology of attacks on Iraqi pipelines, oil installations, and oil personnel, see http://www.iags.org/iraqpipelinewatch.htm.

169. T. Christian Miller, "Task force shield not successful, audit finds," *Los Angeles Times*, April 30, 2006.

170. Suzanne Goldenberg, "US soldier's family brings legal action against British private security firm," *The Guardian*, October 30, 2007.

171. Ibid.

172. "More men for Iraq," www.fijilive.com, October 26, 2004; and "Firm denies expiry of contracts in Iraq," *Fiji Times*, October 26, 2004.

173. Kalinga Seneviratne, "Fijian deaths in Iraq revive mercenaries' issue," *Inter Press Service*, June 12, 2006.

174. Michael Field, "Soldiers pull in the cash," *The Press* [Christchurch, New Zealand], November 24, 2005, p. B4.

175. "Iraq recruiter warns Fiji remittances 'will not last forever,'" *Fijilive* Web site, Suva, in English, June 15, 2006.

176. Nic Maclellan, *Fiji, the War in Iraq, and the Privatisation of Pacific Island Security*, Austral Policy Forum 06-11A, April 6, 2006.

177. "Former Fijian solders sue over Iraq contracts," April 16, 2004, http://home. nzcity.co.nz/news/default.asp?id=38606&cat=1032&c=w.

178. Malakai Veisamasama, "Fjian ex-peacekeepers to boost security in Iraq," Reuters, September 5, 2003.

179. "Don't call us mercenaries, says British company with lucrative contracts and cheap labour," *The Guardian* [London], May 17, 2004, p. 4.

180. "Millions pour in through GRS," *Fiji Times*, May 26, 2004.

181. "Strike shuts Baghdad airport to civilian traffic," Reuters, June 24, 2005. See also David Phinney, "Contract quagmire in Iraq," *CorpWatch*, April 27, 2005.

182. "Baghdad airport closed in row over unpaid bills," Reuters, September 9, 2005.

183. Richard A. Oppel Jr., "Security company closes Baghdad airport over pay," *New York Times*, September 10, 2005.

184. "World risk: Alert—Private firms move to fill Iraq's security vacuum," EIU RiskWire, September 30, 2003. Kroll set up a new subsidiary, Kroll Security International, whose chairman and CEO is Alastair Morrison. Morrison, a British Special Air Service (SAS) veteran and founder of Defence Systems Ltd, one of the first PMCs, later sold DSL to Armor Holdings.

185. http://www.krollworldwide.com/investor.

186. Robert Fisk and Severin Carrell, "Occupiers spend millions on private army of security men," *The Independent*, March 28, 2004.

187. "Private firms move to fill Iraq's security vacuum."

188. "En route to Baghdad," *Indian Ocean Newsletter*, No. 1073, January 24, 2004.

189. Antony Barnett, Solomon Hughes, and Jason Burke, "Mercenaries in 'coup plot' guarded UK officials in Iraq: Shocked MP demands a rethink of the way government awards its security contracts," *The Observer*, June 6, 2004. See also "Meteoric fall of an SA firm," *News24.com*, August 8, 2004, http://www.news24.com/News24/Africa/Zimbabwe/0,,2-11-259_1569960,00.html.

190. Michael Gilbert, "Getting ready to supply Iraq," *News Tribune*, November 25, 2003. See also Steve Liewer, "In Kuwait, 1st ID trains for convoy," *Stars and Stripes*, European Edition, March 6, 2004; and Jim Krane, "Troops train to fight Iraqi guerrillas," *Mercury News* (Associated Press), February 24, 2004.

191. http://www.mpri.com/site/int_mideast.html.

192. http://www.publicintegrity.org/wow/docs/ContractorsBattlefield.pdf.

193. Jonathan Werve, "Contractors Write the Rules: Army policy governing use of contractors omits intelligence restrictions," June 30, 2004, Center for Public Integrity, http://www.publicintegrity.org/wow/report.aspx?aid=334&sid=100.

194. Dean Calbreath, "A blueprint for a nation: The Pentagon leans on San Diego's SAIC in rebuilding Iraq; the sole-source contracts are lucrative and controversial," *San Diego Union-Tribune*, July 4, 2004.

195. Robert Collier, "S.F. agency has guns, will travel: With guards and investigators for hire, Steele Foundation keeps busy in Iraq," *San Francisco Chronicle*, June 25, 2004.

196. Collier, "Global security firms."

197. Greg Jaffe, David S. Cloud, and Gary Fields, "Legal loophole arises in Iraq: Abuse case raises question of how to prosecute civilian workers," *Wall Street Journal*, May 4, 2004, p. 4. For background on Titan, see Pratap Chatterjee, "Titan's translators in trouble," *CorpWatch*, May 7, 2004, http://warprofiteers.com/article.php?id=11284.

198. Bruce V. Bigelow, "Translation service pays off big for Titan," *San Diego Union-Tribune*, August 11, 2004. See also Renae Merle, "Prisoner-abuse report adds to Titan's troubles: Lockheed plan to buy firm already stalled," *Washington Post*, May 7, 2004, p. E3.

199. The following job description is from Titan Corp.'s Web site. "Provide operational contract linguist support to reconstruction efforts in Iraq. Provide general linguistic support for military operations and interpret during interviews, meeting, and conferences. Interpret and translate written and spoken communications. Transcribe and analyze verbal communications. Perform document exploitation. Scan, research, and analyze foreign language documents for key information. Translate and gist foreign language documents. Identify and extract information components meeting military information requirement list criteria. Provide input to reports. Linguists are required to work 12-hour shifts and in excess of 60-hour weeks in order to provide continuous contract linguist support that this 24 × 7 operation requires. Linguists must be available for worldwide deployment as the mission dictates.

Minimum required: Native proficiency in the Arabic/Iraqi dialect (Interagency Language Roundtable skill level 4–5). Must be capable of providing idiomatic translations of non-technical material using correct syntax and expression from English to the native language or vice versa; ability to conduct consecutive, accurate translations/interpretation of ongoing conversations/activities; must be capable of providing cultural social, ethnic context of translations and interpretations, and advise supported organization on the cultural, social and ethnic significance of conversations, situations, documents, etc., in one or more Iraqi cultural traditions and or regions; must be familiar with the local culture, conduct oneself in accordance with local customs, and deal unobtrusively with the populace; must be familiar with and adhere to U.S. Army standards of conduct and the laws of the host nation in performing work assignments; must have good interpersonal skills and ability to work as part of a civil-military team in an unstructured environment; must be willing and capable to live and work in a harsh environment. Desired: University degree from accredited North American or European university." Source: http://www.titan.com/careers/list.html?req=3979&callid=2.

200. "Titan competing with Northrop, L-3 to keep its largest contract," *Bloomberg News*, June 7, 2004.

201. Tony Capaccio, "Titan Payments Withheld over Iraq Billing Dispute," *Bloomberg.com*, March 12, 2004.

202. Bruce V. Bigelow, "Titan to repay Army $937,000 for translators," *San Diego Union-Tribune*, June 16, 2004.

203. "U.S. military interpreter charged as fraud," *The Smoking Gun*, October 17, 2005, http://www.thesmokinggun.com/archive/1017051malki1.html.

204. "Titan Wins $170 Million NORAD/NORTHCOM Integration and Operational Information Technology Support Contract," Source: The Titan Corporation; issued October 18, 2004.

205. Edmond Lococo, "U.S. Army to extend Titan translation contract," *Bloomberg.com*, June 28, 2005; and David Washburn, "Titan gets extension on interpreters contract," *San Diego Union-Tribune*, July 20, 2005.

206. "The Titan Corporation Announces Expiration of Hart-Scott-Rodino Act Waiting Period for Proposed Merger with L-3 Communications Corporation," Titan Corporation press release, issued July 14, 2005.

207. "L-3 out, Dyncorp-McNeil in for $4.65B Iraq translation contract?" *Defense Industry Daily*, December 10, 2007; and "L-3 challenges Army's contract with Dyncorp," *San Diego Union-Tribune*, December 15, 2007.

208. David Washburn and Bruce V. Bigelow (Associated Press), *Union-Tribune*, July 24, 2005.

209. Paul Martin, "Green Zone security switch causes anxiety," *Washington Times*, November 4, 2005, p. 15.

210. C. J. Chivers, "Contractor's boss in Iraq shot at civilians, workers' suit says," *New York Times*, November 17, 2006, p. 16; Tom Jackman, "U.S. contractor fired on Iraqi vehicles for sport, suit alleges," *Washington Post*, November 17, 2006, p. A20.

211. Steve Fainaru, "A chaotic day on Baghdad's airport road," *Washington Post*, April 15, 2007, p. 1.

212. Isabel Ordonez, "Iraq, Afghanistan lure poor Latin American guards," Reuters, August 21, 2006.

213. "Triple Canopy Inc.," *SourceWatch*, http://www.sourcewatch.org/index.php?title=Triple_Canopy_Inc; and Daniel Bergner, "The Other Army," *New York Times Magazine*, August 14, 2005.

214. Steven Rosenfeld, "Forget Halliburton," originally published in Tom Paine, http://progressivetrail.org/articles/040117Rosenfeld.shtml.

215. Dean Calbreath, "Iraqi army, police force fall short on training," *San Diego Union-Tribune*, July 4, 2004.

216. Geoff S. Fein, "Training Iraqi Army is a 'wild card,'" *National Defense*, December 2003.

CHAPTER 4

1. Thomas Catan, "Call to vet security companies working overseas," *Financial Times*, September 29, 2004.

2. "Regulation—an ArmorGroup Perspective," ArmorGroup International plc, September 27, 2004: A statement of its position on the regulation of Private Security Companies ("PSCs") and Private Military Companies ("PMCs") that are based in the United Kingdom and operate in areas of diminished law and order and civil strife around the world, http://www.privatemilitary.org/industrydocuments.html.

3. Clayton Hirst, "Dogs of war to face new curbs in Foreign Office crackdown: Regulation planned for security firms amid claims that 'any Joe Public can get a Kalashnikov and work abroad,'" *The Independent*, March 13, 2005.

4. Ollie Stone-Lee, "Bouncer body 'to vet Iraq guards,'" *BBC News*, March 15, 2006.

5. Statement of Robert Rosenkranz, president, International Technical Service, DynCorp International, before the Committee on House Government Reform, Subcommittee on National Security, Emerging Threats, and International Relations, June 13, 2006.

6. Statement of Ignacio Balderas, former CEO and current Board of Directors member, Triple Canopy, before the Committee on House Government Reform, Subcommittee on National Security, Emerging Threats, and International Relations, June 13, 2006.

7. Statement of William M. Solis, director, Defense Capabilities and Management, United States Government Accountability Office, to the Committee on House Government Reform, Subcommittee on National Security, Emerging Threats, and International Relations, June 13, 2006.

8. "Utahn gets 'rush' as bodyguard," *Deseret Morning News*, May 19, 2006.

9. Clayton Hirst, "No more must they cry havoc and let slip the dogs of war," *The Independent*, November 28, 2004.

10. Barry Yeoman, "Dirty Warriors: How South African Hit Men, Serbian Paramilitaries, and Other Human Rights Violators Became Guns for Hire for Military Contractors in Iraq," *Mother Jones*, November–December 2004.

11. Karen Robb, "Contracting agency offers hiring perks for Iraq work," *Marine Corps Times*, October 8, 2004.

CHAPTER 5

1. The best account from soldiers of American torture in Vietnam is "Winter Soldier Investigation" (Detroit, January 31–February 2, 1971), the complete transcript of which was introduced into the Congressional Record by Senator Mark Hatfield of Oregon. See Veterans Testimony on Vietnam, 92nd Congress, 1st sess., Congressional Record, 117, part 8 (April 5–19, 1971), 9947-10055. The edited version is available under Vietnam Veterans against the War (VVAW), *The Winter Soldier Investigation* (Boston: Beacon Press, 1972). Also valuable is Mark Lane's "Conversations with Americans and House Committee on Government Operations," Subcommittee on Government Operations, U.S.

Assistance Programs in Vietnam: Hearings, 92nd Cong., 1st sess., 1971; James Ron, *Frontiers and Ghettos*: State Violence in Serbia and Israel (Berkeley: University of California Press, 2003); Darius Rejali, *Torture and Democracy* (Princeton: Princeton University Press, 2005); and Edward Peters, *Torture*, 2nd ed. (Berkeley: University of California Press, 1989).

On the legal debate on "ill treatment" versus "torture," the best recent discussion is in John Conroy's *Unspeakable Acts, Ordinary People* (Berkeley: University of California Press, 2001).

The best recent study of U.S. interrogation manuals and methods was conducted by the *Baltimore Sun* in the 1990s, and the declassified material is available at the National Security Archives at George Washington University. A recent analysis of what is permitted during interrogation is Jennifer K. Elsea, *Lawfulness of Interrogation Techniques under the Geneva Conventions*, Congressional Research Service, U.S. Library of Congress, RL32567, September 8, 2004.

2. William Neikirk, "Use of contractors for military purposes under scrutiny," *Chicago Tribune*, May 9, 2004.

3. Julian Borger, "'Cooks and drivers were working as interrogators': Witness: Private contractor lifts the lid on systematic failures at Abu Ghraib jail," *The Guardian*, May 7, 2004.

4. Hearing of the Senate Armed Services Committee, "Mistreatment of Iraqi Prisoners," Washington, D.C., May 7, 2004.

5. http://www.house.gov/apps/list/press/il09_schakowsky/pr5_04_2004iraq.html.

6. Human Rights Watch letter to General Jay Garner on Human Rights priorities during Iraqi reconstruction, http://www.hrw.org/press/2003/04/iraq42403ltr.htm.

7. Joshua Chaffin, "Contractor defers billings for Abu Ghraib work," *Financial Times*, June 16, 2004.

8. Jonathan Karp, "As Titan mutates to meet needs of Pentagon, risks become clear," *Wall Street Journal*, June 28, 2004, p. 1.

9. "Titan Wins $255 Million Department of Defense Joint Intelligence Support Contract," Titan Corp., July 23, 2004, http://www.defense-aerospace.com/cgi-bin/client/modele.pl?prod=43022&session=dae.4430928.1090888536.QQWjWMOa9dUAAHexZYY&modele=jdc_1.

10. Christopher Deliso, "Tales from the Titan's Mouth: An Iraq Contractor Speaks," *Antiwar.com*, October 15, 2004, http://www.antiwar.com/deliso/?articleid=3786.

11. CACI's Web site has a FAQ list, "CACI in Iraq—Frequently Asked Questions and Special Information" at http://www.caci.com/iraq_news.shtml.

12. Reinhardt Krause, "Giving them what they need," *Investor's Business Daily*, July 21, 2005.

13. *Marketplace*, National Public Radio, May 3, 2004.

14. "CACI Completes Acquisition of Premier Technology Group, Inc.: Expands CACI Support for Military Intelligence and Information Technology," CACI News Release, May 15, 2003, http://www.caci.com/about/news/news2003/05_15_03_NR.html. For details on how CACI became involved in intelligence work, see Ellen McCarthy, "Intelligence work comes to CACI via acquisitions," *Washington Post*, July 8, 2004, p. E1.

15. Scott Shane, "Some US prison contractors may avoid charges," *Baltimore Sun*, May 24, 2004, p. 1A.

16. http://www.caci.com/about/ethics.shtml.

17. Matt Kelley, "Iraq interrogator contracts blocked," Associated Press, May 26, 2004.

18. "Review of 12 Procurements Placed under General Services Administration Federal Supply Schedules 70 and 871 by the National Business Center" (Assignment No. W-EV-OSS-0075-2004), United States Department of the Interior, Office of Inspector General, Memorandum, July 16, 2004, http://www.oig.doi.gov/upload/CACI%20LETTER. txt; and Ellen McCarthy, "Interior Dept. inquiry faults procurement," *Washington Post*, July 17, 2004.

19. Ellen McCarthy, "CACI gets new interrogation contract," *Washington Post*, August 5, 2004, p. E5. The contract, for a period of four months, was worth $15.3 million and had two optional extensions worth up to $3.8 million each, for a total value of $23 million. CACI noted that the contract was issued directly by the Army and not through any other government organization. The interrogation support services would continue to be provided under the direction of the U.S. military in Iraq. Source: "CACI Receives Contract Extension for US Army Interrogation Support in Iraq," August 10, 2004, http://biz. yahoo.com/prnews/040810/dctu005_1.html.

20. David Phinney, "DoD tightening contracting rules after Iraqi prison scandals," *Federal Times*, June 7, 2004, p. 4; and Shane Harris, "Defense Tightens Reins on Outside Contracts," *GovExec.com*, June 17, 2004.

21. Ellen McCarthy, "Contractors sometimes stretch their deals: Iraq work done beyond scope of agreements," *Washington Post*, May 31, 2004, p. E1.

22. Neil King Jr. and Christopher Cooper, "Army hired Cuba interrogators via same disputed system in Iraq," *Wall Street Journal*, July 15, 2004, p. 4. See also Pratap Chaterjee, "Meet the new interrogators: Lockheed Martin," *CorpWatch*, November 4, 2005.

23. Ibid.

24. Shane Harris, "GSA Queries Lockheed Martin on Interrogation Contracts," *GovExec.com*, July 29, 2004.

25. Gail Gibson and Scott Shane, "Contractors act as interrogators," *Baltimore Sun*, May 4, 2004.

26. "Outrage," *Nightline*, ABC News Transcripts, May 5, 2004.

27. Joel Brinkley, "Private contractor use violated Army's policy," *New York Times*, June 12, 2004.

28. William Matthews, "The Deal on Contractors: How Much Is Too Much in Providing DoD Services?" *Armed Forces Journal* (November 2004).

29. Memo from Patrick T. Henry, Office of the Assistant Secretary, Manpower and Reserve Affairs, Department of the Army, December 26, 2000, http://www.publicintegrity. org/wow/docs/25-d_intelligence.pdf.

30. Hearing of the Senate Armed Services Committee, "The Army Inspector General's Report on the Abuse in Abu Ghraib Prison and Detention Operations Doctrine and Training." Witnesses: Les Brownlee, acting secretary of the Army; General Peter Schoonmaker, chief of staff of the Army; Lieutenant General Paul Mikolashek, inspector general of the Army, July 22, 2004.

31. The Church report on detainee interrogation and incarceration was completed under the direction of Vice Admiral Albert T. Church, an officer in the United States Navy. Church was then the naval inspector general. His mandate was to investigate the interrogation and incarceration of detainees in the United States "war on terror" in Afghanistan, Iraq, and Guantanamo Bay. The inquiry was initiated on May 25, 2004. A version of its report was finished on March 2, 2005. An unclassified 21-page executive summary, http://cryptome.org/church-report.htm, was circulated. The full 368-page report is classified. Human Rights Watch reported that the Church inquiry didn't interview any detainees. Source: http://en.wikipedia.org/wiki/Church_Report_on_detainee_interrogation.

CACI issued a press release stating that it was pleased that the Church report "recognized the value and diligent service of civilian interrogators provided by CACI and other private contractors," even though it acknowledged that it had access only to the executive summary of the report and did not know if the "very few instances" of contractor abuses involved CACI employees. Source: "CACI Says Church Report Underscores Critical Value of Interrogation Services to Saving Military Lives and National Security," Press Release, CACI International Inc., PRNewswire-FirstCall, March 10, 2005.

32. "The Final Report of the Independent Panel to Review DoD Operations," p. 21, and Appendix B, p. 1, http://www.dod.gov/news/Aug2004/d20040824finalreport.pdf. Details of past and ongoing investigations can also be read in the August 25 "Background Briefing on Investigations at Abu Ghraib," http://www.defenselink.mil/transcripts/2004/tr20040825-1222.html.

33. Ellen McCarthy, "Changes behind the barbed wire: New standards are in place for the oversight of contract workers at Abu Ghraib prison," *Washington Post*, December 13, 2004, p. E1.

34. Ibid.

35. For records related to the Taguba Report that were released under the Freedom of Information Act, see http://www.aclu.org/safefree/torture/torturefoia.html. Note that many documents are still being withheld by the U.S. government.

36. Seymour M. Hersh, "Torture at Abu Ghraib," *New Yorker*, May 10, 2004.

37. Stephanowicz, 34, enlisted in the U.S. Naval Reserve in February 1998, according to records from the Navy. He served in Muscat, Oman, for most of 2002, and his rank is listed as intelligence specialist 3rd class. Stephanowicz, who received a number of military awards, including a medal for meritorious service, left his last post, at Willow Grove, Pennsylvania, in September 2003. Source: Ellen McCarthy, "CACI worker did nothing wrong, lawyer says," *Washington Post*, May 11, 2004, p. 13.

38. *Article 15-6 Investigation of the 800th Military Police Brigade*, http://cryptome.org/army-report.htm.

39. "Private Contractors Directed Some Iraqi Prisoner Abuse," *Capitol Blue*, June 15, 2004, http://www.capitolhillblue.com/artman/publish/article_4692.shtml; and Scott Shane, "Civilian interrogator denies promoting physical abuse of Abu Ghraib prisoners," *Baltimore Sun*, June 15, 2004.

40. Pratap Chatterjee, "Intelligence, Inc.: Military interrogation training gets privatized," *CorpWatch*, March 7, 2005.

41. Mark Benjamin and Michael Scherer, "'Big Steve' and Abu Ghraib," *Salon*, March 31, 2006.

42. Mark Benjamin, "No Justice for All," *Salon*, April 14, 2006.

43. Leon Worden, "Abu Ghraib translator unschooled in Geneva Conventions," *The Signal*, April 21, 2005; and Leon Worden, "From Santa Clarita to Abu Ghraib, one year later," *The Signal*, April 24, 2005.

44. Renae Merle, "Contractor investigated by Justice: Criminal inquiry targets civilian," *Washington Post*, May 22, 2004, p. A17; and Joel Brinkley, "US civilian working at Abu Ghraib disputes army's version of his role in abuses," *New York Times*, May 26, 2004.

45. Deborah Avant, "What are those contractors doing in Iraq?" *Washington Post*, May 9, 2004, p. B01.

46. Peter Singer on *All Things Considered*, National Public Radio, May 3, 2004.

47. Brinkley, "U.S. civilian working at Abu Ghraib."

48. Joel Brinkley, "200,000 employees awaiting clearance to work for military," *New York Times*, May 12, 2004.

49. Joel Brinkley and James Glanz, "Civilian employees: Contractors in sensitive roles, unchecked," *New York Times*, May 7, 2004.

50. Wade-Hahn Chan, "OMB: Security clearance backlog will be under control this year," *Federal Computer Week*," February 15, 2008.

51. Joel Brinkley, "The civilians: 9/11 set army contractor on path to Abu Ghraib," *New York Times*, May 19, 2004.

52. "The Sky's the Limit," Blog: The Daily Outrage, *The Nation*, January 13, 2005.

53. Ellen McCarthy, "Changes behind the barbed wire: New standards are in place for the oversight of contract workers at Abu Ghraib prison," *Washington Post*, December 13, 2004, p. E1.

54. Peter Singer of the Brookings Institution discussed the role of private military contractors working at Abu Ghraib in Iraq on *Fresh Air*, National Public Radio, May 11, 2004.

55. Jonathan Karp, "Titan fires translator accused of mistreating Iraqi prisoners," *Wall Street Journal*, May 24, 2004, p. 7.

56. This was the written statement, made two hours before Nakhla's second interview, by Kasim Mehaddi Hilas. Hilas identified the rapist only by the pseudonym Abu Hamid. The man was a translator, recalled Hilas. He was also large ("not skinny or short"), and his accent was Egyptian.

In the CID report, Nakhla is never mentioned by the detainees in Tier 1, even though the translator had been reassigned there. When asked about Nakhla, Nelson says that he didn't really know the man. "He would have had much more interaction with the M.P.'s," Nelson said, "and especially the Tier 1 M.P.'s."

Although Nakhla's name is absent from the detainee claims of abuse, there are references to a man named Abu Hamid (sometimes spelled Abu Hamed by an interpreter). Hayder Sabbar Abd was one of the six victims of the November night of torture and humiliation that was documented in photographs and that caused outrage around the world: pictures of men naked, hooded with sandbags, forced to form a human pyramid, to ride on each other's backs, and to simulate oral sex. Abd, whose prison number was 13077, said in his sworn statement that a translator named Abu Hamed was there, translating the commands of Abd's tormentors. In May, after Abd was released, he told a *New York Times* reporter the same thing. The translator's name is not mentioned in the *Times* piece, only the fact that the man was Egyptian.

Source: Osha Gray Davidson, "Contract to Torture," *Salon.com*, August 9, 2004, http://oshadavidson.com/contractors_salon.pdf.

Note that the Fay report also said that an interpreter "allegedly raped a 15–18 year old male detainee," according to another detainee. The report says the description of the interpreter "partially matches" that of a Titan interpreter, Civilian 17. The report says the Titan interpreter allegedly involved in the rape also was "present during the abuse of detainees depicted in photographs." Source: McCarthy, "Changes behind the barbed wire."

57. Tara McKelvey, "The Unaccountables," *American Prospect*, September 7, 2006.

58. Nelson was mistakenly identified in the report as a Titan employee when he actually worked for CACI.

59. Pratap Chatterjee, "An Interrogator Speaks Out," *AlterNet*, March 7, 2005.

60. Julian Borger, "Private contractor lifts the lid on systematic failures at Abu Ghraib jail," *The Guardian*, May 7, 2004.

61. Robert Lusetich, "Private firms at centre of very public scandal," *Weekend Australian*, May 8, 2004, p. 11.

62. Printed in the *Guardian*'s Corrections and Clarifications column, Friday, May 14, 2004, http://www.guardian.co.uk/international/story/0,3604,1211351,00.html.

63. "CACI Emphasizes Facts Presented during Congressional Testimony on Iraq Prison Investigation and Requirements Related to Company's US Military Contract," http://www.caci.com/about/news/news2004/05_09_04_NR.html.

64. Griff Witte, "Contractors were poorly monitored, GAO says: Report contends CACI performed jobs in Iraq meant for government," *Washington Post*, April 30, 2005, p. E1; and Shane Harris, "Oversight of interrogation contracts broke down, GAO finds," *Government Executive*, May 4, 2005.

65. Ellen McCarthy, "CACI defense contracts hazy on civilian authority: Language reserves direction for military," *Washington Post*, July 29, 2004, p. E5.

66. Jason Vest, "Haunted by Abu Ghraib," *Government Executive*, April 1, 2006.

67. Roeseanne Gerin, "How Do You Respond?" *Washington Technology* 20, no. 4 (February 21, 2005). For a view that reflects CACI's position that it was unfairly tarred by the media, see J. Phillip London, *Our Good Name: A Company's Fight to Defend Its Honor and Get the Truth Told about Abu Ghraib* (Washington, DC: Regnery Publishing, 2008).

68. Ellen McCarthy, "CACI plans to drop interrogation work: Firm was entangled in Abu Ghraib," *Washington Post*, September 15, 2005, p. D4. See also "The Center for Constitutional Rights Credits Pressure from Advocacy Group and Public with CACI International Withdrawal from Iraq," Center for Constitutional Rights Press release, September 21, 2005, http://www.commondreams.org/cgi-bin/newsprint.cgi?file=/news2005/0921-05.htm.

69. David Johnston and Neil A. Lewis, "U.S. examines role of C.I.A. and employees in Iraq deaths," *New York Times*, May 6, 2004.

70. Department of the Army, the Inspector General, *Detainee Operations Inspection*, July 21, 2004, http://www4.army.mil/ocpa/reports/ArmyIGDetaineeAbuse/DAIG%20Detainee%20Operations%20Inspection%20Report.pdf.

71. "CACI Clarifies Information about Its Interrogation Services for US Army: Army Inspector General Report Determines CACI Interrogators Met Army Statement of Work (Work Order) Criteria," July 26, 2004, http://www.caci.com/about/news/news2004/07_26_04_NR.html.

72. Shane Harris, "Contractors Were Hired to Oversee Interrogations," *GovExec. com*, July 27, 2004, http://www.govexec.com/story_page.cfm?articleid=29096&dcn=todaysnews. Eleven work orders worth $66.2 million awarded to CACI were obtained by the Center for Public Integrity in Washington, D.C., and can be viewed at http://www.publicintegrity.org/wow/printer-friendly.aspx?aid=361.

73. Department of the Army, the Inspector General, *Detainee Operations Inspection*, pp. 87–89.

74. Ibid, p. 89.

75. Matt Andrejczak, "Army Asks CACI Interrogators to Leave," *CBS.Market-Watch.com*, August 12, 2004.

76. "CACI Reports Preliminary Findings of Internal Investigation: Company Provides Information about Its Interrogator Support Personnel in Iraq, No Evidence of Abusive Wrongdoing Uncovered," http://caci.com/about/news/news2004/08_12_04_NR.html.

77. Walter Pincus, "As army adds interrogators, it outsources training," *Washington Post*, September 23, 2006, p. A14.

78. "SCV Newsmaker of the Week: Brig. Gen. Janis Karpinski, Fmr. Commander, 800th Military Police Brigade," presented by the SCV Press Club and Comcast. Hosted by Signal City editor Leon Worden (telephone interview conducted June 29, 2004), printed in *The Santa Clarita Signal*, July 4, 2004.

79. Mark Bowden, "The Ploy," *Atlantic Monthly*, May 2007.

80. June 3 letter to President Bush by Representatives Henry Waxman, John Conyers Jr., David R. Obey, Ike Skelton, Tom Lantos, and Jane Harman, http://www.house.gov/lantos/releases/PR_040603_Iraq_PrisonScandal.html.

81. David Phinney, "Contract meals 'disaster' for Iraqi prisoners," *CorpWatch*, December 9, 2004, http://www.corpwatch.org/article.php?id=11744.

82. Phillip Carter, "How to discipline private contractors: What consequences do the companies involved in Abu Ghraib face?" *Slate*, May 4, 2004.

83. Ibid.

84. For details, see Anthony J. Sebok, "What Tort Claims, If Any, Can Be Brought by the Inmates Who Were Tortured in Iraq?" May. 17, 2004, http://writ.news.findlaw.com/sebok/20040517.html.

85. Renae Merle, "CACI and Titan sued over Iraq operations: Legal center alleges abuse of prisoners," *Washington Post*, June 10, 2004, p. E3. See also Deborah Hastings, "Former Iraqi prisoners sue: Abuse victims file longshot cases against companies who provided civilian workers," Associated Press, October 24, 2004.The actual filing, *United States* v. *David F. Passaro* (June 17, 2004), can be accessed at http://www.ccr-ny.org/v2/legal/september_11th/docs/Al_Rawi_v_Titan_Complaint.pdf.

86. http://www.burkepyle.com/Saleh/rico-case-statement.pdf.

87. Eric Fair, "An Iraq interrogator's nightmare," *Washington Post*, February 9, 2007, p. A19.

88. Gina Holland, "Supreme Court rejects human rights suit," *The Guardian*, June 29, 2004, http://www.guardian.co.uk/uslatest/story/0,1282,-4258365,00.html. See the Court decision in *Sosa* v. *Alvarez-Machain* at http://wid.ap.org/documents/scotus/040629sosa.pdf. See also Anthony J. Sebok, "The Alien Tort Claims Act: How Powerful a Human Rights Weapon Is It?" Findlaw's Writ, Legal Commentary, July 12, 2004, http://writ.news.findlaw.com/sebok/20040712.html.

89. *Ilham Nassir Ibrahim* v. *Titan Corp.* (July 27, 2004), "Iraqi Plaintiffs Sue Private US Contractors under the Alien Tort Claims Act and RICO Laws, Seeking Damages for Alleged Torture by Defendants Working in Iraq," http://news.findlaw.com/hdocs/docs/torture/ibrahimtitan72704cmp.html.

90. "Edmond & Jones, LLP: Iraqi Civilians File Claim against Private US Firms, Claiming Murder, Torture and Abuse in Abu Ghraib Prison," July 27, 2004, *PR Newswire*, http://www.prnewswire.com/cgi-bin/stories.pl?ACCT=109&STORY=/www/story/07-27-2004/0002218903&EDATE=.

91. *Ilham Nassir Ibrahim, et al., Plaintiffs,* v. *Titan Corporation, et al., Defendants. Saleh, et al., Plaintiffs,* v. *Titan Corporation, et al., Defendants*, Civil Action No. 04-1248 (JR), Civil Action No. 05-1165 (JR), United States District Court for the District of Columbia, 2007 U.S. Dist. Lexis 81794, November 6, 2007, FILED.

92. Lara Jakes Jordan, "Judge allows abuse lawsuit against firm," Associated Press, November 6, 2007; and Josh White, "Judge allows Abu Ghraib lawsuit against contractor," *Washington Post*, November 7, 2007, p. A13.

93. Dan Eggen and Walter Pincus, "Ashcroft says US can prosecute civilian contractors for prison abuse," *Washington Post*, May 7, 2004, p. 18.

94. Kathleen Cahill, "Outside contractors, outside military law," *Washington Post*, May 9, 2004, p. B5; and Joanne Mariner, *Private Contractors Who Torture*, May 10, 2004, http://writ.news.findlaw.com/scripts/printer_friendly.pl?page=/mariner/20040510.html.

95. BOFAXE, Prosecuting private contractors under US law for the mistreatment of detainees in Abu Ghraib, No. 272E, May 17, 2004, http://www.ifhv.de.

96. "Sec. 506. Torture Convention Implementation," Foreign Relations Authorization Act, Fiscal Years 1994 and 1995, http://thomas.loc.gov/cgi-bin/query/F?c103:6:./temp/~c103XuDdI2:e263954.

97. Charlie Savage, "Justice Dept. can target war crime: Scholars cite way to punish abuse of Iraqis," *Boston Globe*, May 12, 2004.

98. For details on MEJA, see Major Joseph R. Perlak, "The Military Extraterritorial Jurisdiction Act of 2000: Implications of Contractor Personnel," *Military Law Review* 169 (September 2001): 92–140; and Captain Glenn R. Schmitt (USAR), "The Military Extraterritorial Jurisdiction Act: The Continuing Problem of Criminal Jurisdiction over Civilians Accompanying the Armed Forces Abroad—Problem Solved?" *Army Lawyer* (December 2000).

99. See *Report of the Advisory Committee on Criminal Law Jurisdiction over Civilians Accompanying the Armed Forces in Time of Armed Conflict (Overseas Jurisdiction Advisory Committee)*, April 1997, http://www.fas.org/irp/doddir/dod/ojac.pdf.

100. For background, see Military Extraterritorial Jurisdiction Act of 1999, Hearing before the Subcommittee on Crime of the Subcommittee on the Judiciary, House of Representatives, One Hundred Sixth Congress, Second Session, on H.R. 3380, March 30, 2000, http://commdocs.house.gov/committees/judiciary/hju64399.000/hju64399_0.htm.

101. The term "employed by the Armed Forces outside the US" means "employed as a civilian employee of DoD, as a DoD contractor or as an employee of a DoD contractor, who is present or residing outside the US in connection with such employment, and is not a national of or ordinarily resident in the host nation." The term "accompanying the Armed Forces outside the US" means a family member of a member of the Armed Forces, a civilian employee of the DoD, a DoD contractor, or an employee of a DoD contractor, not a national of or ordinarily resident in the host nation. See http://www.dscp.dla.mil/contract/doc/contractor.doc.

102. Seth Stern, "Contractors Hover in Gray Area Regarding Legal Liability," *Congressional Quarterly Weekly*, May 8, 2004.

103. Jessica Iñigo, "In first use of jurisdiction act, USAF spouse to be tried in husband's death," *Stars and Stripes*, European edition, June 5, 2003, http://www.estripes.com/article.asp?section=104&article=15275&archive=true. See also Gail Gibson, "Prosecuting abuse of prisoners," *Baltimore Sun*, May 29, 2004; and David Rosenzweig, "Air Force wife guilty in spouse's fatal stabbing," *Los Angeles Times*, October 16, 2004.

104. This is taken from a May 11, 2004, e-mail sent to the author.

105. Drawn from Fredrick A. Stein, "Have We Closed the Barn Door Yet? A Look at the Current Loopholes in the Military Extraterritorial Jurisdiction Act," *Houston Journal of International Law* (Spring 2005).

106. Gibson, "Prosecuting abuse of prisoners." According to Rep. Price:

"I also authored an amendment to the National Defense Authorization Act of 2005 to ensure that civilian contractors are not above the law. The amendment would have clarified that the Military Extraterritorial Jurisdiction Act (MEJA) applies to all civilian contractors supporting US military missions overseas, even if they are subcontractors or foreign nationals. It also would have delineated the enforcement responsibilities of the

Departments of Justice and Defense. Unfortunately, the Rules Committee decided not to allow the House to debate this amendment. I have introduced the amendment as a stand-alone bill, HR 4390, and have also introduced a companion bill, HR 4749, which would set standards for contracting and require that the government collect basic information from its contractors to ensure accountability. I will be working to enact both into law in the remaining months of the 108th Congress." Source: http://price.house.gov/UploadedFiles/abu%20ghraib.doc.

107. "Meehan Introduces Legislation to Increase Private Contractor Accountability," May 18, 2004, http://www.house.gov/apps/list/press/ma05_meehan/NR040518Iraq Contractors.html. The bill can be accessed at http://thomas.loc.gov/home/gpoxmlc108/h4387_ih.xml. See also "Price Introduces New Bill on Civilian Contractors," http://price.house.gov/News/DocumentSingle.aspx?DocumentID=4875.

108. R. J. Hillhouse, "Congress Implies CIA Contractors Involved in Criminal Activities in Iraq," *The Spy Who Billed Me*, October 5, 2007, http://www.thespywhobilledme.com/the_spy_who_billed_me/2007/10/congress-implie.html.

109. Spencer Ackerman, "Today's must read," *TPM Muckraker*, October 4, 2007, http://www.tpmmuckraker.com/archives/004373.php.

110. Michael Sirak, "ICRC Calls for Contractor Accountability in War," *Jane's Defence Weekly*, May 19, 2004, p. 4.

111. John Liang, "DOD Revamping Contracting Guidelines in the Wake of CACI Interrogation Scandal," *InsideDefense.com*, October 25, 2004.

112. Michael Hardy, "DOD Works to Get Contracting Right," *Federal Computer Week*, November 15, 2004, p. 10.

113. Karen Robb, "GSA contracts lose favor with DoD managers," *Federal Times*, November 8, 2004.

114. Richard Sammon, "Pentagon to Rein in Private Companies," *Kiplinger Business Forecasts* 2004, no. 0521 (May 18, 2004).

115. Shane Harris, "Lack of Personnel, Expertise Impede Iraq Reconstruction," *Government Executive*, November 11, 2004, http://www.govexec.com/dailyfed/1104/111104h1.htm.

CHAPTER 6

1. See, for example, Paul Jackson, "'War Is Much Too Serious a Thing to Be Left to Military Men': Private Military Companies, Combat and Regulation," *Civil Wars* 5, no. 4 (Winter 2002): 30–55.

2. See Jennifer Elsea and Nina M. Serafino, *Private Security Contractors in Iraq: Background, Legal Status, and Other Issues*, Congressional Research Service, RL32419, May 28, 2004. Some illustrative articles from law journals are Devin R. Desai, "Have Your Cake and Eat It Too: A Proposal for a Layered Approach to Regulating Private Military Companies," *University of San Francisco of Law Review*, 39 U.S.F. L. Rev. 825, Summer 2005; James R. Coleman, "Constraining Modern Mercenarism, *Hastings Law Journal*, 55 Hastings L.L. 1493, June 2004; Mark W. Bina, "Private Military Contractor Liability and Accountability after Abu Ghraib," *The John Marshall Law Review*, 38 J. Marshall L. Rev. 1237, Summer 2005; Martha Minow, "Outsourcing Power: How Privatizing Military Efforts Challenges Accountability, Professionalism, and Democracy," *Boston Law College*

Review, 46 B.C.L. Rev 989, September 2005; and Laura A. Dickinson, "Government for Hire: Privatizing Foreign Affairs and the Problem of Accountability under International Law, *William & Mary Law Review*, 47 Wm and Mary L. Rev. 135, October 2005.

3. For details, see Major Todd S. Milliard, "Overcoming Post-Colonial Myopia: A Call to Recognize and Regulate Private Military Companies," *Military Law Review* 176 (June 2003): 19–76; and Peter Singer, "War, Profits, and the Vacuum of Law: Privatized Military Firms and International Law," *Columbia Journal of International Law* 42, no. 2, Spring 2004.

4. Jackie Spinner, "Private security crews emerge as another feared element in Baghdad," *Washington Post*, November 28, 2005, p. 16.

5. Awadh al-Taee and Steve Negus, "Shoot first, pay later culture pervades Iraq," *Financial Times*, March 18, 2005.

6. Mark Townsend, "Fury at 'shoot for fun' memo: Outburst by US security firm in Iraq is attacked by human rights groups," *The Observer*, April 3, 2005.

7. Warden Message: U.S. Government Temporary Suspension of Personal Security Detail Operations in Erbil, Iraq, Consular Affairs Bulletin Middle East/N. Africa–Iraq, July 20, 2005.

8. Jonathan Finer, "Security contractors in Iraq under scrutiny after shootings," *Washington Post*, September 10, 2005, p. 1.

9. Andrew J. Bacevich, "What's an Iraqi life worth?" *Washington Post*, July 9, 2006, p. B1.

10. Jonathan Finer, "State Department contractors kill 2 civilians in N. Iraq," *Washington Post*, February 9, 2006, p. 18.

11. Sean Rayment, "'Trophy' video exposes private security contractors shooting up Iraqi drivers," *London Telegraph*, November 27, 2005.

12. David Phinney, "From mercenaries to peacemakers?" *CorpWatch*, November 29, 2005.

13. Jonathan Finer, "Contractors cleared in videotaped attacks: Army fails to find 'probable cause' in machine-gunning of cars in Iraq," *Washington Post*, June 11, 2006, p. 18.

14. Matt Armstrong, "Holding Contractors Accountable," *MountainRunner*, September 20, 2007, http://mountainrunner.us/2007/09/holding_contractors_accountabl.html.

15. Ken Silverstein, "Six Questions for Robert Young Pelton," Washington Babylon, *Harper's Magazine*, September 7, 2006, http://harpers.org/archive/2006/09/sb-six-questions-robert-young-pelton-1157654152.

16. John Accola, "Private security guard sues after reporting claims of 'unprofessional conduct,'" *Rocky Mountain News*, December 15, 2005; and Alan Prendergast, "Blackwater isn't the only security contractor with something to hide," *Denver Westworld*, October 25, 2007.

17. Nick Butterly, Sam Riches, "Aussie dies in bungle Baghdad security mix-up," *Hobart Mercury*, March 30, 2006, p. 4.

18. Jay Price, "Hired guns unaccountable," *News&Observer* [Raleigh, North Carolina], March 23, 2006, p. A1.

19. "Hired guns; U.S.-paid private security contractors in Iraq seem to work almost literally without oversight. That could be big trouble," *News&Observer* [Raleigh, North Carolina], March 25, 2006, p. A18.

20. Karen DeYoung, "State Department struggles to oversee private army," *Washington Post*, October 21, 2007. p. 1.

21. Yochi J. Dreazen, "New scrutiny for Iraq contractors: Killing by Blackwater worker poses dilemma for U.S. authorities," *Wall Street Journal*, May 14, 2007, p. 4; John M. Broder, "Ex-paratrooper is suspect in a Blackwater killing," *New York Times*, October 4, 2007.

22. "Contractor Involved in Iraq Shooting Got Job in Kuwait," *CNN.com*, Oct. 4, 2007.

23. "Blackwater CEO Testifies on Hill," *Jim Lehrer Newshour*, October 2, 2007.

24. Eric Schmitt, "Report details shooting by drunken Blackwater worker," *New York Times*, October 2, 2007.

25. Ned Parker and Raheem Salman, "Blackwater under scrutiny in Iraq," *Los Angeles Times*, September 21, 2007, p. 1.

26. Steve Fainaru, "How Blackwater sniper fire felled 3 Iraqi guards," *Washington Post*, November 8, 2007, p. A1.

27. Steve Fainaru and Saad al-Izzi, "U.S. security contractors open fire in Baghdad," *Washington Post*, May 27, 2007, p. A1.

28. Steve Fainaru and Amit R. Paley, "Private guards fire on Taxi; three Iraqis hurt, police say," *Washington Post*, October 19, 2007, p. A16.

29. R. J. Hillhouse, "Help Wanted for Controversial Blackwater Contract," *The Spy Who Billed Me*," October 19, 2007.

30. Steve Fainaru, "Guards in Iraq cite frequent shootings," *Washington Post*, October 3, 2007.

31. The following five paragraphs are taken from David Isenberg, "Dogs of war: More oversight needed," *UPI*, February 8, 2008.

32. http://www.cpa-iraq.org/regulations/20040627_CPAORD_17_Status_of_Coalition__Rev__with_Annex_A.pdf.

33. Ibid.

34. CPA Order 17, *Wikipedia*, http://en.wikipedia.org/wiki/CPA_Order_17.

35. Katherine McIntire Peters, "Buck Private: Meet the new face of the armed forces in Iraq: A security contractor," *Government Executive*, October 1, 2004. What Professor Avant is referring to is a statutory change made by the USA PATRIOT Act, passed in October 2001. A little-noticed section of that omnibus bill changed the federal criminal jurisdiction statute, 18 U.S.C. § 7, to include "the premises of United States diplomatic, consular, military or other United States Government missions or entities in foreign States . . . irrespective of ownership." In essence, this change extends U.S. federal criminal jurisdiction to follow the flag wherever U.S. diplomats and soldiers may operate.

36. This information on the limitation of the AECA is taken from Constantine Golowinski, *Access to Information: The Case of Private Military Contractors*, J440 Controls of Information. Accessed March 18, 2008, via the Wayback machine, http://web.archive.org/web/*/http://foi.missouri.edu/controls/golowinski.doc.

37. Ibid., Sec. 3 (b).

38. Renae Merle, "Pentagon revises contractor rules," *Washington Post*, May 7, 2005, p. E1.

39. Nathan Hodge, "Despite new rules, military contractors overseas still in 'gray area,'" *Defense Daily*, May 10, 2005.

40. Sharon Behn, "Iraq security companies lobby for heavy arms," *Washington Times*, June 6, 2005, p. 1.

41. (P.L.109–364). See "The Law Catches Up to Private Militaries, Embeds," *DefenseTech.org*, http://www.defensetech.org/archives/003123.html; and William Matthews, "Law subjects contractors to military justice," *Federal Times*, January 15, 2007.

42. Mark Hemingway, "Blackwater's Legal Netherworld," *National Review Online*, September 26, 2007.

43. Jenny Mandel, "Military justice code now covers some contractors," *Government Executive*, January 9, 2007.

44. Lieutenant Junior Grade David A. Melson, JAGC, USN, "Military Jurisdiction over Civilian Contractors: A Historical Overview," *Naval Law Review* 52 (2005): 277.

45. Jonathan Finer, "Recent Developments: Holstering the Hired Guns: New Accountability Measures for Private Security Contractors," *Yale Journal of International Law* 33 (Winter 2008): 259.

46. "Civilian Contractors in Iraq: Accountability and the Uniform Code of Military Justice," International Peace Operations Association Press Release, January 11, 2007. See also Griff Witte, "New law could subject civilians to military trial," *Washington Post*, January 15, 2007, p. A1.

47. Nathan Hodge, "Private Security Firms Weigh Impact of US Law Change," *Jane's Defence Weekly*, January 31, 2007.

48. "UCMJ Jurisdiction over DOD Civilian Employees, DOD Contractor Personnel, and Other Persons Serving with or Accompanying the Armed Forces Overseas during Declared War and in Contingency Operations," March 10, 2008, http://www.pscouncil.org/pdfs/DoDUCMJMemo03-10-08.pdf.

49. Jim Wolf, "US Lacks Standardized Rules for Iraq Contractors," *ABC News*, http://www.abcnews.go.com/wire/US/reuters20040624_514.html, June 24, 2004.

50. For example, see "Contractors on the Battlefield," *Air Force Journal of Logistics* (October 1999); Air Force General Counsel Guidance Document, Department of the Air Force, *Deploying with Contractors: Contracting Considerations*, November 2003; HQ AFMC Contingency Contracting Web site, https://www.afmc-mil.wpafb.af.mil/HQ-AFMC/PK/pko/gotowar.htm; Army Field Manual 4-100.2 (FM100-10-2), *Contracting Support on the Battlefield*, August 4, 1999; Army Regulation 715-9, *Contractors Accompanying the Force*, October 29, 1999: Army Materiel Command Pamphlet 715-18, *AMC Contracts and Contracting Supporting Military Operations*, June 16, 1999; *Concept for Managing Weapon System Contractors during Military Operations*, Draft, June 16, 1999; Department of the Army Pamphlet 715-16, *Contractor Deployment Guide*, February 27, 1998; Army Field Manual 3-100.21 (FM100-21), *Contractors on the Battlefield*, March 21, 2000; "Institutionalizing Contractor Support on the Battlefield," *Army Logistician* 32, no. 4 (July–August 2000): 12–15, 22; Joe A. Fortner, "Managing, Deploying, Sustaining, and Protecting Contractors on the Battlefield," *Army Logistician* 32, no. 5 (September–October 2000): 3–7; P.L.106-523, *Military Extraterritorial Jurisdiction Act of 2000*; and OMB Circular No. A-76, "Performance of Commercial Activities," August 4, 1983 (Revised 1999); and the bibliography *Contractors on the Battlefield*, Library Notes, Naval War College, October 2003, Vol. 32, No. 2, http://www.nwc.navy.mil/library/3Publications/NWCLibraryPublications/LibNotes/libContractors.htm.

51. Fawzia Sheikh, "Uncertainty Still Surrounds Application of UCMJ Law to Contractors," *Inside the Army*, March 5, 2007.

52. Ibid.

53. David Phinney, "DoD rule would permit arming of contractors," *Federal Times*, March 29, 2004, p. 1. See also *Federal Register* 69, no. 56 (March 23, 2004): 13500–13503 [Proposed Rules]: SUMMARY: DoD is proposing to amend the Defense Federal Acquisition Regulation Supplement (DFARS) to address issues related to contract performance outside the United States. The proposed rule contains a clause for use in

contracts that require contractor employees to accompany a force engaged in contingency, humanitarian, peacekeeping, or combat operations.

54. Ibid.

55. Jason Sherman, "New Defense Policy to Guide Role of Contractors on the Battlefield," *Inside the Pentagon*, October 20, 2005.

56. http://www.acq.osd.mil/dpap/dars/dfars/html/current/tochtml.htm.

57. http://www.cpa-iraq.org/regulations/20031231_CPAORD3_REV__AMD_.pdf.

58. http://www.cpa-iraq.org/regulations/20030822_CPAMEMO_5_Implementation_of_Weapons_Control_with_Annex_A.pdf.

59. Statement of Chris Taylor Vice, president, Blackwater USA, to the Committee on House Government Reform, Subcommittee on National Security, Emerging Threats, and International Relations, June 13, 2006.

60. Peter Spiegel, "U.S. is faulted for using private military workers," *Los Angeles Times*, May 24, 2006.

61. Peter W. Singer, *Humanitarian Principles, Private Military Agents: Some Implications of the Privatized Military Industry for the Humanitarian Community*, Brookings Institution, http://www.brookings.edu/views/articles/singer20060307.pdf.

62. *Iraq Reconstruction: Lessons in Human Capital Management, Special Inspector General for Iraq Reconstruction*, January 2006, http://www.sigir.mil/reports/pdf/Lessons_Learned_Feb16.pdf.

63. James Glanz, "Modern mercenaries on the Iraqi frontier," *New York Times*, April 4, 2004.

64. Michael Schwartz, "A government with no military and no territory: Iraq's sovereignty vacuum (Part 1)," *TomDispatch.com*, March 9, 2006, http://www.tomdispatch.com/index.mhtml?pid=66969.

65. This section on the ICC is derived from Heather Carney, "Prosecuting the Lawless: Human Rights Abuses and Private Military Firms," *George Washington Law Review* (February 2006).

CHAPTER 7

1. For details on the past activities of Executive Outcomes, see Al J. Venter, *War Dog: Fighting Other People's Wars* (Drexel Hill, PA: Casemate, 2006).

2. Jennifer Elsea and Nina M. Serafino, "Private Security Contractors in Iraq: Background, Legal Status and Other Issues," Congressional Research Service, May 28, 2004, RL 32419, http://www.opencrs.com/rpts/RL32419_20040528.pdf.

3. July 11, 2006, phone conversation with a man who used to be in management for a major private security contractor that still operates in Iraq.

4. Seth Borenstein, "Insurance, security prove costly for contractors in Iraq," *Knight Ridder/Tribune News Service*, April 1, 2004.

5. Rowan Scarborough, "Iraqi construction funds go to security," *Washington Times*, February 9, 2006, p. 1.

6. Vivienne Morgan, "£100m Spent on Iraq Private Security Firms," Press Association Newsfile, February 27, 2006.

7. See Charlotte Eagar, "A game of tisk," *Evening Standard* [London], March 31, 2006; and Jonathan Guthrie, "Tim Spicer finds security in the world's war zones," *Financial Times* [London], April 7, 2006, London Edition 1, p. 21.

8. Robert Verkaik, "The war dividend," *The Independent* [London], March 13, 2006, p. 1.

9. Bradley Graham and Glenn Kessler, "Iraq security for U.S. teams uncertain: Use of reconstruction coordinators has been approved," *Washington Post*, March 3, 2006, p. 11. See also Fred Burton, "Iraq: Leaving the Green Zone," *Stratfor*, April 6, 2006, http://www. libertypost.org/cgi-in/readart.cgi?ArtNum=135746.

10. "The Swiss Guard of Baghdad," March 3, 2006, http://www.strategypage.com/ htmw/htinf/articles/20060303.aspx.

11. Subcontractors were Military Professional Resources Inc., Science Applications International Corp., Eagle Group International Inc., Omega Training Group, and World-wide Language Resources Inc.

12. Ariana Eunjung Cha, "Recruits abandon Iraqi Army: Troubled training hurts key component of Bush security plan, *Washington Post*, December 13, 2003, p. A1.

13. Michael Hirsh, "Iraq: Breaking the Silence: A Prominent Former Insider Is Criticizing the Administration's Handling of Iraq's Reconstruction. And There's More to Come," *Newsweek*, March 22, 2006.

14. See Eric J. Fredland, "Outsourcing Military Force: A Transactions Cost Perspective on the Role of Military Companies," *Defence & Peace Economic* 15, no. 3 (June 2004): 205–219.

15. See Moshe Adler, "Sometimes, government is the answer," *Los Angeles Times*, March 4, 2006.

16. Deborah D. Avant, *The Market for Force: The Consequences of Privatizing Security*, (New York: Cambridge University Press, 2005), 48.

17. Walter F. Roche Jr., "Documents describe US auditors' battles with Halliburton," *Los Angeles Times*, March 29, 2006; Griff Witte, "Documents trace KBR billing problems," *Washington Post*, March 29, 2006, p. 7; and "Billions Wasted in Iraq?" *CBS News*, February 12, 2006, http://www.cbsnews.com/stories/2006/02/09/60minutes/ main1302378.shtml.

18. James Glanz, "U.S. should repay millions to Iraq, a U.N. audit finds," *New York Times*, November 5, 2005.

19. IAMB press conference, United Nations, December 28, 2005, http://www.iamb. info/trans/tr122805.htm. The IAMB's mandate was due to expire on December 31, 2005, but was extended by the UN Security Council to the end of 2006.

20. IAMB press release, January 20, 2006, http://www.iamb.info/pr/pr013006.htm.

21. See http://en.wikipedia.org/wiki/Custer_Battles; and Charles R. Babcock, "Contractor accused of profiteering," *Washington Post*, February 16, 2006, p. D2.

22. For details, see David Isenberg, "The Good, the Bad, and the Unknown: PMC in Iraq," http://basicint.org/pubs/2006PMC.htm. This paper was written and presented at the "Guns'n gates: The role of private security actors in armed violence," Cost Action 25 Working Group 3 roundtable, held in Bonn, Germany, February 9–10, 2006.

23. Peter W. Singer, *Can't Win with 'Em, Can't Go to War without 'Em: Private Military Contractors and Counterinsurgency*, Foreign Policy at Brookings, Policy Paper #4, September 2007. See also P. W. Singer, "Sure, he's got guns for hire. But they're just not worth it," *Washington Post*, October 7, 2007.

24. These suggestions are taken from Malcolm Nance, "All Hands on Deck—Radically Reorienting Private Security in Iraq," *Small Wars Journal Blog*, September 22, 2007, http://smallwarsjournal.com/blog/2007/09/all-hands-on-deck-radically-re/.

25. August Cole, "Fresh bid to lift veil on security work: More disclosure sought from armed contracting firms," *MarketWatch*, May 16, 2005.

26. Jason Sherman, "DoD Revises 'Law of War' Program, Adds Requirements for Contractors," *Inside the Pentagon*, May 18, 2006.

27. David DeVoss, "Iraq's 'Dirty Harrys': The swagger and tactics of private security guards are doing more harm than good," *Los Angeles Times*, September 23, 2007.

28. Kinsey, op. cit.

29. http://iraq.usembassy.gov/iraq/iraq_pco.html.

30. This point comes from William Moloney, *What has been the experience of the Private Military Industry in Iraq and what are the possible lessons for future deployments?* Master's Dissertation, 2004, War Studies Department, Kings College, London, unpublished research paper, p. 15.

31. Ibid.

32. Kinsey, op. cit.

33. Portions of this section are taken from David Isenberg, "Dogs of war: The importance of oversight," *UPI*, February 1, 2008.

34. Hearing on Contracting in Iraq, Subcommittee on Defense, House Appropriations Committee, May 10, 2007.

35. Renae Merle, "Government short of contracting officers," *Washington Post*, July 5, 2007, p. E8.

36. *Urgent Reform Required: Army Expeditionary Contracting: Report of the Commission on Army Acquisition and Program Management in Expeditionary Operations* ("Gansler Commission" Report on Contracting), October 31, 2007, https://acc.dau.mil/CommunityBrowser.aspx?id=179150. See also Eric Schmitt, "Panel faults Army's wartime contracting," *New York Times*, November 1, 2007, p. 12.

37. Stephen Barr, "Contractors, the Army's neglected stepchildren," *Washington Post*, November 5, 2007, p. D4.

38. Charles R. Babcock, "Contractor bilked U.S. on Iraq work, federal jury rules," *Washington Post*, March 10, 2006, p. 14; Laura Parker, "Jury fines defense contractor in Iraq $10M," *USA Today*, March 10, 2006, p. 3A; and T. Christian Miller, "U.S. contractor found liable for fraud in Iraq," *Los Angeles Times*, March 10, 2006.

39. William C. Peters, "On Law, Wars and Mercenaries: The Case for Court-Martial Jurisdiction over Civilian Contract Misconduct in Iraq," *Brigham Young University Law Review* (2006): 2:367–414.

40. *Reid* v. *Covert*, 354 U.S. 1, 9 (1956). Carney, op. cit. (author's note 139).

Bibliography

BOOKS

Ashcroft, Capt. James. 2006. *Making a Killing: The Explosive Story of a Hired Gun in Iraq.* London: Virgin Books Ltd.

Avant, Deborah D. 2005. *The Market for Force: The Consequences of Privatizing Security.* NY Cambridge University Press.

Bryden, Alan, and Marina Caparini, eds. 2006. *Private Actors and Security Governance.* Zurich: Lit Verlag.

Chesterman, Simon, and Chia Lenhardt, eds. 2007. *From Mercenaries to Market: The Rise and Regulation of Private Military Companies.* New York: Oxford University Press.

Cole, Robert. 2007. *Under the Gun in Iraq: My Year Training the Iraqi Police.* Amherst, MA: Prometheus Books.

Cross, J. P., and Buddhiman Gurung, eds. 2007. *Gurkhas at War: Eyewitness Accounts from World War II to Iraq.* London: Greenhill Books/Lionel Leventhal Ltd.

Drohan, Madelaine. 2003. *Making a Killing: How Corporations Use Armed Force to Do Business.* Guilford, CT: The Lyons Press.

Geddes, John. 2006. *Highway to Hell: An Ex-SAS Soldier's Account of the Extraordinary Private Army Hired to Fight in Iraq.* London: Century.

Jäger, Thomas, and Gerhard Kümmel, eds. 2007. *Private Military and Security Companies: Chances, Problems, Pitfalls and Prospects.* Wiesbaden, Germany: Vs Verlag.

Kershaw, Alex. 2006. *The Few: The American "Knights of the Air" Who Risked Everything to Save Britain in the Summer of 1940.* Philadelphia: Da Capo Press.

Kinsey, Christopher. 2006. *Corporate Soldiers and International Security: The Rise of Private Military Companies.* Abingdon, VA: Routledge.

Lanning, Michael Lee. 2005. *Mercenaries: Soldiers of Fortune, from Ancient Greece to Today's Private Military Companies.* New York: Ballantine Books.

London, J. Phillip. 2008. *Our Good Name: A Company's Fight to Defend Its Honor and Get the Truth Told About Abu Ghraib.* Washington: Regnery Publishing.

Maogoto, Jackson, and Benedict Sheehy. 2008. *Legal Control of the Private Military Corporation: Belling the Cheshire Cat.* New York: Palgrave Macmillan.

Morgan, Cynthia I. 2006. *Cindy in Iraq: A Civilian's Year in the War Zone.* New York: Free Press.

Pelton, Robert Young. 2006. *Licensed to Kill: Hired Guns in the War on Terror.* New York: Crown Publishers.

Robins, Nick. 2006. *The Corporation That Changed the World: How the East India Company Shaped the Modern Multinational.* London: Pluto Press.

Rosen, Fred. 2005. *Contract Warriors: How Mercenaries Changed History and the War on Terrorism.* New York: Penguin Group.

Scahill, Jeremy. 2007. *Blackwater: The Rise of the World's Most Powerful Mercenary Army.* New York: Nation Books.

Schumacher, Col. Gerald, USA (ret.). 2006. *A Bloody Business: America's War Zone Contractors and the Occupation of Iraq.* St. Paul, MN: Zenith Press.

Singer, Peter W. 2003. *Corporate Warriors: The Rise of the Privatized Military Industry.* Ithaca, NY: Cornell University Press.

Stoker. Donald ed. 2008. *Military Advising and Assistance: From Mercenaries to Privatization, 1815–2007.* New York: Routledge.

Urban, William. 2006. *Medieval Mercenaries: The Business of War.* London: Greenhill Books.

Venter, Al J. 2006. *War Dog: Fighting Other People's Wars.* Philadelphia: Casemate.

Wulf, Herbert. 2005. *Institutionalizing and Privatizing War and Peace.* New York: Palgrave Macmillan.

JOURNAL ARTICLES

Abrahamsen, Rita, and Michael C. Williams. 2008. "Selling security: Assessing the impact of military privatization." *Review of International Political Economy* 15:131–146.

Adams, Thomas K. 1999. "The New Mercenaries and the Privatization of Conflict." *Parameters* 29:103–116.

Addicott, Jeffrey F. 2006. "Contractors on the 'Battlefield': Providing Adequate Protection, Anti-Terrorism Training and Personnel Recovery for Civilian Contractors Accompanying the Military in Combat and Contingency Operations." *Houston Journal of International Law* 28:323.

Avant, Deborah. 2004. "The Privatization of Security and Change in the Control of Force." *International Studies Perspectives* 5:153–157.

———. 2006. "The Implications of Marketized Security for IR Theory: The Democratic Peace, Late State Building, and the Nature and Frequency of Conflict." *Perspectives on Politics* 4:507–528.

———. 2006. "The Privatization of Security: Lessons from Iraq." *ORBIS* 50:327–342.

———. 2007. "Contracting for Services in U.S. Military Operations." *PS: Political Science and Politics* 40:457–460.

Avery, Abigail H. 2006. "Weapons of Mass Construction: The Potential Liability of Halliburton under the False Claims Act and the Implications to Defense Contracting." *Alabama Law Review* 57:827.

Bina, Mark W. 2005. "Private Military Contractor Liability and Accountability After Abu Ghraib." *The John Marshall Law Review* 38:1237.

Bjork, Kjell, and Richard Jones. 2005. "Overcoming Dilemmas Created by the 21st Century Mercenaries: Conceptualising the Use of Private Security Companies in Iraq." *Third World Quarterly* 26:777–796.

Blyth, Christina M. 2008. "Minding the Liability Gap: American Contractors, Iraq, and the Outsourcing of Impunity." *University of Miami Law Review* 62:651.

Brooks, Doug, and Jim Shevlin. 2005. "Reconsidering Battlefield Contractors." *Georgetown Journal of International Affairs* 6:2.

Calaguas, Mark. 2006. "Military Privatization: Efficiency or Anarchy?" *Chicago-Kent Journal of International and Comparative Law* 6:58–81.

Cameron, Lindsey. 2006. "Private military companies: Their Status under International Humanitarian Law and Its Impact on Their Regulation." *International Review of the Red Cross* 863:573–598.

Carmola, Kateri. 2006. "It's All Contracts Now: Private Military Firms and a Clash of Legal Culture." *Brown Journal of World Affairs* 13:161–173.

Carney, Heather. 2006. "Prosecuting the Lawless: Human Rights Abuses and Private Military Firms." *George Washington Law Review* 74:317.

Castillo, Lt. Col. Lourdes A., USAF. 2000. "Waging War with Civilians: Asking the Unanswered Questions." *Aerospace Power Journal* 14:26–31.

Casto, William R. 2006. "Regulating the New Privateers of the Twenty-First Century." *Rutgers Law Journal* 37:671–702.

Catera, Elise. 2008. "ATCA: Closing the Gap in Corporate Liability for Environmental War Crimes." *Brooklyn Journal of International Law* 33:629.

Charles, Valerie C. 2006. "Hired Guns and Higher Law: A Tortured Expansion of the Military Contractor Defense." *Cardozo Journal of International and Comparative Law* 14:593.

Clapham, Andrew. 2006. "Human Rights Obligations of Non-state Actors in Conflict Situations." *International Review of the Red Cross* 863:491–523.

Cockayne, James. 2006. "The Global Reorganization of Legitimate Violence: Military Entrepreneurs and the Private Face of International Humanitarian Law." *International Review of the Red Cross* 863:459–490.

Coleman, James R. 2004. "Constraining Modern Mercenarism." *Hastings Law Journal* 55:493.

Corn, Geoffrey S. 2008. "Bringing Discipline to the Civilianization of the Battlefield: A Proposal for a More Legitimate Approach to Resurrecting Military-Criminal Jurisdiction over Civilian Augmentees." *University of Miami Law Review* 62:491.

Cottier, Michael. 2006. "Elements for Contracting and Regulating Private Security and Military Companies." *International Review of the Red Cross* 863:637–662.

Davidson, Michael. 2000. "Ruck Up: An Introduction to the Legal Issues Associated with Civilian Contractors on the Battlefield." *Public Contract Law Journal* 29:233.

Deavel, R. Philip. 1998. "The Political Economy of Privatization for the American Military." *Air Force Journal of Logistics* 22:3.

Desai, Devin R. 2005. "Have Your Cake and Eat It Too: A Proposal for a Layered Approach to Regulating Private Military Companies." *University of San Francisco Law Review* 39:825.

Dickinson, Laura A. 2005. "Government for Hire: Privatizing Foreign Affairs and the Problem of Accountability under International Law." *William and Mary Law Review* 47:135.

———. 2006. "Public Law Values in a Privatized World." *Yale Journal of International Law* 31:383–426.

———. 2006. "Symposium: 'Torture and the War on Terror': Torture and Contract." *Case Western Reserve Journal of International Law* 37:267–275.

Donnelly, Robin M. 2006. "Civilian Control of the Military: Accountability for Military Contractors Supporting the U.S. Armed Forces Overseas." *Georgetown Journal of Law and Public Policy* 4:237.

Douglas, Karen L. 2004. "Contractors Accompanying the Force: Empowering Commanders with Emergency Change Authority." *Air Force Law Review* 55:127.

Doyle, Roger. 2007. "Contract Torture: Will Boyle Allow Private Military Contractors to Profit from the Abuse of Prisoners?" *Pacific McGeorge Global Business and Development Law Journal* 19:467.

Faite, Alexandre. 2004. "Involvement of Private Contractors in Armed Conflict: Implications under International Humanitarian Law." *Defence Studies* 4:166–183.

Fallah, Katherine. 2006. "Corporate Actors: The Legal Status of Mercenaries in Armed Conflict." *International Review of the Red Cross* 863:599–611.

Fallon, Andrew D., and Capt. Theresa A. Keene. 2001. "Closing the Legal Loophole? Practical Implications of the Military Extraterritorial Jurisdiction Act of 2000." *The Air Force Law Review* 51:271.

Fergusson, James. 2006. "War Dog: Fighting Other People's Wars—The Modern Mercenary in Combat." *Perspectives on Political Science.* 35:176–177.

Finer, Jonathan. 2008. "Recent Developments: Holstering the Hired Guns: New Accountability Measures for Private Security Contractors." *Yale Journal of International Law* 33:259.

Fredland, J. Eric. 2004. "Outsourcing Military Force: A Transactions Cost Perspective on the Role of Military Companies." *Defence and Peace Economics* 15:205–219.

Freeman, Jody. 2000. "The Contracting State." *Florida State University Law Review* 28:155.

Fricchione, Kristen. 2005. "Casualties in Evolving Warfare: Impact of Private Military Firms Proliferation on the International Community." *Wisconsin International Law Journal* 23:731.

Frye, Ellen L. 2005. "Private Military Firms in the New World Order: How Redefining 'Mercenary' Can Tame the 'Dogs of War.'" *Fordham Law Review* 73:2607–2664.

Garmon, Tina. 2003. "Domesticating International Corporate Responsibility: Holding Private Military Firms Accountable under the Alien Tort Claims Act." *Tulane Journal of International and Comparative Law* 11:325.

Gaston, E. L. 2008. "Mercenarism 2.0? The Rise of the Modern Private Security Industry and Its Implications for International Humanitarian Law Enforcement." *Harvard International Law Journal* 49:221.

Giardino, Capt. Anthony E. 2007. "Using Extraterritorial Jurisdiction to Prosecute Violations of the Law of War: Looking beyond the War Crimes Act." *Boston College Law Review* 48:699.

Gillard, Emanuela-Chiara. 2006. "Business Goes to War: Private Military/Security Companies and International Humanitarian Law." *International Review of the Red Cross* 863:525–572.

Greenstock, Jeremy. 2006. "Private Security Companies in an Insecure World." *Royal Uniformed Services Institute (RUSI) Journal* 151.

Guillory, Maj. Michael E. 2001. "Civilianizing the Force: Is the United States Crossing the Rubicon?" *The Air Force Law Review* 51:111.

Gul, Saad. 2006. "The Secretary Will Deny All Knowledge of Your Actions: The Use of Private Military Contractors and the Implications for State and Political Account-ability." *Lewis and Clark Law Review* 10:287.

Hamaguchi, Cara-Ann M. 2008. "Between War and Peace: Exploring the Constitu-tionality of Subjecting Private Civilian Contractors to the Uniform Code of Military Justice During 'Contingency Operations.'" *North Carolina Law Review* 86:1047.

Harney, Maj. Mary E. 1998. "The Quiet Revolution: Downsizing, Outsourcing, and Best Value." *Military Law Review* 158:48.

Heaton, Maj. J. Ricou. 2005. "Civilians at War: Reexamining the Status of Civilians Accompanying the Armed Forces." *The Air Force Law Review* 57:155.

Heibel, Matt. 2006. "Military Inc.: Regulating and Protecting the 'A-Teams' of the Post-Modern Era." *Pace International Law Review* 18:531.

Hellinger, Daniel. 2004. "Humanitarian Action, NGOs and the Privatization of the Military." *Refugee Survey Quarterly* 23: 4 pp.

Hemingway, Tom. 2006. "Outsourcing of War: The Role of Contractors on the Battlefield." *Humanitäres Völkerrecht* 19:129–132.

Jackson, Katherine. 2007. "Not Quite a Civilian, Not Quite a Soldier: How Five Words Could Subject Civilian Contractors in Iraq and Afghanistan to Military Jurisdiction." *Journal of the National Association of Administrative Law Judiciary* 27:255.

Joseph, Jeremy. 2007. "Striking the Balance: Domestic Civil Tort Liability for Private Security Contractors." *Georgetown Journal of Law and Public Policy* 5:691.

Kassebaum, David. 2000. "A Question of Facts—The Legal Use of Private Security Firms in Bosnia." *Columbia Journal of Transnational Law* 38:51.

Kierpaul, Ian. 2008. "The Mad Scramble of Congress, Lawyers, and Law Students After Abu Ghraib: The Rush to Bring Private Military Contractors to Justice." *University of Toledo Law Review* 39:407.

Kinsey, Christopher. 2003. "International Law and Control of Mercenaries and Private Military Companies." *Cultures et Conflits* 52:91–116.

———. 2005. "Examining the Organizational Structure of UK Private Security Compa-nies." *Defence Studies* 5:188–212.

———. 2005. "Regulation and Control of Private Military Companies: The Legislative Dimension." *Contemporary Security Policy* 26, no. 1:84–102.

———. 2005. "Challenging International Law: A Dilemma of Private Security Compa-nies." *Conflict, Security and Development* 5:269–293.

Krahmann, Elke. 2005. "Private Military Services in the UK and Germany: Between Partnership and Regulation." *European Security* 14:277–295.

———. 2005. "Regulating Private Military Companies: What Role for the EU?" *Contem-porary Security Policy* 26:103–125.

Kritsiotis, Dino. 1998. "Mercenaries and the Privatization of Warfare." *Fletcher Forum of World Affairs* 22:11–25.

Kummel, Gerhard. 2005. "The Privatization of Security: Private Military and Security Companies in International Relations." *Zeitschrift fur Internationale Beziehungen* 12:141–169.

Leander, Anna. 2005. "The Power to Construct International Security: On the Significance of Private Military Companies." *Millennium: Journal of International Studies* 33:803–826.

Liebl, Ryan J. 2005. "Rule of Law in PostWar Iraq: From Saddam Hussein to the American Soldiers Involved in the Abu Ghraib Scandal, What Law Governs Whose Actions?" *Hamline Law Review* 28:91.

Lindemann, Marc. 2007. "Civilian Contractors under Military Law." *Parameters* 37 (Autumn 2007): 83–93.

Logan, Ryan P. 2006. "The Detainee Treatment Act of 2005: Embodying U.S. Values to Eliminate Detainee Abuse by Civilian Contractors and Bounty Hunters in Afghanistan and Iraq." *Vanderbilt Journal of Transnational Law* 39:1605.

Lytton, Christopher H. 2006. "Blood for Hire: How the War in Iraq Has Reinvented the World's Second Oldest Profession." *Oregon Review of International Law* 8:307.

Maclellan, Nic. 2006. "From Fiji to Fallujah: The War in Iraq and the Privatization of Pacific Security." *Pacific Journalism Review* 12:47–65.

———. 2007. "Fiji, Iraq and Pacific island security." *Race and Class* 48:47–62.

Mandel, Robert. 2001. "The Privatization of Security." *Armed Forces and Society* 28:129–151.

Mandernach, Christopher J. 2007. "Warriors Without Law: Embracing a Spectrum of Status for Military Actors." *Appalachian Journal of Law* 7:13.

Maogoto, Jackson Nyamuya, and Benedict Sheehy. 2006. "Contemporary Private Military Firms under International Law: An Unregulated 'Gold Rush.'" *Adelaide Law Review* 26:245–269.

Markusen, Ann R. 2003. "The Case against Privatizing National Security." *Governance: An International Journal of Policy, Administration, and Institutions* 16:471–501.

Martin, Jennifer S. 2007. "Contracting for Wartime Actors: The Limits of the Contract Paradigm." *New England Journal of International and Comparative Law* 14:11.

Mathonniere, Julien. 2004. "Soldiers for Sale: The Privatization of War?" *Defense nationale*. 60, no. 7:67–79.

McCormack, Shawn. 2007. "Private Security Contractors in Iraq Violate Laws of War." *Suffolk Transnational Law Review* 31:75.

Melson, Lt. (JG) David A. 2005. "Military Jurisdiction over Civilian Contractors: A Historical Overview." *Naval Law Review* 52:277–321.

Micallef, Ryan. 2006. "Liability Laundering and Denial of Justice Conflicts Between the Alien Tort Statute and the Government Contractor Defense." *Brooklyn Law Review* 71:1375.

Michaels, Jon D. 2004. "Beyond Accountability: The Constitutional, Democratic, and Strategic Problems with Privatizing War." *Washington University Law Quarterly* 82:1001–1127.

Milliard, Maj. Todd S. 2003. "Overcoming Post-Colonial Myopia: A Call to Recognize and Regulate Private Military Companies." *Military Law Review* 176:1–95.

Minow, Martha. 2005. "Outsourcing Power: How Privatizing Military Efforts Challenge Accountability, Professionalism, and Democracy." *Boston College Law Review* 46:989.

Mlinarcik, J. T. 2006. "Private Military Contractors and Justice: A Look at the Industry, Blackwater and the Fallujah Incident." *Regent Journal of International Law* 4:129.

Mongelard, Eric. 2006. "Corporate Civil Liability for Violations of International Humanitarian Law." *International Review of the Red Cross* 863:665–691.

Morgan, Richard. 2008. "Professional Military Firms under International Law." *Chicago Journal of International Law* 9:213.

Morris, Jessica C. 2007. "Civil Fraud Liability and Iraq Reconstruction: A Return to the False Claims Acts War-Profiteering Roots?" *Georgia Law Review* 41:623.

Newell, Virginia, and Benedict Sheehy. 2006. "Corporate Militaries and States: Actors, Interactions and Reactions." *Texas International Law Journal* 41:67.

Newton, Michael A. 2006. "Symposium: 'Torture and the War on Terror': War by Proxy: Legal and Moral Duties of 'Other Actors' Derived from Government Affiliation." *Case Western Reserve Journal of International Law* 37:249.

Nitzschke, Lt. Col. Stephen G. 2005. "The Adaptable Force: Privatization and the Public Military." *Information Age Warfare Quarterly* 1:1.

Oulton, Donald P., and Alan F. Lehman. 2001. "Deployment of U.S. Military, Civilian and Contractor Personnel to Potentially War Hazardous Areas from a Legal Perspective." *DISAM Journal* 23:15–21.

Parrillo, Nicholas. 2007. "The De-Privatization of American Warfare: How the U.S. Government Used, Regulated, and Ultimately Abandoned Privateering in the Nineteenth Century." *Yale Journal of Law and the Humanities* 19:1.

Percy, Sarah V. 2003. "This Gun's for Hire: A New Look at an Old Issue." *International Journal* 58:721–736.

Perlak, Maj. Joseph R. 2001. "The Military Extraterritorial Jurisdiction Act of 2000: Implications for Contractor Personnel." *Military Law Review* 169:92–140.

Perrin, Benjamin. 2006. "Promoting Compliance of Private Security and Military Companies with International Humanitarian Law." *International Review of the Red Cross* 863:613–636.

Peters, William C. 2006. "On Law, Wars and Mercenaries: The Case for Courts-Martial Jurisdiction over Civilian Contractor Misconduct in Iraq." *Brigham Young University Law Review* 2:367–414.

Pfanner, Toni. 2006. "Interview with Andrew Bearpark." *International Review of the Red Cross* 863:449–457.

Rakowsky, Kateryna L. 2006. "Military Contractors and Civil Liability: Use of the Government Contractor Defense to Escape Allegations of Misconduct in Iraq and Afghanistan." *Stanford Journal of Civil Rights and Civil Liberties* 2:365.

Rehman, Atif. 2006. "The Court of Last Resort: Seeking Redress for Victims of Abu-Ghraib Torture through the Alien Tort Claims Act." *Indiana International and Comparative Law Review* 16:493.

Renou, Xavier. 2005. "Private Military Companies against Development." *Oxford Development Studies*. 33:107–115.

Rosemann, Nils. 2005. "The Privatization of Human Rights Violations—Business Impunity or Corporate Responsibility? The Case of Human Rights Abuses and Torture in Iraq." *Journal of Non-State Actors and International Law* 5:77–100.

Rosky, Clifford J. 2004. "Force Inc.: The Privatization of Punishment, Policing, and Military Force in Liberal States." *Connecticut Law Review* 36:879.

Ruys, Tom. 2005. "Attacks by Private Actors and the Right of Self-Defense." *Journal of Conflict and Security Law* 10:289.

Sapone, Montgomery. 1999. "Have Rifle with Scope, Will Travel: The Global Economy of Mercenary Violence." *California Western International Law Journal* 30:5.

Schneiker, Andrea. 2005. "Privatization of the Military? Private Military Companies as an Actor in US Foreign Policy." *WeltTrends* 49:135–143.

Schmitt, Maj. Glenn R. 2001. "Closing the Gap in Criminal Jurisdiction over Civilians Accompanying the Armed Forces Abroad—A First Person Account of the Creation of the Military Extraterritorial Jurisdiction Act of 2000." *Catholic University Law Review* 51:55.

————. 2005. "Amending the Military Extraterritorial Jurisdiction Act (MEJA) of 2000: Rushing to Close an Unforeseen Loophole." *Army Lawyer*, June 2005:41–47.

Schmitt, Michael N. 2005. "War, International Law, and Sovereignty: Reevaluating the Rules of the Game in a New Century: Humanitarian Law and Direct Participation in Hostilities by Private Contractors or Civilian Employees." *Chicago Journal of International Law* 5:511–546.

Schooner, Steven L. 2005. "Contractor Atrocities at Abu Ghraib: Comprised Accountability in a Streamlined Outsourced Government." *Stanford Law and Policy Review* 16:549.

Scoville, Ryan M. 2006. "Toward an Accountability-Based Definition of 'Mercenary.'" *Georgetown Journal of International Law* 37:541–581.

Sifton, John. 2006. "United States Military and Central Intelligence Agency Personnel Abroad: Plugging the Prosecutorial Gaps." *Harvard Journal of Legislation* 43:487–516.

Singer, Peter W. Winter 2001–2002. "Corporate Warriors: The Rise of the Privatized Military Industry and Its Ramifications for International Security." *International Security* 26:186–220.

————. 2004. "Profits, and the Vacuum of Law: Privatized Military Firms and International Law." *Columbia Journal of Transnational Law* 42:521–549.

————. 2005. "Outsourcing War." *Foreign Affairs* 84:2.

Smith, Eugene B. Winter 2002–2003. "The New Condottieri and US Policy: The Privatization of Conflict and Its Implications." *Parameters* 32:104–119.

Sjoberg, Gideon. 2005. "The Corporate Control Industry and Human Rights: The Case of Iraq." *Journal of Human Rights* 4:95–101.

Spearin, Christopher. 2004. "The Emperor's Leased Clothes: Military Contractors and Their Implications in Combating International Terrorism." *International Politics* 41:243–264.

————. 2007. "Contracting a Counterinsurgency? Implications for US Policy in Iraq and Beyond." *Small Wars and Insurgencies* 18:541–558.

Stein, Frederick A. 2005. "Have We Closed the Barn Door Yet? A Look at the Current Loopholes in the Military Extraterritorial Jurisdiction Act." *Houston Journal of International Law* 17:579–608.

Stinnett, Nathaniel. 2005. "Regulating the Privatization of War: How to Stop Private Military Firms from Committing Human Rights Abuses." *Boston College International and Comparative Law Review* 28:211–224.

Strydom, Hennie. 2005. "Private Military Companies: Some Legal Issues." *Strategic Review for Southern Africa* 27:85.

Taulbee, James L. 1998. "Reflections on the Mercenary Option." *Small Wars and Insurgencies* 9:145–163.

Terry, Bryan. 2007. "Private Attorneys General v. 'War Profiteers': Applying the False Claims Act to Private Security Contractors in Iraq." *Seattle University Law Review* 30:809.

Tiefer, Charles. 2007. "The Iraq Debacle: The Rise and Fall of Procurement-Aided Unilateralism as a Paradigm of Foreign War." *University of Pennsylvania Journal of International Economic Law* 29:1.

Turner, Maj. Lisa L., and Maj. Lynn G. Norton. 2001. "Civilians at the Tip of the Spear." *The Air Force Law Review* 51:1.

Verkuil, Paul R. 2006. "Public Law Limitations on Privatization of Government Functions." *North Carolina Law Review* 84:397.

Waits, K. Elizabeth. 2006. "Avoiding the 'Legal Bermuda Triangle': The Military Extrater-ritorial Jurisdiction Act's Unprecedented Expansion of U.S. Criminal Jurisdiction over Foreign Nationals." *Arizona Journal of International and Comparative Law* 23:493.

Walker, Clive, and Dave Whyte. 2005. "Contracting Out War? Private Military Companies, Law and Regulation in the United Kingdom." *International and Comparative Law Quarterly* 54:651–690.

Wen Abigail Hing. 2003. "Suing the Sovereign's Servant: The Implications of Privatiza-tion for the Scope of Foreign Sovereign Immunities." *Columbia Law Review* 103:1538.

Whyte, David. 2003. "Lethal Regulation: State-Corporate Crime and the United Kingdom Government's New Mercenaries." *Journal of Law and Society* 30:575–600.

Wither, James K. 2005. "European Security and Private Military Companies: The Prospects for Privatized 'Battlegroups.'" *PfP Consortium Quarterly Journal* 4:107–128.

Wolf, Antenor Hallo de. 2006. "Modern Condottieri in Iraq: Privatizing War from the Perspective of International and Human Rights Law." *Indiana Journal of Global Legal Studies* 13:315–356.

Zarate, Juan Carlos. 1998. "The Emergence of a New Dog of War: Private International Security Companies, International Law, and the New World Order." *Stanford Journal of International Law* 34:75–156.

PAPERS

Armstrong, Matthew. 2007. "Is the Privatization of Force Organic to Western Liberal Democracy?" Conference Papers—Midwestern Political Science Association; 2007 Annual Meeting.

Avant, Deborah, and Lee Siegelman, "What Does Private Security in Iraq Mean for Democracy at Home?" January 2008. http://www.international.ucla.edu/cms/files/PrivateSecurityandDemocracy.pdf.

Bereziuk, Bryan. 2004. "The Corporation: A New State Actor in the International Political System." For partial completion of the MA in War Studies Programme.

Beutel, Dee. 2006. "Power Reconsidered: The Effects of Private Military Companies and the Need for Regulation through International Collaboration." Paper presented at the annual meeting of the American Political Science Association, Marriott, Loews Philadelphia, and the Pennsylvania Convention Center, Philadelphia, PA, 2006-08-31.

Blakely, Gregg. 2006. "Marketized Soldiering: How Private Military Companies Chal-lenge Global Governance, Erode Accountability and Exacerbate Conflict." Simon Fraser University. http://ir.lib.sfu.ca/retrieve/4187/etd2603.pdf.

Brandle, Shawna. 2007. "Closing the Loophole: Finding a Place for Private Military Firms in the Laws of War." Conference Papers—Northeastern Political Science Association; 2007.

Cameron, Lindsey. 2006. "Private Military Companies: International Humanitarian Law Considerations Affecting Their Regulation." Paper from Nonstate Actors in Standard Setting—The Erosion of the Public-Private Divide conference, held in Basel, Switzerland, on 8–9 February 2007. http://www.baselgovernance.org/fileadmin/docs/pdfs/Nonstate/Cameron.pdf.

Carette, Alexandre. 2006. "New and Emerging Threats: Are Private Military Firms up to the Challenge?" Paper presented at the Revolution or Evolution? Emerging Threats to Security in the 21st Century, First Annual Graduate Symposium, Dalhousie University, Halifax, Nova Scotia, Canada, March 25, 2006.

Carmola, Kateri. 2007. "Privatized Actors and the Ethics of Contemporary Warfare." Conference Papers—International Studies Association; 2007 Annual Meeting.

———. 2006. "Abu Ghraib, the US Military and the Complications of Responsibility." Conference Papers—International Studies Association, 2006 Annual Meeting.

———. 2005. "Global Warriors: Private Companies and the Ambiguities of National Strategy." Conference Papers—American Political Science Association, 2005 Annual Meeting.

———. 2004. "Outsourcing Military Action: The Legal and Ethical Consequences of Private Military Corporations." Conference Papers—International Studies Association, 2004 Annual Meeting.

Clark, Martha K. 2007. "Soldier and the Contractor: The Interactions of Military and Private Security Company Personnel in the Field of Combat." Paper prepared for the Annual Meeting of the International Studies Association Chicago, Illinois February 28–March 3, 2007.

DeWinter, Rebecca. 2007. "From Mercenaries to Corporate Actors: Processes of Legitimizing Private Military and Security Companies." Conference Papers—International Studies Association; 2007 Annual Meeting.

Fitzsimmons, Scott. 2007. "The Art of Private Warfare: A Military Culture Theory of the Military Performance of Modern Mercenary Forces." Conference Papers—International Studies Association; 2007 Annual Meeting.

Hedahl, Capt. (USAF) Marc O. "Outsourcing the Profession: A Look at Military Contractors and Their Impact on the Profession of Arms." Paper presented at the Joint Services Conference on Professional Ethics (JSCOPE) 2005 conference, Springfield, Virginia. http://www.usafa.edu/isme/JSCOPE05/Hedahl05.html.

Holmqvist, Caroline. 2005. "Private Security Companies: The Case for Regulation." Stockholm International Peace Research Institute Policy Paper No. 9. http://www.sipri.org/contents/conflict/SIPRI_PolicyPaper9.pdf.

Isenberg, David. 1997. "Soldiers of Fortune Ltd.: A Profile of Today's Private Sector Corporate Mercenary Firms." Center for Defense Information Monograph. http://www.cdi.org/issues/mercenaries.

———. 2004. "A Fistful of Contractors: The Case for a Pragmatic Assessment of Private Military Companies in Iraq." BASIC Research Report 2004.2, September 27, 2004. http://basicint.org/pubs/Research/2004PMC.htm.

———. 2006. "The Good, the Bad, and the Unknown: PMCs in Iraq." Presentation given at the "Guns 'n gates: The role of private security actors in armed violence" Cost Action 25 Working Group 3, Bonn, Germany, February 9–10, 2006. http://basicint.org/pubs/2006PMC.htm.

———. 2006. "A Government in Search of Cover: PMCs in Iraq." Paper presented to the "Market Forces: Regulating Private Military Companies" Institute for International Law and Justice conference at the New York University School of Law, March 23–24, 2006. http://basicint.org/pubs/Papers/pmcs0603.htm.

———. 2006. Chapter Eight, "Challenges of Security Privatisation in Iraq." Pp. 149–166 in *Private Actors and Security Governance*. Edited by Alan Bryden and Marina Caparini, Geneva Centre for the Democratic Control of Armed Forces (DCAF), LIT Verlag, October 2006.

————. 2007. Chapter Five, "A Government in Search of Cover: Private Military Compa-
nies in Iraq." Pp. 82–93 in *From Mercenaries to Market: The Rise and Regulation of
Private Military Companies*. Edited by Simon Chesterman and Chia Lehnardt. New
York: Oxford University Press, 2007.

Kidwell, Deborah C. 2005. "Public War, Private Fight? The United States and Private
Military Companies." Global War on Terrorism Occasional Paper 12, Combat
Studies Institute Press, Army Command and General Staff College, Fort Leaven-
worth, KS.

Krahmann, Elke. 2006. "'The Soldier and the State' in the New Millennium: From Citizen-
Soldier to Entrepreneur." Conference Papers—International Studies Association,
2006 Annual Meeting.

Lawyer, Jared F. 2003. "The Role of Private Military Corporations in Failing Nation
States." Presented at the Conference on Multinational Corporations, Development
and Conflict, Queen Elizabeth House, Oxford, December 6, 2003.

Leander, Anna. 2004. "The Power to Construct International Security: On the Significance
of the Emergence of Private Military Companies." Paper presented at the Facets of
Power in International Relations conference, Session 5, London School of Economics,
October 30–31, 2004.

————. 2004. "Private Agency and the Definition of Public Security Concerns: The Role
of Private Military Companies." Political Science Publications No. 8/2004, Syddansk
Universitet (University of Southern Denmark).

Lee, Simon W. 2007. "Making a Killing on the Battlefield: Private Military Companies and
Their Status under International Law." Paper submitted for the Francis Lieber Prize,
2007.

Mandel, Robert. 2006. "Robots, Mercenaries, and Soldiers: The Comparative Utility of
Future Fighting Forces." Conference Papers—International Studies Association;
2006 Annual Meeting.

Marshall, Robert. 2006. "Militarizing P3s: The State, New Public Management and
Outsourcing War." Paper presented to the session "A Second Look at Public-Private
partnerships," Annual Meeting of the Canadian Political Science Association, York
University, Toronto, Ontario, May 27–June 3, 2006.

Messner, J. J., and Ylana Gracielli. 2007. "State of the Peace and Stability Operations
Industry, Second Annual Survey 2007." Peace Operations Institute.

Mingst, Karen A. 2005. "Security Firms, Private Contractors and NGOs: New Issues
About Humanitarian Standards." Paper presented at the International Studies Association Convention, Honolulu, Hawaii, March 5, 2005.

Møller, Bjørn. 2005. "Privatisation of Conflict, Security and War." Danish Institute for
International Studies Working Paper 2005/2.

Möller, Sara. 2006. "Private Military Contractors in Iraq—Legal Status and State Responsibility." Master's thesis, Faculty of Law, University of Lund, Spring 2006.

Moloney, William. 2004 "What Has Been the Experience of the Private Military Industry
in Iraq and What Are the Possible Lessons for Future deployments?" Master's dissertation, War Studies Department, Kings College, London.

Nitzschke, Stephen G. 2004. "The Adaptable Force: Privatization and the Public Military."
Naval War College, October 14, 2004.

Sakamoto, E. Elize. 2006. "Governing the Provision of Arms in International Private Security Services." Paper for the British International Studies Association Annual Conference University of Cork, December 18–20, 2006. http://www.bisa.ac.uk/2006/pps/
sakamoto.pdf.

Schreier, Fred, and Marina Caparini. 2005. "Privatising Security: Law, Practice and Governance of Private Military and Security Companies." Geneva Centre for the Democratic Control of Armed Forces Occasional Paper No. 6, March 2005.

Singer, Peter W. 2007. "Can't Win with 'Em, Can't Go to War without 'Em: Private Military Contractors and Counterinsurgency." Foreign Policy at Brookings, Policy Paper #4, September 2007. http://www.brookings.edu/~/media/Files/rc/papers/2007/0927militarycontractors/0927militarycontractors.pdf.

"State of the Peace and Stability Operations Industry 2006." 2006. International Peace Operations Association.

Stollenwerk, Michael F. 1998. "LOGCAP: Can Battlefield Privatization and Outsourcing Create Tactical Synergy?" School of Advanced Military Studies (SAMS) Monograph, US Army Command and General Staff College (CGSC), Fort Leavenworth, KS.

Voelz, Glenn James. 2006. "Managing the Private Spies: The Use of Commercial Augmentation for Intelligence Operations." Center for Strategic Intelligence Research, Joint Military Intelligence College.

Wallwork, Maj. Richard D. 2005. "Operational Implications of Private Military Companies in the Global War on Terror." School of Advanced Military Studies, United States Army Command General Staff College, Fort Leavenworth, KS.

Welborne, Bozena C. 2006. "Blood for Money: The Subcontracting of Defense in the Developing World." Paper presented at the annual meeting of the American Political Science Association, Marriott, Loews Philadelphia, and the Pennsylvania Convention Center, Philadelphia, PA, 2006-08-31.

PERIODICAL LITERATURE

Alden, Diane. 1999. "Soldiers R Us: The Corporate Military." SpinTech (September 12).

Althouse, James E. 1998. "Contractors on the Battlefield: What Doctrine Says, and Doesn't Say." Army Logistician 30:14–17.

Avant, Deborah. 2002. "Privatizing Military Training." Foreign Policy in Focus 7, no. 6. http://www.foreignpolicy-infocus.org/briefs/vol7/v7n06miltrain.html.

Baer, Robert. 2007. "Iraq's Mercenary King." Vanity Fair (April).

Bergner, Daniel. 2005. "The Other Army." New York Times Magazine (August 14).

Bowman, Marion E. "Spike." 2007. "Privatizing While Transforming." Defense Horizons, no. 57:1–7.

Brooks, Doug, and Gaurav Larola. 2005. "Privatized Peacekeeping." The National Interest (Summer).

Cahlink, George. 2002. "Army of Contractors." Government Executive 34:2.

Campbell, Gordon L. 2000. "Contractors on the Battlefield: The Ethics of Paying Civilians To Enter Harm's Way and Requiring Soldiers to Depend upon Them." Springfield, VA: Joint Services Conference on Professional Ethics, 2000.

Carafano, James Jay. 2005. The Pentagon and Postwar Contractor Support: Rethinking the Future. The Heritage Foundation, No. 958, February 1, 2005. www.heritage.org/research/nationalsecurity/em958.cfm.

Castillo, Lourdes A. 2002. "Waging War with Civilians: Asking the Unanswered Questions." Aerospace Power Journal 14:26–31.

Chiarotti, Charles G. 2000. "Joint Contractor Logistics Support Doctrine: Ensuring Success on the 21st Century Battlefield." Newport, RI: Naval War College.

Croft, Christopher D. 2001. "Contractors on the Battlefield: Has the Military Accepted Too Much Risk?" Fort Leavenworth, KS: Army Command and General Staff College. School of Advanced Military Studies.

Database of Researchers on International Private Security, International Peace Institute. http://www.ipinst.org/our-work/coping-with-crisis/grips/.

Department of Defense Privatization and Outsourcing. 2003. "A Bibliography." Maxwell Air Force Base, AL: Air University Library.

Flynn, Sean. 2006. "The Day the War Turned." *GQ* February: 106–111, 163–164.

Fortner, Joe A. 2004. "Managing, Deploying, Sustaining, and Protecting Contractors on the Battlefield." *Army Logistician* (September/October 2004). http://www.almc.army.mil/ALOG/issues/SepOct00/MS571.htm.

Foster, Susan C. 1998. "Contractors on the Battlefield: Force Multipliers or Detractors?" Carlisle Barracks, PA: U.S. Army War College.

Friedman, Robert M. Civilian Contractors on the Battlefield: A Partnership with Commercial Industry or Recipe for Failure? Carlisle Barracks, PA: U.S. Army War College, 2002.

Goddard, Maj. S., Maj. RA INF, Australia. 2001. *The Private Military Company: A Legitimate International Entity Within Modern Conflict*. A thesis presented to the Faculty of the U.S. Army Command and General Staff College in partial fulfillment of the requirements for the degree Master of Military Arts and Sciences.

Grant, Bruce D. 1998. "U.S. Military Expertise for Sale: Private Military Consultants as a Tool of Foreign Policy." In Essays 1998: Chairman of the Joint Chiefs of Staff Strategy Essay Competition, 89–113. Washington, DC: National Defense University, Institute for National Strategic Studies.

Gutman, Huck. 2004. "Soldiers for Hire." *Monthly Review* (June).

Harris, Marilyn. 2000. "LOGCAP: The Nation's Premier Contingency Contracting Program for Force XXI." Carlisle Barracks, PA: U.S. Army War College.

International Consortium of Investigative Journalists. 2002. *The Business of War*.

Isenberg, David. 2003. "There's No Business Like Security Business." *Asia Times* (April 30).

———. 2003. "The Secret World of Corporate Mercenaries." *Asia Times* (December 19).

———. 2004. "Corporate Mercenaries: Part 1: Profit Comes with a Price." *Asia Times* (May 19).

———. 2004. "Corporate Mercenaries: Part 2: Profit Comes with a Price." *Asia Times* (May 20).

———. 2005. "America's Unsung War Dead." *Asia Times* (November 30).

———. 2007. "Emerging Threats—Analysis: Blackwater—Guilty as charged?" *UPI* (September 20).

———. 2007. "Law Is Clear: Blackwater Is Not above It." *Asia Times* (October 16).

———. 2007. "Ghost of Outsourcing Yet to Come." *UPI* (December 27).

———. 2008. "Dogs of War: Here to Stay." *UPI* (January 25).

———. 2008. "Dogs of War: The Importance of Oversight." *UPI* (February 1).

———. 2008. "Dogs of War: The Pay Gap Myth." *UPI* (February 15).

———. 2008. "Dogs of War: Modest Proposals for Reform." *UPI* (February 22).

———. 2008. "Dogs of War: No Stinkin' Oversight Needed." *UPI* (February 29).

———. 2008. "Dogs of War: Round Laws, Square Holes." *UPI* (March 7).

———. 2008. "Dogs of War: Employees, What Employees?" *UPI* (March 14).

———. 2008. "Dogs of War: Life Imitating Art." *UPI* (March 21).

————. 2008. "Dogs of War: No Gravy Train for PMC Grunts." *UPI* (March 28).

————. 2008. "Dogs of War: Military Justice and PMCs." *UPI* (April 11).

————. 2008. "Dogs of War: Cost-effective: Myth or Fact?" *UPI* (April 25)

————. 2008. "Dogs of War: Insurance? What Insurance?" *UPI* (May 2)

————. 2008. "Dogs of War: Inherently Governmental?" *UPI* (May 9)

————. 2008. "Dogs of War: Blackwater, Najaf—Take Two," *UPI* (May 16)

————. 2008. "Dogs of War: Defense Base Act Revisited," *UPI* (May 23)

————. 2008. "Dogs of War: The Holy Grail, Part Four," *UPI* (June 6)

————. 2008. "Dogs of War: Two Little Words," *UPI* (June 13)

————. 2008. "Dogs of War: CACI—Some Publicity Is Bad," *UPI* (June 20)

————. 2008. "Dogs of War: A Small Step for Contractors," *UPI* (June 27)

————. 2008. "Dogs of War: The Founding Contractors," *UPI* (July 7)

————. 2008. "Dogs of War: Immunity Hype," *UPI* (July 11)

————. 2008. "Dogs of War: The Con Side of Contractors," *UPI* (July 18)

————. 2008. "Dogs of War: Life without Blackwater?" *UPI* (July 25)

————. 2008. "Dogs of War: Are PMCs POWs?" *UPI* (Aug. 1)

————. 2008. "Dogs of War: Blackwater to thr Rescue in Darfur?," *UPI* (Aug. 8)

————. 2008. "Dogs of War: One-stop Shopping at Blackwater," *UPI* (Aug. 18)

————. 2008. "Dogs of War: More Contractors in Iraq," *UPI* (Aug. 22)

————. 2008. "Dogs of War: Contractor Oversight Is Improving," *UPI* (Aug. 29)

————. 2008. "Dogs of War: Micromanaging Security Contractors," *UPI* (Sep. 5)

————. 2008. "Dogs of War: From Mercenary to Security Contractor and Back Again," *UPI* (Sep. 12)

Kinsey, Christopher. 2005. *Private Military Companies: Options for Regulating Private Military Services in the United Kingdom.* BASIC Notes, September 7, 2005. http://www.basicint.org/pubs/Notes/BN050907.htm.

Kochems, Alane. 2006. *When Should the Government Use Contractors to Support Military Operations?* Heritage Foundation Backgrounder No. 1938, May 19, 2006.

Kolling, James G. et al. 1998. "Potential Combat Risks from Outsourcing of Selected Sustainment Functions." Carlisle Barracks, PA: U.S. Army War College.

Kwok, James. 2006. "Armed Entrepreneurs: Private Military Companies in Iraq." *Harvard International Review* 28:34–37.

Mahlon, Apgar IV, and John M. Keane. 2004. "New Business with the New Military." *Harvard Business Review* (September).

Mailander, David J. 2002. "Battlefield Contractors: Assessing the Benefits and Weighing the Risks." Carlisle Barracks, PA: U.S. Army War College.

McCormick Tribune Conference Series. 2006. *Understanding the Privatization of National Security.* Chicago: McCormick Tribune Foundation. http://www.mccormicktribune.org/publications/privatization2006.pdf.

McKenna, Long, and Aldridge LLP. 2007. "Civilians Accompanying Forces in the Field Now Subject to U.S. Military Justice." *Government Contracts Advisory* 5, no. 5 (January 29). http://www.mckennalong.com/attachment/499/GC%20Advisory%201-29-07%20UCMJ%20Jurisdiction.pdf.

Ortiz, Carlos. 2004. "Regulating Private Military Companies: States and the Expanding Business of Commercial Security Provision." In *Global Regulation. Managing Crises after the Imperial Turn.* Edited by Libby Assassi, Duncan Wigan and Kees van der Pijl. New York: Palgrave Macmillan, pp. 205–219.

Percy, Sarah. 2006. "Domestic Regulation in the United States, South Africa, and the United Kingdom." International Institute for Strategic Studies Adelphi Paper Series, Regulating the Private Security Industry, 2006.

Peters, Katherine M. 1996. "Civilians at War." *Government Executive* 28, no. 7 (July).

"The Privatized Military: The Unmonitored, Unregulated and Unchecked Global Growth of Private Military Firms: An Interview with Peter W. Singer." *Multinational Monitor*, March 2004: 25–29.

Ries, Maj. Mark A. 2008. "Contingency Contractor Personnel." *Army Lawyer* (January).

Schmitt, Glenn R. 2005. "Amending the Military Extraterritorial Jurisdiction Act of 2000: Rushing to Close an Unforeseen Loophole." *Army Lawyer* (June).

Schreier, Fred, and Marina Caparini. 2005. "Privatising Security: Law, Practice and Governance of Private Military and Security Companies." The Geneva Centre for the Democratic Control of Armed Forces, DCAF Occasional Paper 6, March 2005. http://www.globalpolicy.org/nations/sovereign/military/0305privatisingsecurity.pdf.

Singer, Peter W. 2003. "Peacekeepers, Inc." *Policy Review*, no. 119 (June and July).

Smith, Eugene B. 2002–2003. "Condotierri and US Policy: The Privatization of Conflict and Its Implications." *Parameters* 32:104–119.

Tiron, Roxana. 2003. "Army Not Equipped to Manage Contractors on the Battlefield." *National Defense* 88, no. 598 (September): 32–33.

Transcript of "Iraq reconstruction funds." 2005. File On 4, BBC (February 1). http://news.bbc.co.uk/nol/shared/bsp/hi/pdfs/08_02_05_fileonfouriraq.pdf.

U.S. Department of the Army. *Contracting Support on the Battlefield*. Washington, D.C.: Department of the Army. Headquarters, 4 August 1999. Field Manual No. 100-10-2 (formerly FM 4-100.2). Army's first capstone doctrinal manual for acquiring contractor support: focuses more on acquisition of contract support than on contractor operational support. *Policy Memorandum—Contractors on the Battlefield*, 12 December 1997, is found in Appendix F.

U.S. Department of Defense. Continuation of Essential DoD Contractor Services during Crises. Washington, D.C.: DoD, 16 November 1990. DoD Instruction 3020.37. Incorporates change 1, 26 January 1996. http://www.dtic.mil/whs/directives/corres/html/302037.htm.

Uttley, Matthew. 2006. "Private Contractors on Deployed Military Operations: Inter-Agency Opportunities and Challenges." Heritage Lecture No. 972 (June 15).

Yeoman, Barry. 2004. "Dirty Warriors." *Mother Jones* (November/December): 30, 32–35.

REPORTS

Camm, Frank A., and Victoria A. Greenfield. 2005. "How Should the Army Use Contractors on the Battlefield? Assessing Comparative Risk in Sourcing Decisions." RAND, MG-296-A, 245pp.

"Civilian or Military? Assessing the Risk of Using Contractors on the Battlefield." 2005. RAND Research Brief.

"Compliance with Contract W911S0-04-C-0003." 2005. Audit Report, Office of the Special Inspector General for Iraq Reconstruction, Report Number 05-005, April 20, 2005.

"Contractors Accompanying the Force Overview Training Support Package, 151M001/Version 2." 2007. U.S. Army Combined Arms Support Command CSS Collective Training Division Training Directorate, 12 March 2007.

"Contractors on the Battlefield, FM 3-100.21 (100-21)." 2003. Headquarters, Department of the Army (January).

"Contracts Awarded for the Coalition Provisional Authority by the Defense Contracting Command-Washington." 2004. Office of the Inspector General, Department of Defense, (March 18).

Cullen, Patrick, and Peter Ezra Weinberger. 2007. "Reframing the Defense Outsourcing Debate: Merging Government Oversight with Industry Partnership." Peace Operations Institute.

"Dollars, Not Sense: Government Contracting under the Bush Administration." 2006. Minority Staff, Special Investigations Division, House Government Reform Committee (June).

"Expert Meeting on Private Military Contractors: Status and State Responsibility for Their Actions." 2005. Organized by the University Center for International Humanitarian Law, Geneva. Convened at International Conference Centre, Geneva, August 29–30, 2005.

Grasso, Valery Bailey. 2007. "Defense Contracting in Iraq: Issues and Options for Congress." Congressional Research Service (January 26).

"Interim Audit Report on Inappropriate Use of Proprietary Data Markings by the Logistics Civil Augmentation (LOGCAP) Contractor." 2007. SIGIR-06-035 (October 26).

"Interim Review of DynCorp International, LLC, Spending under Its Contract for the Iraqi Police Training Program." 2007. Office of the Special Inspector General for Iraq Reconstruction, SIGIR-07-016 (October 23).

Jennings, Kathleen M. 2006. "Armed Services: Regulating the Private Military Industry." FAFO Report 532.

Kosar, Kevin R. 2006. "Privatization and the Federal Government: An Introduction, Congressional Research Service." (December 28).

Leander, Anna. 2006. "Eroding State Authority? Private Military Companies and the Legitimate Use of Force." Centro Militare di Studi Strategici (CeMiSS), Rome, Italy. www.difesa.it/SMD/CASD.

Mathieu, Fabien, and Nick Dearden. 2006. "Corporate Mercenaries: the Threat of Private Military and Security Companies." War on Want, October 30.

National Defense University, Industrial College of the Armed Forces. 2006. "Industry Study Final Report: Private Military Operations." http://www.ndu.edu/icaf/industry/reports/2006/pdf/2006_PMOIS.pdf.

Private Military Contractors in Iraq: An Examination of Blackwater's Actions in Fallujah. 2007. Majority Staff, House Oversight and Government Reform Committee (September).

"Private Security Contractors at War: Ending the Culture of Impunity." 2008. Human Rights First. http://www.humanrightsfirst.info/pdf/08115-usls-psc-final.pdf.

"Progress on Recommended Improvements to Contract Administration for the Iraqi Police Training Program." 2008. Office of the Special Inspector General for Iraq Reconstruction (SIGIR) (April 22). http://www.sigir.mil/reports/pdf/audits/08-014.pdf.

Smith, Richard Victor. 2004. "Can Private Military Companies Replace Special Operational Forces?" CDAI-DCFAI 7th Annual Graduate Student's Symposium, RMC, October 29–30, 2004.

Spear, Dr. Joanna. 2006. "Market Forces: The Political Economy of Private Military Companies." FAFO Report 531, 72 pp.

Tipling, Dustin M. 2006. "The Military Extraterritorial Jurisdiction Act and Its Implications for Private Military Companies." The Berkeley Electronic Press, Paper 1393.

"Report of the Defense Science Board Task Force on Outsourcing and Privatization." 1996. Office of the Under Secretary of Defense for Acquisition and Technology (August).

"Report of the Secretary of State's Panel on Personal Protective Services in Iraq." October 2007.

"Report on Allegations Regarding State Department Inspector General Howard Krongard." 2007. Majority Staff, House Oversight and Government Reform Committee (November).

"A Review of ICITAP's Screening Procedures for Contractors Sent to Iraq as Correctional Advisors." 2005. Office of the Inspector General, U.S. Department of Justice (February).

"Urgent Reform Required: Army Expeditionary Contracting, Report of the 'Commission on Army Acquisition and Program Management in Expeditionary Operations.'" October 31, 2007.

U.S. Defense Science Board. 1996. "Report of the Defense Science Board Task Force on Outsourcing and Privatization." Washington, D.C.: Office of the Undersecretary of Defense for Acquisition and Technology.

U.S. GOVERNMENT

Congressional Hearings

Hearing of the House Oversight and Government Reform Committee, Hearing on *Iraqi Reconstruction: Reliance on Private Military Contractors*, February 7, 2007. http://oversight.house.gov/story.asp?id=1165.

Hearing of the House Oversight and Government Reform Committee, Hearing on *Private Security Contracting in Iraq and Afghanistan*, October 2, 2007. http://oversight.house.gov/story.asp?ID=1509.

Hearing of the House Judiciary Subcommittee on Crime, Terrorism, and Homeland Security, Hearing on *Enforcement of Federal Criminal Law to Protect Americans Working for U.S. Contractors in Iraq*, December 19, 2007. http://judiciary.house.gov/oversight.aspx?ID=401.

Hearing of the Senate Committee on Homeland Security and Governmental Affairs, *An Uneasy Relationship: U.S. Reliance on Private Security Firms in Overseas Operations*, February 27, 2008.

Hearing of the House Committee on Oversight and Government Reform, *Defense Base Act Insurance: Are Taxpayers Paying Too Much?* May 15, 2008.

Congressional Budget Office

"Logistics Support for Deployed Military Forces." October 2005.

Congressional Research Service

"Defense Outsourcing: The OMB Circular A-76 Policy." 2005. RL 30392 (April 21).
"Iraq: Frequently Asked Questions About Contracting." 2005. RL32229 (March 18).
"Private Security Contractors in Iraq: Background, Legal Status, and Other Issues." 2007. RL32419 (June 21). http://www.fas.org/sgp/crs/natsec/RL32419.pdf.
"Proposed Federal Income Tax Exclusion for Civilians Serving in Combat Zones." 2006. RL 33230 (January 10).

Government Accountability Office

"Contract Management: Opportunities to Improve Surveillance on Department of Defense Service Contracts." 2007. GAO-05-274 (March).
"Defense Base Act Insurance: Review Needed of Cost and Implementation Issues." 2005. GAO-05-280R (April 29).
"Defense Budget: Trends in Operation and Maintenance Costs and Support Services Contracting." 2007. GAO-07-631 (May 18).
"Defense Contracting: Additional Personal Conflict of Interest Safeguards Needed for Certain DOD Contractor Employees." 2008. GAO-08169 (March).
"Defense Contracting: Army Case Study Delineates Concerns with Use of Contractors as Contract Specialists." 2008. GAO-08-360 (March 26).
"Defense Contracting: Progress Made in Implementing Defense Base Act Requirements, but Complete Information on Costs Is Lacking." 2008. GAO-08-772T (May 15).
"Defense Management: DOD Needs to Reexamine Its Extensive Reliance on Contractors and Continue to Improve Management and Oversight." 2008. GAO-08-572T (March 11).
"Federal Contracting: Use of Contractor Performance Information, by William T. Woods, director, acquisition and sourcing management, before the Subcommittee on Government Management, Organization, and Procurement, House Committee on Oversight and Government Reform." 2007. GAO-07-1111T (July 18).
"Interagency Contracting: Problems with DOD's and Interior's Orders to Support Military Operations." 2005. GAO-05-201 (April).
"Iraq Contract Costs: DoD Consideration of Defense Contract Audit Agency's Findings." 2006. GAO-06-1132 (September).
"Operation Iraqi Freedom: DoD Should Apply Lessons Learned Concerning the Need for Security over Conventional Munitions Storage Sites to Future Operations Planning." 2007. GAO-07-444 (March).
"Military Operations: Background Screenings of Contractor Employees Supporting Deployed Forces May Lack Critical Information, but U.S. Forces Take Steps to Mitigate the Risk Contractors May Pose." 2006. GAO—06-999R (September 22).
"Military Operations: DOD's Extensive Use of Logistics Support Contracts Requires Strengthened Oversight." 2004. GAO-04-854 (July).
"Military Operations: High-Level DOD Action Needed to Address Long-Standing Problems with Management and Oversight of Contractors Supporting Deployed Forces." GAO-07-145.
"Rebuilding Iraq: Actions Needed to Improve the Use of Private Security Providers." 2005. GAO-05-737 (July).

"Rebuilding Iraq: Actions Still Needed to Improve the Use of Private Security Providers."
   2006. GAO-06-865T (June 13).
"Rebuilding Iraq: Continued Progress Requires Overcoming Contract Management Chal-
   lenges." 2006. GAO-06-1130T (September 28).
"Rebuilding Iraq—Status of DoD's Reconstruction Program." 2006. GAO-07-30R
   (December 15).
"Rebuilding Iraq—DOD and State Department Have Improved Oversight and Coordina-
   tion of Private Security Contractors in Iraq, but Further Actions Are Needed to Sus-
   tain Improvements." 2008. GAO-08-966 (July 31).
"Securing, Stabilizing, and Rebuilding Iraq: GAO Audit Approach and Findings." 2007.
   GAO-07-385T (January 18).
"Stabilizing and Rebuilding Iraq: Actions Needed to Address Inadequate Accountability
   over U.S. Efforts and Investments." 2008. GAO-08-568T (March 11).

Index

About the Author

DAVID ISENBERG is an independent analyst specializing in military, foreign policy, and national and international security issues. He previously worked with the British American Security Information Council (BASIC), the Center for Defense Information, and DynCorp. He is also an adjunct scholar with the Cato Institute, a research fellow at the Independent Institute, a columnist for UPI, and a U.S. Navy veteran. He lives in the Washington, D.C., area.